CW01655948

Contemporary Kiln-formed Glass

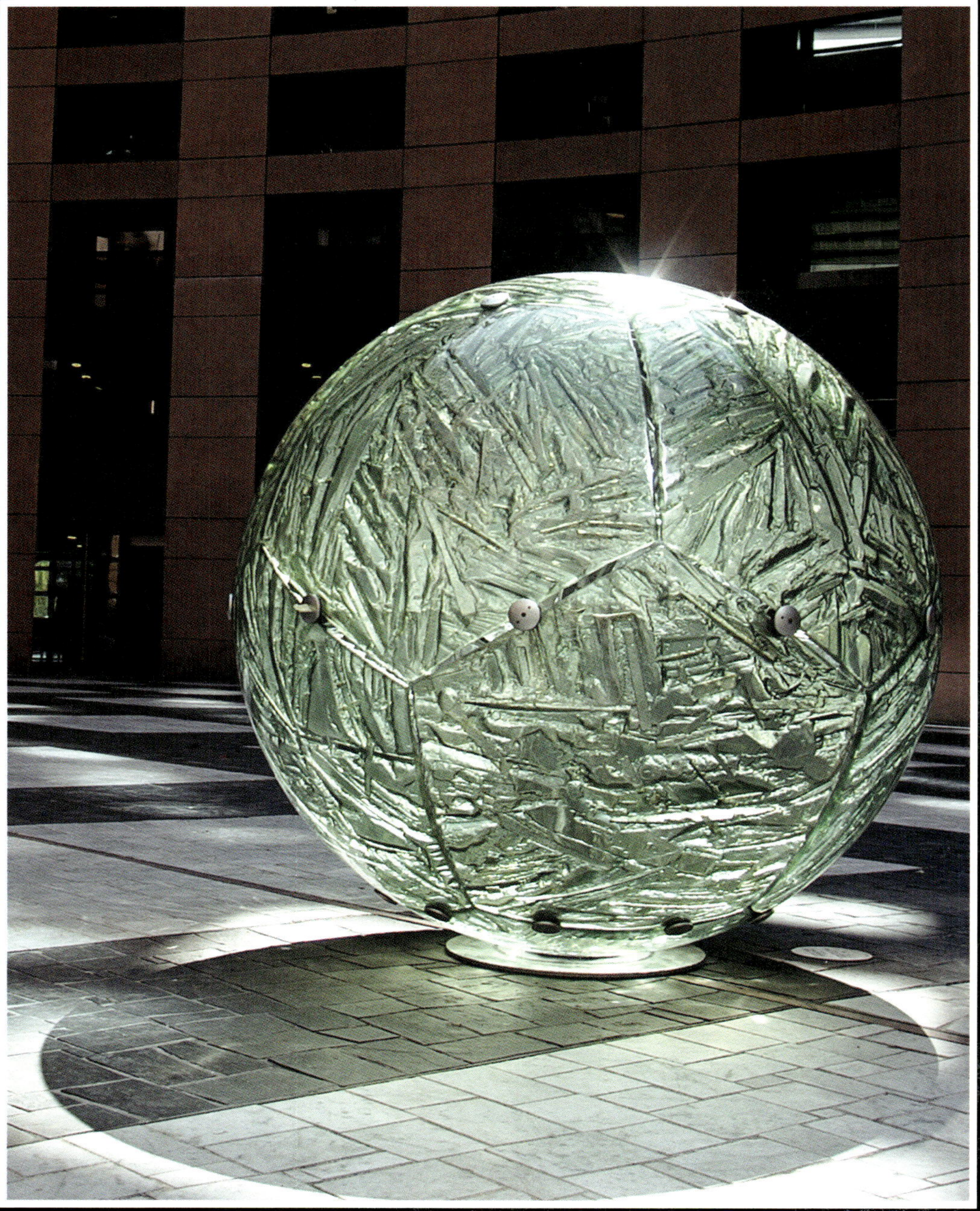

Contemporary Kiln-formed Glass

Keith Cummings

A&C Black • London

University of Pennsylvania Press • Philadelphia

COVER
Sundowner 12, Galia Amsel, 2007. W. 60 cm (23⅝ in.), H. 54 cm (21¼ in.), D. 15 cm (6 in.).
Photo: the artist.

FRONTISPIECE
United Earth, Tomasz Urbanowicz, 2004. Located at the European Parliament at Strasbourg. D. 180 cm (71 in.).

First published in 2009 by
A&C Black Publishers
36 Soho Square
London W1D 3QY
www.acblack.com

ISBN 978-1-408-10075-2

Published simultaneously in the USA by
University of Pennsylvania Press
3905 Spruce Street
Philadelphia, Pennsylvania 19104-4112

ISBN 978-0-8122-4232-4

© Keith Cummings, 2009

CIP Catalogue records for this book are available from the British Library and the US Library of Congress.

Keith Cummings has asserted his right under the Copyright, Design and Patents Act 1988 to be identified as the author of this work.

All rights reserved. No part of this publication may be reproduced, stored in a retrieval system, or transmitted in any form or by any means, electronic, mechanical, photocopying, recording or otherwise, without prior permission in writing from the publisher.

Book design by Penny Mills
Cover design by Sutchinda Rangsi Thompson

Printed and bound in China

Acknowledgements

I would like to thank the following people:

Tina Oldknow and Jill Thomas-Clark of Corning Museum NY; as well as Max Stewart, Simon Bruntnell, Paddy Hartley and all of the artists who so generously allowed me access to images of their work, but also provided me with highly personal statements which revealed so much about their thoughts, creative methods and innermost motivations.

Keith Cummings

Contents

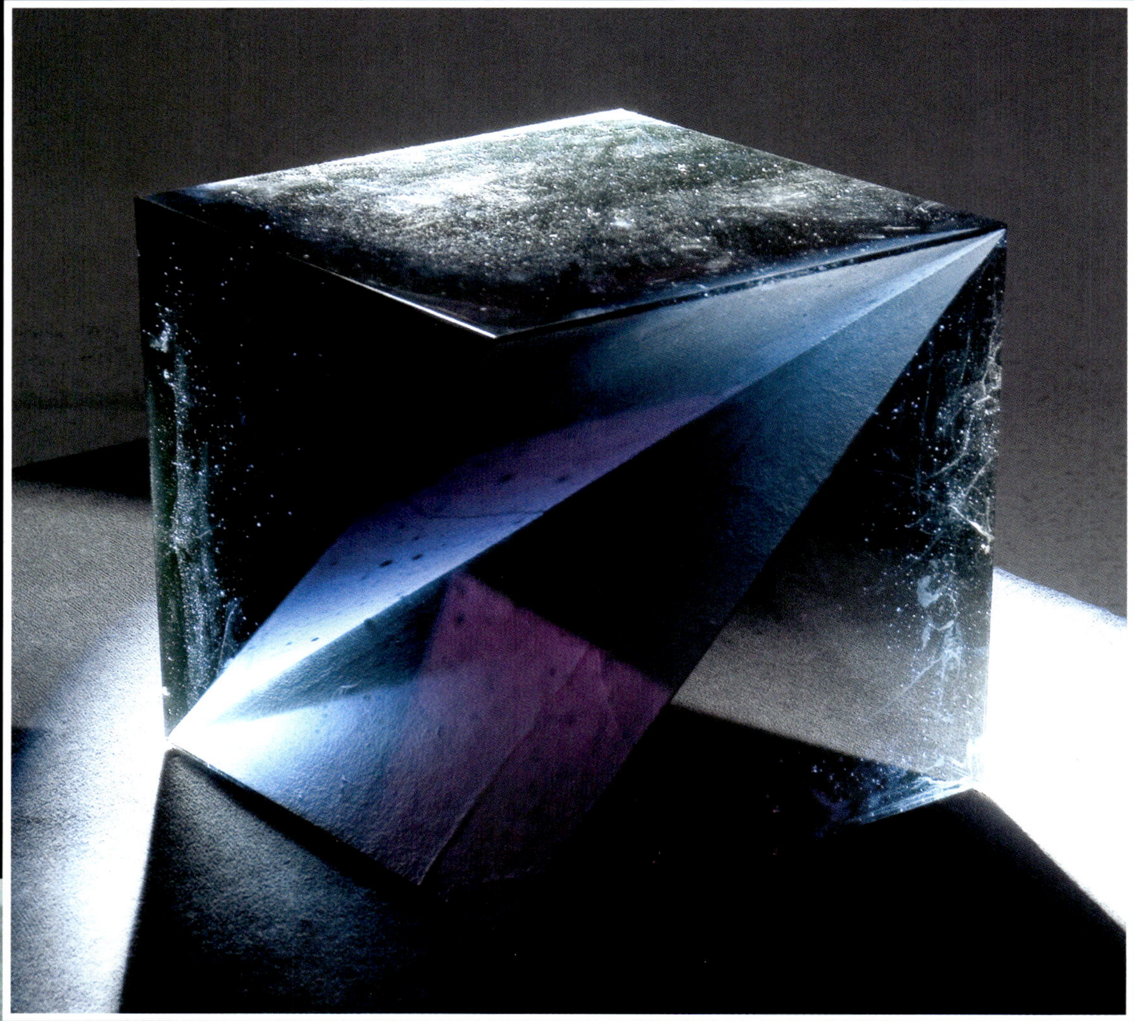

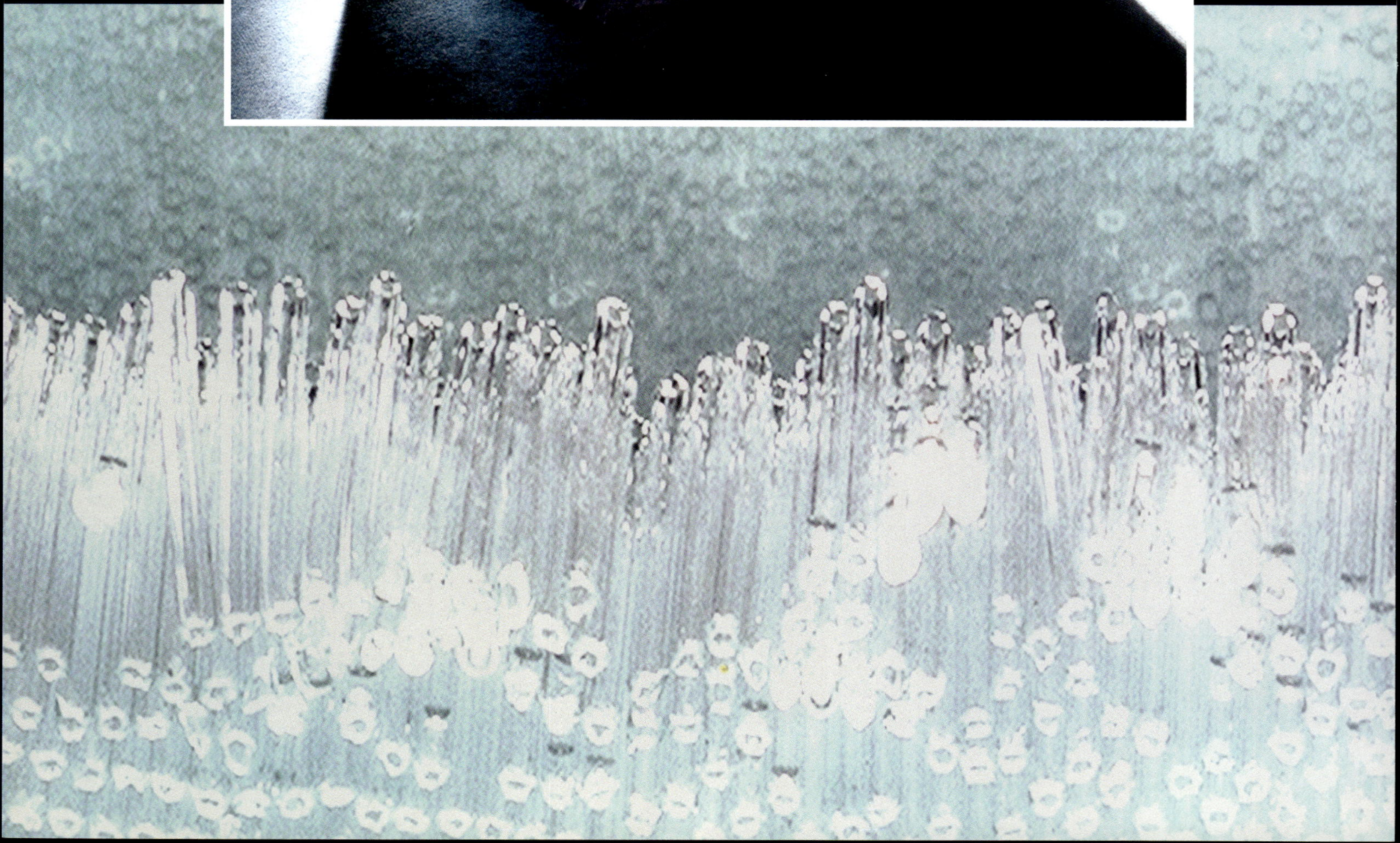

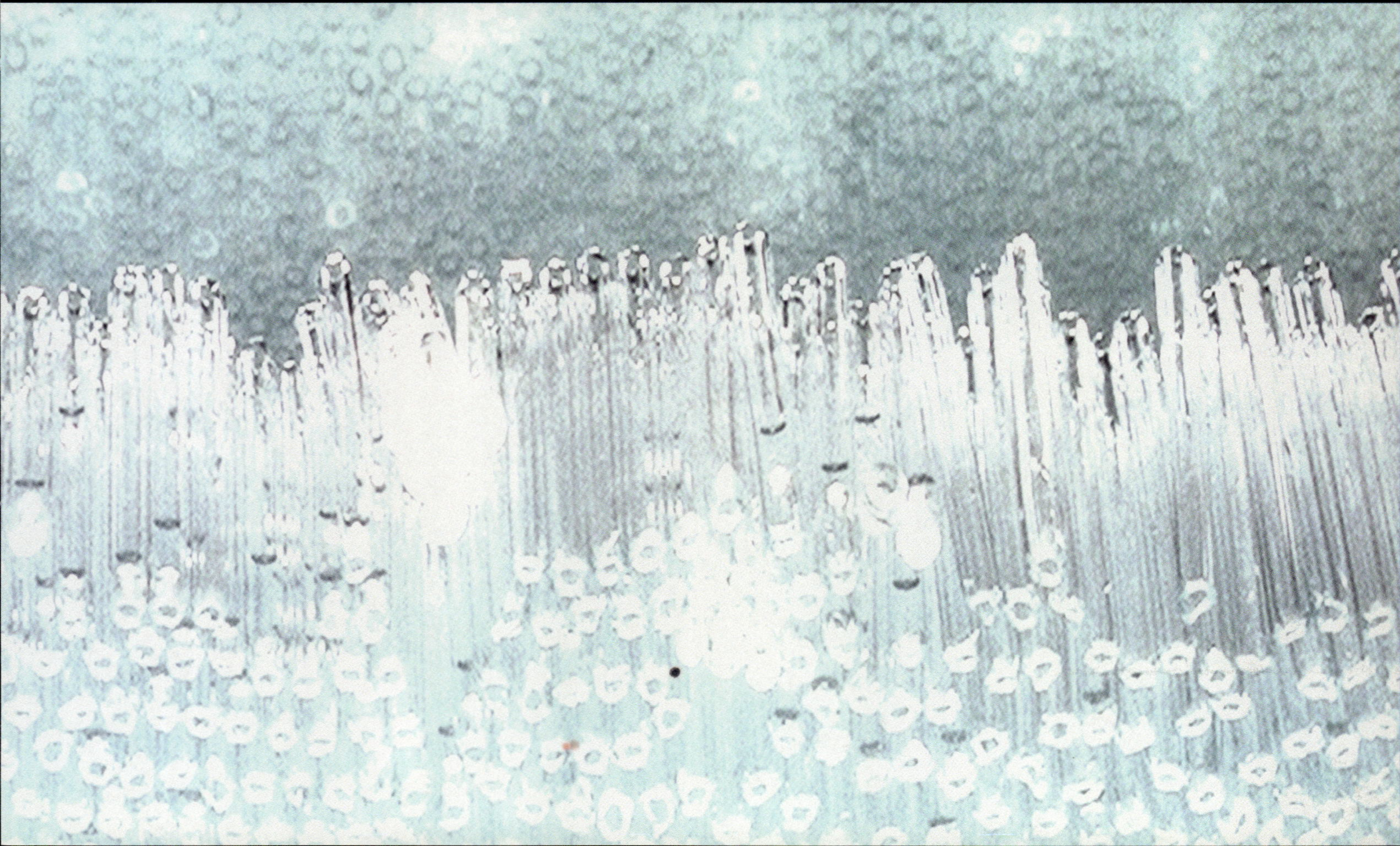

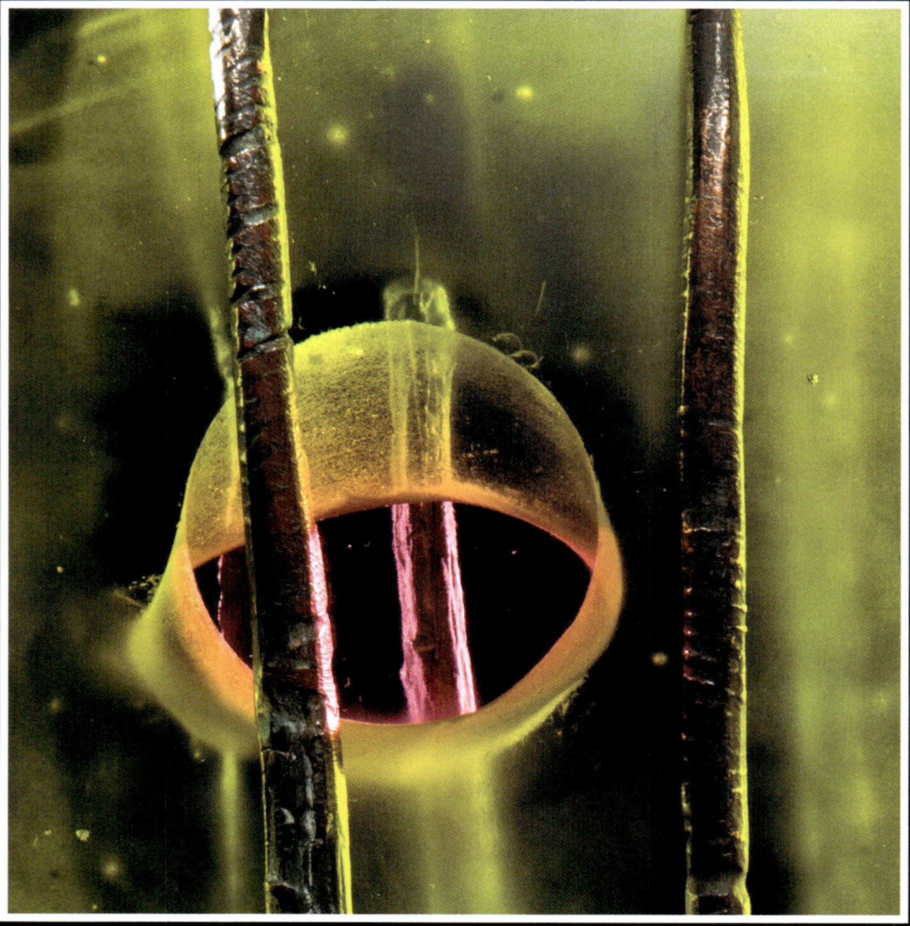

This book appears, by its title, to be limited to a single material, glass, and to a specific group of forming methods – kiln-forming. However, interested as I am in kiln-forming, having devoted over forty years of my life to its development and use, I do not wish to present process and technique in isolation from the creative imperatives that drive its uses, and which ultimately determine the end product.

Glass is a material, and not a subject until certain choices are made; so to devote a book to only half the equation seems to miss the opportunity to present and discuss the whole rather than the part.

To decide to kiln-form glass is to embrace a whole language of form, qualities of colour and texture, in addition to a set of limitations in terms of the scale and repeatability of particular pieces. These factors mean that its use is predominantly to further artistic enquiry in terms of individual creativity rather than for multiple reproductions. More people worldwide are now using glass in this way than at any time during the five millennia since the material was first developed. Their motives, their personal philosophies and their creative aspirations are what raise their making activities above the level of mere technique applied to material.

In this book I want to discuss kiln-forming as a distinctive means of giving shape, internal structure, colour and texture to glass. The range of qualities and the richness of potential objects mean that examples vary from large-scale architectural features to jewellery, and from decorative, domestic-scale craftworks to sculpture, often involving a variety of other materials in combination with glass.

The choice of material and process is, in some sense, analogous to a composer`s choice of instrumentation, selected for its aesthetic vocabulary. The music score is, however, the determining force in such a creative partnership, and I wanted to include the visual artist`s equivalent as part of the remit of this book. For this reason I have chosen to illustrate and describe much of the best of current practice through the works of a number of artists, selected for their quality and creative individuality. Their kiln-forming range stretches across the full temperature spectrum, from enamelling to casting, and includes many highly personal procedures. Because of this I did not want to centre my discussion on images of finished works alone, no matter how beautiful these were. The artists' own presentation of their work via their individual websites has made the

PREVIOUS PAGE
Cube 2, Stepan Pala, 2007. 30 x 30 x 30 cm (11¾ x 11¾ x 11¾ in.).
Photo: courtesy of the artist.

Although his work sits within the tradition of Czech glass, Stepan Pala extends its range and repertoire through his use of strong colour and texture.

◄ *Ember* (detail), Keith Cummings, 2007. Kiln-formed and cast glass, and bronze. W. 22 cm (8¾ in.), H. 19 cm (7½ in.), D. 9 cm (3½ in.).
Photo: Simon Bruntnell.

high-quality image of the finished piece an essential and central part of the publicity and commercial exchange of the art object. In fact critical discussion is often centred on such images, particularly with a material as photogenic as glass. For this reason I have asked contributing artists, wherever possible, to let me have a philosophic statement, and an image or two, relating to their technical and creative practice. These generously given insights have allowed me to do two things: to discuss firstly the relationships the practitioner has with their chosen material, their own creative process and their sources of inspiration; and secondly the crucial development of the object through its various stages, from idea to finished piece, illustrating on the way some of the most personal and sophisticated kiln-forming techniques in use today. Many of these techniques have been hard-won through years of individual endeavour, and I am indebted to the artists who have so generously allowed me both to feature their works and to tell some of the stories behind them.

Background

Much is made of the uniqueness of glass as a material, sometimes to its detriment, in the sense that it can seem to exist in isolation from other materials, and from the art & craft movements of which it is undoubtedly a part. It is possible, for example, to argue that a phrase like 'glass artist` is a contradiction in terms, because what is actually being described is an artist or craftsperson working *in* and *through* glass.

In conducting a survey of kiln-formed glass in the early years of the 21st century I feel it is imperative to place it within the context and history of the arts & crafts in general, and to position it in relation to specific movements. The influences that have acted together to shape the nature of creative activity in the plastic arts act as a powerful background against which practitioners operate, and as such these influences contribute to the type of work produced. Their individual effects are as important as their interaction. No artist works in a vacuum except through ignorance, whether accidental or deliberate. Surely the best way to exercise the maximum creative control over a chosen medium is to understand the landscape within which you operate, and the features that contribute to it?

The craft movement, in which glass is, and was, a major influence, began, paradoxically, in the wake of the Industrial Revolution. Once machine production had taken over the role of the traditional hand crafts in the manufacture of large numbers of reasonably priced everyday objects, hand-directed skills were pushed to the margins of society and apparently threatened with extinction. That they did not die out is surely indicative of the importance of individual products, from both the maker's and the consumer's points of view. In fact the crafts enjoyed a creative swansong in the various craft movements (Arts and Crafts and Art Nouveau) at the very point when their ability to supply society's more basic product needs was disappearing. This shift in the late 19th century was to result in the gradual repositioning of many crafts, notably silversmithing, jewellery, fine woodwork, wrought iron, stone carving and glassmaking, into a movement that is now 150 years old and counting.

There were two main radical forces within this fledgling movement. First was the emergence of the artist/craftsman, who blurred the traditional line between designer and maker by combining both roles, often further complicating matters by having a university or art-school education. This

Jeremy Lepisto, photo of a road surface.
Photo: Paul Foster.

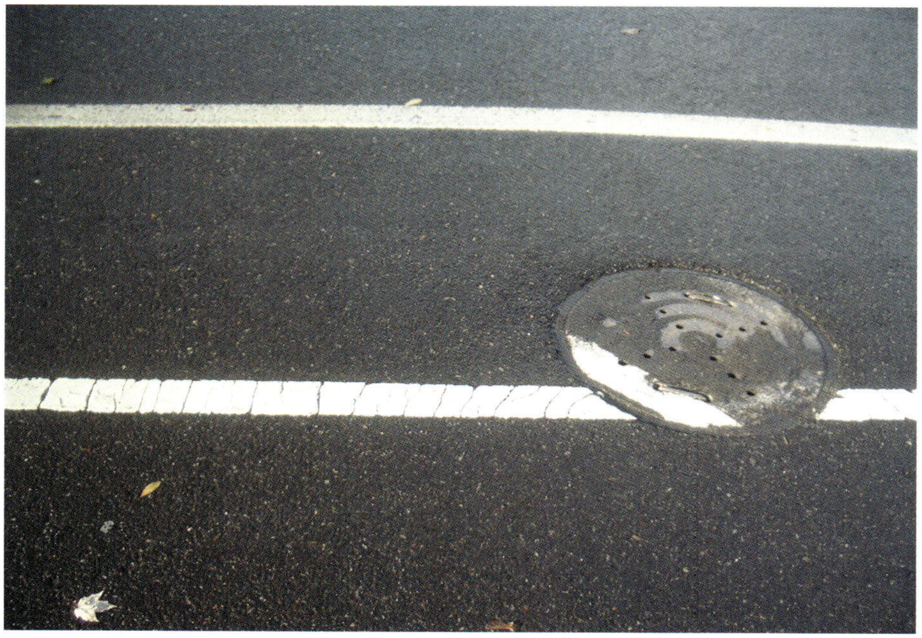

Jeremy Lepisto, 2007
Photo: Paul Foster.

Insight and Development from the *Span* series. Both W. 120 cm (48 in.), H. 15 cm (6 in.).

An example of an artist gaining inspiration from an unexpected source, in this case misaligned road markings.

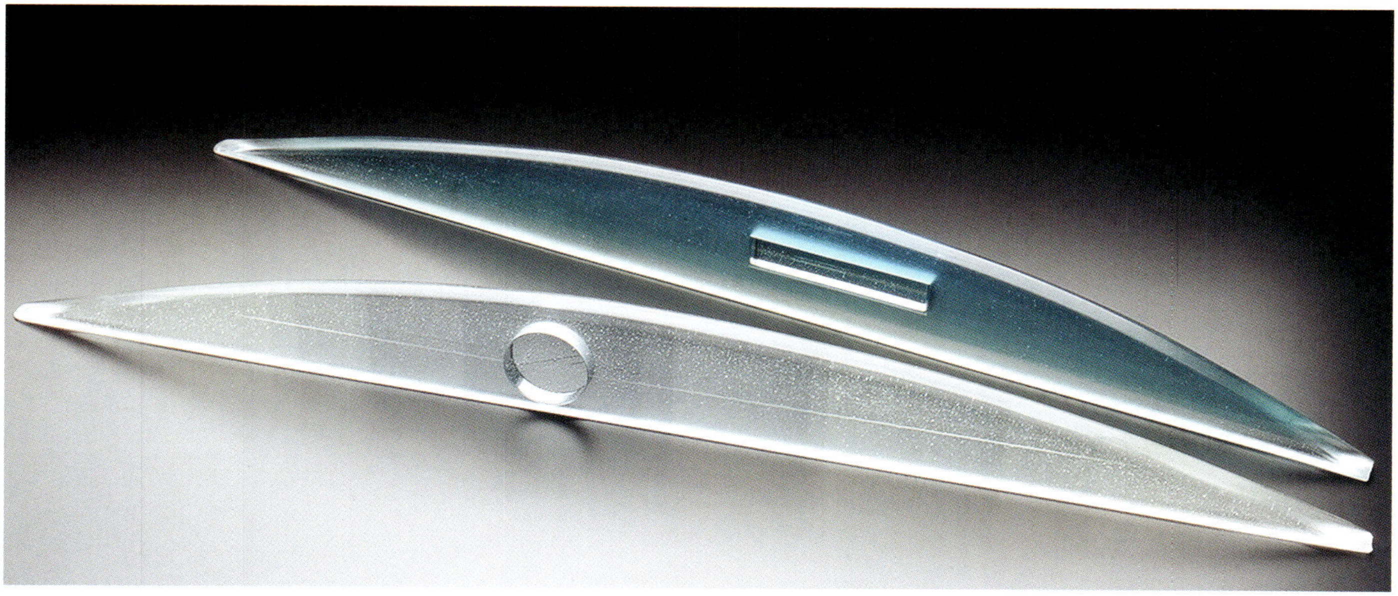

in turn led directly to the birth of the production of the single, signature artefact. The public began to identify objects by association with their maker, which was in direct contrast to both the traditional demarcation between the designer, on the one hand, and the craftsman, on the other, who carried out the designer's wishes by following highly detailed drawings, a partnership exemplified by the presence of high-quality craft skills in the field of building construction. Architects like Gaudí and Horta, for example, knew that they could call on teams of skilled formers of wood, metal, stone and glass to realise their complex drawings. The resulting edifices were credited to their designers, with the actual makers remaining anonymous.

From this background, a coherent international craft movement gradually emerged, centred on individually recognised practice, in which the functions of design and making are performed by the same individual.

The background against which this movement began exercised a profound effect on its development and direction, with the result that many of its early attitudes are still evident even within contemporary practice. The character of the 19th-century pioneers varied from mainstream artists drawn to the creative potential of craft production, to artisans seeking greater control over their own skills.

As the movement came of age it finally found its intellectual voice; practitioners began to articulate and share creative, stylistic, aesthetic and philosophic issues developed from individual studio practice. The growth of an ancillary area devoted to the commercial exchange, collection and criticism of the outcomes saw the setting-up of specialist galleries, periodicals, collections (and collectors), critics and, latterly, museums and nationally funded organisations, all devoted to the crafts.

The fact that this was most in evidence in advanced post-industrial societies shows that the extent of the shift in perception of the crafts has been greatest in areas where it is no longer essential to manufacturing. This is most evident in the way makers now think of themselves, often adopting an approach to their practice, and their end products, that used to be the exclusive realm of the fine artist. It is no accident that so many craft practitioners are happy to provide statements in support of their objects which articulate a personal philosophic approach to making. This is indicative of two things: their need to develop a creative language with which to engage with their material, and a perception that this is an essential part of their dialogue with those who are confronted by their works. This, of course, follows a pattern long established by sculptors and painters, and is further evidence of the blurring of boundaries.

I have drawn heavily on the statements supplied by artists featured in this volume, for they reveal much about both the individuals and the discourse they engage in with themselves and their public. I include myself as a practitioner in this need to explain my work – to myself first and the public second. It has become an accepted part of the marketing and sale of one's work, a little like the expectation that each piece will have a separate title, or that the artist will turn up at the opening of an exhibition to meet and encourage buyers!

An important part of this ongoing debate about the crafts is related to their cultural and financial status within societies where they are increasingly traded as commodities.

Glass

Before moving on to discuss glass in general and kiln-forming in particular, it is worth reiterating that both, but especially kiln-forming, are embedded within wider aesthetic, material, cultural, economic and philosophic contexts. My reasons for constantly stressing this danger of glass becoming, in the words of Steve Linn, one of the artists in this book, 'a ghetto subject' is because history tells us that glass flourishes in vibrant, mixed economies where its constant interaction with other materials, technologies and attitudes is mutually beneficial; by contrast, it dwindles in isolation.

This isolation is especially likely where so much emphasis is placed on the unique and special nature of glass, a fact evident in much contemporary glass marketing and display. To ignore this pitfall, and to fail to acknowledge that glass is a mere material (albeit a very special one) and kiln-forming a mere process, ignores the wider contexts, to the material's lasting detriment. Although the function of this volume is to present developments in technique, I cannot omit discussions of form, motivation, aesthetic intent, visual language and creative methods.

A major feature of the development of glass-forming since the establishment of the global studio glass movement in the 1960s has been an increasingly sophisticated technical control of the medium, as each generation has built on the accumulated knowledge of previous practitioners. This has been a rapid process, which nevertheless shows no sign of slowing down. By choosing as exemplars the works of high-calibre artists, I hope simultaneously to show technical excellence and also innovation in the service of high-quality creativity and concepts. Harvey Littleton's famous dictum 'Technique is cheap' still resonates, for no amount of clever or virtuoso making can cover up a lack of imagination and insight.

The artists chosen cover the full range of ages, from established figures whose work never ceases to surprise, to individuals who are relative newcomers, with all the variations in between. Many countries are represented, ranging from the likes of the USA, where the studio movement originated, to new regions where creative glass-forming has begun to flourish. The objects I have chosen exist as complex, quality artefacts that just happen to be made from glass by kiln-forming. I want to present technique and information in ways that will act as a catalyst for future progress; and the best way to do this is surely to show how it has been used in the service of genuinely creative enquiries.

Glass and kiln-forming function like the vocabulary of a writer or the instrument of the musician: conduits through which ideas are shaped and expressed, partners in the whole act of thinking and making, with each advance in technique adding to the total vocabulary of glass available to artists worldwide, nowadays easily so via the internet.

The injection of intellectualism into the craft movement by pioneers like William Morris and C.R. Ashbee has grown to the point where art has become absorbed into the educational mainstream, culminating in our own era in the inclusion of craft making in the curricula of many universities. It was unthinkable even a few years ago that a craft skill such as glass-blowing could be used as a pathway to BA, MA, even doctorate-level study. Any critical survey of end products must surely take this into consideration.

The global studio glass movement owes much of its existence and dynamism to the energy and example of its pioneers, most of whom are still very much alive at the time of writing. Prime movers like Harvey Littleton and Dale Chihuly in America, and Erwin Eisch and Bertil Vallien in Europe, set up centres like Pilchuck, Wisconsin and Frauenau in Germany, which acted as crucibles of excellence, experiment and dissemination. Much of the energy of this period centred on the manipulation of hot glass direct from the furnace, through blowing and sand-casting, with kiln-forming only gradually appearing as the movement spread. However, kiln-forming in the work of the pâte-de-verre artists of 19th-century France had pre-dated the studio movement by over a hundred years. Unfortunately, the handful of exponents of this technique had died out by the late 1950s, and their technical expertise had died with them. The complex procedures they had developed of casting with coloured glass grains had to be patiently rediscovered before pâte-de-verre could become a major part of the studio movement. Iconic pieces made by artists like Décorchement, Argy-Rousseau and Walter remained as supreme examples of what could be achieved, acted as stimuli for a new generation, and continue to inspire and inform contemporary practice.

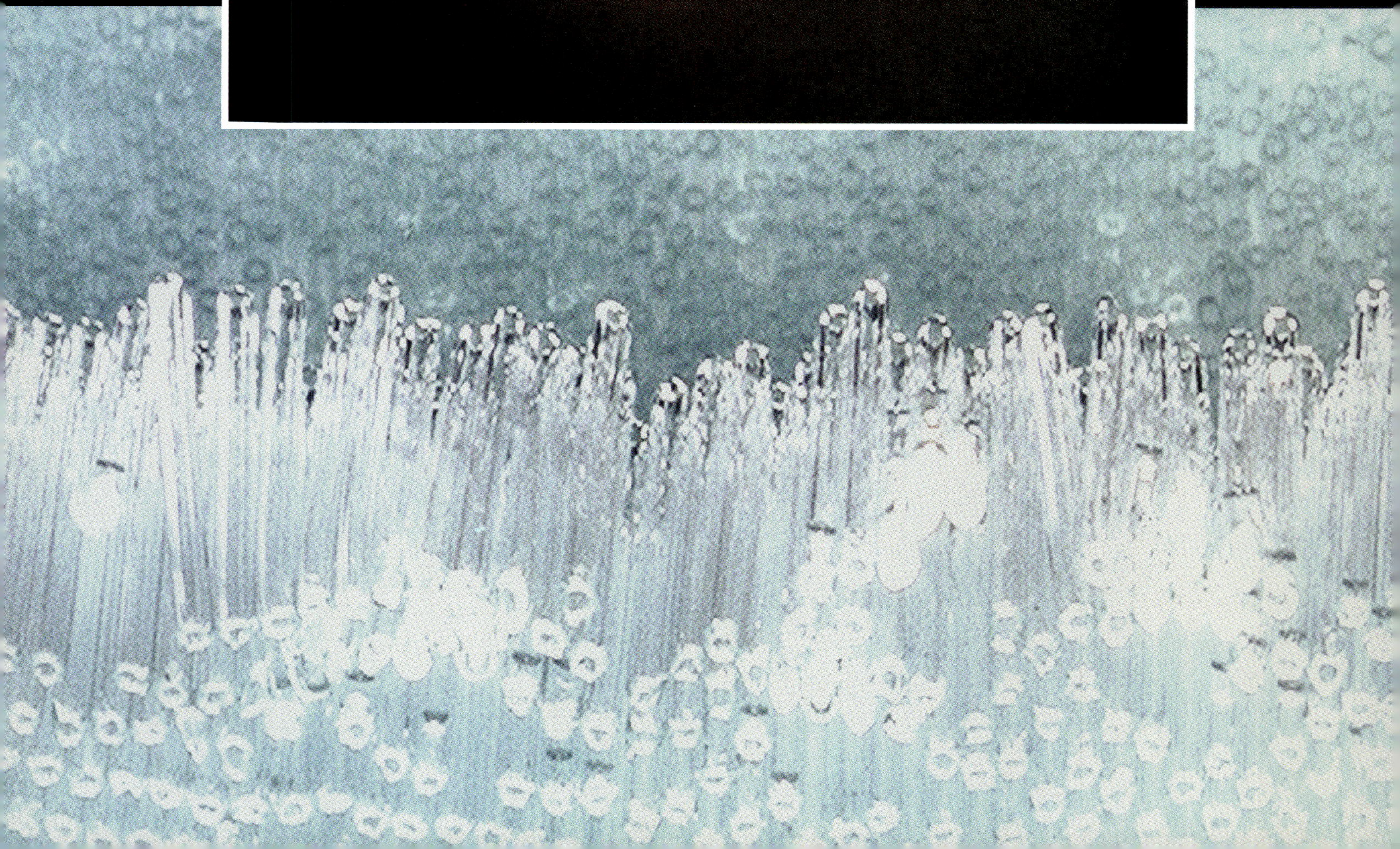

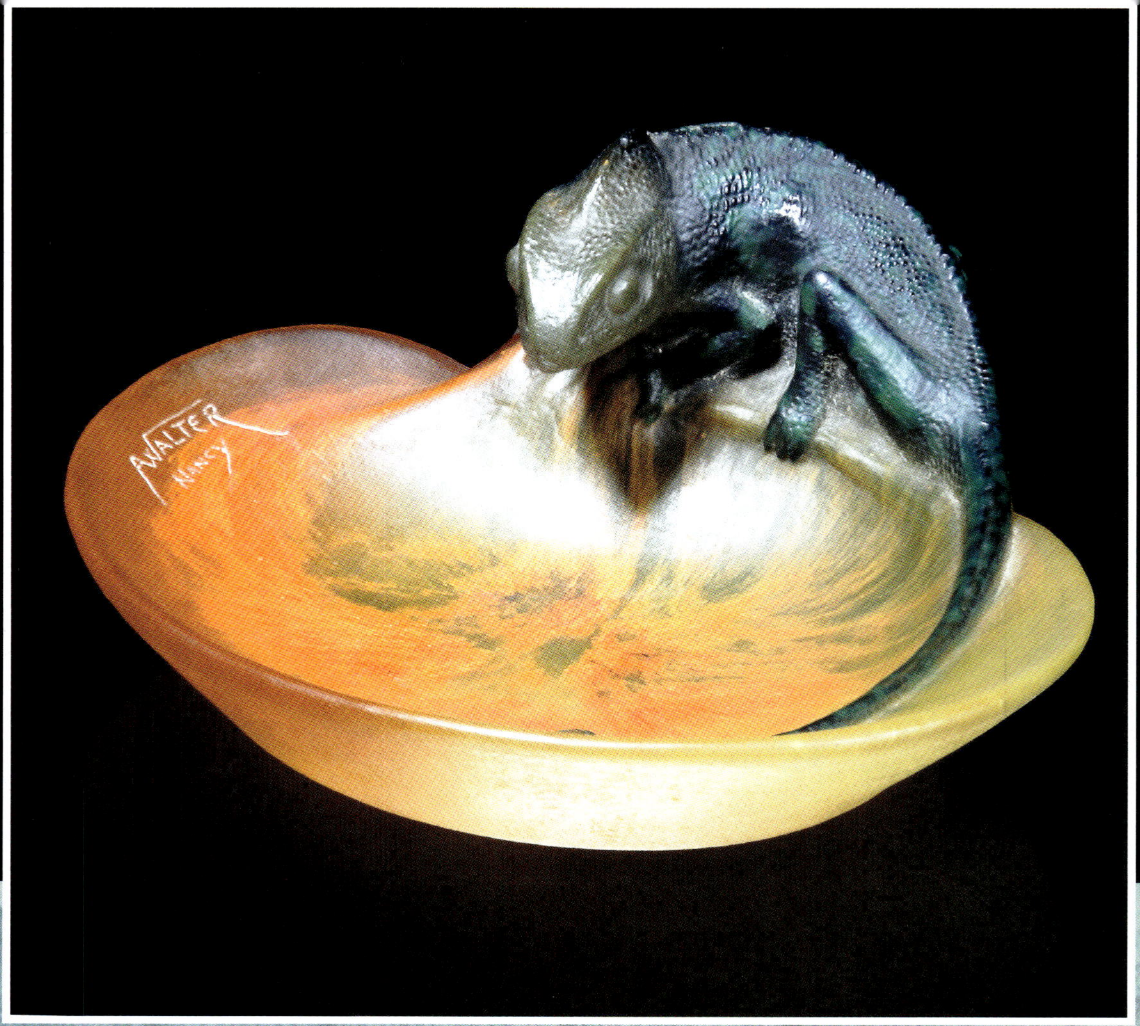
AWALTER
NANCY

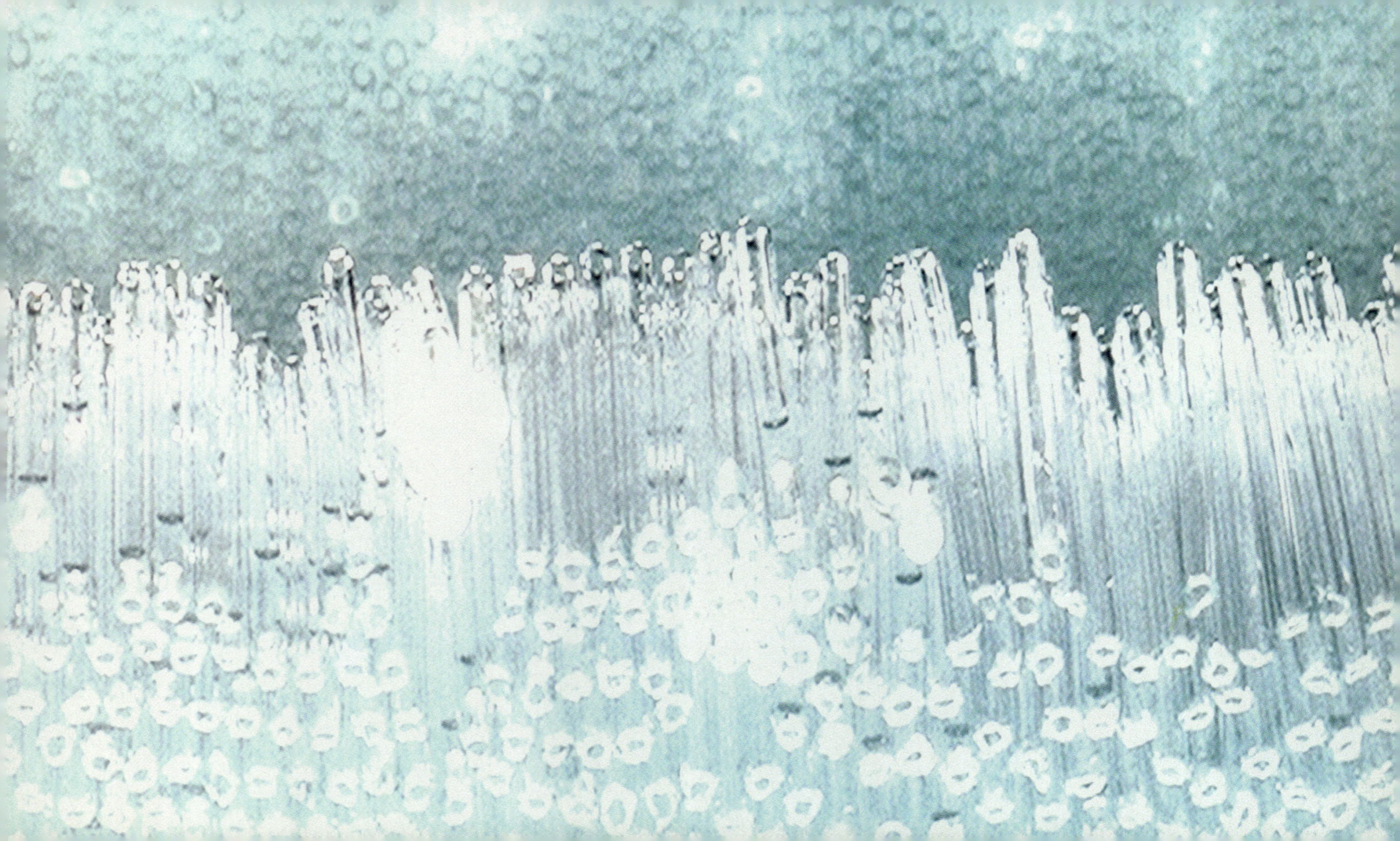

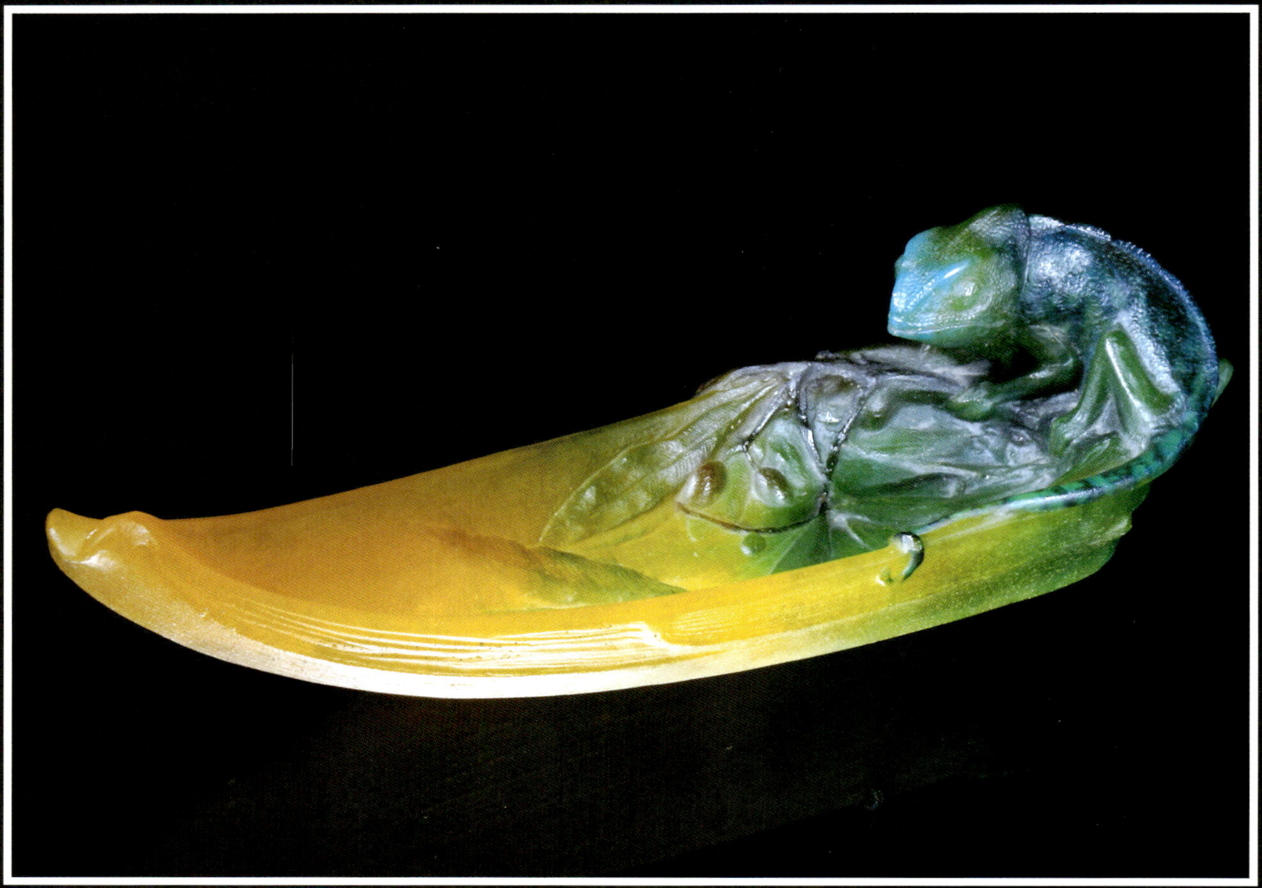

The Development

Although most European countries were affected by the Industrial Revolution, France was perhaps the first country in which its impact prompted shifts in craft production, particularly in relation to glass. The main centres for this development were the ceramic and glass factories, particularly Sèvres, with its national training school for artists and artisans, which trained apprentices in all aspects of ceramic design and manufacture. The accent was on the acquisition and development of high-level hand skills, including observational drawing, painting and modelling, in addition to all aspects of enamelling, from mixing to application and firing.

Courses were long and rigorous. Crucially, an element of research through practical experiment seems to have been fostered in addition to traditional practices. It must be remembered that in the latter part of the 19th century France was home to three major art movements – Impressionism, Post-Impressionism and Art Nouveau – and this larger context is the creative environment within which the first major craft glass technique of the modern era developed, namely pâte de verre.

The kiln-forming process known by this generic title has had a strange relationship with the modern studio glass movement since its emergence in the third quarter of the 19th century. It flourished from the 1880s until the 1930s, lasting effectively just one generation, before disappearing completely with the deaths of its main exponents. If it had remained a dead process there would be no justification for including a detailed account of it in this volume; however, there are currently more artists worldwide shaping glass by this and other closely allied means than there ever were during its first flowering. This makes its history and description essential to the understanding of contemporary practice.

When the studio glass movement began in the wake of the Second World War, pâte de verre was a mysterious process with no contemporary exponents and no written accounts which would allow its replication. It had to be reinvented from scratch by artists like Diana Hobson, with only the examples in museums made by the pioneers to provide inspiration and, within their forms and textures, clues as to its manufacture. Gradually, its secrets have been rediscovered by the accumulated research of many artists, to the point where it is practised globally by thousands, dwarfing the handful who initially developed and used it.

Its contemporary exponents include Antoine Leperlier, a grandson of

PREVIOUS PAGE
Amalric Walter, chameleon dish. Marked 'A. Walter Nancy & Bergé'. H. 9 cm (3½ in.), W. 18 cm (7 in.), D. 16 cm (2⅜ in.).
Photo: Simon Bruntnell.

An early example of Walter's use of a range of grain sizes in a single cast; from the fine detail of the painted surfaces to the contrasting heavier textures in the main body of the cast. The model of the chameleon is used in combination with a variety of bases to create different items.

◄ Chameleon dish, Amalric Walter, *c.* 1909. Marked 'Daum Nancy'. H. 9 cm (3½ in.). W. 29 cm (11½ in.) D. 9 cm (3½ in.).
Photo: Simon Bruntnell.

One of the earliest pieces of Walter's mature style, and a characteristic example of his mastery of the techniques of pâte de verre. He took the basic process developed by Henri Cros at Sèvres, and produced a more sophisticated and controllable version based on ceramic painting using enamels.

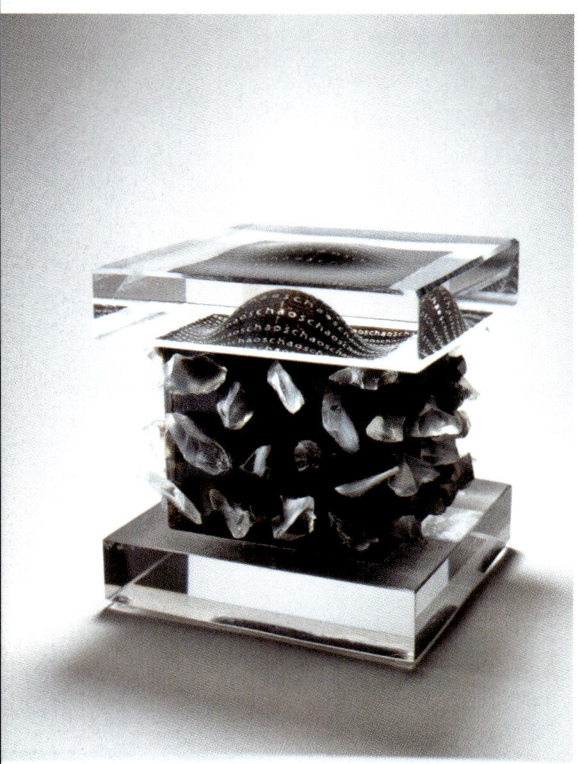

▲ *L'Instant Just Avant VIII*, Antoine Leperlier, 2003. H. 20 cm (8 in.), W. 18 cm (7 in.), D. 18 cm (7 in.).
Photo: courtesy of the artist.

A sculptural approach to the process of kiln-casting by a grandson of one of the major early 20th-century practitioners of pâte de verre, Francois Décorchement. Antoine Leperlier not only continues the tradition but constantly adapts and contributes to it.

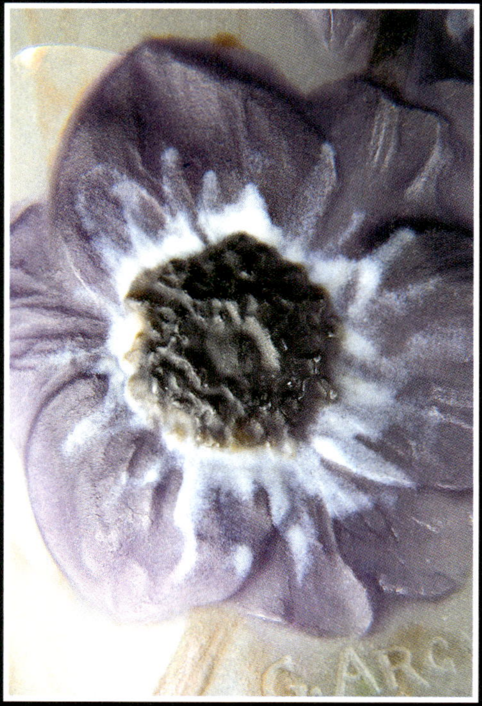

◄ Detail of an anemone nightlight shade from the mid-1920s by Gabriel Argy-Rousseau.
Photo: Simon Bruntnell.

Argy-Rousseau's technique differed from that of Walter in a significant way. Whereas Walter used extremely finely crushed glass mixed with a medium to paint in the surface details, giving an effect analogous to enamel painting, Argy-Rousseau pressed coarser grains of glass into the mould's details (rather than mixing them with an oil medium and painting them with a brush), resulting in a more translucent effect.

Francois Décorchemont, who, utilising his grandfather's notebooks, has carried on the family tradition and become a major artist in his own right.

An important feature of pâte(s) de verre, to give it its proper title, both in its first manifestation and in contemporary terms, is that it is not actually a single process at all, but a series of individual variations on a central theme. Each slight shift in any of the factors involved – mould, glass type, filling and firing – acts as a personal version of the process, giving each practitioner`s works a particular set of qualities.

A major distinction lies in the designations 'pâte' or its plural 'pâtes', translating literally into 'paste' or 'pastes'; this describes the use of a single grain size and colouring, or the use of a range of different grain sizes and colouring methods. The differences can clearly be seen by comparing the work of two near contemporaries.

This piece by Argy Rousseau shows in close-up that the mould has been filled with crushed coloured glasses of the same consistency.

On the other hand this piece by Amalric Walter clearly displays a different approach. He designated his work as 'pâtes' – plural (see the 'point of sale plate', on p.26). He ground very finely selected coloured glass that he had founded himself from raw ingredients, and, after mixing it with oil, used it like a paint, applying it with a brush to the top surface of the mould, which created the characteristic multicoloured painterly details of his sculptural pieces, particularly those which included animals and insects. As the mould was filled, larger and larger grains were employed, hence the plural 'pastes'.

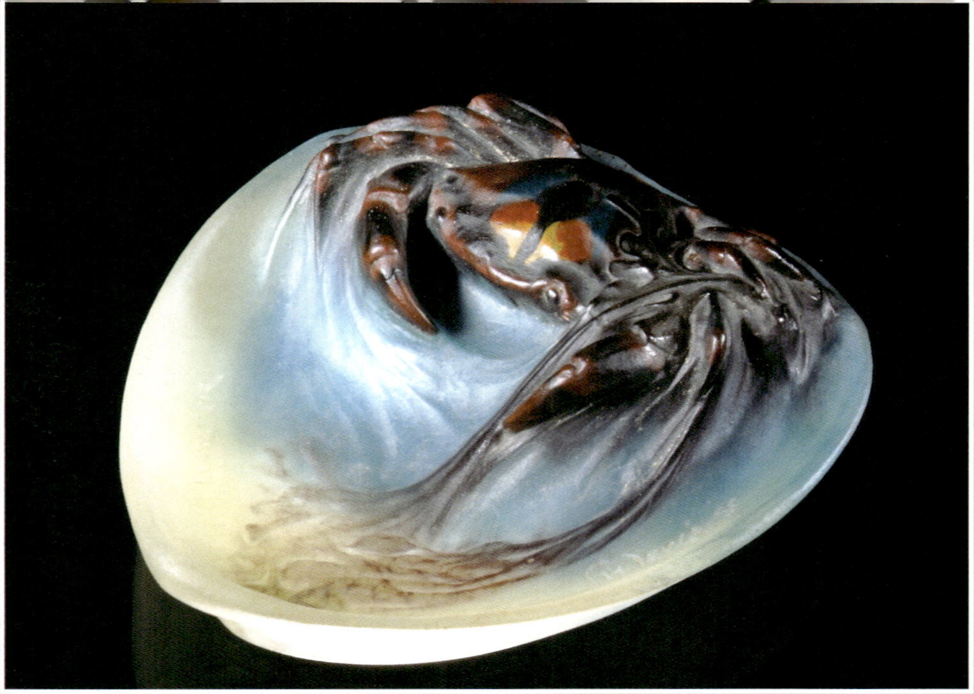

Crab dish, Amalric Walter, 1920s. Marked 'A. Walter & Bergé *sc.*'. H. 7 cm (2¾ in.), W. 17 cm (6⅝ in.), D. 19 cm (7½ in.).
Photo: Simon Bruntnell.

In contrast with Argy-Rousseau's use of translucent glass, Walter's technique resembles the fine ceramic enamel painting that inspired it. In his pâte de verre casts, however, the details were painted onto the interior of the mould before firing, rather than onto the surface after casting.

A major feature of the work of this seminal generation during the period 1880–1930 is that like Walter they all founded, coloured and ground their own glass. This naturally led to a great understanding of, and control over, their individual palettes, and lent greater personal character to their work. There is a great difference between this approach and the contemporary, ready availability of standard glass colours in grain and ingot form which can bring a sameness to pieces produced worldwide. One is put in mind of Henri Matisse`s late paper cut-outs, which were all made from his hand-painted sheets of paper. Much of the quality of this work depends on the individual colours that this method provided.

Another change from earlier practice is the growing tendency for artists to have their work cast by specialist foundries, which are capable of taking a form in plaster or another solid, and casting it in a single-colour glass. This is identical to the age-old practice of bronze-casting, but whereas this has been in existence for millennia, the commercial casting of glass sculpture is a relatively recent phenomenon, and one which adds an important new factor to glass as an art and craft material. It has grown from the practice in former Communist Czechoslovakia of the state sponsorship of artists and the centralisation of the means of production in factory facilities. This led to the development of a unique system, whereby high-quality, large-scale casting facilities were placed at the service of identified artists like Libensky and Brychtová. Since the break-up of the Communist bloc this expertise has been transformed into the establishment of privately run casting studios.

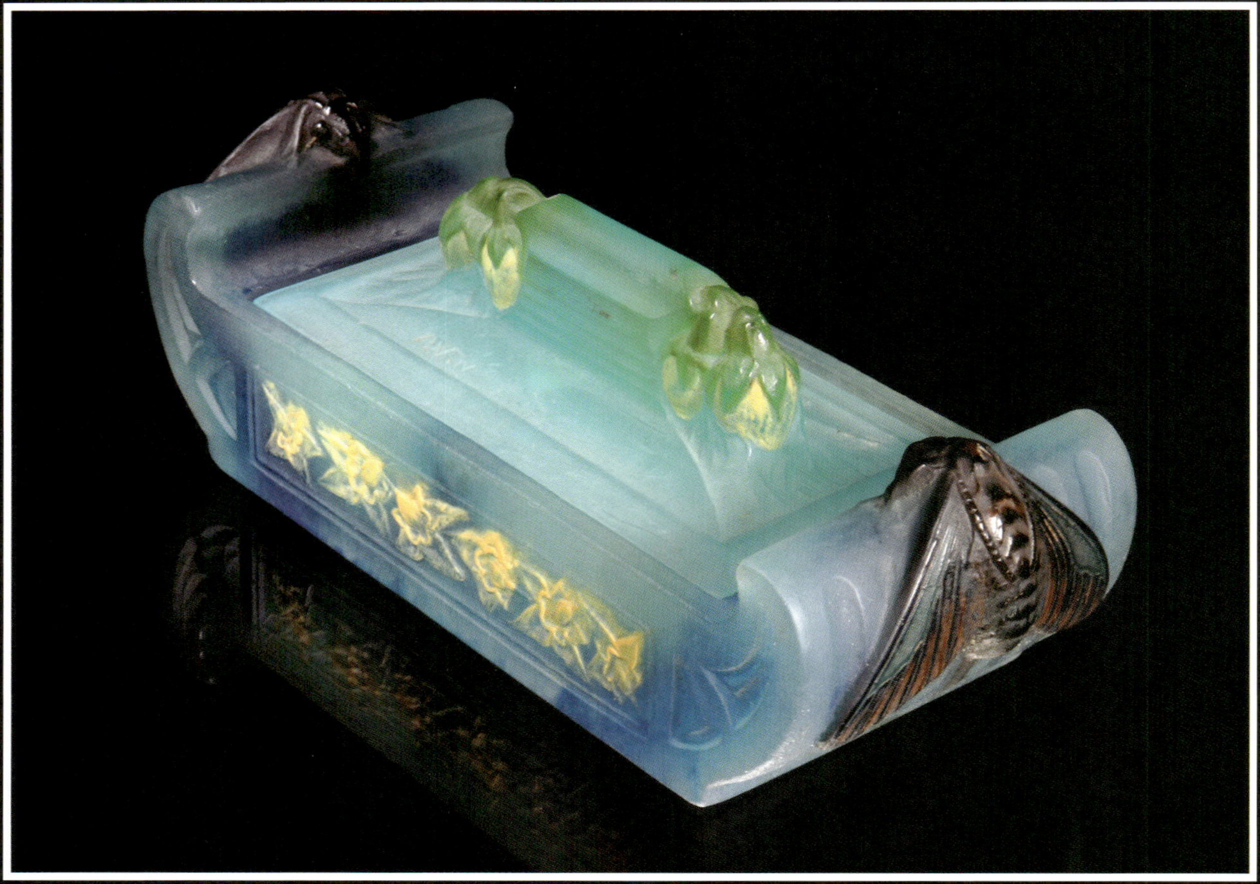

At Sèvres

The inspiration behind the invention of pâte(s) de verre was provided by Henri Cros (1840–1907), a sculptor who, inspired by classical sculpture and vase painting, sought to develop a truly polychromatic modelling material, where local colour within the forms was integral to the material rather than added afterwards as a surface, like paint or enamel. (I use the term 'invention' deliberately despite the fact that the pioneers claimed to be merely rediscovering an ancient process. In fact, apart from some fairly simple glass-casting, there was nothing like pâte de verre in the ancient world; it was without doubt the first new glass craft process for 2000 years.) After experimenting with a number of media, including encaustics, where colour is embedded within hot wax, Cros transferred the same concept to glass, carrying out the bulk of his work at the Sèvres factory.

Sèvres provided Cros with a studio and furnaces, and the factory background was to play a crucial role in the direction of his experiments, and therefore in their outcome. A major part of the output of Sèvres consisted of high-quality decorated ceramics, centred on the painting and firing of coloured enamels onto fine ceramic bodies. Enamels are basically low-temperature glasses crushed and ground in a ball mill to a fine floury consistency and, after mixing this with organic oil, applied by brush to the surfaces of ceramic forms, then fired in a kiln to melt the enamel and to fix it onto the surface of the fired clay body. Sèvres produced its own range of enamel colours, controlling all aspects of its manufacture, including the range of colours, which were created by adding oxides to the glass in crucibles during founding.

The genius of Cros lay in the way he transferred this knowledge to his search for a new material, adapting it to the creation of multicoloured reliefs. He took the soft, low-firing, enamel-glass colours, and from them created a new process. The major obstacle he had to overcome was how to give shape to the different glass colours as they fused in the kiln, a task that clearly gave him some problems. Many of his pieces take the form of plaques; flat on the back with some low-relief modelling on the front. These were effectively two-dimensional forms, and as such they were much easier to cast than fully modelled three-dimensional artefacts.

◀ Covered box with moths, Amalric Walter, *sc.* 1920s. Marked 'A. Walter Nancy & Bergé'. H. 8 cm (3⅛ in.), W. 23 cm (9 in.), D. 9 cm (3½ in.).

Photo: Simon Bruntnell.

The box form with a close-fitting lid presented a particular problem in terms of pâte-de-verre casting. Walter overcame this without compromising his control over surface colour and detail.

To shape a glass mass as it fuses, it needs to be fully supported as it softens in the kiln into a single viscous mass before cooling restores its rigidity. A flat low-relief mould of the kind used by Cros, created from a clay or wax original, has a large opening created by the back of the form, into whose shallow depressions the fine, granular glass colours can be accurately placed. Once fired to a temperature high enough to fuse the glass grains into a solid mass, the result is a two-dimensional form with a multicoloured, homogeneous character. The palette of different-coloured glasses that Cros used was created by founding and fritting quite small amounts of clear glass mixed with colouring agents, and was a time-consuming process.

Once established, the basic process was refined and customised by Cros's followers. Although pâte de verre was not on the curriculum at the school at Sèvres, Cros's constant presence in his studio there meant that the technique exerted an influence on students, with some, notably Amalric Walter (1870–1959), developing their careers through its practice. The process became more sophisticated and varied in the hands of this next generation. Different ways of filling moulds and firing them led to a range of variations within the generic process, and a greater complexity of form, with fully realised three-dimensional shapes being achieved. This meant that instead of being limited to flat plaque-like forms, hollow vases and even lidded boxes could be produced (see the photo on p.22).

One advance that made this possible was the use of binding agents to help the glass granules cling to vertical surfaces during firing. Another was the use of internal cores to press glass into the desired shape and, after firing and their removal, to leave behind the internal spaces needed for a hollow form like a vase. However, despite the sophistication of the work of his followers, full credit must go to Cros for his original research and insight. Although in its mature form the process invariably shapes the glass within a mould, I am of the opinion that a small number of Cros's low reliefs may have been formed freely, directly onto a ceramic bat, which would have supported it while in the kiln. The glass grains would have been mixed with water and modelled with wooden tools.

I mention this to indicate a path which has never to my knowledge been explored, and which may lead someone to a new, looser version of the process. Clearly, working like this would result in soft, imprecise contours (a characteristic of some of Cros's pieces), and three-dimensional forms would be, to say the least, difficult. However, as an area for experiment it surely has potential, and if successful would yield a different set of possibly more painterly qualities when compared with the mould-formed version. Generally speaking, the so-called secrets of pâte de verre have been solved, and there are thousands of artists worldwide working in a variety of ways that are linked to the generic process, in stark contrast to its origins, where there were very few.

Perhaps of all the artists who practised pâte de verre in the generation that came after Cros, none came closer to realising his original vision of a truly polychromatic, translucent material used in the production of sculptural form than Amalric Walter. His methods were arguably the most complex and detailed of all, and were the subject of a research project I set up and directed at the University of Wolverhampton in 2005/6, with the support of a grant from the Arts and Humanities Research Council. The aim of the project was to create, through research, an exact model of Walter's methods, and to use it to recreate facsimiles of his work. A major reason for undertaking this project was to place the findings in the public domain so as to inform, and hopefully inspire, a new generation of artists. Much of this information is new and therefore, in the spirit of this book, I feel its description in detail is merited.

The account that follows is of research carried out by Max Stewart, who worked with me on the project, and is taken from his research report with his permission.

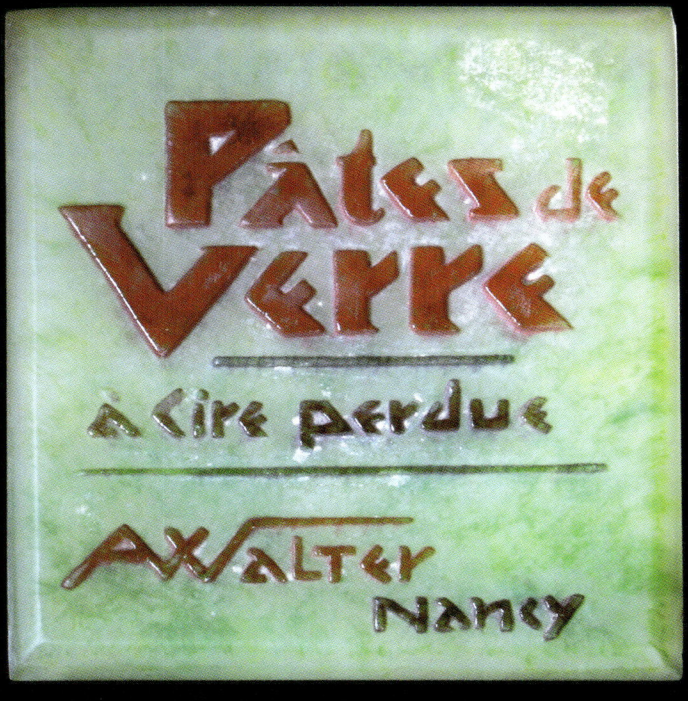
Pâtes de
Verre
à cire perdue
AWalter
Nancy

Amalric Walter

Walter was born in 1870 in Sèvres, and enrolled in 1885 at the factory school to follow in his father's and grandfather`s footsteps and train as a ceramic enamel painter, a long and rigorous four-year course. Although not on the official curriculum, pâte(s) de verre was practised at Sèvres by Henri Cros and his son, who was a contemporary of Walter's. Walter stayed at Sèvres for 15 years, during which time he became adept at the pâte(s) de verre process, working as an assistant to his erstwhile teacher, Professor Gabriel Lévy, in the production of a range of experimental products, some of which were exhibited at national exhibitions, winning a number of awards. These products demonstrated an updated version of Cros's original process, which was used in the realisation of predominantly architectural features like tiles, as well as one-off items.

◄ Amalric Walter, rectangular 'point of sale' plate, date unknown. W. 11 cm (4⅜ in.), D. 12 cm (4¾ in.).

Photo: Simon Bruntnell.

Interesting on a number of levels, this small plaque showed Walter's interest in the marketing of his work. It also uses the plural spelling of 'pâtes', derived from his use of a variety of different grades of crushed glass within his pieces.

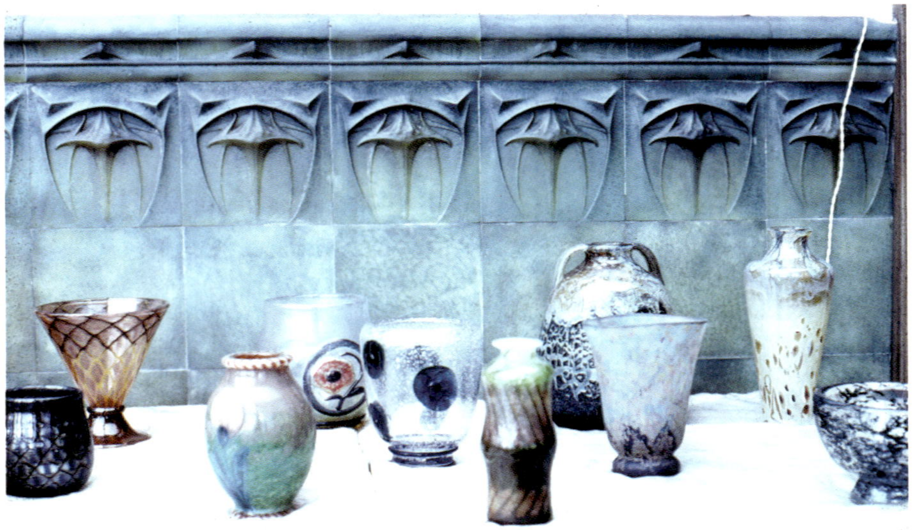

◄ Experimental cast wall tiles, produced while Walter was employed at Daum, *c.* 1909.

Photo: unknown.

During this crucial, formative period, pâte de verre was used in the production of a variety of experimental objects, many of which were exhibited in national exhibitions.

Although the exact terms of his employment at Sèvres are unclear, his association with the process, and his expertise, led in 1904 to an approach by the Nancy glass factory Daum, who invited him to join the staff as a specialist in this new process. Walter stayed at Daum until the outbreak of the First World War, acting predominantly as a facilitator, producing works in pâte de verre for a range of artists. However, he also developed a crucial friendship and collaboration with the modeller Henri Bergé, and with him produced pieces which as early as 1908 established the main characteristics of his mature style.

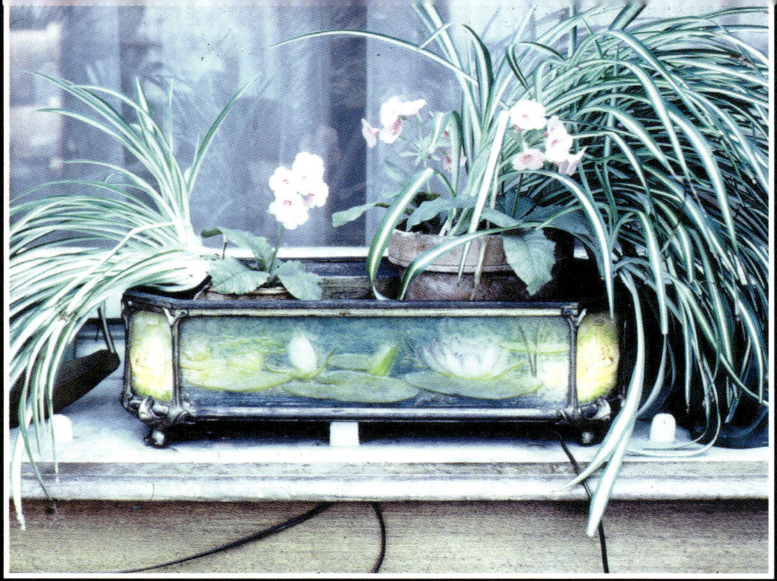

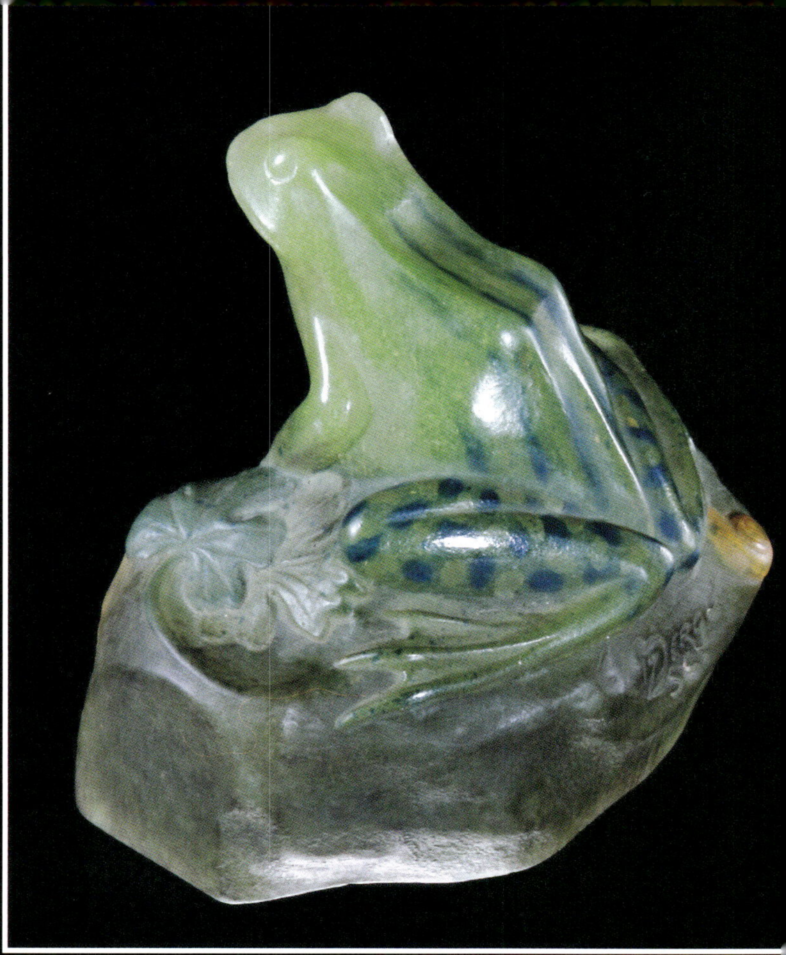

▲ Jardinière, Amalric Walter, *c.* 1909.

Photo: unknown.

Pâte-de-verre panels set into a pewter frame, produced at Daum. Walter was employed by Daum to develop pâte de verre as a viable process. While he developed his personal style, he was also used as a facilitator for other artists' designs. This piece, which remained at the factory, was almost certainly a one-off.

After service in the First World War, Walter decided not to return to Daum, instead setting up his own studio in Nancy, which was to remain in operation until 1937. Crucially, the split with Daum was entirely amicable; he was allowed to take his master models with him, and to pursue his collaboration with Bergé, which continued until Bergé's death in 1937.

All of these ingredients – the training in ceramics, a detailed knowledge of enamels, and a continuing source of basic glass from the Daum factory – came together in Walter's mature work. A hallmark of his oeuvre is the control he exercised over the detailed surface colouring of his pieces. This developed from his extensive training as an enamel painter on ceramics, which simply and effectively he transferred to his glass, thereby extending the vocabulary of Cros's original process to achieve a closer approximation to his original aims. I would even go further and say that Walter came nearest to realising Cros's vision of a truly multicoloured sculptural material.

Walter's surface patterns, which are often dense or opaque, are supported by background layers of less dense, more translucent-coloured

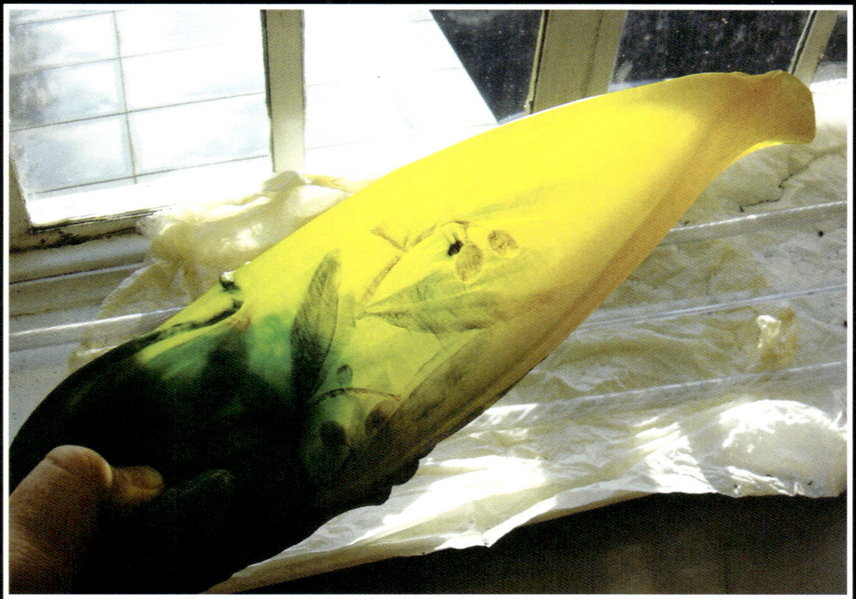

Large frog paperweight, Amalric Walter, *c.* 1920. Marked Walter & Bergé, *sc.* H. 9 cm (3½ in.), W. 10 cm (4 in.), D. 7 cm (2¾ in.).

Photo: Simon Bruntnell.

The different grades of crushed glass can clearly be seen in this piece. The fine blue stripes on the frog's skin still show their original brush marks, while the main body of the frog displays the coarser texture created by the use of coarser green granules. This model of an individual creature was employed in the production of many objects, from paperweights to dishes.

Detail of chameleon dish.

Photo: courtesy of the University of Wolverhampton.

The painted nature of the surface details can be seen in the way that the delicate greenery has been brushed onto the mould's surface in finely crushed glass mixed with an oil medium.

glass, which help to create depth within the pieces. His formal language – a fusion of traditional and contemporary French styles – together with his extensive use of reptile, insect and amphibian motifs, conveyed a signature sculptural presence across his entire output.

In seeking to understand and replicate Walter's methods, we were extremely fortunate to have access to an extensive private collection of original pieces. This allowed us to study and photograph the detailed surfaces of over 150 pieces, and provided us with vital clues to direct the practical research. The point of departure for these investigations centred on the highly detailed surfaces of the pieces, which, unlike the work of Walter's contemporaries, had a strong painterly quality.

In addition, close examination revealed a movement from the surface of the cast back into the interior. A similar pattern is evident in the surface decoration of an example of the famous chameleon boat form (see photo on p.18). (Incidentally, this one is marked 'Daum', which puts it in the period 1904–18, and shows that Walter's style and technique were well established even early in his career.)

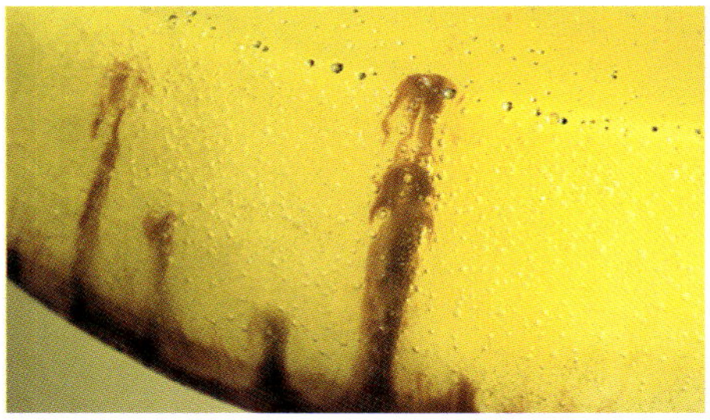

Detail of the rim of a Walter dish. ➤

Photo: courtesy of the University of Wolverhampton.

The finely crushed-glass rim colour rising through the body colour; this is caused by the oil medium burning during firing.

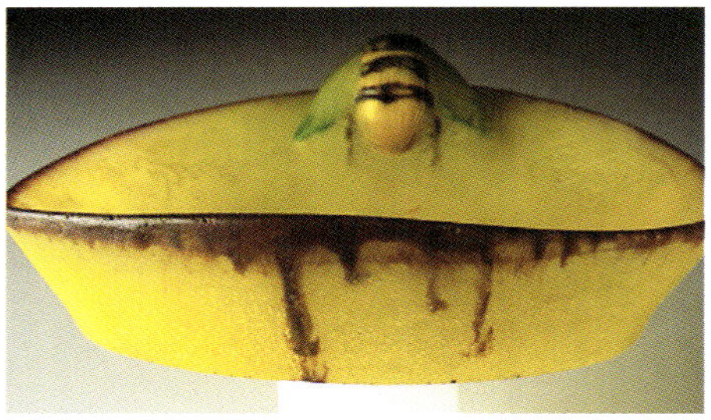

Rim detail as it appears. ➤➤

Photo: courtesy of the University of Wolverhampton.

As the dish is fired upside down, the bleeding colour appears to run down from the rim when the dish is placed upright.

The colour seems to bleed back into the yellow backing glass. Again, on this bee dish the colour painted on the edge looks as if it is being dragged back from the rim.

The dish, held the right way up, looks as if the rim colour has dribbled down the side; however, this is misleading, as this piece, like all of Walter's output, was actually cast the other way up, to allow glass to flow down from the flat base into the form. Viewed from this perspective these are revealed as risers; the colour has floated back from the surface during firing. Experiments revealed that this was caused by a characteristic of enamel painting on ceramics, namely the presence of a painting medium, an organic oil which binds the colouring agents together and allows them to be brushed onto the surface before being burnt off during firing. When this technique was transferred to glass, however, the oil, buried within a mass of glass, could not burn off; instead its presence created bubbles in the soft glass mass, which rose up and drew away some of the colour from the rim.

This is such a characteristic of Walter's glass that it is certain he both understood the phenomenon and welcomed it as an important part of his glass vocabulary. Walter was actually working in a reverse version of ceramic painting. In ceramics the enamel is applied last, to the stable, exposed ceramic surface; in Walter's glass the colour is painted first, onto the inner surfaces of the mould, and backed up with the glass that makes up the main body of the piece. This is why the ground and the painted surface details soften back into the larger grain support glasses that make up the bulk of the body. Prior to our research there had been some speculation that Walter enamelled his pieces after manufacture, which would have resulted in a totally different quality.

The start for each form was the master model in plaster. This one, which is characteristic, shows a number of the standard aspects of the procedure: the decoration is fully modelled; Walter's signature and that of the modeller are impressed into the surface; and the model sits on a deep base form, which, as part of the mould, will act as a reservoir for extra glass during the firing process.

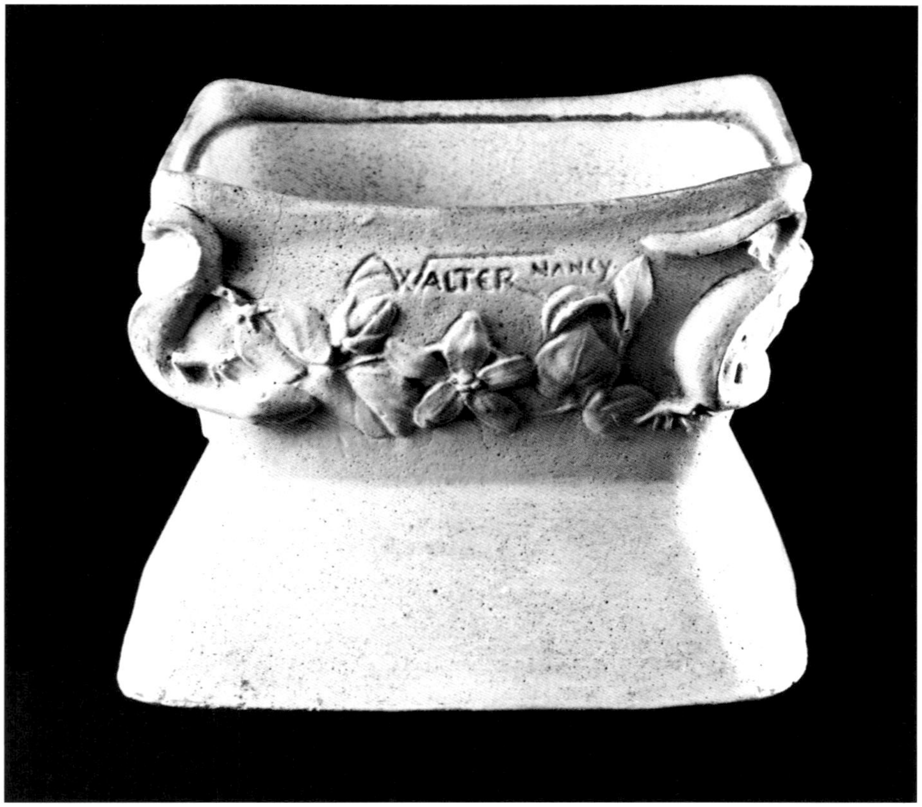

➤ An original plaster model of one of Walter's containers, *c.* 1920.

Repr. D. Bastien © INVERNTAIRE GENERAL/ADAGP (collection particulière – touts droites réservés.)

This would have served as the master form from which the multi-part wax mould would have been cast. Walter's signature trademark has been incorporated into the surface. The piece includes a deep base, to act as a reservoir for the extra glass that will be needed to fill the mould during the settling of the loose grains during firing.

The plaster original was used to make a multi-part hollow plaster exterior, from which any number of wax versions of the piece could be made. This of course utilised a ceramic technique – a multi-part mould from which large numbers of slipcast ceramic forms could be made – which would have been part of Walter's training at Sèvres.

The moulds for glass-casting were made by encasing individual waxes in a special refractory mix and melting out the wax in a low-temperature oven. This is in strict contrast with most contemporary artists, who tend to favour steaming, as it carries a lower risk of damaging the mould. Each casting mould could be used only once; after firing it had to be broken away to reveal the glass. (It is interesting to note that the images supplied by artists in this book show that present practice is identical.)

Walter, despite over twenty years' experience of commercial production, preferred the more intimate scale of the studio to that of the factory, and never employed more than a dozen or so workers. One reason for this could have been a desire to retain personal control over all of his production. One contemporary account states that he painted all of the details of the top surface of his casts himself. This would certainly account for the consistency apparent in his output for over two decades.

This attention to detail, and the one-off nature of the casting process,

Amalric Walter, two uses of the same model, both 1920s: mallard paperweight. H. 6 cm (2⅜ in.), W. 6 cm (2⅜ in.), D. 10 cm (4 in.); mallard dish. H. 6 cm (2⅜ in.), W. 14 cm (5½ in.), D. 20 cm (8 in.). Both marked 'A. Walter. Nancy'.

Photo: Simon Bruntnell.

The mallard would have been modelled as a separate form; in these two items by Walter, it is used on its own as a paperweight, and as an addition to a dish. In each instance the decoration has been varied, exploiting the fact that each piece had to have its surface colours and patterns applied by hand.

meant that he was never a rich man. It also meant that, without compromising quality, he was forced to take whatever steps he could to rationalise his methods. An account of his working method is surely of more than historical interest alone, addressing as it does issues which still confront all those who seek to sustain a satisfying and meaningful practice in the 21st century.

Even in the early years of the 20th century the serial creation of what were essentially one-off pieces was financially a risky business, and Walter had to address this in his production system. We have already seen that he used master moulds from which he could cast large numbers of waxes, but he did not stop there. He devised systems of components – individual creatures, for example – combining them in different ways with a variety of bowl, tray and dish forms. It is possible to see the fettling marks made by the action of the serrated modelling tool where the different sections have been joined. Basic dish forms were customised by the addition of

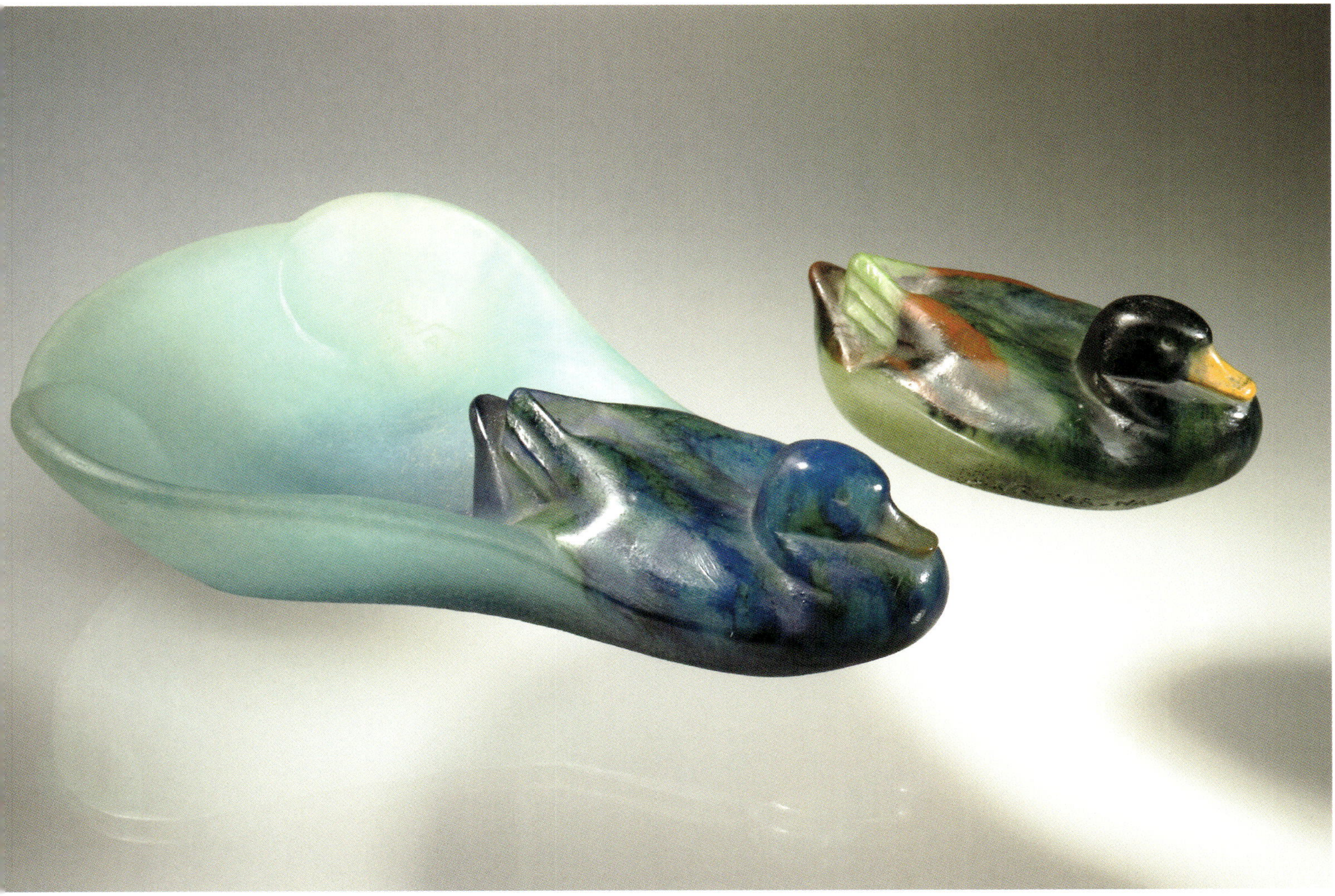

low-relief motifs, like sprigs of leaves and berries, in addition to the more sculptural animal and insect forms. In these ways he created a whole range of artefacts from a number of components. He was further able to increase the individualism of each piece by overseeing and varying the painting in of the surface details. In this way he ensured that even if two casts were identical in shape, their individual colouring made them unique.

The use of the mallard duck on its own and as a component of a dish is an example of this process, as are the variations in individual colouring and uses of the same chameleon cast (as can be seen in the dishes below). Whilst Walter made his pieces in the form of semi-functional objects, there is little evidence of everyday use – marks or other signs of wear – on surviving examples. This would seem to indicate that their owners valued them as small-scale, decorative sculptures rather than utilitarian objects, a fact that clearly has resonance for kiln-formers seeking to maintain a practice in the 21st century.

Amalric Walter, two versions of the chameleon dish.

Photo: courtesy of the University of Wolverhampton.

These four casts all use the same basic chameleon model. The two versions on the left are from different decades but were obviously cast from the same master. In addition to the variations in colour some loss of surface crispness is evident in the later version on the extreme left.

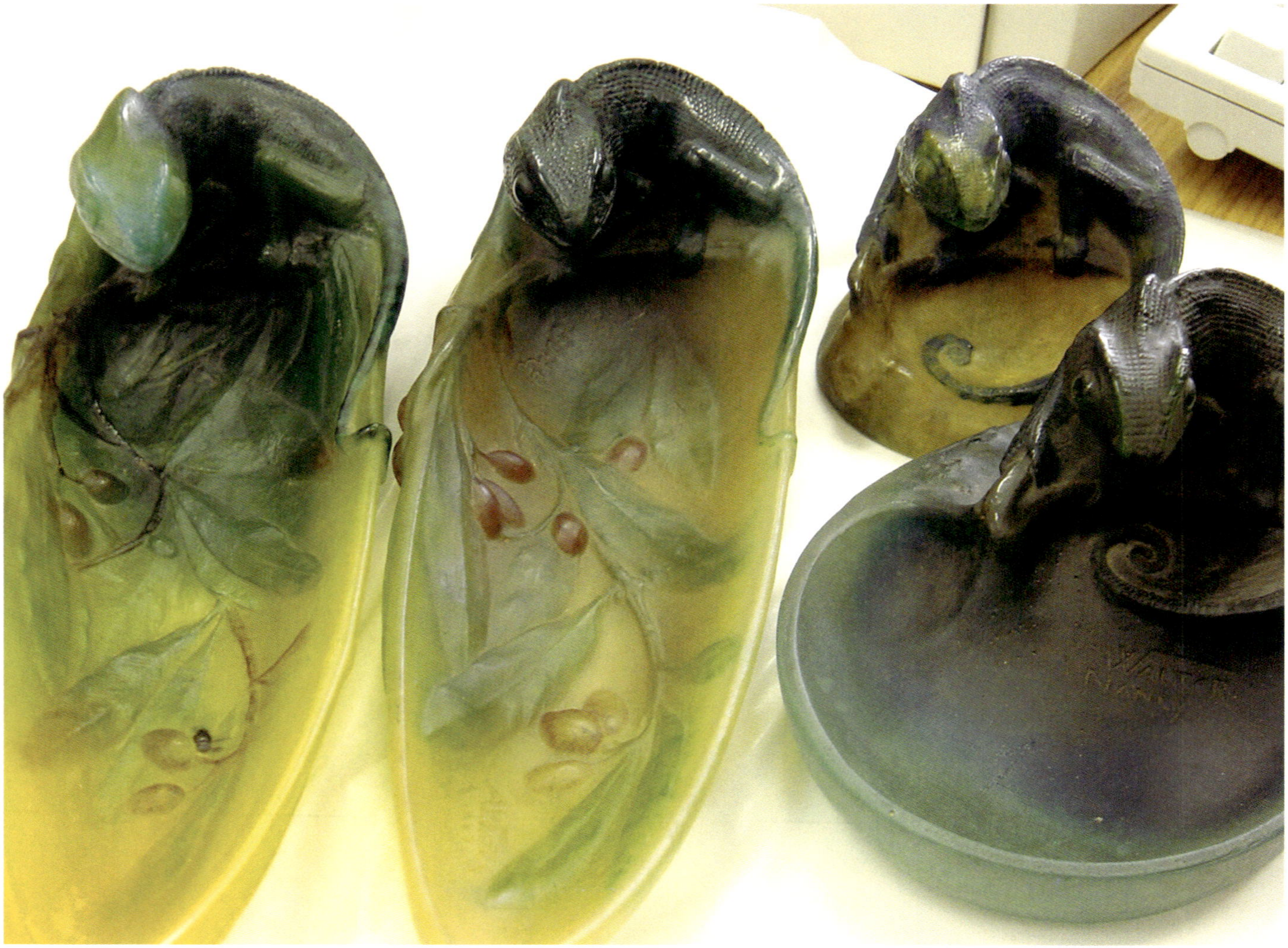

The manufacturing process

Before any of Walter`s pieces could be cast in wax, up to ten stages were needed to create a mould.

1 A maquette of the finished piece was modelled up from a watercolour design to give a good impression of its scale and mass. This was usually done in a material similar to modern plasticine, i.e. a mixture of powdered clay and linseed oil.
2 The maquette would then be broken down into its component parts: main shape, three-dimensional decorative elements (e.g. creature) and surface details.
3 These would be modelled separately.
4 The base form, devoid of detail, would be cast in plaster and worked, shaped and polished until it was ready to receive the decoration, while still in the soft clay and linseed mix. The large reservoir would be incorporated at this stage.
5 A multi-part mould would be made of the larger sculptural decoration, to allow for its production as a separate glass cast. There are numerous examples of paperweights by Walter of single animals, which are also used as three-dimensional elements adorning trays and dishes.
6 The production of, for example, the boat-shaped form with the chameleon would have proceeded as follows: the two positives, dish and chameleon, would have been fitted together, and the join marks fettled with a modelling tool, evidence of which is frequently seen on finished glass casts. Any extra low-relief details (e.g. foliage) would be either added directly onto the plaster form or pulled in clay form from a plaster sprig mould before being added.
7 This final assemblage would be the subject of a multi-part plaster mould.
8 A plaster positive was then cast from this mould.
9 This was now subjected to a thorough refining of the overall finish and detailing, before being sealed with shellac. It was then used to make a multi-part mould, which functioned as the mould from which all subsequent waxes were produced for the lost-wax, glass-casting process. The original or master form was preserved and not used again unless something happened to the wax reproduction mould, or through overuse its detailing became eroded.
10 Waxes were cast from the mould, each wax being used, like the casting mould, just once.
Each wax was subjected to a final finish before being set into refractory mix. Any blemishes that could be removed at this stage would mean less work on the actual glass cast (see the photos of Daum's present production on p.53, p.55 and pp.58–9). An overall softness could be imparted to the wax by gently rubbing with a heated linen cloth.

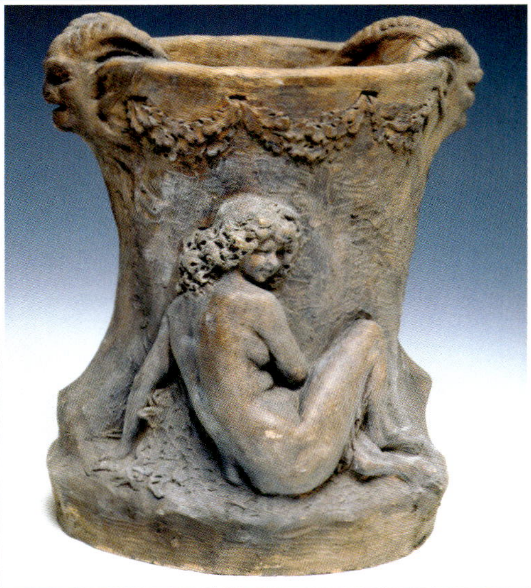

Amalric Walter? A plaster model from the Daum years, 1903–14.

Repr.D. Bastien © INVERTAIRE GENERAL/ADAGP (collection particulière – tous droits resérvés).

It is unlikely that this was designed by Walter, but it is typical of the master forms from which the multipart plaster moulds for the production of the wax multiples were made.

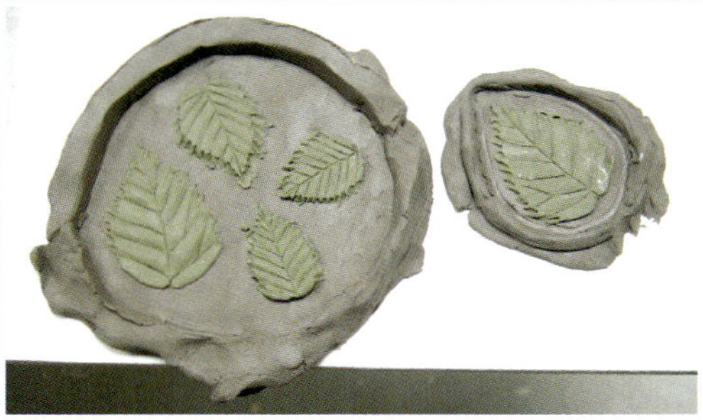

Details ready to be cast in plaster (after Walter).

Photo: courtesy of the University of Wolverhampton.

Walter's practice was to combine a range of elements to create the largest number of variations of items. Not only were larger forms like individual reptiles added to basic container forms, but smaller details like leaves were also used to vary the changes.

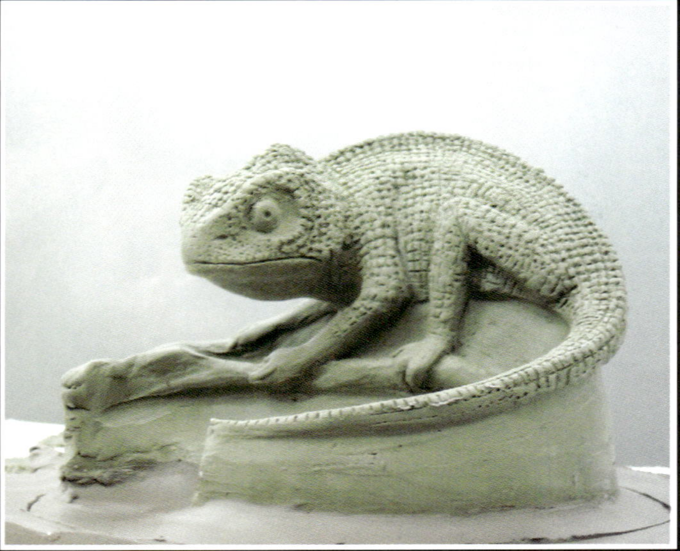

▲ A clay model of a chameleon (after Walter), ready to be cast in plaster, from which a master form would be created.

Photo: courtesy of the University of Wolverhampton.

The multipart mould made from this master would wear after producing a certain number of waxes, but the plaster master means that the precision of the original will not be lost.

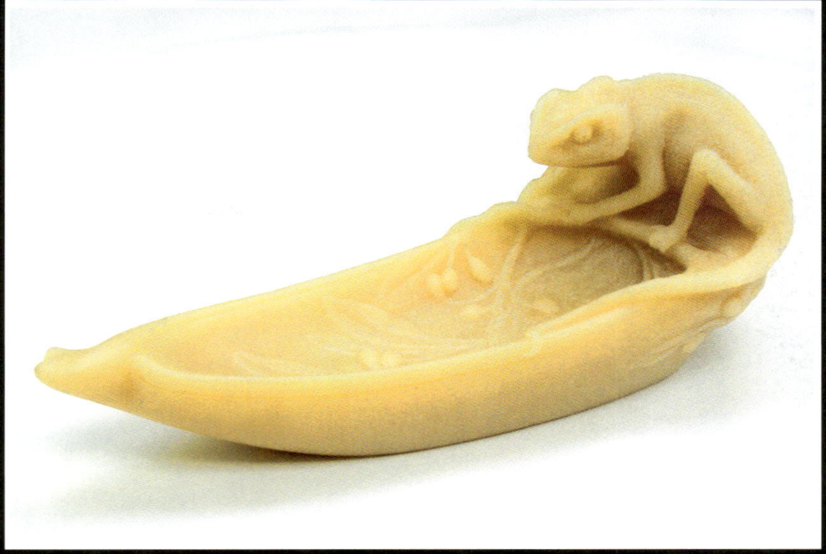

▲ A wax model of the chameleon dish (reproduction).

Photo: courtesy of the University of Wolverhampton.

Cast from a multipart plaster mould made from the master model, each glass cast required the use of a wax original like this one, which was then 'lost', i.e. melted from the refractory mould to allow the glass to be inserted prior to firing.

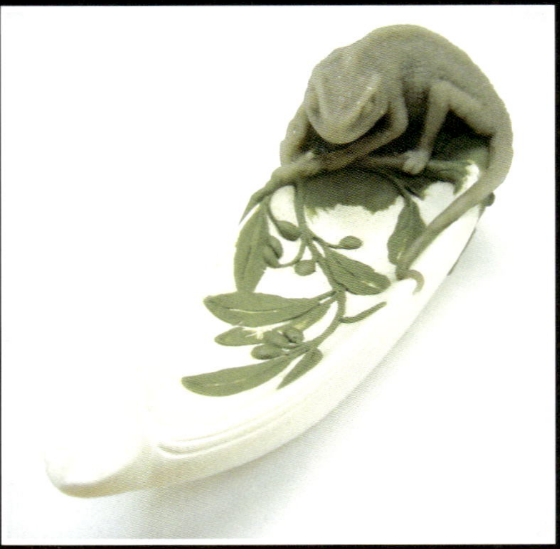

▲ A composite form.

Photo: courtesy of the University of Wolverhampton.

Various elements are brought together to create a version of the chameleon dish. All of the individual elements can be found in different combinations in the production of other items.

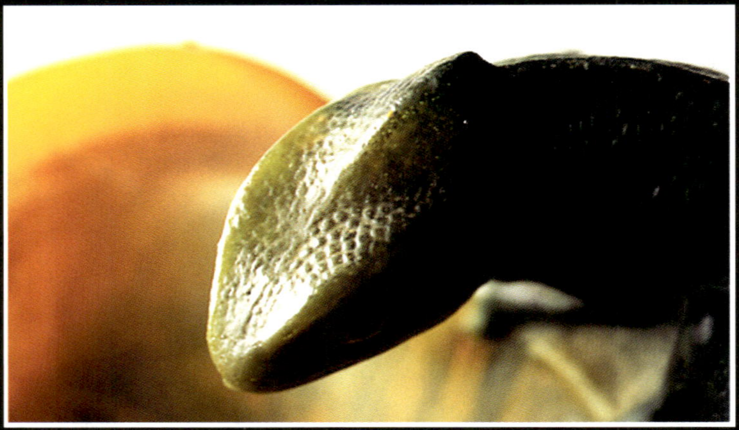

▲ Detail of a chameleon dish (Walter).

Photo: courtesy of the University of Wolverhampton.

This close-up of a chameleon's head from a cast dish clearly shows the seam line left on the wax by the two-part plaster mould, and is still evident in the glass cast.

All the pieces Walter made in his studio from 1918 onwards bore his signature and, generously, the signature of the modeller of the original. In the majority of cases this was Walter`s lifelong friend and collaborator Henri Bergé,

The refractory mix

There are no records of the precise make-up of Walter's mould mix, but from records left by his contemporaries we can speculate that it followed a similar pattern, give or take some minor variations:

Plaster	28%
Calcined kaolin (china clay)	22%
Kaolin	3%
Ground sand	10%
Sand in grains	37%

The mix was measured by weight, and once the sieved ingredients were amalgamated it was put through a wooden ball mill and sieved again. It was then gently added to water until the bulk of the mix sat just below the surface. It was allowed to thoroughly soak in before being manually agitated to a thick cream-like consistency. A cylinder of linoleum was placed around the wax model, leaving a minimum of 1 cm (⅜ in.) between cylinder and model. The mixture was poured in and allowed to set.

There is little evidence that Walter used any kind of supporting jacket to prevent the fragile mould mix from developing fissures during firing, but given that a majority of present-day practitioners do, it is a fair bet that he did. I have personally used the mix outlined above, and found it to be even more fragile than its 21st-century equivalents. The only possible clue to answering this question lies in a description of Walter's process by his employer, Antonin Daum, who stated that the moulds were covered in fireclay prior to firing. I have not personally tested this technique, but Daum's account does at least indicate that some kind of support was used. It is clear that the moulds themselves could not have been made from fireclay. The use of grog by some of today's artists as a constituent of moulds to give strength suggests that this was what Antonin Daum may have seen. Although there are a huge variety of kiln-casting mixes in use, they are all variations on this basic theme.

Although Walter's likely mix differs in some of its elements from those in use today, the similarities are more significant than the differences. Any casting mix must reach a compromise between strength and softness to enable it to withstand the rigours of the firing process and yet remain soft enough for it to fall away from the glass after casting.

Once the wax was melted from the mould, any cracks that had appeared in the delicate casting surface were made good by the application of a little fresh mixture, preferably before the mould had dried out.

When dry, the entire inner surface of the mould was coated with a layer of shellac. It is worth describing the use and application of shellac in some detail, because, like so much of this historical research, it has strong contemporary applications. Shellac is an organic secretion from the shell of the insect *Coccus Lacca*, which, diluted with methylated spirit, is brushed onto the surfaces of the mould that will come into contact with the glass during casting. This coating, which, being organic, burns away entirely, brings a number of benefits to the kiln-mix surface, and its use today is recommended.

1 It toughens the surface layer of the mould.
2 It stabilises the dry surface, and prevents dust from contaminating the glass.
3 The shellac seals the mould, and prevents it from absorbing moisture from delicate applications of ground-glass colours, making the details easier to brush on and control afterwards.
4 Because the mould mix is sealed, it effectively has less direct contact with the glass during firing, and has less opportunity to contaminate the glass or to adhere to it. The surface of the glass is, as a result, smoother.
5 After firing the mould is easier to break away from the glass, which in turn needs less cleaning.

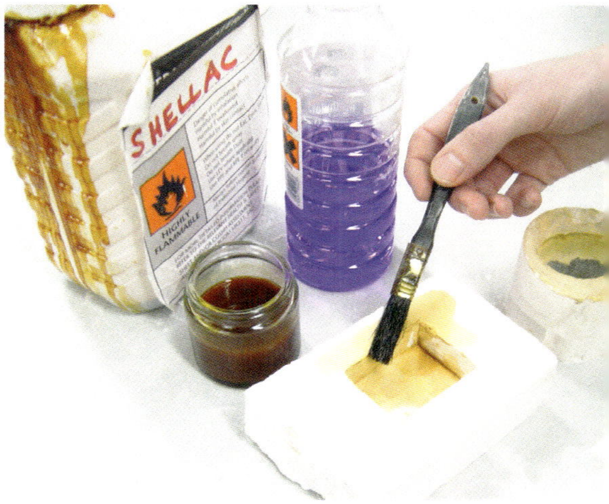

▲ The use of shellac to seal the mould's surface.

Photo: courtesy of the University of Wolverhampton.

The organic origins of shellac (it is derived from beetles' shells) and the fact that it can be diluted with methylated spirit mean that it burns away without leaving any residue to contaminate the glass. It is excellent for sealing the delicate surface of the mould, and also aids the removal of the mould from the glass after casting.

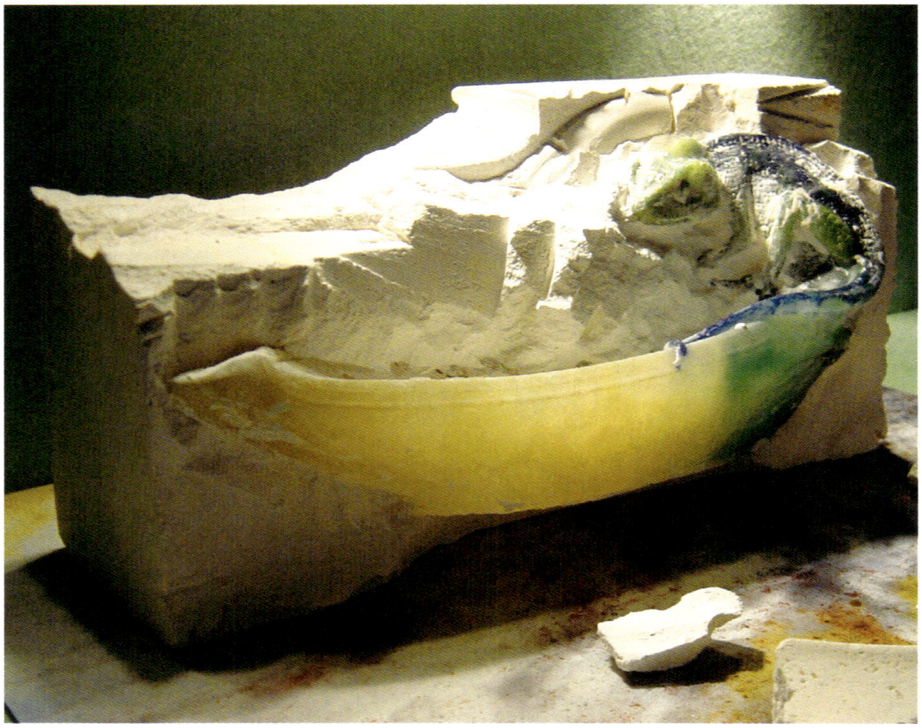

◄ Removing the glass cast from the mould.

Photo: courtesy of the University of Wolverhampton.

Each glass cast was unique, and required the destruction of the refractory mould material to release it. This still seems to be common practice today.

The coloured glasses

Walter, like his contemporaries, made his own colours, starting with a basic, soft, clear glass. He almost certainly bought this from his erstwhile employers and proceeded to create from it his signature palette. It is interesting to contrast this with contemporary practice, where the global availability of off-the-peg coloured glass ranges has, in addition to making life easier, perhaps at the same time taken away some of the individuality. Not for the first time, Walter and his circle have more to offer us than mere historical interest.

The colourless base glass from which all of the colours were made was a very soft lead glass with up to 40% lead content. This made it extremely easy to cast at fairly low temperatures (around 800°C/1472°F, as opposed to 950°C/1742°F for harder, soda glasses). Walter could do this because his items were decorative rather than utilitarian, and his pieces derived their strength from both their mass and their simple profiles.

The colouring agents are basically metallic oxides, mixed individually with the colourless glass at a founding temperature of 1240°C (2264°F). The primary oxides were:

copper – for turquoise
cobalt – for blue
chrome – for green
manganese – for brown-violet
iron – for yellow-red

Examples of the blue-green-yellow range of Walter's palette. ➤

Photo: Simon Bruntnell.

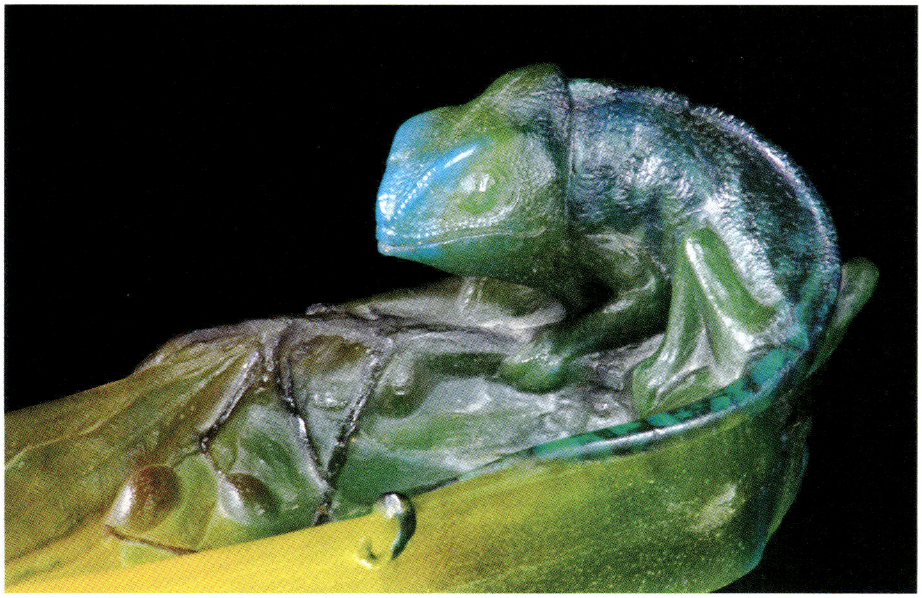

Walter made his colours from scratch, adding a range of colouring oxides to a basic lead batch he obtained from Daum. Although his range was restricted (certainly in contrast with the vast ranges now available commercially), it had the advantage of being under his control, and as a result highly personal.

Colour Range

Based on the mixing of 100 g (3½ oz) of basic 40% lead glass grains with the amount of oxide indicated, this mixture is placed in separate crucibles (one for each colour) and fired to 1240°C (2264°F) before being removed from the kiln and poured into water. The glass in the samples quoted in this list (below) is in granular form, equivalent to D3.

1	Turquoise clear	copper oxide 0.2 g
2	Grey-blue clear	cobalt oxide 0.1 g + chrome oxide 0.1 g
3	Brown-violet	manganese 3 g
4	Blue	cobalt 1.4 g
5	Green	chrome 0.01 g
6	Grey-blue	cobalt 0.1 g + chrome 0.014 g
7	*Brown-yellow	iron 3 g + manganese 3 g
8	Clear violet	cobalt 0.5 g + manganese dioxide 0.5 g
9	Clear yellow-brown	iron 0.3 g + manganese 0.3 g
10	Gold ruby	gold chloride 0.8 g
11	Blue	cobalt 1.4 g

* Colours 7 and 9 require a slightly higher temperature to strike – in the region of 1270/80°C (2318/36°F).

The temperature is held at a constant level for an hour, during which each crucible in turn is removed and stirred with a real potato on a stick (a traditional method) to ensure that the oxide is well integrated. The crucibles are placed back in the kiln to return them to top temperature for

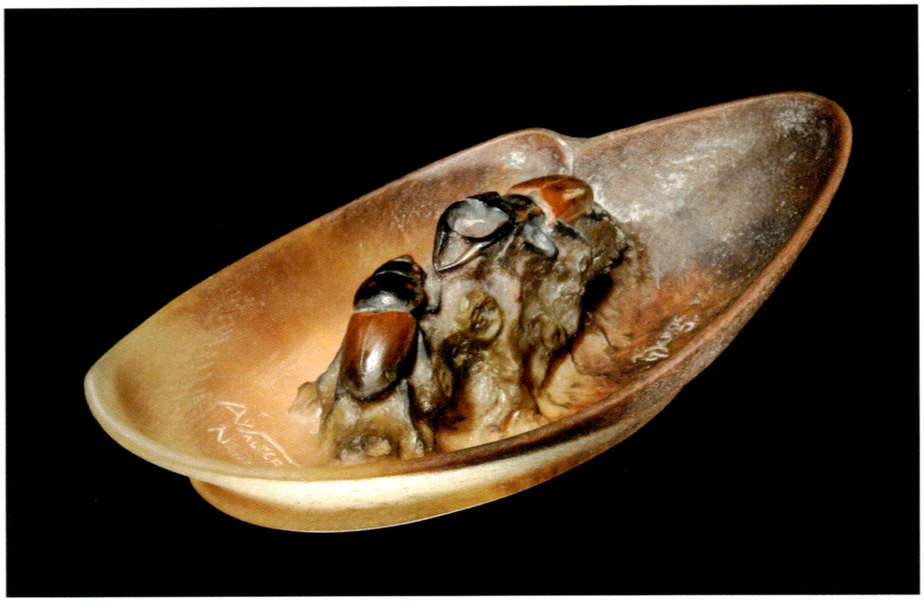

Examples of the red-brown-black range of Walter's palette.

Photo: Simon Bruntnell.

The darker blacks and browns betray through their density and the matt surfaces they impart to the glass, the large amounts of oxide used in their manufacture.

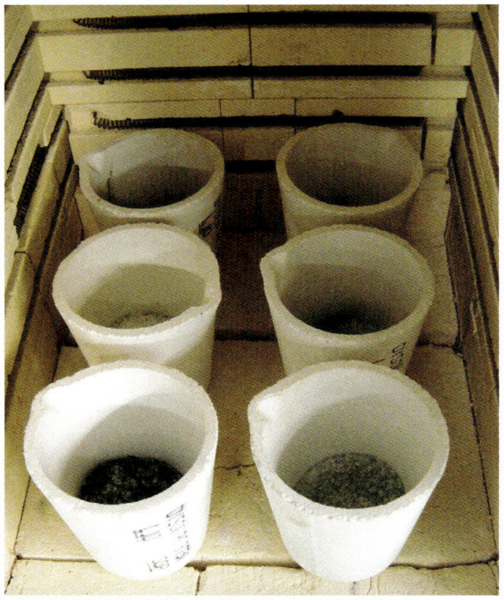

▲ Crucibles ready to fire.

Photo: courtesy of the University of Wolverhampton.

Each crucible is charged with different oxides mixed with the same basic clear lead batch to create a range of compatible colours, and placed in a kiln to fire.

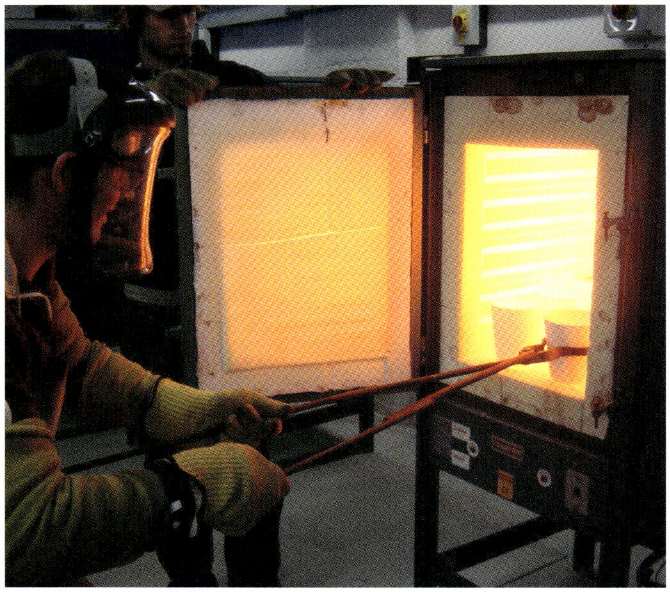

▲ The crucibles are fired to 1240°C (2264°F).

Photo: courtesy of the University of Wolverhampton.

At this temperature the oxides and the base glass have combined to create a specific coloured glass.

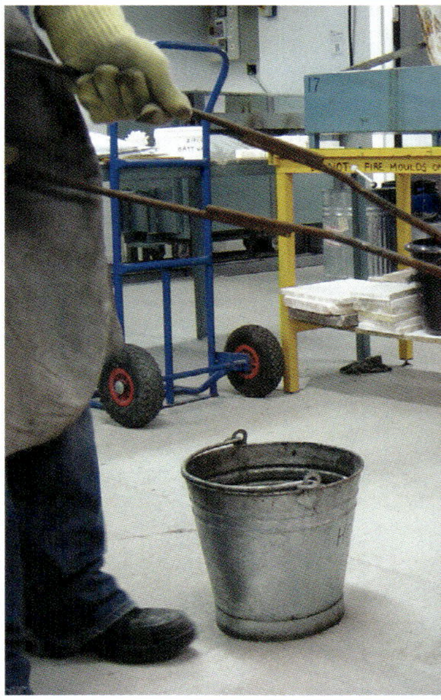

▲ Pouring the molten glass into water.

Photo: courtesy of the University of Wolverhampton.

Each crucible in turn is removed from the kiln and poured into water. A separate container is used for each colour to prevent contamination, and care is taken to ensure that a large enough quantity of water is used to prevent scalding.

long enough to ensure maximum pourability, whereupon they are removed and their contents poured into water.

This rapid cooling delivers such a thermal shock to the glass that it shatters into fragments, with the colour appearing as it cools.

Amongst the grains are also long ribbons of glass, which must be broken by direct pressure while still under water; it has to be water because the strings have tensions built into them, like the Prince Rupert's Drops they resemble, and fragment dangerously if broken in the air. The glass is then washed, strained and dried, whereupon it is ready for use.

Glass fritted in this way is, in many ways, more suitable for pâte-de-verre work than grains that are manually crushed.

This is because the individual glass fragments are cleaner, with no dust to muddy the cast, and have sharp, bright, surfaces which tend to lock

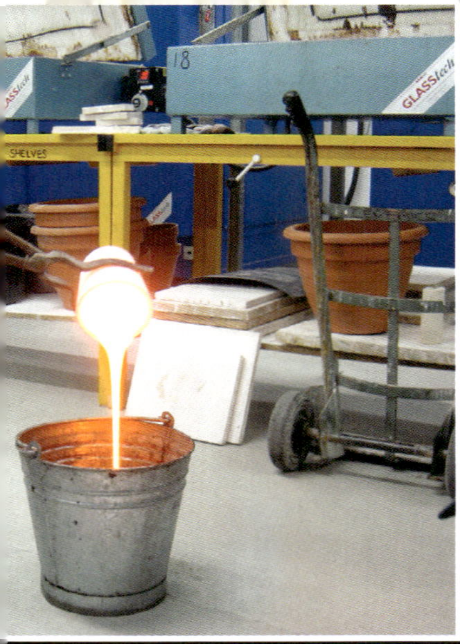

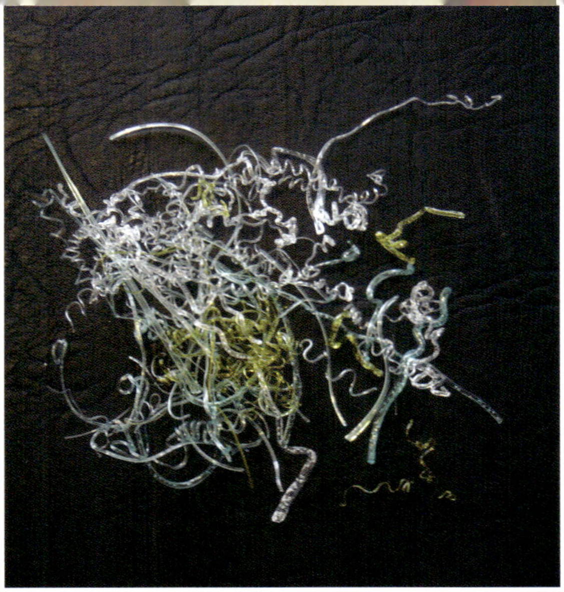

▲ Strings of glass caused by the thermal shock.

Photo: courtesy of the University of Wolverhampton. T

The molten glass reacts to the rapid drop in temperature in two distinct ways. These threads are full of tension, like toughened glass, and care must be taken when breaking them.

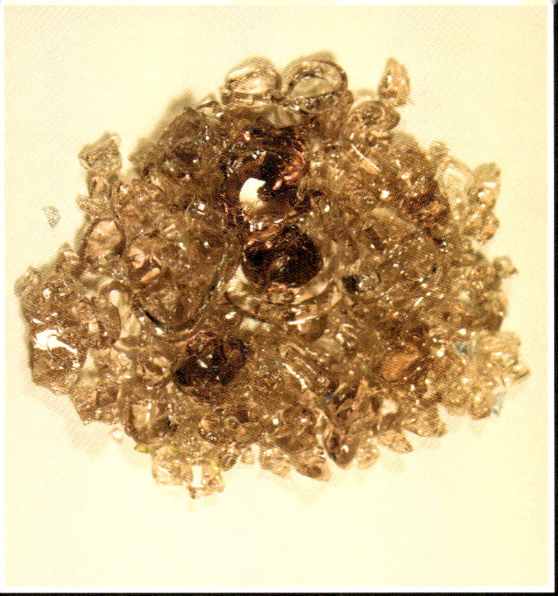

▲ Shattered fragments of glass.

Photo: courtesy of the University of Wolverhampton.

This is the other form that the glass takes on contact with the water.

Amalric Walter, chameleon dish. Marked 'A. Walter Nancy & Bergé'. H. 9 cm (3½ in.), W.18 cm (7 in.), D. 16 cm (2⅜ in.). ➤

Photo: Simon Bruntnell.

An early example of Walter`s use of a range of grain sizes in a single cast; from the fine detail of the painted surfaces, to the contrasting heavier textures in the main body of the cast. The model of the chameleon is used in combination with a variety of bases to create different items.

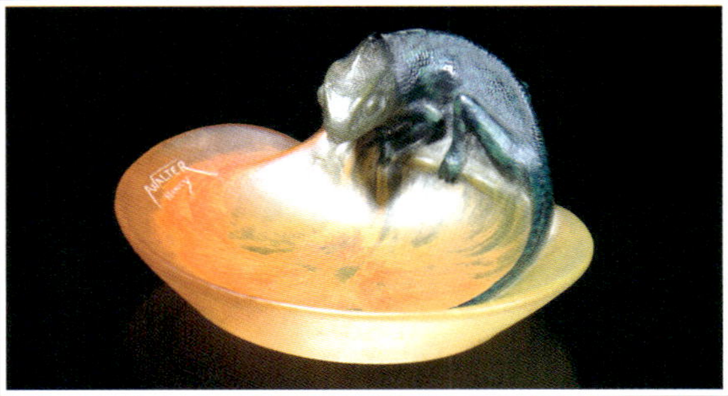

together well. The size of the grains used in the creation of colour at 1240°C (2264°F) is immaterial, as at this temperature any traces of the original grains simply disappear.

However, the casting of pâte de verre with lead-based glass was carried out at only 800°C (1472°F), and at this temperature different sizes of grain yield different effects within the body of the cast. This can clearly be seen in Walter's work, and it would seem that in addition to the finely ground, brush-applied colour, he used a range of mesh sizes between 7 and 100.

Generally speaking, the finer meshes are used at the surface of the cast, with coarser grains in the main body. This is obviously related to the greater detail and use of colour at the surface, with the main body often comprising a single colour.

The preparation of glass for pâte de verre

This method prepares the fritted glass for general use. The finer glass for painted details needs a further stage, which is described elsewhere.

1 A quantity of the base clear-glass grains is placed in an over-large container, and covered with water to the point where the ratio of water to glass is 3:1.
2 The mix is agitated, to bring the finer dust particles to the surface, and allowed to settle.
3 The milky residue is poured off, leaving the cleaner grains behind.
4 This process should be repeated three times.
5 The glass frit can then be dried, and is ready for the crucible. The previous list (see p. 39) is of recipes related to a notional 100 g (3½ oz) of glass.

The creation and application of the fine, coloured glass for painted detailing

A quantity of the frit from the crucible firing is ground by pestle and mortar until it is the size of D3 frit.

This is then placed in a ball mill, and left to run for 48 hours.

The powder that emerges is extremely fine, and when mixed with

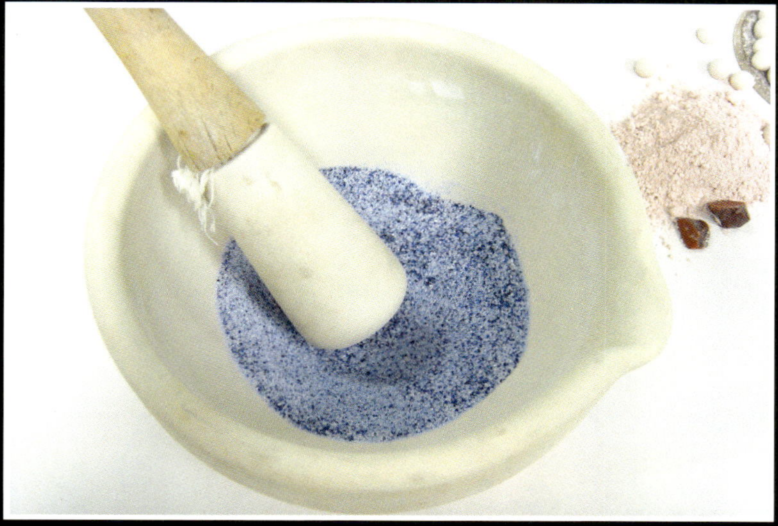

▲ Glass being ground by pestle and mortar.

Photo: courtesy of the University of Wolverhampton.

This is the first stage in the reduction of the water-shattered glass into usable grains. Walter ground his glass into a variety of mesh sizes to achieve different effects within a single cast. **Care must be taken to keep the grains damp to prevent dust inhalation.**

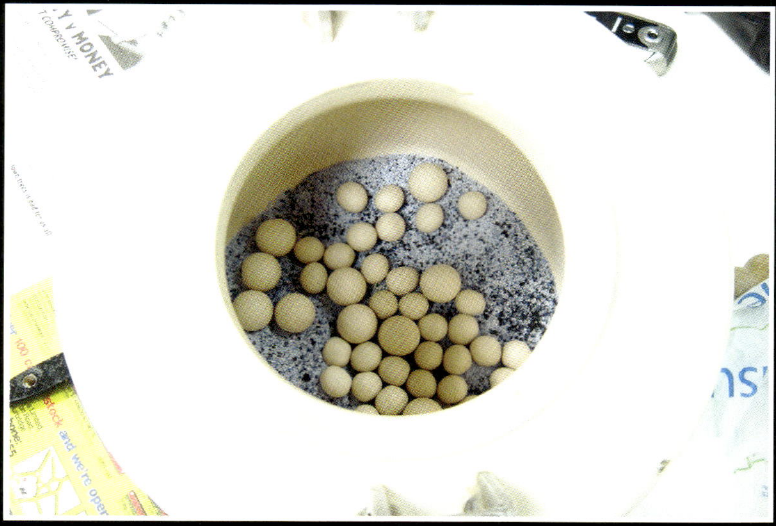

▲ Coarse grains placed in a ball mill.

Photo: courtesy of the University of Wolverhampton.

The glass is subjected to many hours in the mill, which, through the constant action of the porcelain balls, reduces it to an extremely fine consistency.

the fat oil medium produces a soft, paintable mass, which can if necessary be thinned out with pure turpentine.

Fat oil comes in various grades, the one used here being Sennelier's Essence Grasse. This is still used by the porcelain painters of Limoges to bind and apply their ceramic enamel colours. It is pale gold in colour and has a gentle scent, which indicates its purity and thus its tendency to burn off cleanly during firing. The ceramic painters of France all have their own individual preferences, which include oils of aniseed, lavender or orange. However, these are generally too thin for the binding of glass grains, no matter how fine. The procedure is as follows:

1 Place a small quantity of the powdered glass into a small dish, and, while mixing, add the fat oil a little at a time. Once mixed, the prepared paint should be kept in an airtight container to prevent the fat oil from evaporating.
2 The oil should be incorporated into the powder with a wooden tool. Contact with metal should be avoided, as this would change the purity of the colour through contamination.
3 When a good consistency, similar to toothpaste, is obtained, the mixture can be tested by pulling a small amount from the main body to see if it peaks in the same way as when you whip up egg white. If desired it can be slackened with the addition of pure turpentine.

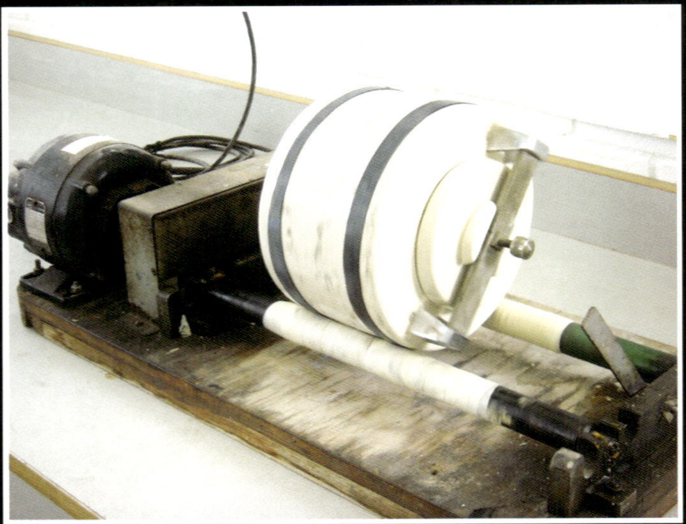

The ball mill in operation.

Photo: courtesy of the University of Wolverhampton.

By varying the length of time the ball mill is kept running, the precise mesh size of the grains can be determined with great precision.

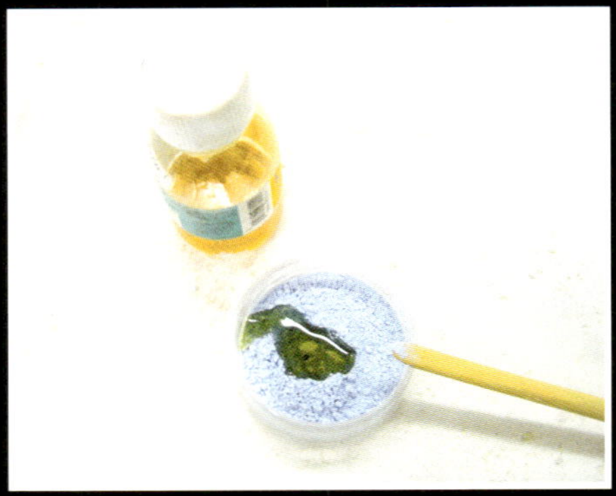

The fine glass grains are mixed with an oil medium.

Photo: courtesy of the University of Wolverhampton.

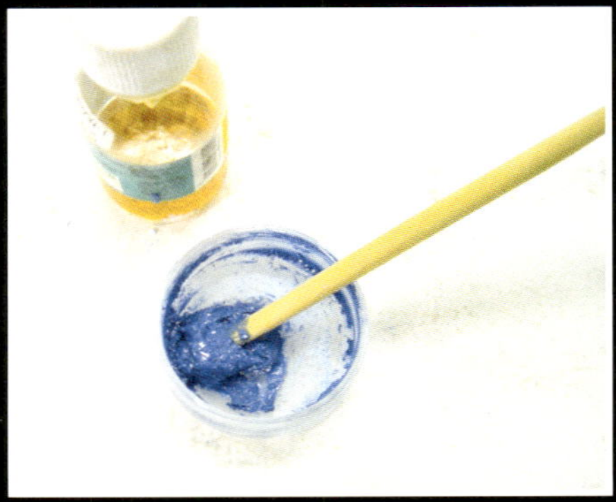

Determining the desired consistency.

Photo: courtesy of the University of Wolverhampton.

The use of wooden tools is essential to avoid contamination that would affect the colour.

Application

With good-quality brushes the paint can easily be applied to small details in the mould.

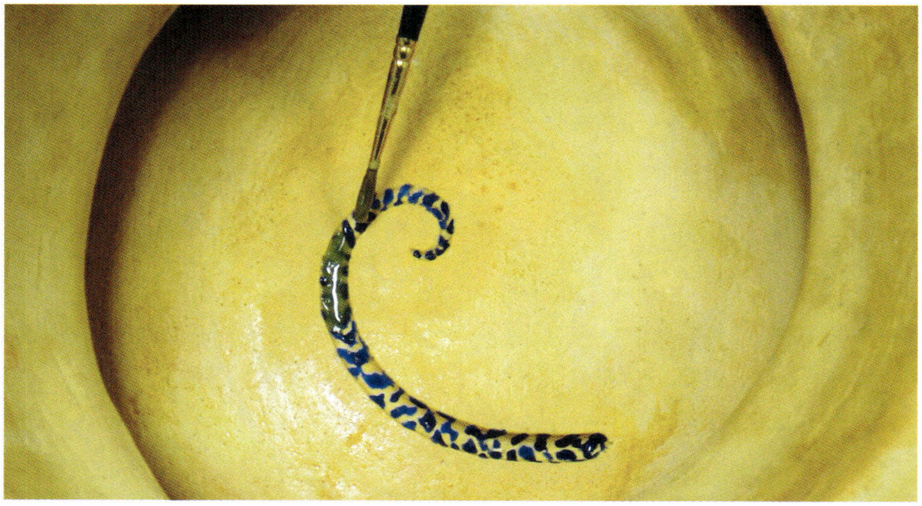

Painting details into the mould.

Photo: courtesy of the University of Wolverhampton.

By varying the amount of oil, a paint can be achieved that can be positioned with great accuracy into the areas of detail.

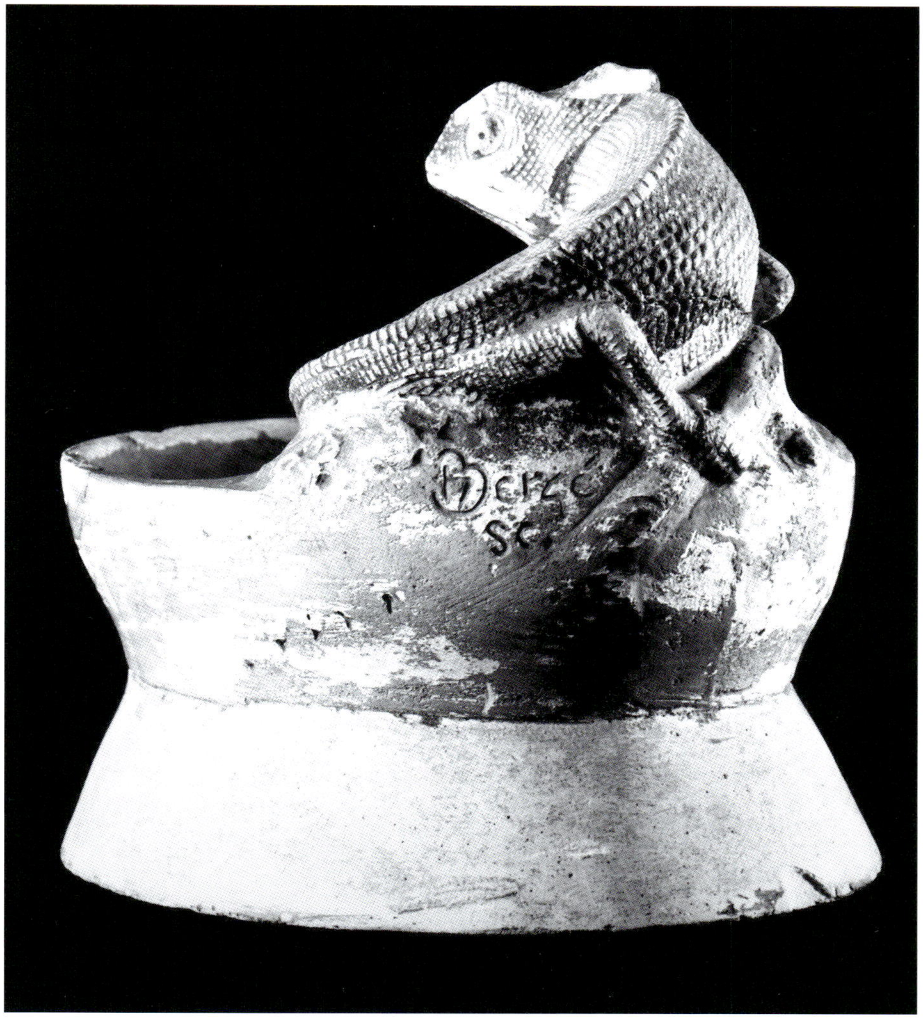

An original plaster model of Walter's (possibly for Chameleon dish, see p.41).

Repr.D. Bastien © INVERNTAIRE GENERAL/ADAGP (collection particulière – tous droits réservés).

Two things are of particular note: the extreme depth of the form, and therefore the difficulty that Walter had in effectively painting the areas of greatest detail at the furthest reaches of the hollow form; and the large reservoir built into the form, which would have carried extra glass to compensate for the settling of the mass of grains during firing.

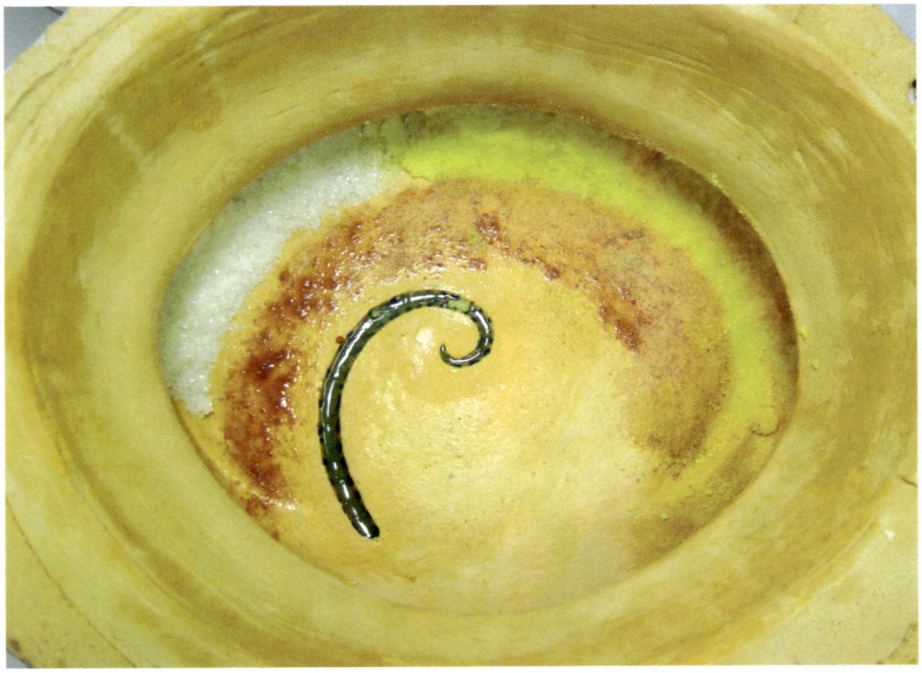

Different layers of colour and grades of glass grain.

Photo: courtesy of the University of Wolverhampton.

Each layer had to be allowed to dry before the next was applied, to avoid movement. As the detailing moved away from the surface larger grains were applied, and the use of the fine brush application stopped, to be replaced by the placing of larger grains.

The shellac coating prevents the oil from soaking into the fabric of the mould. The size of the opening to the mould, by allowing or restricting access, has a bearing on how complex the applications can be. It is surprising, however, just how far it is possible to apply paint to difficult areas. It is interesting to look at an example of Walter's work that has, through its small base, presented him with such problems, and to see just how far he has been able to control the detail in spite of these.

Contemporary accounts suggest that he painted the top details himself, thus exercising maximum control over the most signature characteristic of his output. It is important that layers should be built up slowly, for it is not possible to achieve a thick build-up of pigment in one go. Walter probably countered this problem by working on a number of moulds at the same time. The paint must be given time to lose some medium through evaporation, and therefore to harden off to the point where it retains its precision.

When the paints are sufficiently dried out, it is then possible to back up the detailed areas with the main masses of colour. This is provided by the coarser grains, mixed with water and a *little* gum arabic. This stage involves the careful application of the paste of glass grains, water and gum arabic to gradually cover, and back up, the fine detail. It is important to keep the paste only just damp enough to hold together. Once a layer is in position, a paper towel can be used to remove moisture.

Lost volume during casting

All of Walter`s original models sit on large bases that do not form part of the actual glass cast. This is nevertheless an extremely important part of the process, for when it becomes a void in the mould, the base creates a reservoir for the essential extra glass that will be needed to top up the glass in the mould during the firing stage. This is because, as the individual grains fuse together, the tiny pockets of air between them are driven out, and the mass settles. Of course, this is a problem that is well-known to all kiln-casters, but it is interesting nevertheless to see that a professional of Walter's calibre had to take measures to deal with it.

Up to 50% of the original volume can be lost during firing, an amount that is clearly dependent on the size of granule. The extent to which the grains of glass have moved as they have settled can clearly be seen in this dish of Walter's: the darker grains have traced their path within the lighter yellow.

A detail of the finished piece on p. 41. ➤

Photo: courtesy of the University of Wolverhampton.

Shining a light through the piece, the precise contrast between surface detail and the movement of the coarser grains during firing can be clearly seen. Walter would have deliberately orchestrated these effects, and it shows why he described his technique as *pâtes* in the plural.

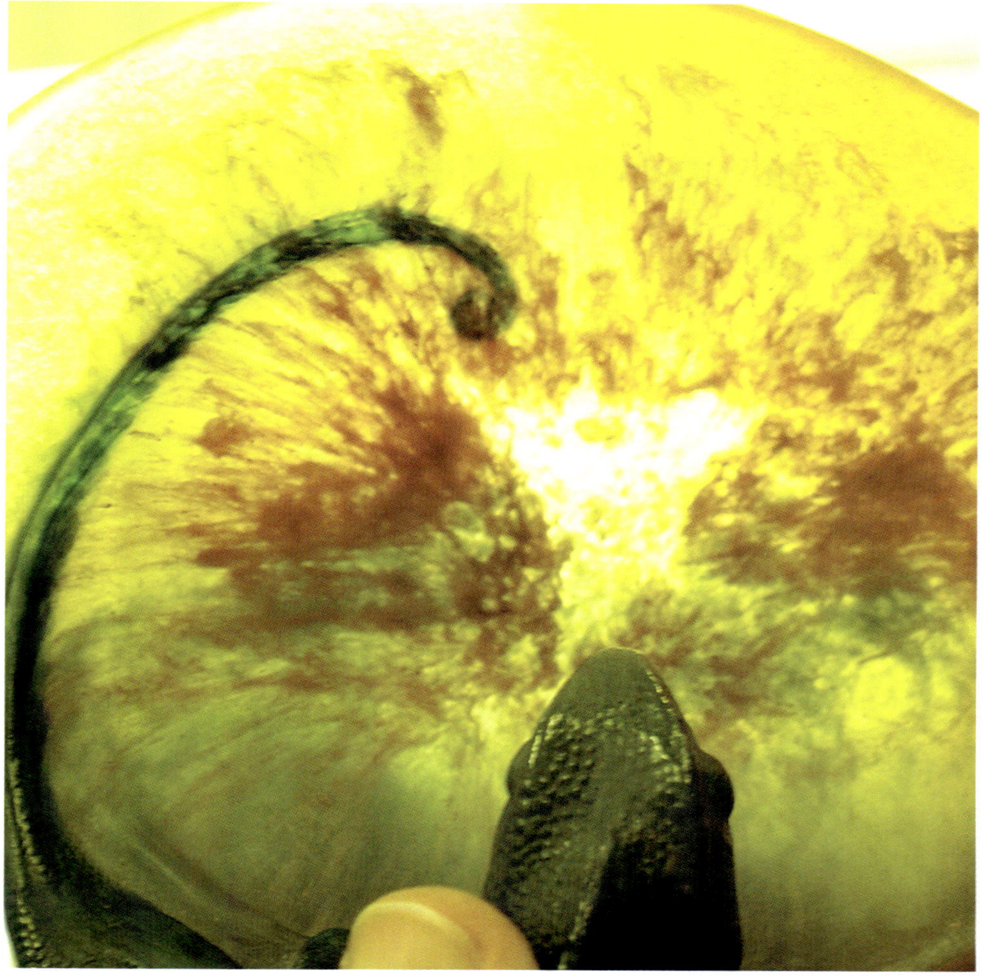

Because of the care taken with the casting process, finishing was kept to a minimum, essential in items where the most important detail is in the top few microns of glass. The finishing that was carried out was restricted to the selective, gentle polishing of highlights, which involved the use of felt or cork wheels, fed with a small amount of pumice or even Vaseline.

Walter's glass, being very, very soft, coupled to the fact that the top surface carried the detail, was highly susceptible to damage. This light buffing of the surface without removing any glass is in strict contrast to much contemporary practice, where the whole top surface is removed, and a completely new one created.

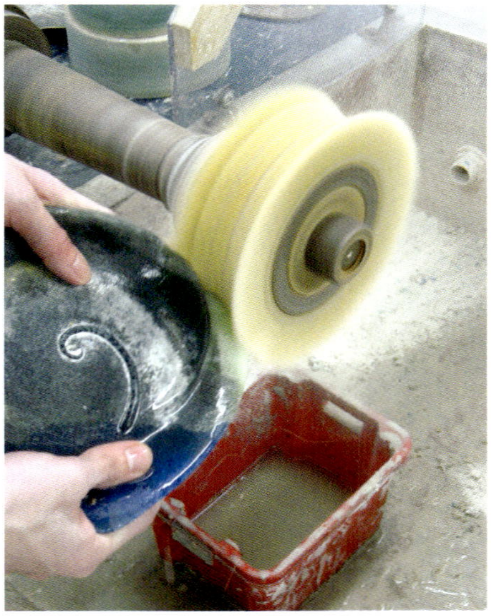

▲ Surface polishing.

Photo: courtesy of the University of Wolverhampton.

Walter used an unprecedented 40% lead glass as the base for his colours. This meant not only that it cast well at low temperatures, but also that its surface was soft and relatively easy to polish. He used polishing very selectively for highlights, and even then preferred a soft sheen to a hard polish. Buffing on a brush wheel with pumice powder or even vaseline was often sufficient.

Future developments

This research project set out with two main aims: to explore the processes of Amalric Walter and, having done so, to place this information in the public domain. There are in our view a number of different constituencies – historians, collectors and especially practitioners – who might have an interest in our findings. By describing in detail how Walter might have gone about his business, we hope to stimulate artists to follow rather than imitate him. This information can, and perhaps should, be taken out of its historical context and applied in part or as a whole to practice as it exists today and, hopefully, tomorrow.

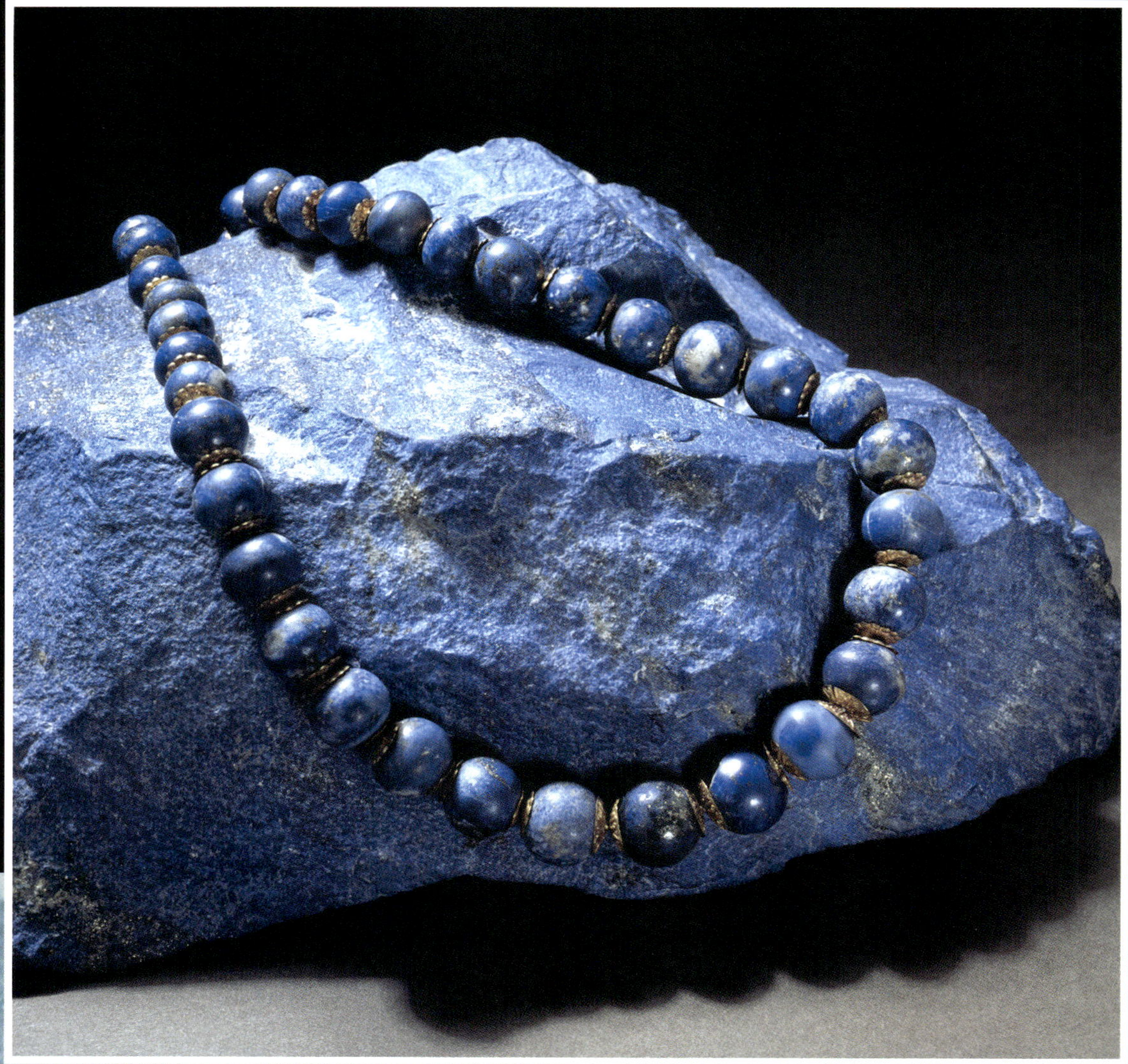
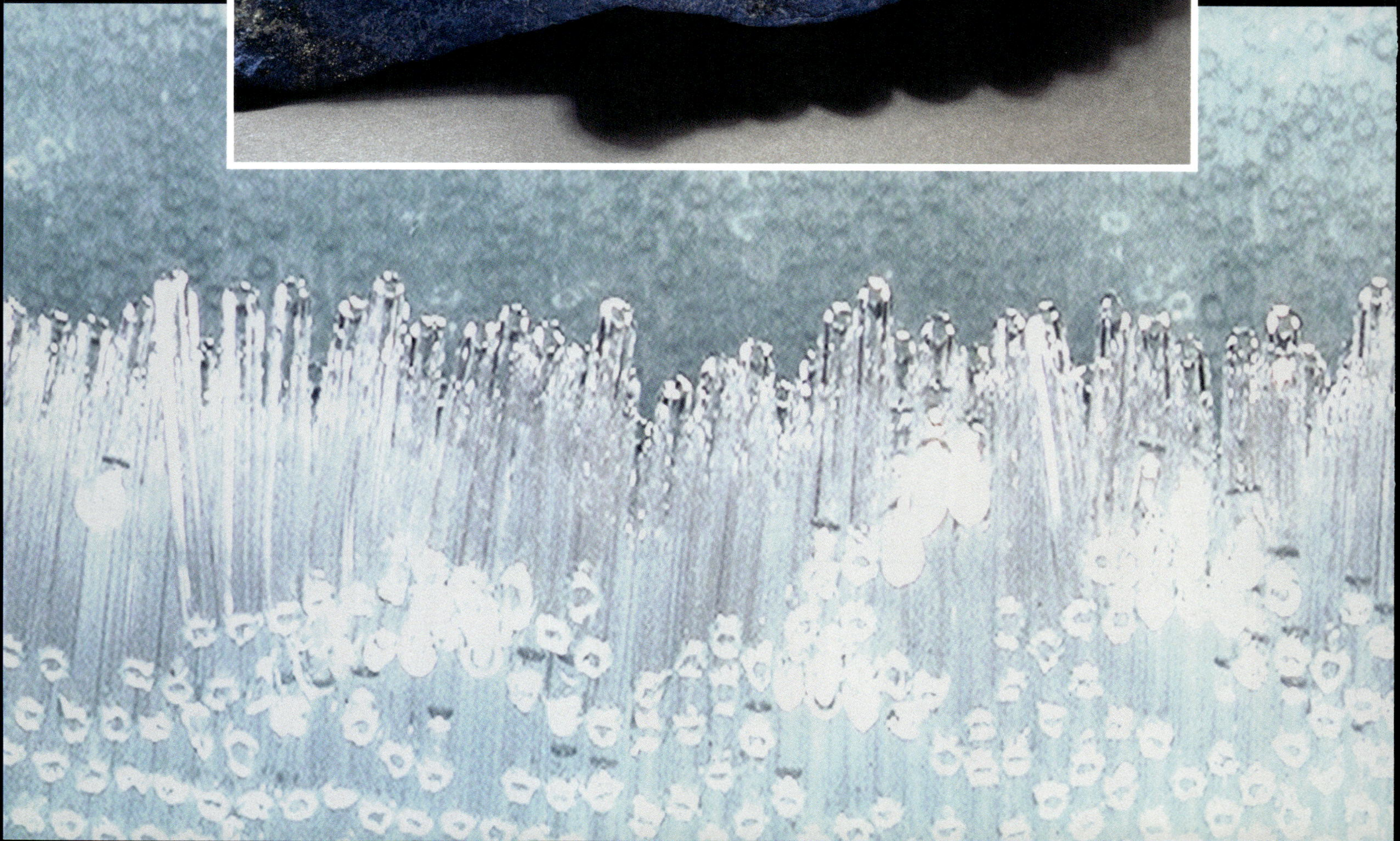

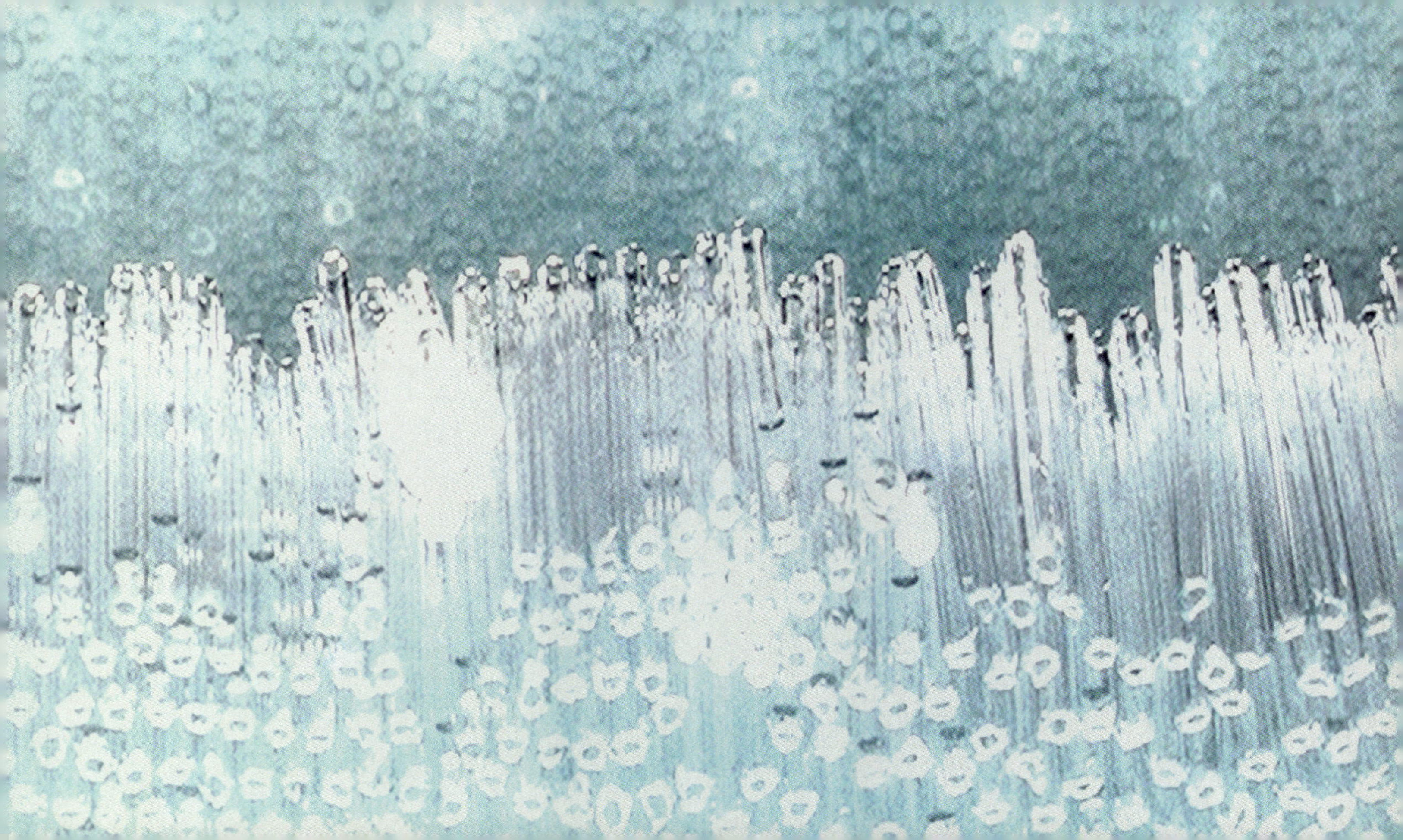

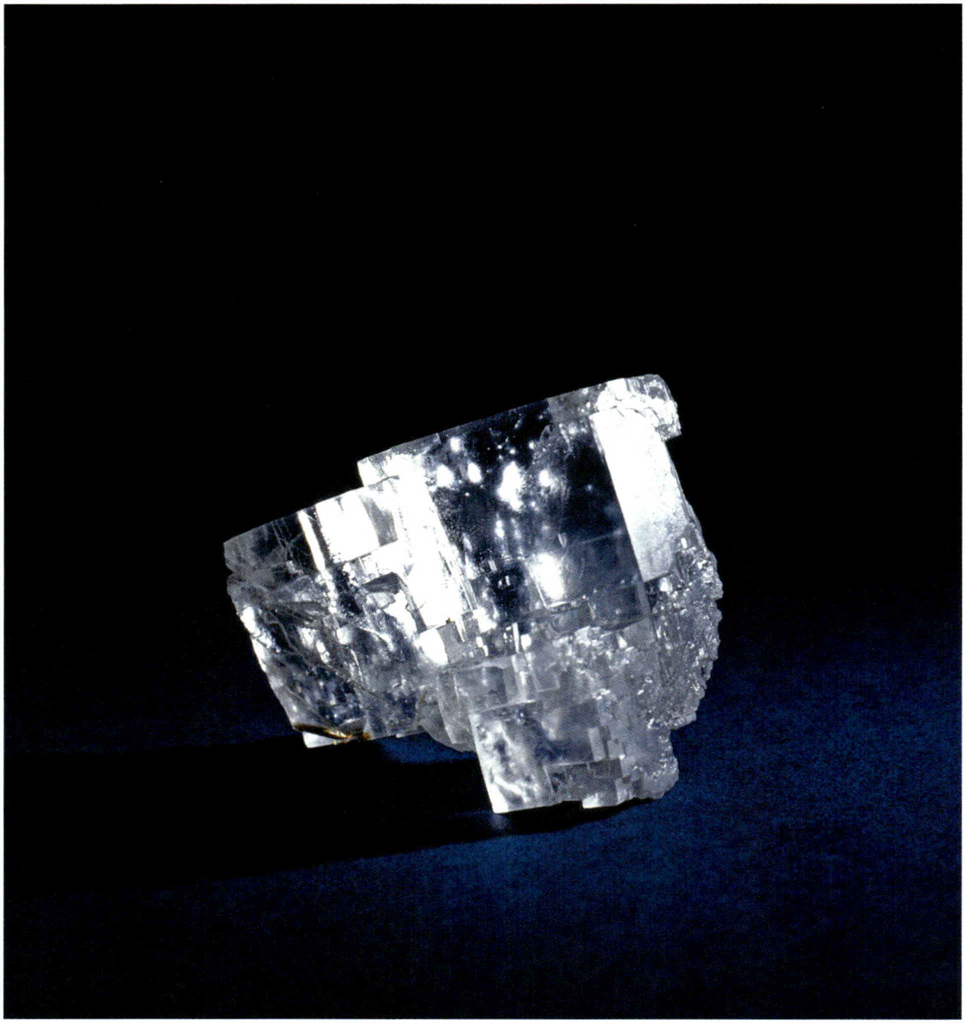

Despite the claims made about the unique qualities of glass when compared with other materials, it has often been used not for its own sake but because of its ability to ape, or act as a substitute for, other materials. There are three main reasons for this. Firstly, glass is a synthetic material; i.e. it has no direct equivalent in the natural world. Secondly, it is, through its physical structure as a solution (rather than the more usual compound), capable of existing in a huge range of formats, each one displaying different properties and qualities: strength or weakness, flexibility or rigidity, opacity or transparency, coloured or clear. Finally, being a purely human construct, it requires the pre-existence of a wide range of sophisticated technologies before it can be produced, let alone shaped. Therefore, it has usually developed late within each culture, long after metals and ceramics technologies, and their patterns of use, have been established. As a result glass has often taken its forms, values and functions from the materials that are already established, something which has obviously had a profound effect on its development.

The fact that Egyptian glass was used as a substitute for semi-precious stones meant that its technical repertoire was explored in a particular direction that exploited its ability to emulate the key qualities of decorative, jewel-like materials. Throughout the ancient world the qualities of opacity, richness of colour and integral patterning were the preferred characteristics of glass, and process and technique were brought to bear on achieving control over the creation and exploitation of these properties. In doing this they ignored the potential of glass to present another face and function – that of the clear, colourless container. It is possible to draw a parallel between glass in Ancient Egypt and its most prized natural hardstone, lapis lazuli, and to claim that this established a view of glass that has formed part of its image to the present.

The qualities that the Egyptians saw in glass have strong echoes in the approach of many contemporary kiln-formers: the creation of rich, dense, textured, precious objects which often share more with prized natural hardstones than with the common contemporary experience and perception of glass as a transparent, colourless material. Strangely enough, this second view of glass is also derived from a naturally occurring hardstone, namely rock crystal.

This provided an ideal towards which the technology of glass was

PREVIOUS PAGE
Lapis lazuli.

Courtesy of the Natural History Museum, London.

A naturally occurring hardstone, lapis was highly prized by the Egyptians, and helped to set the benchmark for their use of glass. Their control over glass was directed at achieving gem-like colours and qualities, with little or no interest in making clear glass.

◄ Natural rock crystal.

Courtesy of the Natural History Museum, London.

A highly sought-after natural quartz, rock crystal became, for many glass-makers, the ideal to which they aspired, and as a result their energies were directed at the achievement of the Holy Grail of a colourless 'crystal' glass.

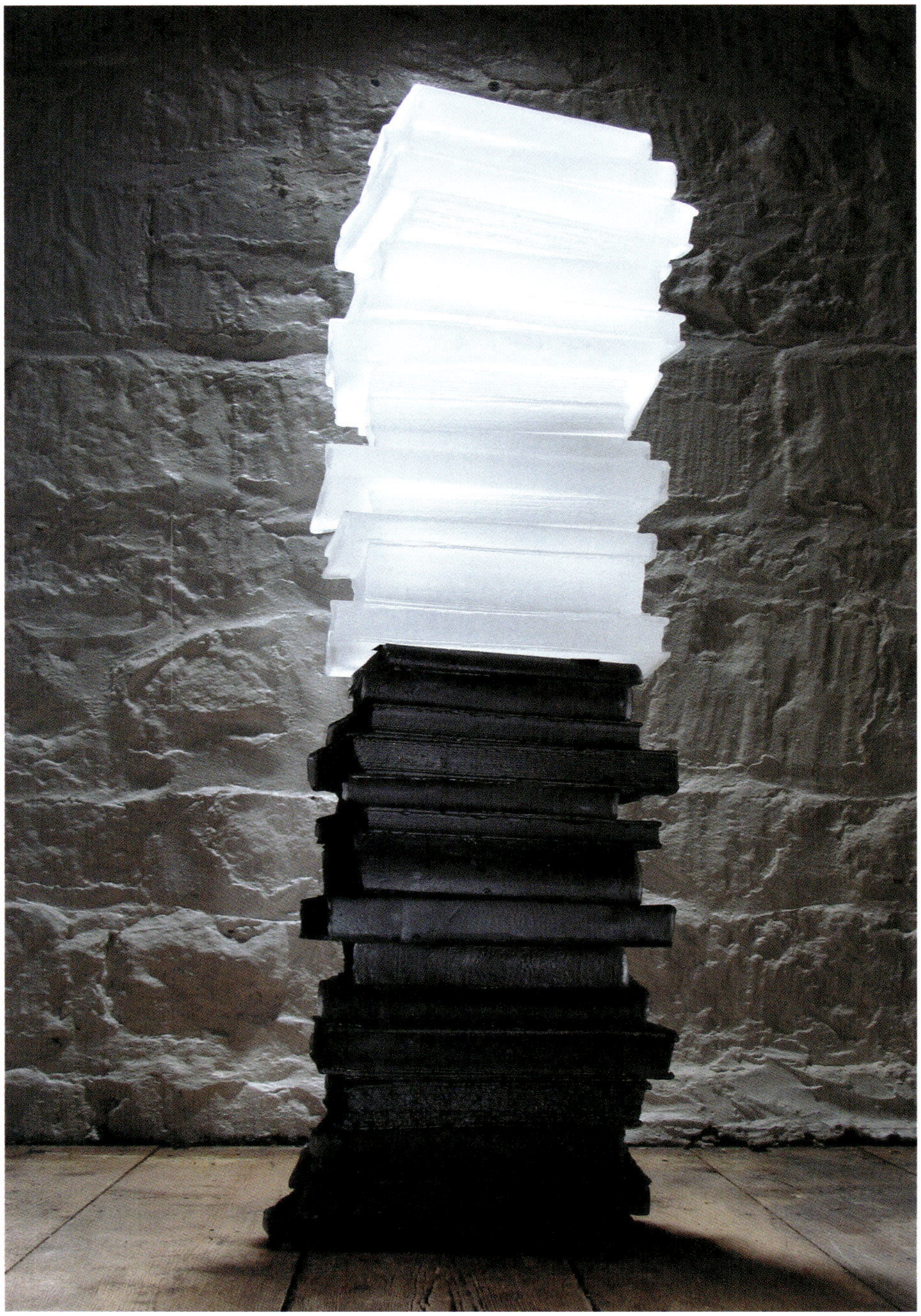

Contrast, Colin Reid, 2007. ➤
H. 82 cm (32½ in.), x W. 25 cm (10 in.), D. 18 cm (7 in.). Kiln-cast optical and float glass.

Courtesy of the artist.

The two attitudes to glass encapsulated within a sculpture by Colin Reid.

driven, once it became established as a transparent material from which containers could be produced. The ideal of a glass that would possess the qualities of rock crystal drove technical research throughout much of its history, providing a counterweight to the earlier aim of a glass that was the equal of an opaque, highly coloured, semi-precious stone. The most common perception of glass in our era, as a clear, bright, shiny refractive material, has obscured its earlier manifestation; this is a pity, because it underlies much of the kiln-former's attitude to glass. How many of us have seen our work questioned because it did not fit the modern ideal of what glass should look like? If rock crystal provides a metaphor for a particular view of glass, then lapis lazuli can stand as marker for another, older view, one that extends from the Egyptians to Walter, Argy-Rousseau, Décorchement and beyond.

Many contemporary practitioners will admit to feeling empathy with ancient glass and its methods. It is obviously true that not all modern kiln-formers seek dense colour, richness of texture and detail (although many do), but even those who employ clear refractive glass in their creations produce works that often have more in common with precious stones than liquid glass.

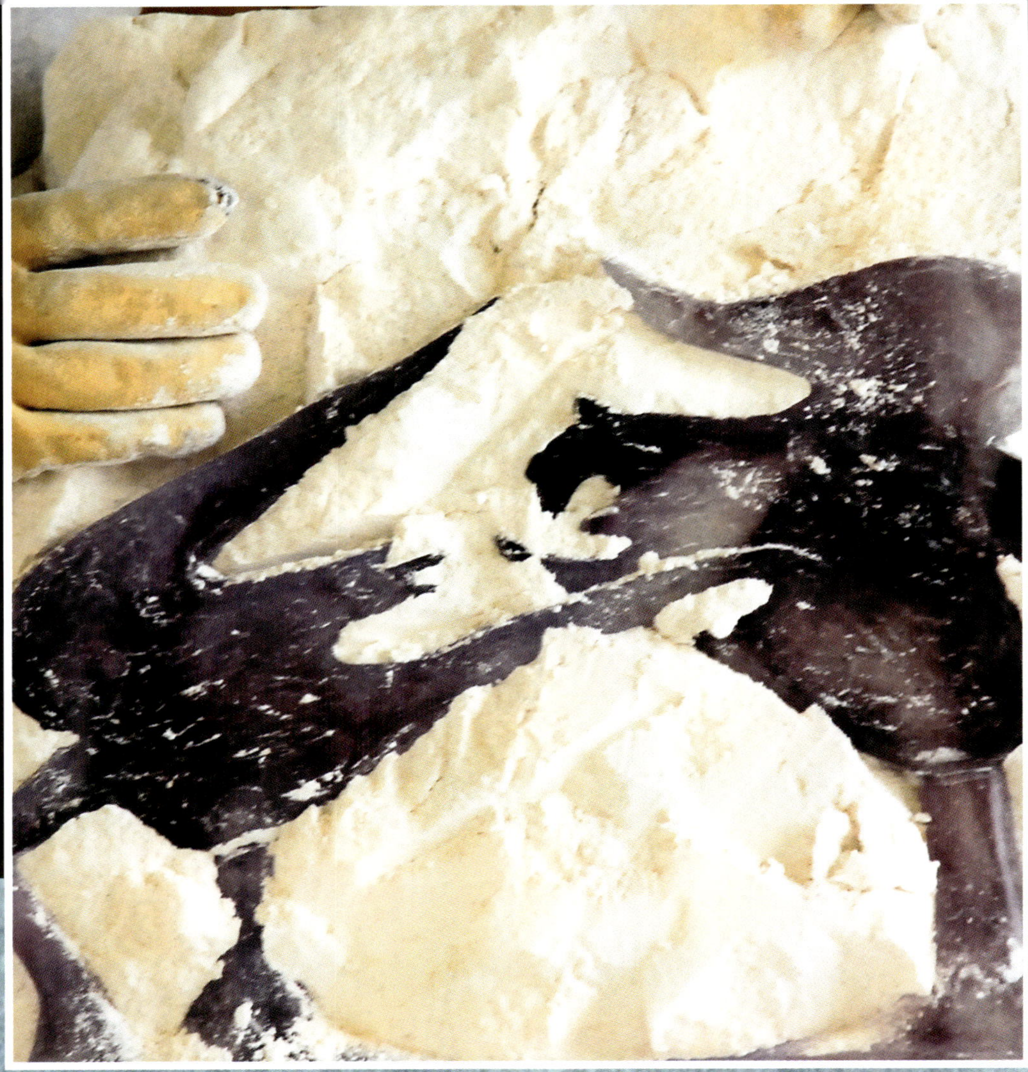

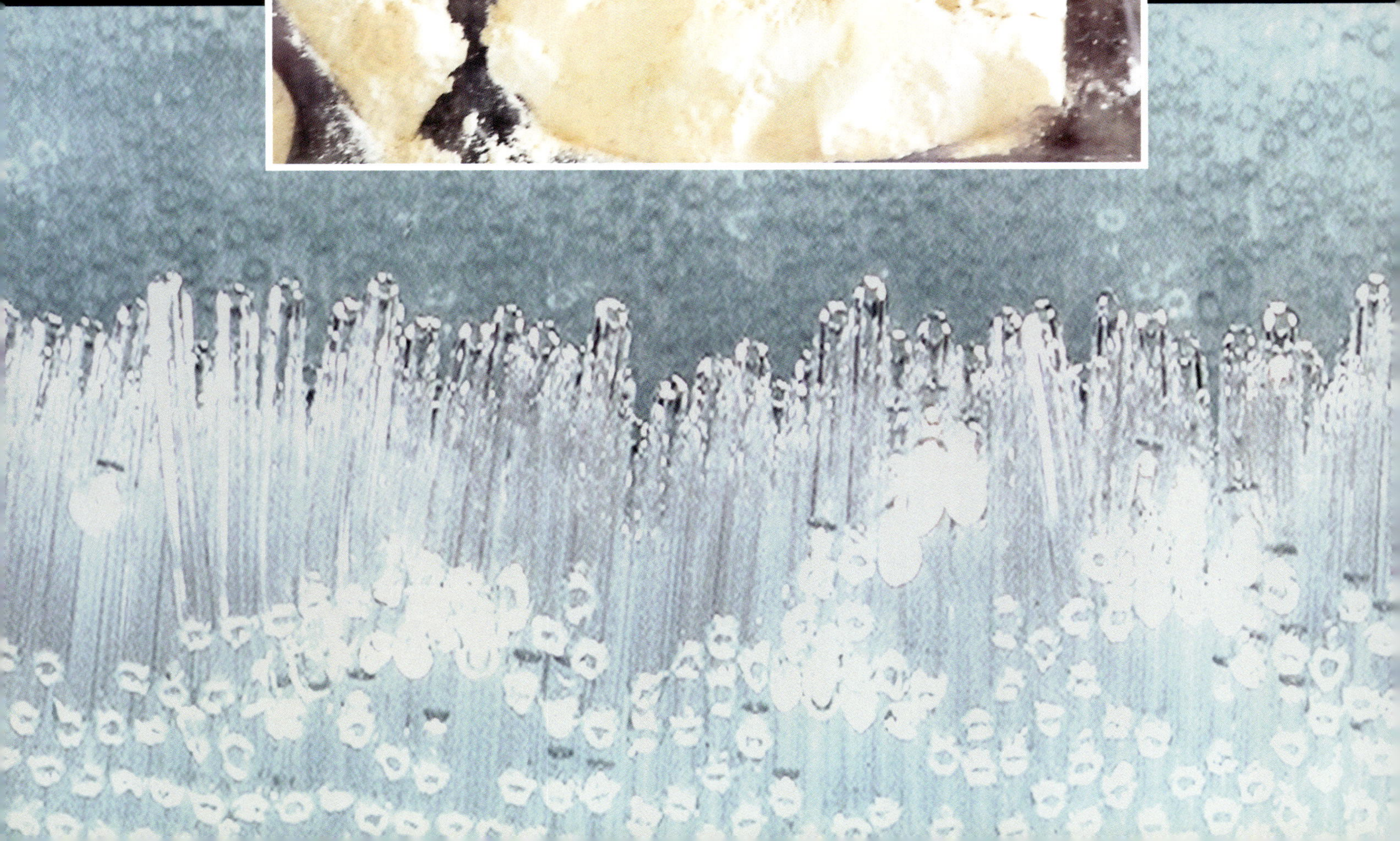

4 The Development of the Studio Movement

'There should be monuments, there should be odes/... to the first flaker of flints/who forgot his dinner.'

W.H. AUDEN, from *Epilogue: Love and do what you will.*

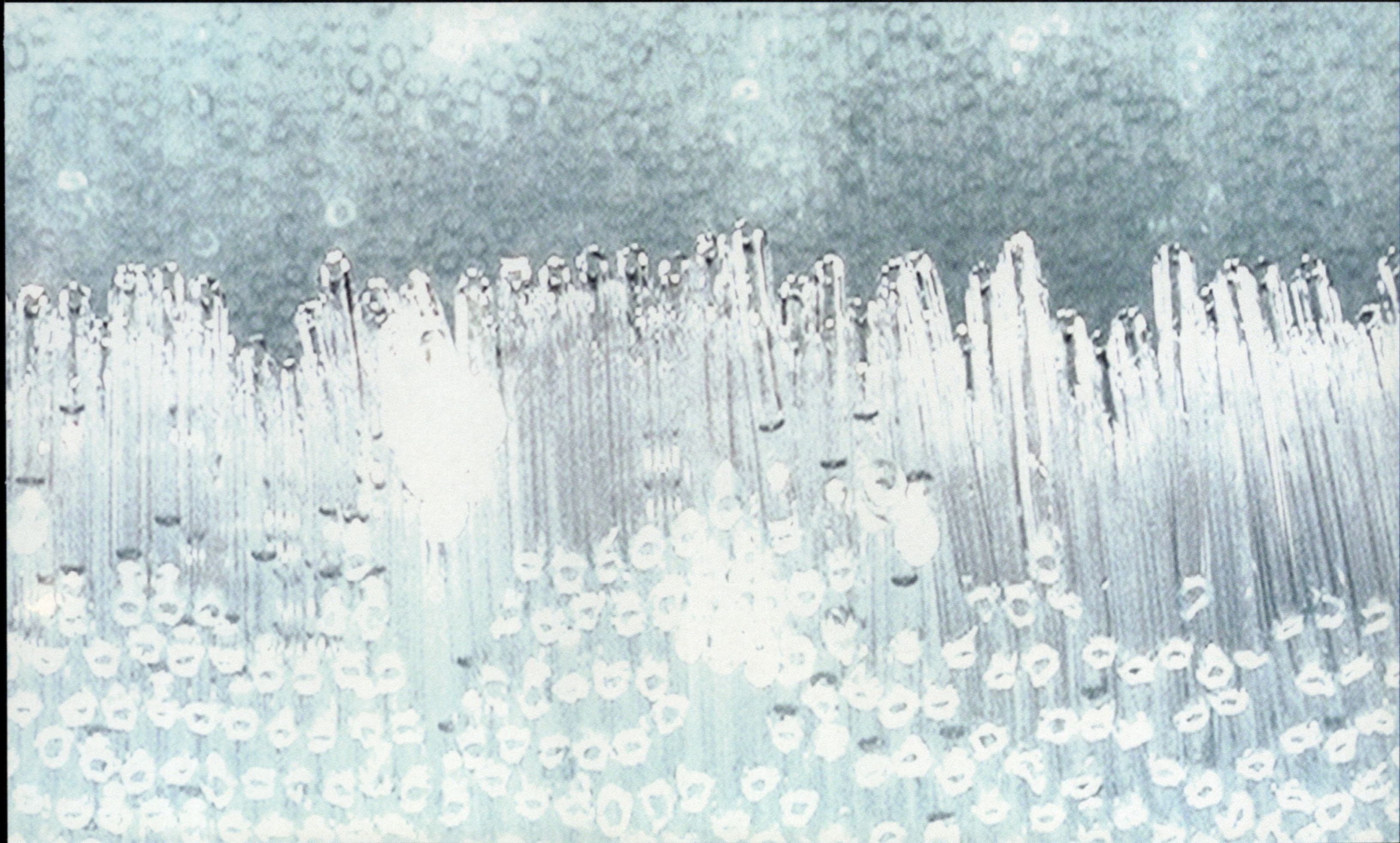

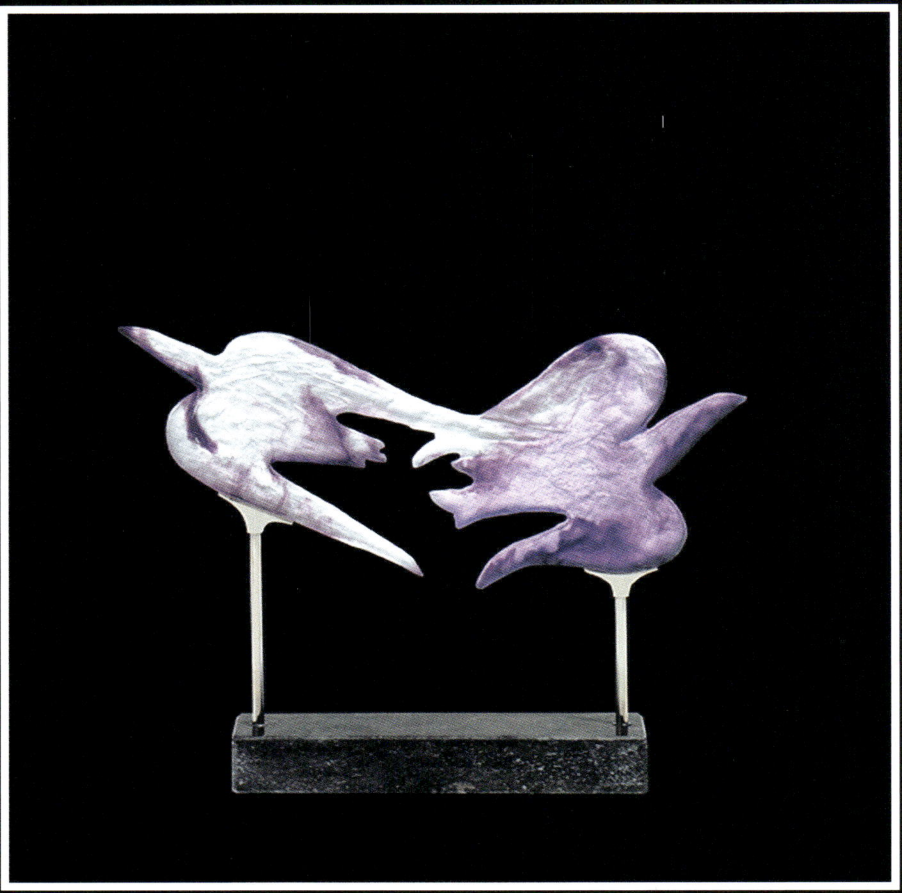

Walter ceased production in 1937, a year after Argy-Rousseau. Both had experienced financial difficulty in the era following the Wall Street crash, which profoundly affected the market for decorative, luxury goods. It is worth examining the circumstances that caused this original, magnificent way of forming glass to last but a few decades, for its bearing on the context in which today`s kiln-formers practice. This is especially relevant, as this aspect of modern kiln-forming evolved from the 1960s as a self-conscious attempt to rediscover what was, by then, seen as a lost art.

The main problems surrounding the production of kiln-formed articles as a life-sustaining activity were the same for Walter and his contemporaries as they are for those in our own era who, in C. R. Ashbee`s famous words, 'seek to relate the creations of their hands to their reasons for existence' – i.e. they try to square this basic wish with the need to be commercial. The processes are difficult, skilled, labour-intensive and *slow*. No stage lends itself to mechanisation, and even attempts to produce batches of similar objects do not result in the production of large numbers of them.

Amalric Walter and Gabriel Argy-Rousseau were the most successful of the early studio-based glass workers. However, despite running individual studios for years, employing (at their peaks) around a dozen workers each, and using moulds to produce editions of each object, their *total* output can be measured only in the tens of thousands. The kinds of artefacts they made – decorative, semi-sculptural, small-scale items with strong personal identities, based round an individual house style – was to a large extent dictated by the limitations of the techniques. These are all issues that those of us who operate as contemporary kiln-formers have to address, and the novel ways in which each artist represented in this book relates to them are implicit within their works and their words.

Objects made by these methods are bound to be expensive, and need to function in specialist contexts, marketed through galleries which exploit their uniqueness and signature identities. A major shift since Walter's day has been the steady move from the decorative domestic item to the stand-alone sculpture.

The cast glass produced by the Daum factory since the early 1960s uses named artists and marketing techniques that stress both the artistic lineage of the process and the signature nature of each piece's origins.

PREVIOUS PAGE
'De-moulding', or removing the cast from the mould material.

Photo: courtesy of Daum.

The cast requires much surface grinding and polishing to remove the marks and slight imperfections caused by casting, and to highlight selected areas.

◄ The finished piece, produced by the Daum factory, 2007.

Photo: courtesy of Daum.

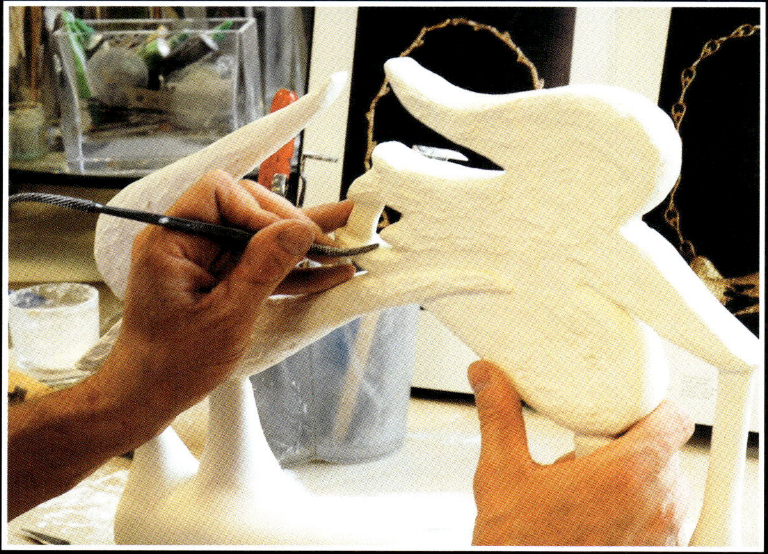

▲ Stages in the production of a piece of contemporary pâte de verre at the Daum factory, 2007.

Photo: courtesy of Daum.

The original plaster model, from a design by Georges Braque, is fettled to achieve the desired finish prior to its replication by the production of a rubber mould.

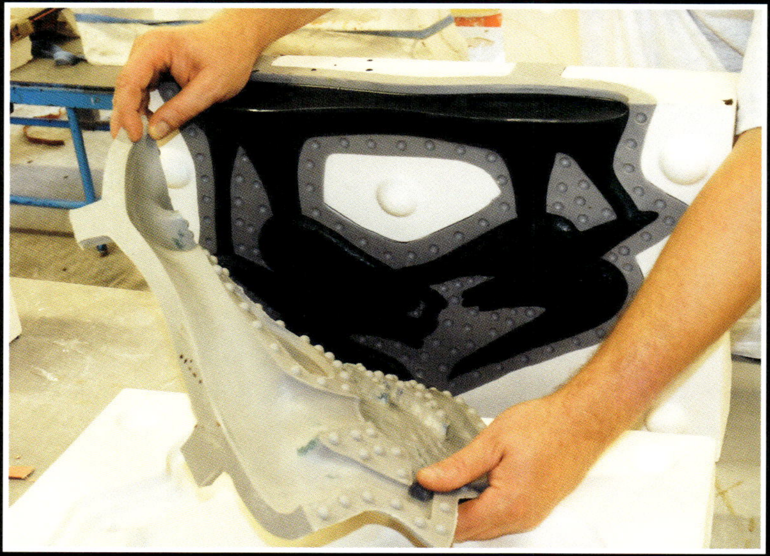

▲ Removing a wax from the two-part rubber mould.

Photo: courtesy of Daum.

Walter developed pâte de verre at the Daum factory before the First World War, and the process used today owes its principles to Walter, although he did not have the benefit of modern aids like castable rubber.

This is evident in their recent collaboration with the estate of Georges Braque to produce an edition of his forms in glass.

The route taken by today's studio-glass artists, although foreshadowed by earlier practitioners like François Décorchement, with their choice of art over craft, is not a straightforward one. The decision to devote oneself to the lifetime practice of a craft discipline in the 21st century is not the same as making that choice in a pre-industrial or even an early post-industrial age. Prior to large-scale mechanisation, craft or, more broadly, skilled, hand-driven methods were simply the only means of production for the goods that society needed. Once these were rationalised into industrial products, made in their millions by machine, craft systems had to adapt in order to survive in any form.

The decorative, the one-off, the high-quality special order – these were the areas left after mass-production systems had taken their toll. Stressing the unique nature of the handmade object became increasingly evident in both process and form, with the expression of the maker's individual vision gradually assuming a leading role. Despite the huge differences between the works of the artists in this volume, two themes are always in evidence, both within their works and within their statements: a unique approach to the forming of glass, albeit within a well-defined

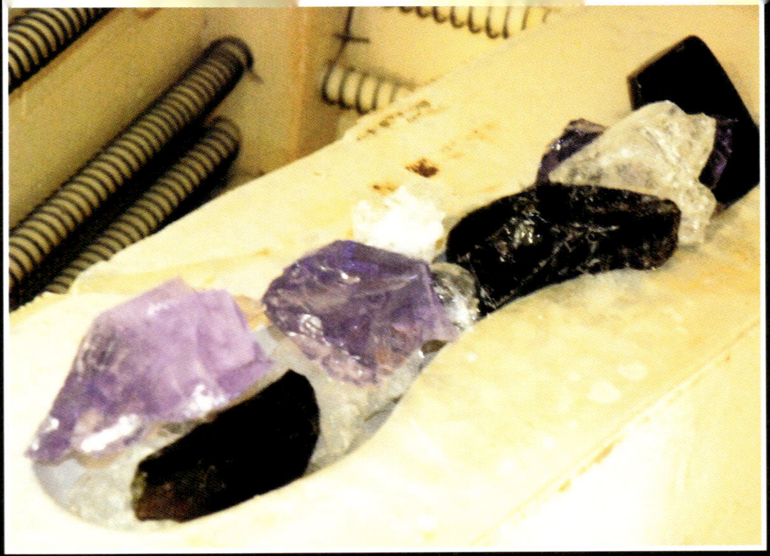

▲ Mould with glass ready for firing.

Photo: courtesy of Daum.

Daum has a large range of colours, and tends to cast with fairly large grains. Walter's careful surface painting is no longer used.

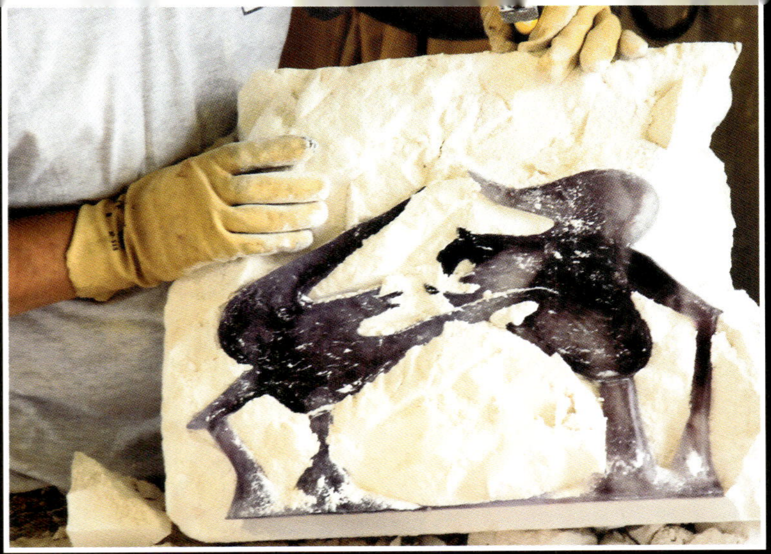

▲ 'De-moulding', or removing the cast from the mould material.

Photo: courtesy of Daum.

The cast requires much surface grinding and polishing to remove the marks and slight imperfections caused by casting, and to highlight selected areas.(See p.56 for the finished work.)

process; and a strong visual identity, expressed through a personal vocabulary of shape, colour and texture. It is often possible to name the artist even from a cursory glance at a piece in a gallery.

The movement from decorative items that make at least a residual nod toward function, to the production of sculpture is indicative of two trends, one commercial, the other artistic. Sculpture carries more status, and therefore a higher potential price tag; and forms which do not pretend to function as vases or dishes can evolve more freely within a wider three-dimensional matrix. These two approaches still coexist, of course, and are reflected in these pages through the decisions of each practitioner, and in turn throughout the craft movement as a whole.

The choice of a life spent in the practice of a craft material discipline is a self-conscious one based on the desire for self-expression. You could say that such a choice determines the lifestyle; two centuries ago the reverse was true. The contexts in which such activities are studied are now the art school and the university department rather than the atelier, workshop or factory. This is an indication of both the changing status of such activities and the uses to which they are put, both in terms of their end products and in the effects that their study have on the individuals who choose to study them.

Craft activity used to lead to anonymity, the individual self hidden within the production of well-prescribed traditional objects, the individual ego subservient to the designs of others, with no room for self-expression. A glance at the statements provided by so many of the artists in these pages shows the extent to which things have changed. To make your mark in craft today it is clearly necessary to develop two things: a personal, philosophic approach to material and process, and a visual vocabulary reflecting this approach, with which your chosen materials are shaped. This, when successful, results in artefacts with a strong, easily identified personal style.

The seeds of this change were evident in the 19th century, affecting the growth and development of the contemporary craft movement, while strong echoes of this change are still evident within current thinking and practice. I do not refer to the age-old circular debate that has bedevilled the studio craft movement – that of craft versus art. As far as I am concerned Kurt Schwitters decided it once and for all with his famous statement that 'Everything an artist spits out is art.'

Clearly, the nature of the artist is what determines the nature of the outcome, not the medium, method or history. However, the issues surrounding language and intent are of interest, in the sense that they shed light on current practice in ways that sterile questions of category do not. The language of craft derives from the interaction of two areas: the vocabulary of forms, colours and textures inherent in the material, and the way in which these are revealed by the manipulation of process. In this sense a decision to kiln-form glass is analogous to that of a musician choosing to learn to master a particular instrument. The initial decision determines the range of effects and qualities available, and contains built-in limits and opportunities.

Throughout the 50-year history of the studio-glass movement, there has been a steep and constant extension of the technical boundaries of the medium, to the extent that pieces from the 1960s often look basic by comparison with contemporary work. Nowhere has this been more apparent than in kiln-forming; and neither is this rate of development showing any signs of slowing, as each new generation of kiln-formers, in stretching the limits of the medium, contributes to the vocabulary of the next.

This is true for kiln-forming in a greater sense than for those glass processes, like blowing, which were based on firm, extant traditional skills and had accessible, well-documented histories. All that was needed was to adapt these skills to an individual's 'search for form', to use Harvey Littleton's classic phrase. By contrast, the basic procedures that now make up kiln-forming – casting, pâte de verre, slumping, etc. – did not exist in any equivalent, adaptable, contemporary form, and thus had to be invented or rediscovered piece by piece.

The only clues to the process of pâte de verre, for instance, lay in museum examples incarcerated within glass cases that prevented anything but visual access. Such information as did exist was often misleading or just plain wrong. When I started to work with glass in the late 1950s, pâte de verre was described in one book as granulated glass, mixed with water, and thrown on a wheel! From these beginnings each artist made a little progress, and through their work, experiments and/or teaching handed on this information to succeeding generations.

There is a greater range of glass processes in use today throughout the studio movement than at any time during glass's 5000-year existence. For by far the greater part of this history, it has been usual for one process to dominate, sometimes to the exclusion of all others. This makes the current era, with its plethora of methods, unique. Most of this is down to the studio movement and its relentless search for originality, its inclusion in educational programmes, and of course, most recently, the individual website.

Of equal (or perhaps greater) importance to novelty in vocabulary through technique is the issue of the artist's motivation and intent, both of which are complex, multilayered and subject to misrepresentation and misunderstanding. Motives clearly include self-expression, satisfaction and, perhaps the most important, the desire to engage with an activity that demands the full range of human skills, incorporating the head, heart and hand. This and its corollary, being in sole charge of a process that runs from first idea to final form, appears high on most studio practitioners' lists when asked about why they choose to spend their lives making.

The desire to be in command of a personal world which revolves around a defined area of endeavour, and which is subject to continual creative cycles of thinking, making and reflection, is a powerful one. This opinion is based on almost five decades of personal practice, teaching and talking to students and fellow makers. Although this is true of any solitary, studio-based activity, I feel that it is especially true of kiln-forming, which with its slow, multi-stage character naturally creates punctuation spaces for constant creative intervention. The need to exist in a commercial context is, for most of the practitioners I have spoken to, secondary, with the marketing and selling of their work undertaken to allow the making to continue, rather than the other way round.

Intent, or why the maker chooses to form his/her creations in a particular way, and to what end, is poorly studied and documented; yet its understanding is a necessary goal, as it is arguably the central issue which drives the practitioner forwards, and which literally shapes their work. The situation which is perhaps of greatest interest would seem to be that in which the artist has the greatest amount of choice over their objects.

This is the manufacture of non-functional artefacts, items for which there is no pre-existing order or commission, which in commercial terms are speculative, and which have to be marketed after manufacture. This is another way in which the contemporary craft makers differ from their pre-industrial counterparts, particularly if you add to this the fact that the majority of today's craft objects are decorative rather than practical and thus are predominantly collector's items.

Most items fit, loosely, within one of two paradigms: the decorative or fine arts. Categories like these are of course highly permeable and subject to revision, of interest only in the sense in which they shed light on their author's original intentions. The decorative arts have evolved against the background of the architectural interior, and are often based on a stylistic updating of a traditional host form, e.g. a vase.

To choose to make a form like this, the intent has to include a reference to the lineage of the borrowed format. This can be positive or negative in spirit, an extension or rejection of history, in which the base form acts as a shared point of reference between maker and viewer. In this, it mirrors a particular kind of improvisational jazz, which develops from a well-known tune, constantly reacting to it to the point of destruction, and at the same time referring back to it at intervals in order to maintain a relationship of mutually held knowledge with the listener. This, I feel, underpins much craft production in general, and glass-making in particular. Forms like the plate and the vase are used as vehicles for personal expression in the knowledge that their recognisable format makes their acceptance (and sale?) more likely. Their domestic scale and echo of function make them easier to display, and their innate, decorative nature reinforces this tendency.

There are, of course, degrees of separation from the original shapes on which they are based, resulting in items that range from those differing only slightly from established families of form, to exercises in abstraction in which the notion of dish, plate or bowl all but disappears. The important point is that the visual umbilical chord can be stretched but never entirely broken.

The other main approach is to conduct the personal search for form in purely sculptural terms. An immediate advantage of this is formal freedom, particularly in the sense of full three-dimensional formal licence. The absence of prescriptive vessel requirements – stability, verticality, internal voids – allows form to develop sculpturally into a fully fledged medium of expression and choice. This clearly does not guarantee the production of sculpture; issues of quality are independent of value judgements, and this section is an examination of intent rather than evaluation. Moreover, the sculptural path is liberally strewn with potential pitfalls and bunkers.

The main criticism levelled at sculptural glass is that it is derivative: that it follows developments in mainstream sculpture, which it can only ever reflect. The answer, while recognising that such views can contain an uncomfortable kernel of truth, is to avoid creative short cuts, and to follow Paul Klee's dictum that 'formation is more important than form'; meaning that form emerges as a result of an immersion in a process of genuine enquiry through a medium rather than in the sterile design and production of self-conscious 'art works'.

To a large extent this entails an open-ended attitude, where the object arises gradually during a series of feedback loops, involving half-truth, discovery and creative reactions to failure. Such a creative process involves a number of linked strands: a journey into unknown areas; an evolution from uncertainty to certainty; and an engagement with glass, its properties, processes and limitations, as a full creative partner in this enquiry but not as an end in itself.

The use of drawing, models and multimedia to identify sources of inspiration, and to sift, combine, generate and select alternatives, is a route which is either truncated or avoided altogether by some glassmakers, such is the allure of the material. A recent film of the architect Frank Gehry[1] shows him engaged in just such an activity. Using simple card and plastic models he explores the ideas suggested by his rough sketches. In my experience artists who do not pay attention to this kind of visual thinking limit their opportunities and significantly increase their chances of producing derivative or stale work.

Fine artists often claim to be independent of material constraints, and as a result are free to interpret their ideas without the limitations of a pre-selected material. Craft makers, by definition, choose to master a particular material through the acquisition of its physical disciplines, often taking years to achieve this mastery. While this is a simplified view, particularly in the light of ongoing shifts of emphasis in both areas, it is still one that the glassmaker needs to be wary of.

Glass by its nature is a mysterious, attractive material with a unique range of forming processes and tools. This can encourage would-be makers to immerse themselves in the material's mystique at the expense of a genuine and full creative enquiry. A look at the work and practice of significant artists who have produced some of the major glass artefacts of the past 40 years is revealing. Artists of the calibre of Dale Chihuly, Erwin Eisch, Bertil Vallien and Ann Wolff have sustained themselves as creative artists over many decades by rich, creative methods that exist separately from their actual glass production, and yet provide much of the inspiration that drives it.

The roots of the studio-glass movement

Kiln-forming is a tributary of the studio-glass movement, which is itself a tributary of the crafts movement as a whole. Individual practitioners, or collective institutions like universities (in terms of where they place studio activities within the syllabus), who treat glass in isolation often fail to understand the history of the movement; this matters because the philosophy that drives the movement is neither static, nor was it inevitable.

Today's vibrant global craft movement developed in the way it did for reasons that are also largely responsible for its creative ethos; its continuing evolution is therefore based upon its origins. By understanding how it began we can make more informed decisions about its future, just as each individual maker has to write (and constantly rewrite) the credo by which they direct their creative progress.

The retrenchment of craft methods after the advent of machine production in the 19th century, epitomised by pioneers like William Morris, brought with it an attitude to craft that was predominantly reactionary. This movement sought to reposition the crafts as an activity that manifested a collective, social conscience. Whilst this was responsible for the initial survival of craft activity into the 20th century, its transformation into an individual lifestyle choice was affected by a mix of other forces. Largely because of Morris and his circle, crafts continued to be taught in art schools, mainly because it was felt that the use of hand skills was an important means of assimilating and developing a creative understanding of materials and processes.

Even the Bauhaus, that icon of modernism, incorporated craft making as a basic ingredient of its curriculum. The exodus of talent from Europe that followed the rise of Hitler included numerous Bauhaus staff and students, many of whom gravitated to the United States. The presence of such luminaries gave the crafts movement in the USA an important boost. The importance of the example set by these artists lay as much in their attitude as their actual presentation of craft itself. It seems to me their innate message was that craft activity could provide a credible and satisfactory outlet for creative energies.

The position that we take for granted, with craft firmly embedded in the educational, commercial and cultural life of so many developed economies around the world, started in America and in Great Britain in the period between the two world wars. In Britain the impetus provided by William Morris was transformed by Bernard Leach in the 20th century into an interest in the mystical, personal nature of making; it was an interest he expressed in his writings and his practice, as well as in his identification with the traditions of Japan, epitomised in his friendship with, and promotion of, Shoji Hamada. This example of the studio-based individual choosing to place their life's energies into the practice of a traditionally based craft transformed the nature of that activity into something that was anything but traditional. As Rose Slivka has written, 'In the isolation of his studio or workshop, the craft maker made objects that related to himself ... He produced objects that contained his ideas.'[2]

Forms were no longer predicated on the accurate reproduction of traditional norms; at best they provided themes within which the practitioner sought their own creative voice and personal, philosophic position. Objects made within such studios became statements too, and, having eschewed mere function, needed the support of a new network of specialist commercial galleries, collectors and publications, and ultimately public recognition. This began to be put in place in earnest in the years immediately following the Second World War. The American Crafts Council held its first conference in 1957. The trailblazing work of practitioners like Peter Voulkos, with his radical approach to ceramics echoing the New York action painters, meant that, by the time of the first glass workshops in Wisconsin, the ethos of the craft movement was well established.

An interesting feature of this period that has only recently been challenged was the unwritten rule stipulating that studio practitioners should make their work entirely unaided. This was clearly an attitude borrowed from the fine arts, and it led to some unusual responses, particularly in glass-blowing, which had traditionally been practised in teams. Stages like the casting on of a foot on a goblet needed some inventive rethinking to allow its fabrication by one person and bring it into this self-imposed restriction. In kiln-forming this meant that the cast glass produced in Czechoslovakia, when exhibited in America in the late 1960s, was, in the words of Susanne Frantz, 'technically and aesthetically far more sophisticated than contemporary American efforts, but was saddled with the caveat "but it is made in a factory", and thus not really studio glass.'[3] Since then, of course, the parameters have shifted and widened.

---

[1] Sydney Pollack, *Sketches of Frank Gehry*, (Sony Picture Classics, 2006).

[2] Rose Slivka, 'The Art/Craft Connection' in *The Eloquent Object*, Marica and Tom Manhart (eds) (Tulsa: The Philbrook Museum of Art, 1987).

[3] Susanne Frantz, *Particle Theories* (Millville, NJ: Museum of American Glass, 2005).

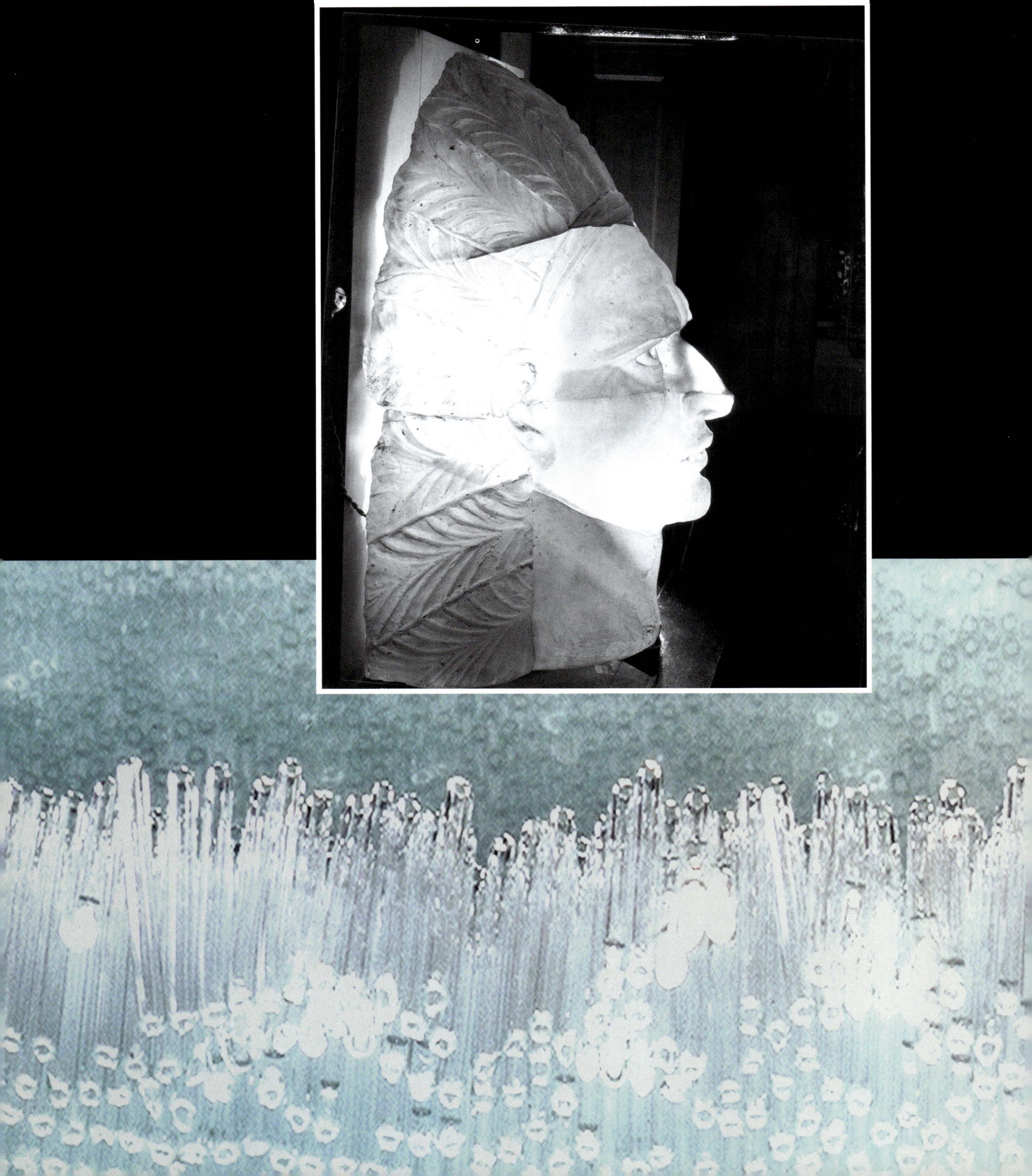

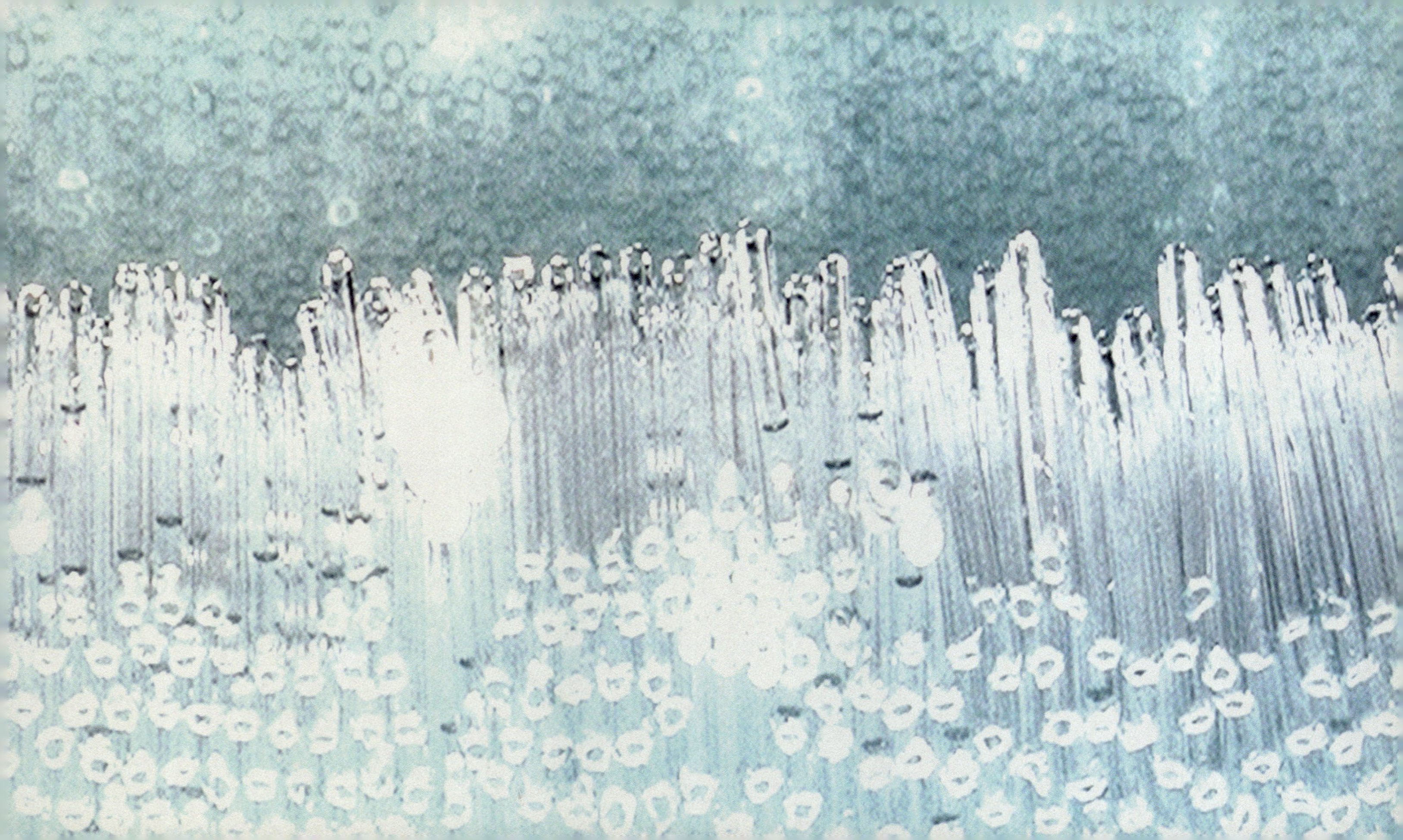

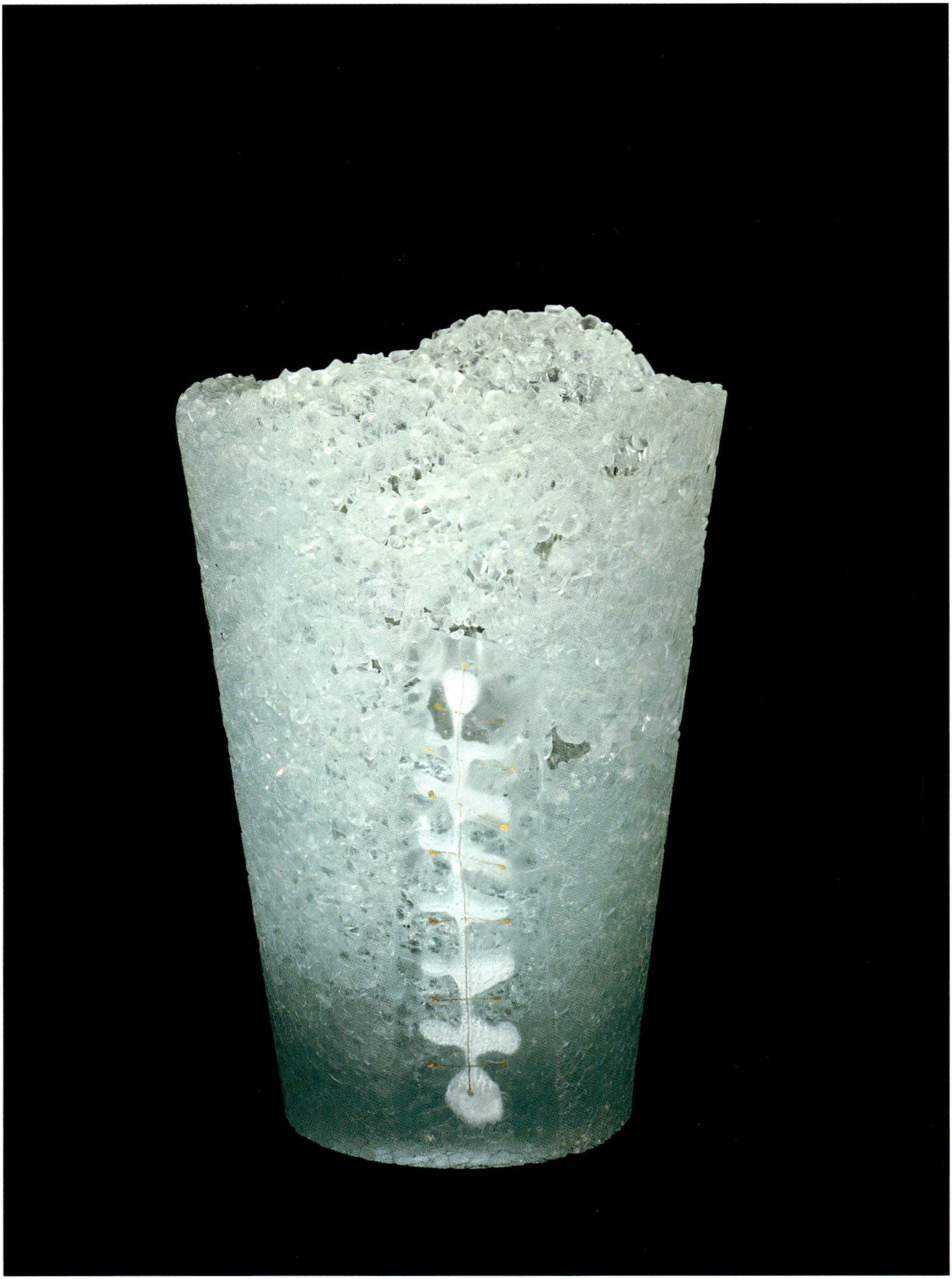

Kiln-forming has natural, in-built limits, in the sense that kilns, annealing schedules and sheer weight make the production of large, single casts difficult, a problem that increases dramatically beyond a certain size. The Mount Palomar reflector, Frederick Carder`s *Indian Head* and the monumental works of artists as diverse as Howard Ben Tré and Stanislav Libensky have pushed the limit, beyond which lurk increasing penalties in terms of weight, time, handling and cost.

Many practitioners are happy to work well within these extremes, content to find their creative vocabulary served by the production of small, discrete objects. However, a characteristic of current practice is the way some artists seek to challenge these natural limitations by approaching them from new directions. This is happening in a number of interesting ways. The artists who are represented in this volume have been included for two interlinked reasons: their quality as artists and their particular approach to the forming of glass. This allows us to see what their range of approaches says about kiln-forming today, particularly the ways in which they both widen and deepen practice (widen in the sense that they extend applications through combination with other materials, both in the kiln and through construction and assemblage).

This attitude can be seen in embryo in the work of the pioneers of kiln-forming, Frances and Michael Higgins, who explored the potential of kiln-forming two decades before the actual studio movement began. They combined pure experiment, carried out in their studio, with the factory production of slumped and enamelled domestic items.

The inclusion of metal clips by fusing them between layers of enamelled and slumped glass is a particular feature of this chandelier (see overleaf) from the 1950s, and their use as essential parts of the design and construction is testament to the far-sightedness of this husband-and-wife team.

The use of kiln-formed elements within larger sculptural wholes has been a feature of the studio movement from its earliest days; and nobody exemplifies this better than Sydney Cash. What sets his work apart is the way in which he uses the spectacular nature of his slumped and stretched forms within wider sculptural assemblages.

Since the early 1970s Mary Schaffer has deformed glass in the kiln with the use of metal armatures which then become part of the finished piece.

Other artists now make more routine use of kiln-formed pieces in mixed-media constructions or assemblages on a wide variety of scales,

PREVIOUS PAGE
Indian Head, monumental cast by Frederick Carder, *c.* 1940. H. approx. 100 cm (39 in.). In the Rockwell Museum, Corning, NY.
Photo: courtesy of the Corning Museum of Glass, New York, USA.

Carder was one of the first artists of the modern era to adopt a constant experimental approach to glass-forming. Throughout his long life, divided equally between England and America, he was a pioneer of casting, among other processes. In the massive *Indian Head* he was attempting to push the barriers of scale and to demonstrate the feasibility of architectural uses for casting. The piece is cracked, due in part to his impatience with the required annealing schedule, as he turned the kiln off after only three weeks.

◄ Fused vessel by Frances Stewart Higgins (1908–2004), *c.* 1955. H. 23.5 cm (9¼ in.).
Courtesy of the Corning Museum of Glass, New York, USA.

The husband-and-wife team Frances and Michael Higgins, who worked in Chicago either side of the Second World War, were genuine pioneers of kiln-forming. They experimented in their studio with enamelling and slumping, foreshadowing many of the techniques that became central to the studio movement from the 1960s onwards.

Dish and slumping mould by Frances and Michael Higgins (1908–1999), 1948. H. 3 cm (1⅛ in.), W. 7.7 cm (3 in.), D. 7.9 cm (3⅛ in.).
Courtesy of Corning Museum of Glass, New York, USA.

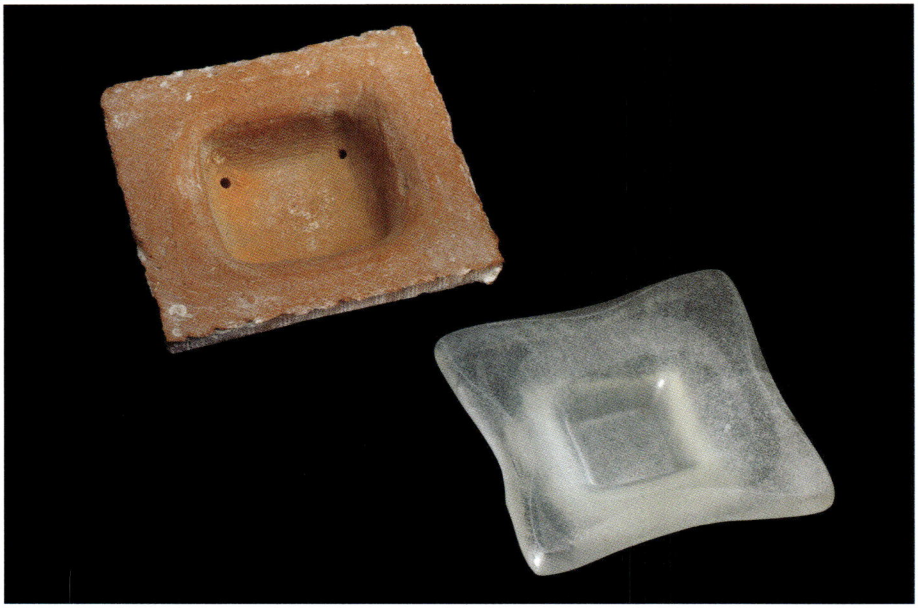

This was the first object made by the Higginses in their apartment studio. It is a simple fused and slumped form made from fused plate glass; the mould is ceramic. Note the small holes in the mould to prevent air becoming trapped during slumping. In addition to their studio experiments the Higginses combined their experimental approach to fusing, enamelling and slumping with an interest in the series production of decorative domestic items. From 1957 to 1966 they were contracted to the Dearborn Glass Co. in Illinois to produce a range of domestic items to their own designs.

Rondelantern, Frances and Michael Higgins, *c.* 1959. A domestic light fitting made by the Dearborn Glass Company, H. 104.5 cm (41⅛ in.), W. 31 cm (12¼ in.), D. 30.8 cm (12⅛ in.).
Courtesy of the Corning Museum of Glass, New York, USA.

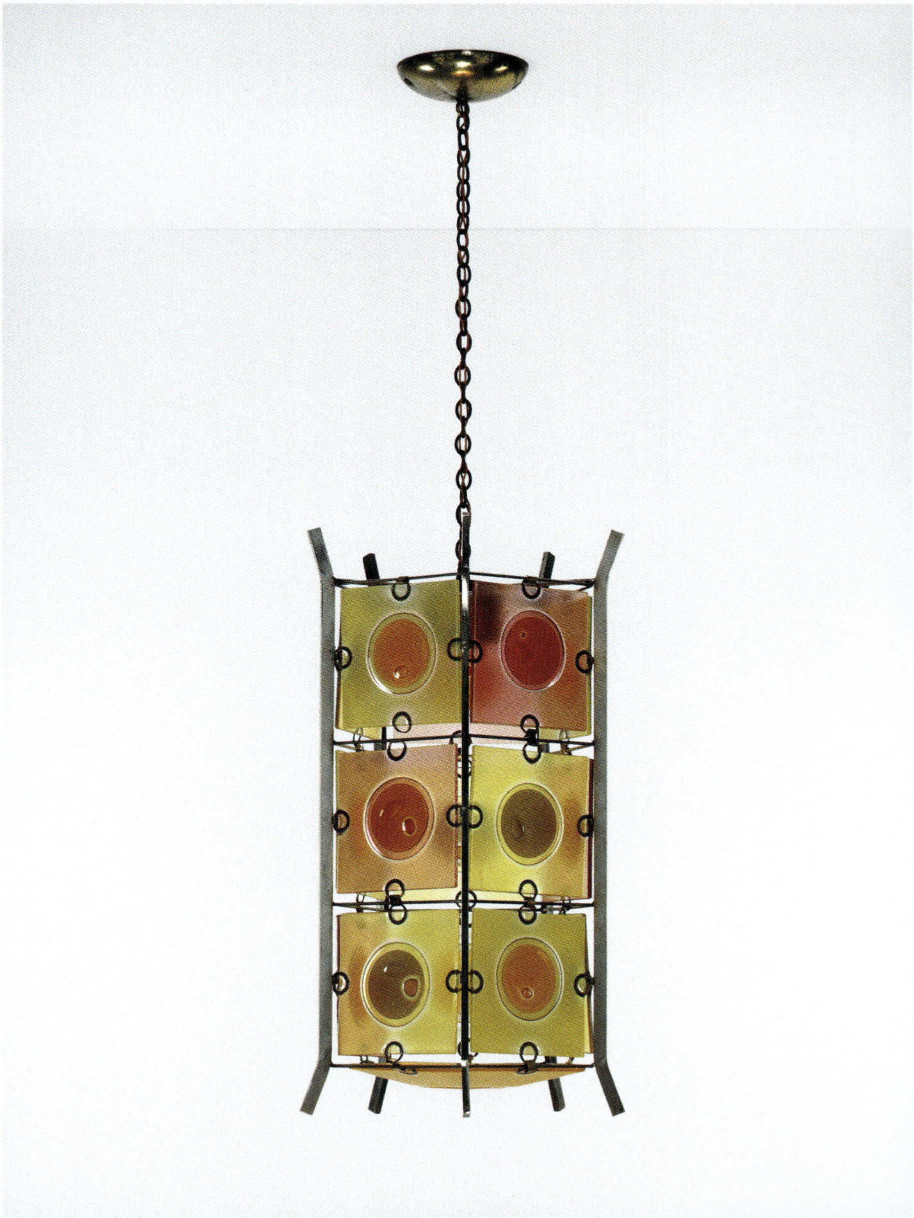

The construction of this piece is particularly interesting. The fused and slumped enamel panels have wires embedded into them during the fusing process. These are then used as anchor points to connect them to the frame.

and to serve a large range of purposes. Such pieces include the delicate jewellery of Linda MacNeil, the monumental architectural schemes of Tomasz Urbanowicz, and the multimedia sculptures of Steve Linn.

I have already touched on the variety of scale and object, qualities that are demonstrated more profoundly by the images themselves than by any descriptions I can offer. Nevertheless, their similarities are also, in their own way, equally eloquent. The objects shown divide themselves broadly into only two main types – the decorative and the sculptural – with architectural features forming an important separate subgroup, Tomasz Urbanowicz, states categorically that his work does not belong in a gallery.

The artists who affirm that their objects are to be seen and judged as sculpture are perhaps best represented by the works of Steve Linn and Janusz Walentynowicz. They have chosen glass as a medium for its ability to express an idea, rather than as an instrument to be exploited for its own sake. Decorative glass, by contrast, involves a celebration of material and form in which the object emerges from a dialogue between the maker and the made. This is not a value judgement, and one is tempted to simply agree with Picasso, who said, 'If it is good it is Art, if it isn't, who cares.' However, I am taking my clues from the intentions of the various artists, expressed in their statements, and in the different characters of the works produced by both types of maker.

This question is clouded by the fact that artists who produce decorative work make reference to at least two different formal traditions in their choice of format. These, as previously mentioned, are the functional and the sculptural. The two types of work are quite distinct, while both remain predominantly decorative in intent and character. I am reminded of the poet Coleridge's statement that, 'Art objects must show likeness and unlikeness, sameness and difference',[1] meaning that all originality must be rooted in certain widely understood conventions in order for its points of departure to be fully appreciated.

While this is true of all art forms, it surely has special relevance for the rapid evolution of crafts in the 20th and 21st centuries, on account of the shift in the relationship of craft activities to society, and to the people who choose to devote their energies to such pursuits. This has made the reference points, Coleridge's 'sameness', more difficult to find, given the way in which, again, in Rose Slivka's words, in this 'identification of work with the process of self-creation' the cultural references rarely come directly from the history of the particular craft as practised, but are more often than not couched in

[1] S.T. Coleridge, 'On Poesy or Art', reprinted in *Biographia Literaria*, vol. 2, J. Shawcross (ed.) (Oxford: Oxford University Press, 1907).

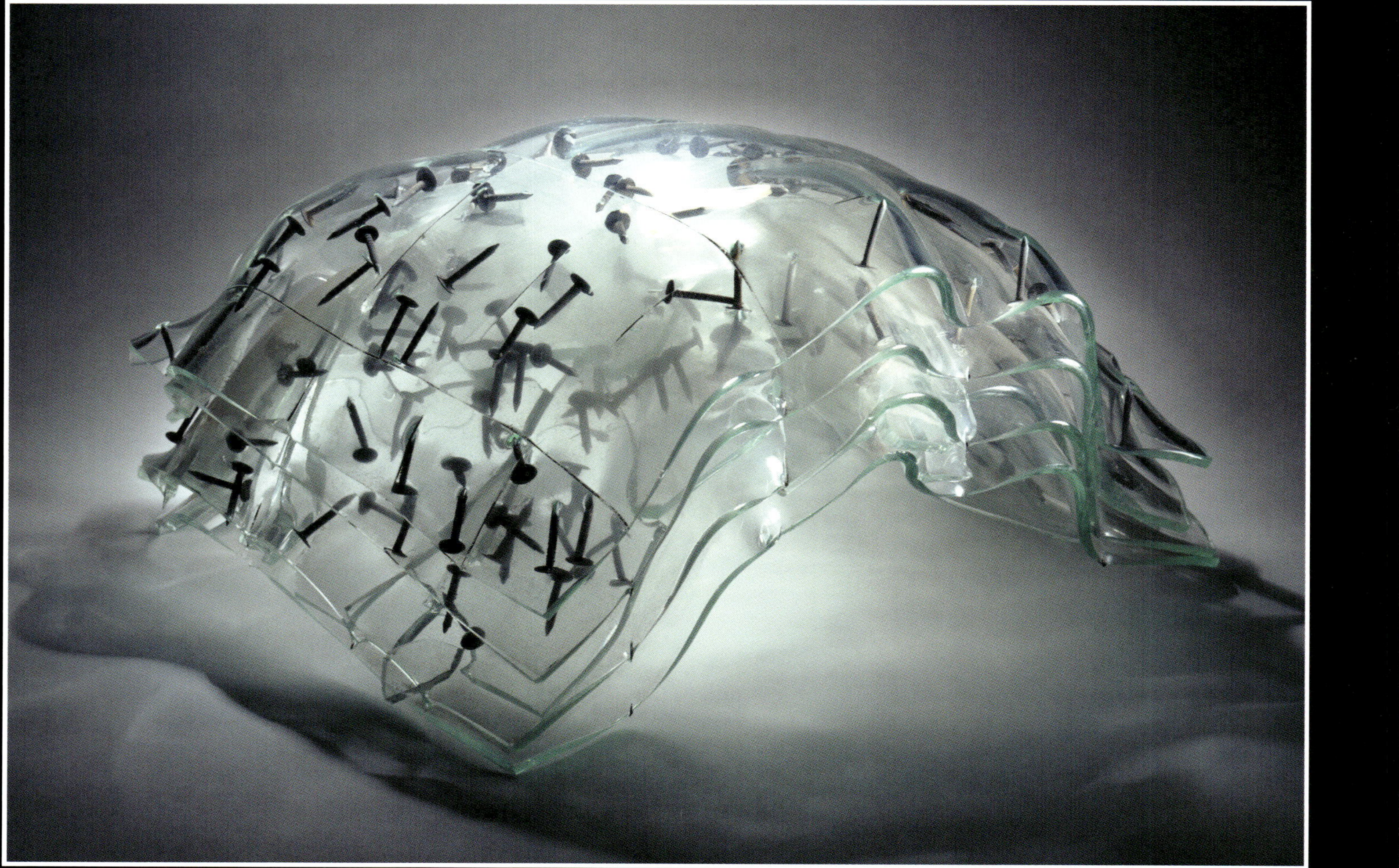

the language of the painter, sculptor or poet. An examination of the statements provided by many of the artists in this book clearly demonstrates this; and their shared ideals tell us as much about the evolving role of craft practice in general as they do about the individuals themselves.

The system by and within which contemporary craft practitioners absorb their skills both reflects and shapes their collective view of themselves. The learning environment has shifted from the workshop apprenticeship to the university department, within which they are 'educated to express themselves',[2] not their culture. This new arrangement is not something to be regretted, being a system through which the crafts have not only survived but are flourishing. The richness of contemporary craft objects, and the fact that so many practitioners survive by selling their work, shows that society values the outcomes of these personal strivings

[2] Lucy Lippard, 'Give and Take Out', in *The Eloquent Object*, Marcia and Tom Manhart (eds) (Tulsa: The Philbrook Museum, 1987).

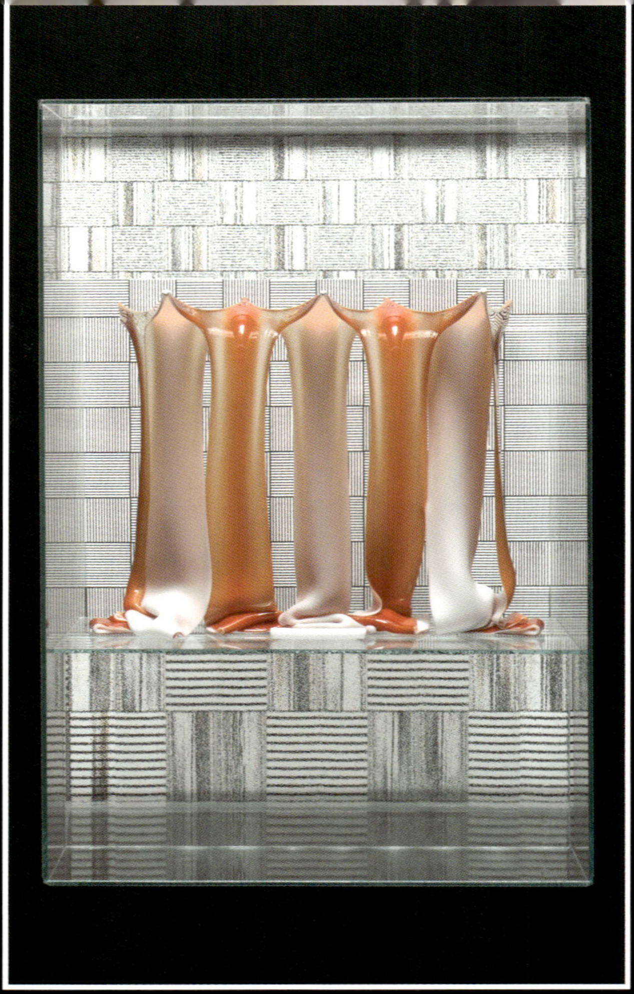

Nail Pillow, Mary Shaffer, 1973. 40 x 40 x 25 cm (15¾ x 15¾ x 9⅞ in.).
Photo: George Erml.

Mary Shaffer was one of the first artists to channel her creative energies through kiln-forming, at the same time challenging the aesthetic expectations that surrounded glass. Her use of metal found objects which combine with and at the same time deform the glass was a radical and original approach to the material. She explains, 'Starting in 1972, I developed "mid-air" slumping. That is, making a structural system that would allow plate glass to soften and move in mid-air. This was the technical basis of all my early work. The process I developed corresponded to my philosophy at that time:

(1) That all points in time were similar; (2) To work in tandem with nature following the female principle. (3) Not to censor my work in any way, but to let it flow directly from my life, feelings, state of being.'

Retread #88.3, Sidney Cash, 1988. Flashed, slumped glass; cut and assembled plate glass; optical glass backed with computer-generated imagery on paper, wire and steel. H. 38.5 cm (15⅛ in.), W. 25.5 cm (10 in.), D. 18 cm (7 in.).
Photo: courtesy of Corning Museum of Glass, New York, USA.

Sydney Cash's use of slumped glass is exercised at the very limits of its temperature range. The glass is allowed to soften and deform from its wire supports to a point where the dynamic distortion is threatened by even the slightest raise in temperature.

for identity, perhaps seeing in them something of their own attempts to come to terms with the forces of modern life.

Another reason why the makers' statements are of interest (and why I chose to include them) is the way they document a fluid and evolving situation. Although the contemporary craft movement clearly has its roots in the period between the two world wars, as can be seen in the activities of individuals like Leach in England and the work of Bauhaus émigrés in America, it was not until the 1950s that this was reflected in the wider cultural landscape.

The starting points of the studio-glass movement are, if anything, even more firmly rooted in the postwar period. Despite the existence of crucial individuals like Marcel Marinot in France, and Frances and Michael Higgins in America, the wider movement can be said to date from the Wisconsin workshops of Harvey Littleton in the early sixties.

Studio-based kiln-forming is even younger, barely fifty years old, coming as it did in the wake of the hot-glass revolution. Obviously, any attempt to identify the philosophic foundations of such a new way of making is obliged to explore the motives and statements of practitioners who have committed themselves to this distinctive art form. Even a cursory glance at the statements in this book reveals a number of important, recurring themes.

Each maker has actively chosen this path from within an informed and liberal context, usually while on a course at an educational establishment, often at degree or higher-degree level. They have made the self-conscious choice of kiln-forming as a means of self-expression, and they describe their creative searches in terms that are redolent of the language of the fine arts, albeit leavened with the vocabulary of their chosen material and that of the decorative arts. The adoption of titles for works is near universal, and is a reflection of both the individual's view of their creative endeavour and the expectations of craft gallery, buyer and specialist publication.

The number of artists who have chosen not to provide a written statement to accompany their work amounts to a few per cent, just as the majority have chosen to provide titles for their objects. The total picture assembled is of a fast-moving series of influences, with the media previously defined as crafts jostling for position with traditional methods of expression within a constantly evolving, complex cultural system. This matters because the insights provided by such statements allow us to see clearly the ways in which a medium like glass, and a forming method like kiln-forming, are being used, taught, described and consumed within contemporary society.

To some extent the seeds of this new self-regard were sown by artists, like Gallé, who in the 19th century described themselves and their work in fully fledged art language, signing pieces with overtly cursive signatures, delivering furniture with accompanying poems, and generally adopting the role of 'Artist' with a capital A. It is significant that Noel Daum, in his book *La Pâte de Verre*, described Walter as 'the Artisan', reserving the title of artist to describe practitioners like Décorchement. It is also significant that Walter did not make any statements about his work, and, unlike other makers, described his objects in the simplest descriptive language.

The search for signature forms and methods, which underlies the endeavours of the artists in this volume, has two aspects: a technical inventiveness, on the one hand, and reference to a wide variety of cultural examples, on the other. As Marcia and Tom Manhart put it, 'Artists now have all but instant access to all the world's cultures'.[3]

[3] Marcia and Tom Manhart, 'The Widening Arc' in *The Eloquent Object*, Marcia and Tom Manhart (eds) (Tulsa: The Philbrook Museum, 1987).

The need for a highly accessible technical approach to glass has driven the incredible rise in sophistication of the work of practitioners since the early, simple experiments that marked the beginning of the studio-glass movement only a few decades ago. The need to exercise a personal aesthetic vocabulary has seen the 'access to all the world's cultures' exploited with great vigour.

Somewhat ironically, at the moment of looking forward, breaking with the restrictions and expectations inherent in the traditional uses of craft skills and materials, many have also looked backwards and sideways for inspiration. Ancient objects, and those drawn from non-industrial societies, freed from their cultural contexts in hermetically sealed museum showcases, have encouraged and inspired the newly self-conscious maker to emulate their sheer formal inventiveness, and to delight in the obvious physical engagement of their original maker with the materials and processes used to make them.

One early and highly significant example of this kind of contemporary reinterpretation of ancient craft objects is Dale Chihuly's series of container forms decorated with patterns derived from Navaho Indian blankets. Influences can be found in the craft objects of industrially advanced countries produced over the past 40 years, which range from Mesopotamia and Egypt to the art of Sub-Saharan Africa and the American Indian. While the spiritual beliefs that originally gave rise to such objects have been jettisoned, the idea that objects made in the 20th and 21st centuries could become vehicles for the expression of personal and universal truths has persisted, and become a major feature of the rationale of the maker's studio.

Methods

The craft ethos that has sustained the survival of the studio-glass movement for over 50 years has owed much of its appeal to the fact that a single maker, working alone, can be in control of the entire system that brings an object into being. This new, integrated practitioner has been called, somewhat clumsily, a designer/maker, although such a designation retains the idea of two separate activities, albeit combined to describe a creative situation in which there is no such separation.

The older system, in which the production of artefacts was divided, with the designer providing the form and the craftsman providing the skill, requires the existence of a complex range of communications

A casting by the studio of Zdeněk Lhotsky. ➤

Photo: courtesy of Lhotsky Studio.

An indication of the expertise and quality of casting facilities available to sculptors who wish to have their work cast commercially is evident in this large-scale, flawless cast by the Lhotsky Studio for sculptor Latchezar Boyadjiev in 2002.

The wax original. ➤

Photo: courtesy of Lhotsky Studio.

A wax original made ready for the refractory stage in the Lhotsky Studio. The piece, *Object Starfish*, 2002. 160 x 120 cm (63 x 47¾ in.). The model, by artist Cestmír Suška, is placed in a wooden mould with metal mesh and strengthening bars to guard against the cracking of the refractory mould during firing.

Removing the mould. ➤

Photo: courtesy of Lhotsky Studio.

The sculpture is carefully removed from the refractory mould after firing.

intended to bridge the gap between them. These vary from diagrams to blueprints to prototypes, but all are meant to enable the maker unambiguously to carry out the wishes of the designer.

In an important sense, the creative journey within such a system

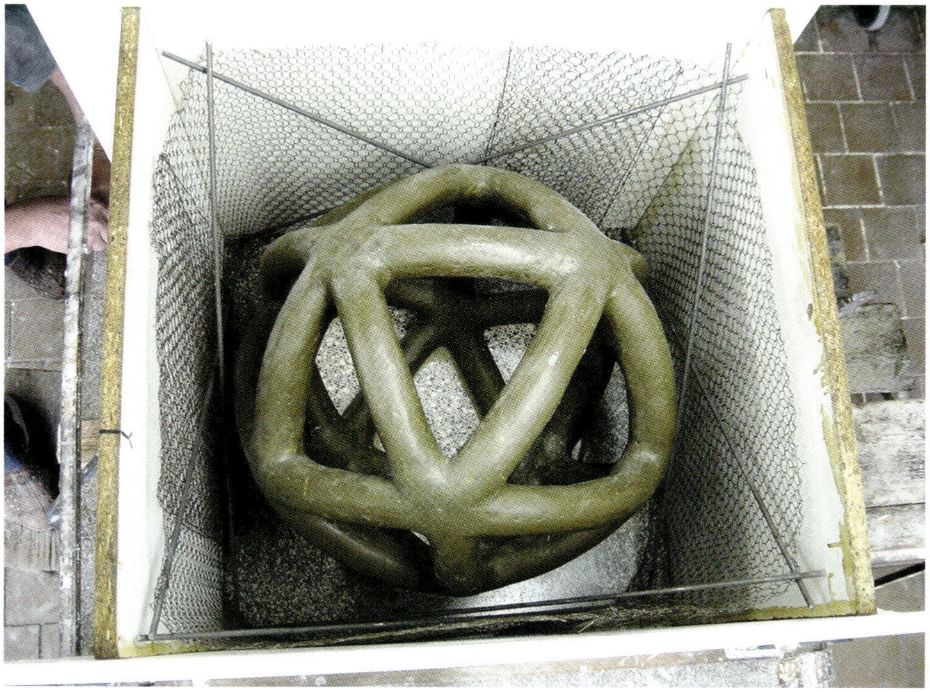

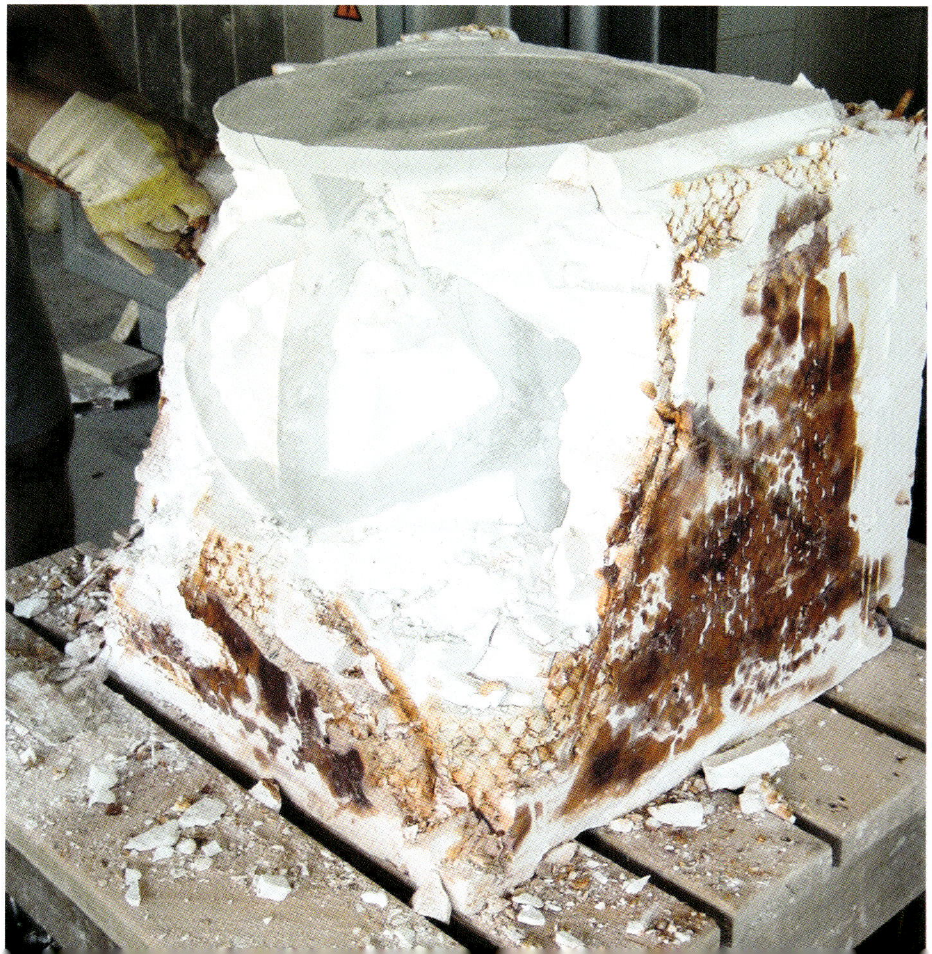

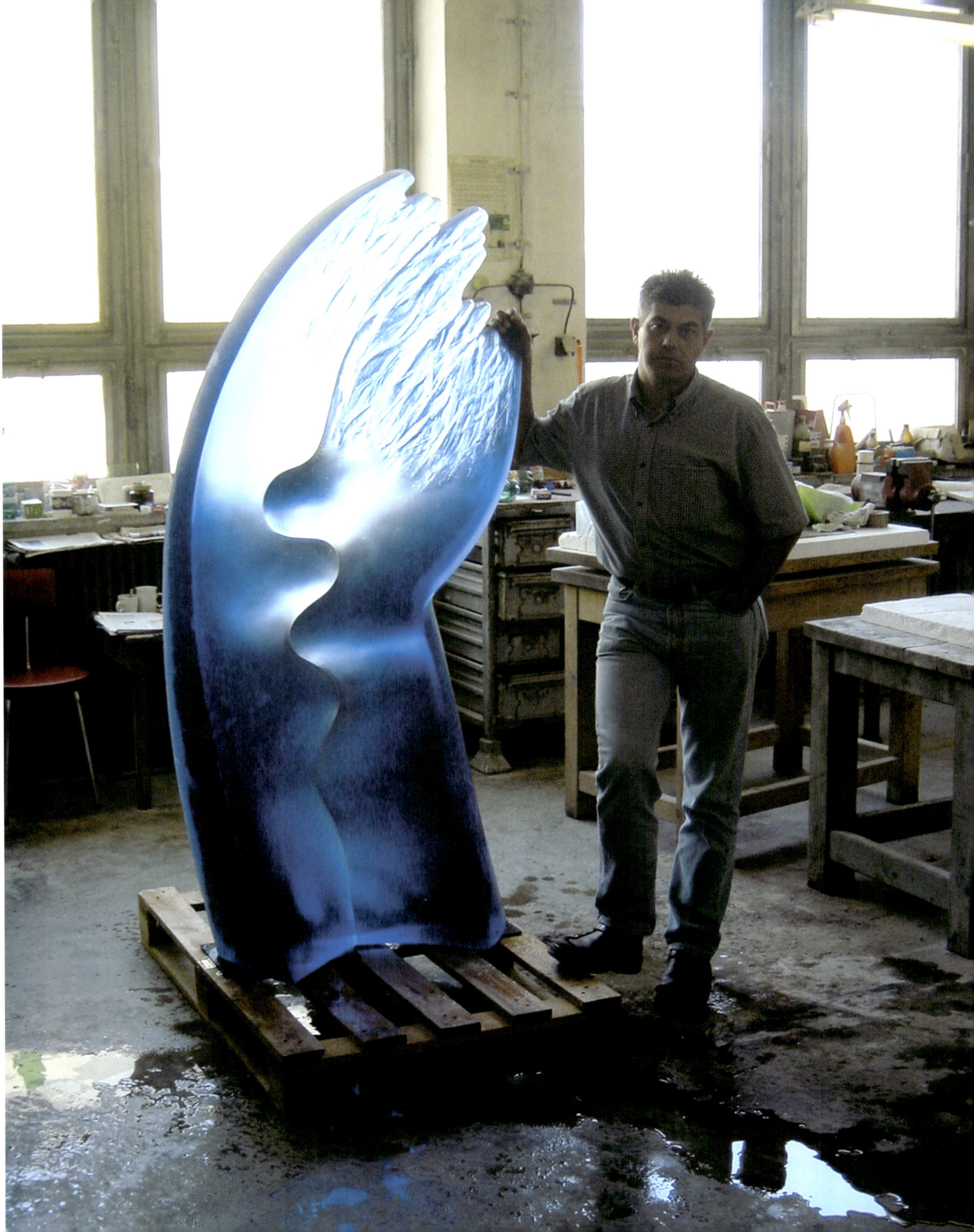

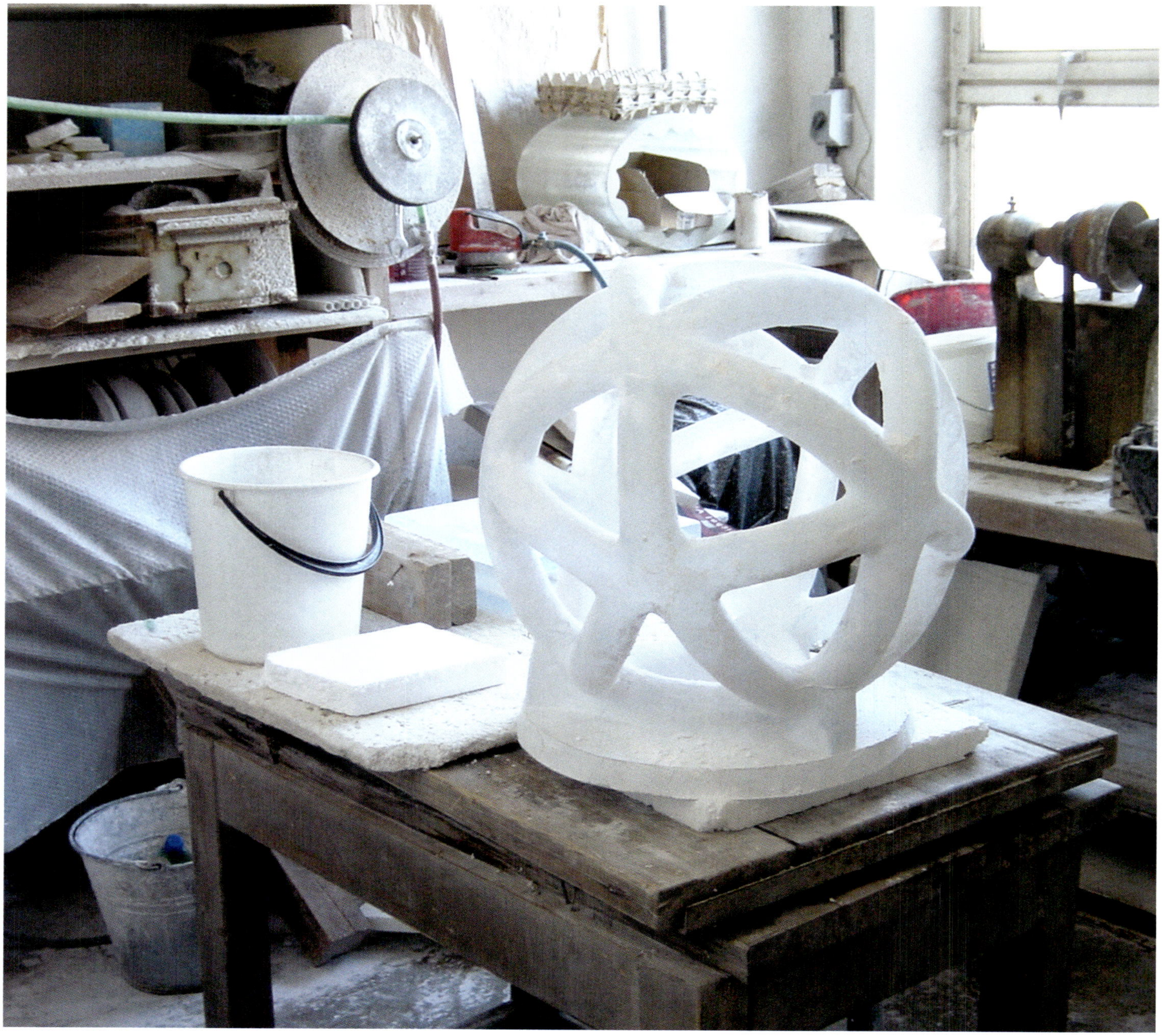

The sculpture before surface finishing.

finishes once the prescription for the form has been created by the designer and handed over to the maker. One of the great attractions of the craft designer/maker system has been the fact that there is no division between an idea and its realisation, as both functions are combined within a single person. In fact the advantage is increased by the fact that the act of creation can continue, via a series of feedback loops, from the earliest idea right up to the moment when the finishing touches are added to the completed piece. This makes the journey from idea to final form into one filled with creative opportunities via constant rethinks and adjustments based on observation.

Kiln-forming, with its many stages and slow accumulation of formal and textural qualities, is well suited to this method of evolving and experiencing the joy of bringing into being new, unique items. In the research for this book, and in the statements and images provided by the artists, it has become clear to me that many feel the same, and have evolved working methods to exploit the potential of the journey. To many, a loss of control over any part of the complete process would be seen as a loss of creative opportunity, and an undermining of their decision to seek this sort of activity in the first place.

However, a recent development has added a new interpretation of the creative equation. A number of companies have set up to offer the same opportunity for glass as has long been available for bronze. In this system the artist provides an original, from which the company proceeds to cast a perfect glass replica in a single colour chosen from a sample range.

This system enables artists who do not possess specialist glass expertise and/or facilities the option of working with the material. This interesting and perhaps overdue development has added a new dimension to kiln-forming, at the same time raising interesting issues about the part played in the kiln-forming of glass by the manufacture of one's own work entirely by oneself.

On one important level this service adds much to the repertoire of kiln-formed glass, with the highly professional production of flawless, large-scale glass casts. The method originated under the Czech state-sponsored art system, where artists like Libensky were given factory-scale facilities to realise their monumental works, and which, since the break-up of the Soviet bloc, has been made available to artists worldwide through these new, dynamic and highly professional, commercial studios.

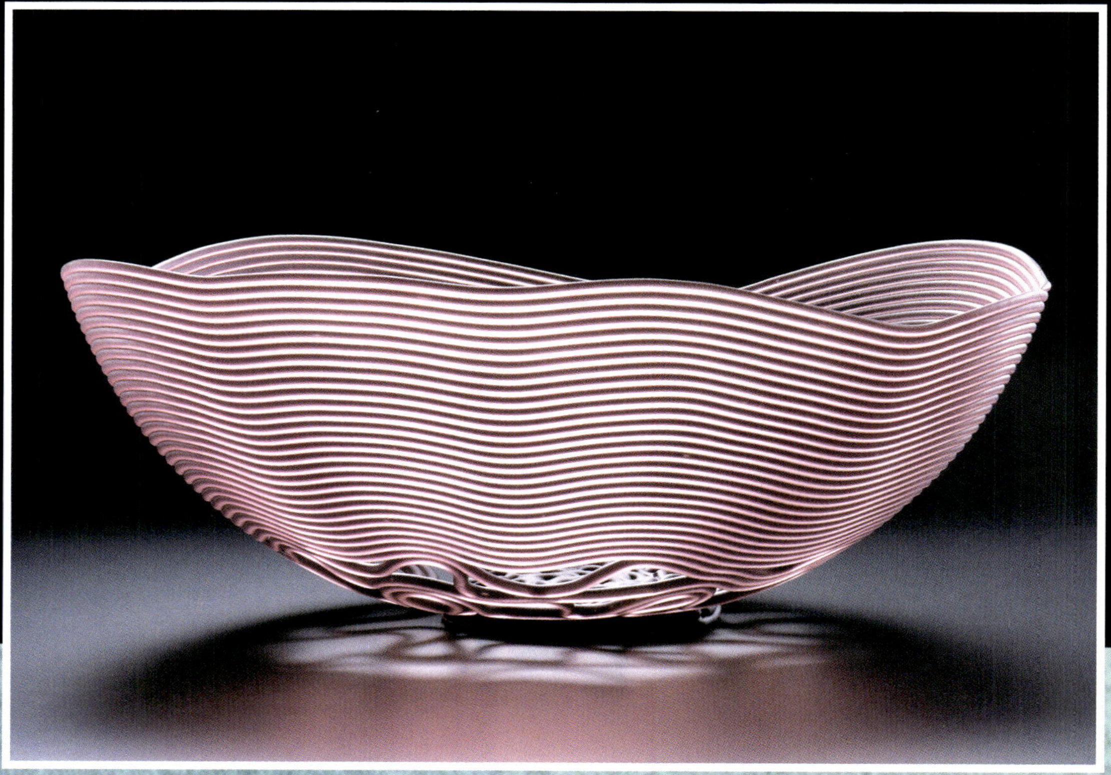

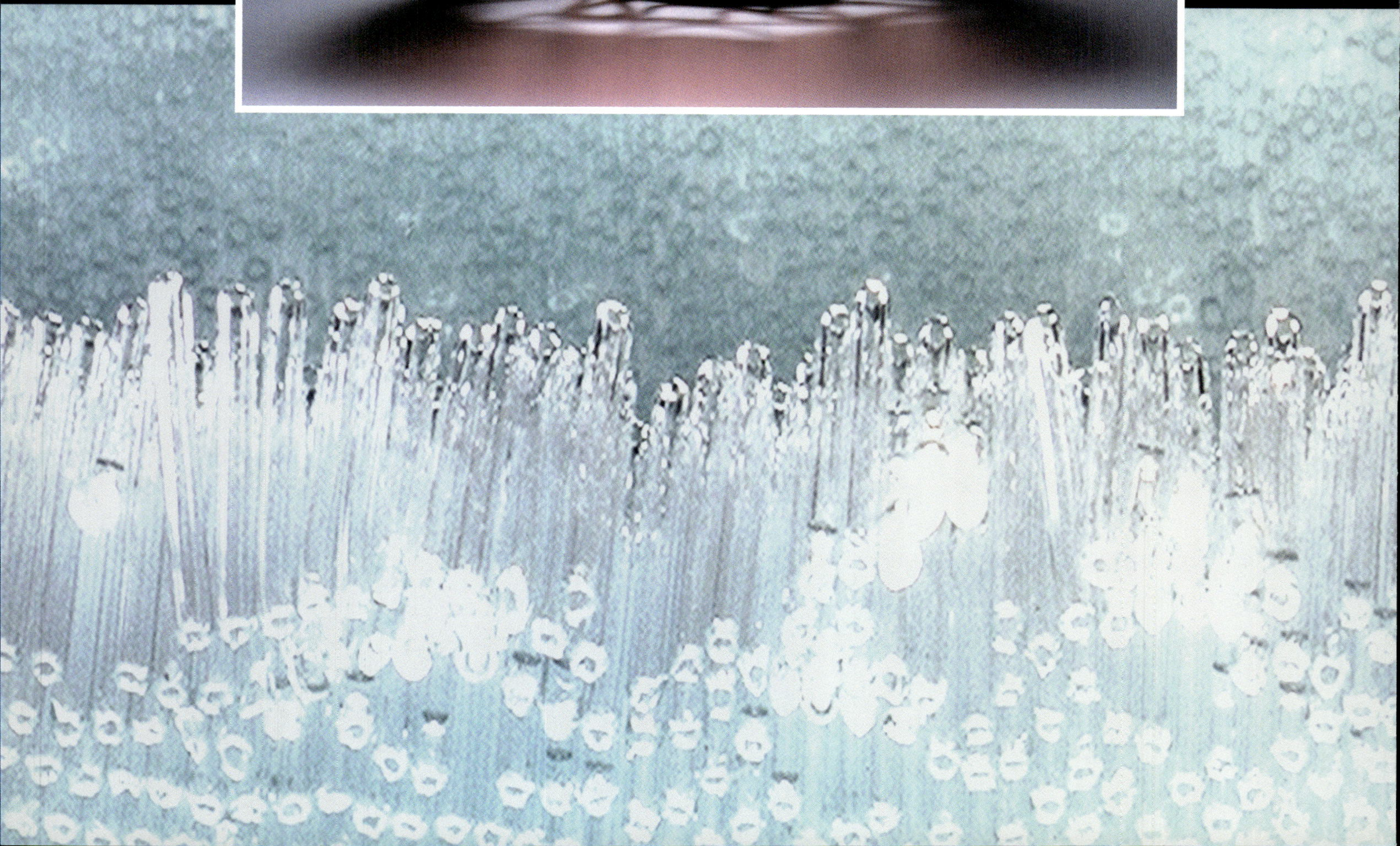

6 *The Nature of Glass*

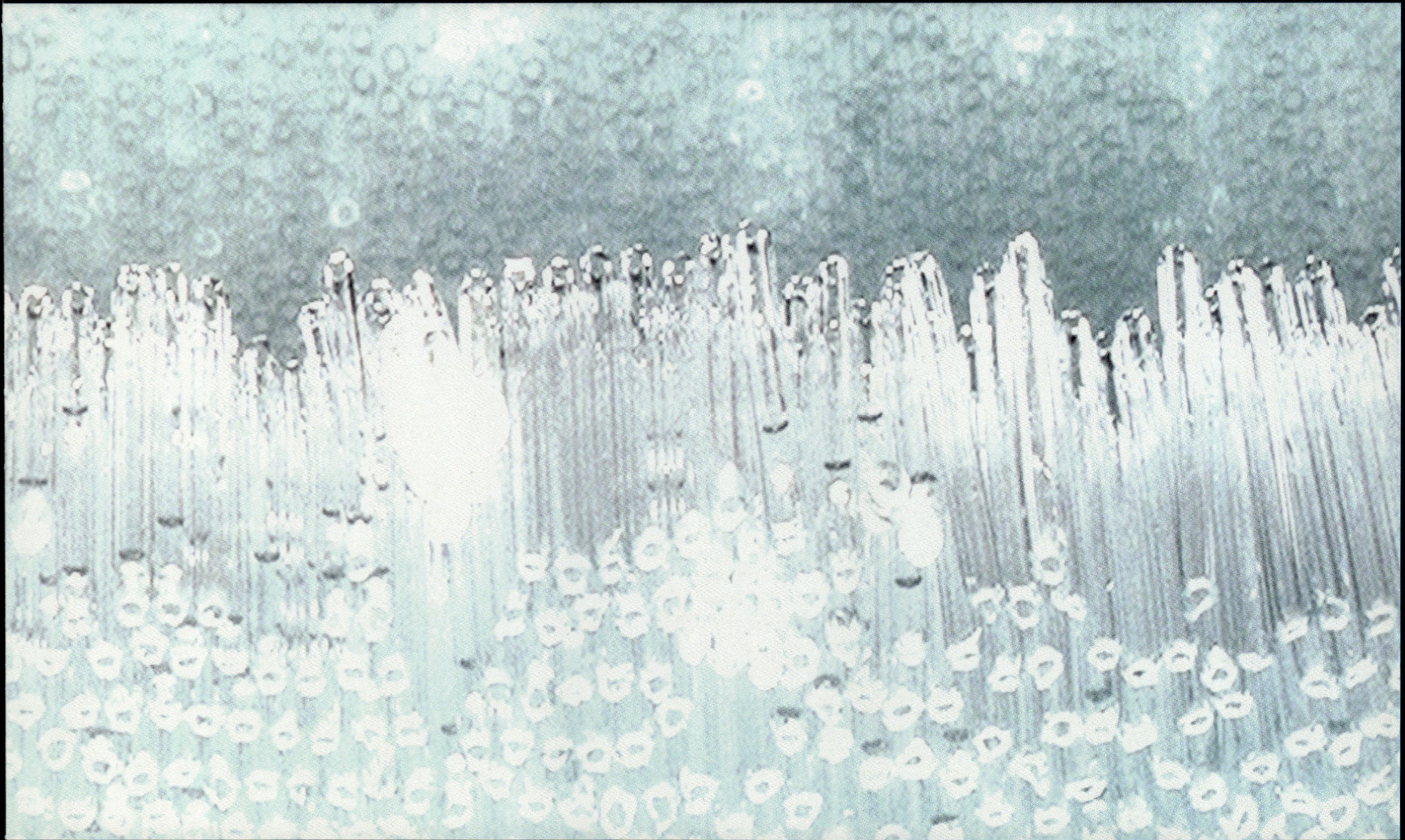

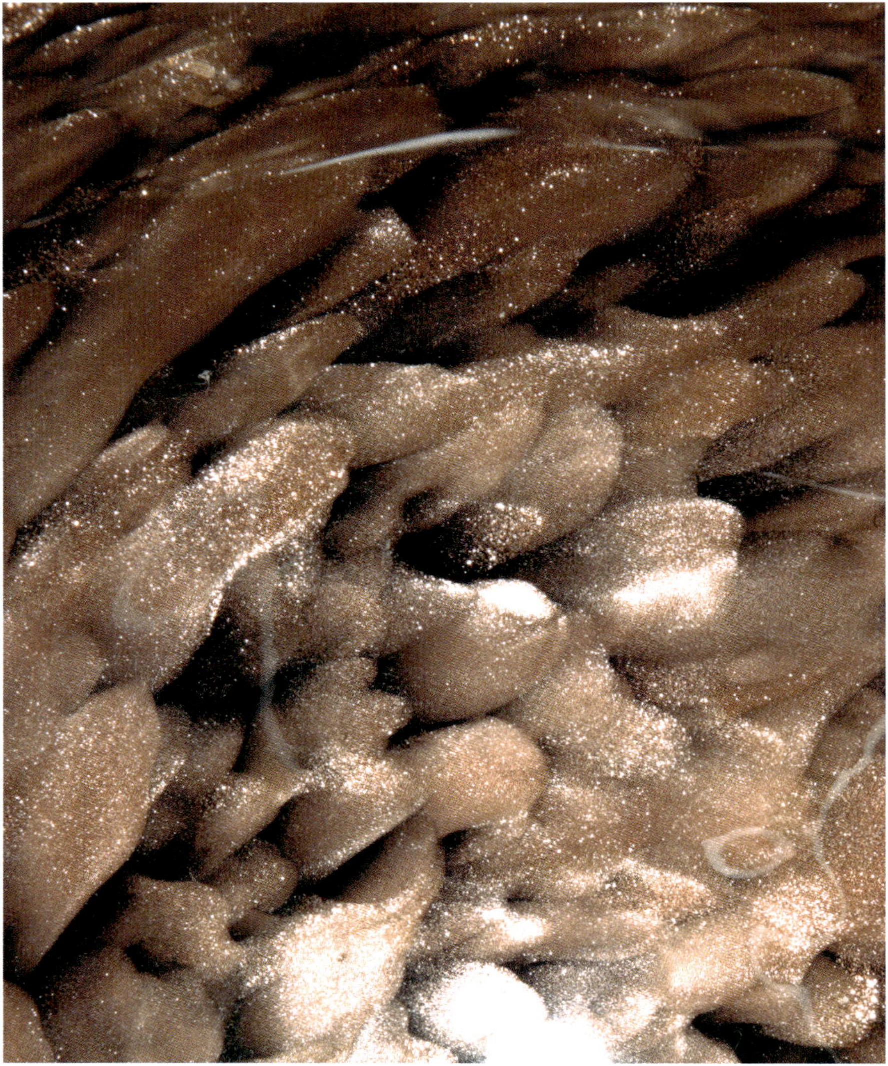

Glass is a unique material, a fact that has been noted so many times and in so many ways that it has been dulled by repetition. I would simply like to add a couple of examples that illustrate a particular aspect of this singularity, and by doing so perhaps shed some light on its various manifestations. Many kiln-formers will, I feel sure, have had the 'glassiness' of their work called into question. Many of the qualities that kiln-formers prize in their work do not match the ideal view of glass held by most non-practitioners, and this often creates barriers to the full appreciation of the work.

The fact is that glass can be made to function in an almost infinite number of ways through the manipulation of its qualities during manufacture. The everyday experience of glass, however, tends to be restricted to a very narrow band among its qualities, centred mainly on transparency and refraction.

Glass is unusual among the raw materials used in craft production in being a solution rather than a compound. As such, it can absorb an almost infinite range of other materials, whose inclusion can dramatically change its qualities but not to the extent that it can no longer function as a glass. This is the behaviour that scientists, engineers and artists – particularly kiln-formers – rely on to exploit in their different, highly personal dealings with it.

Three examples drawn from very different disciplines illustrate this property. The first involves literally saturating the solution of glass to the point where precipitation occurs.

This is the creation of aventurine glass, where copper is added to glass during founding in such large quantities that, instead of achieving a blue or green colouring as normal, the copper crystals are forced to form in the solution. The result is an attractive and unusual glass.

The second is drawn from a completely different field – surgical medicine. Here, the fact that glass is a solution is exploited in a totally novel way, and to achieve a highly specialised result.

It involves a special glass with a very high calcium content from which have been cast glass shapes that are surgically implanted into damaged areas of the skull, where, due to the presence of the calcium and the relatively porous nature of the glass, they become hosts for the regrowth of bone. The calcium that has been added to the glass during its manufacture

PREVIOUS PAGE

Mark Peiser, the cold-stream casting process, 2008. A classic example of an artist developing a unique forming method to realise his creative vision, the cold-stream system is just one example of the inventiveness of the artist Mark Peiser, whose career spans over thirty years. He has moved from kiln-forming to develop ways of casting glass that refuse simple categorisation. The cold-stream system is a brilliant response to the liquidity of molten glass, and harnesses the mobility of a thin stream of glass as it is directed onto a moving surface.

➤

Aventurine glass.

Photo: Simon Bruntnell.

A prime example of the nature of glass as a solution rather than as a compound. Copper is added to the glass during founding until it cannot absorb any more, whereupon the copper precipitates into crystals. This phenomenon is exploited in the production of aventurine glass.

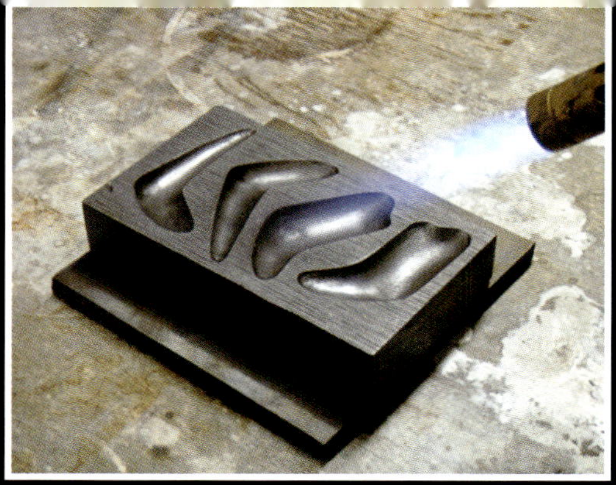

Carved graphite moulds being preheated.
Photo: Paddy Hartley.
This is step one of a process to produce glass casts that are rich in calcium. They are used by Guy's Hospital as implants to replace bone, to which the existing bone can bond.

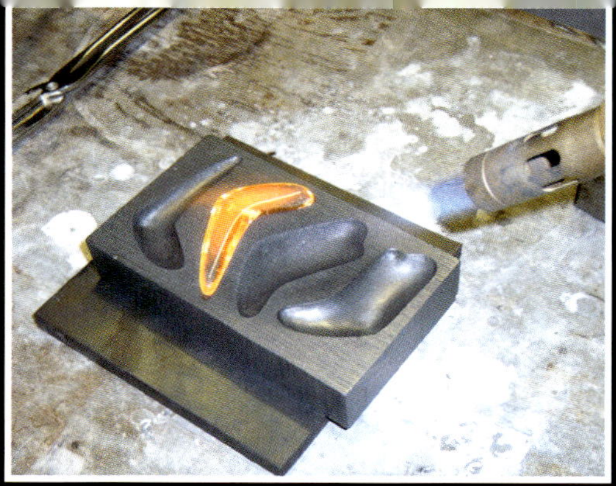

Melting the glass.
Photo: Paddy Hartley.
Calcium-rich Bioglass ingots are then melted into the preheated mould.

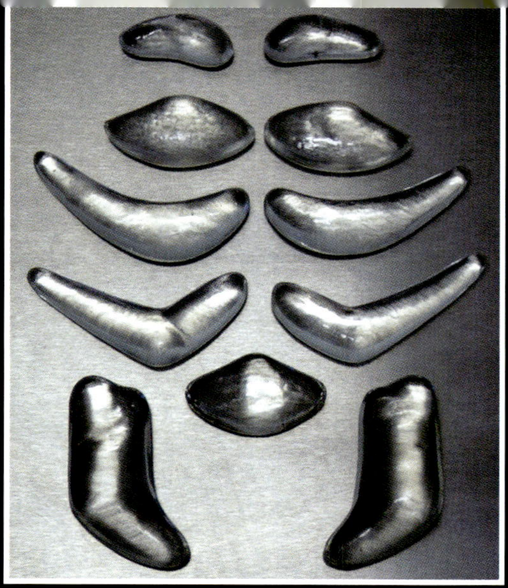

Finished glass implants.
Photo: Paddy Hartley.
A selection of Paddy Hartley's finished Bioglass implants, used for medical purposes.

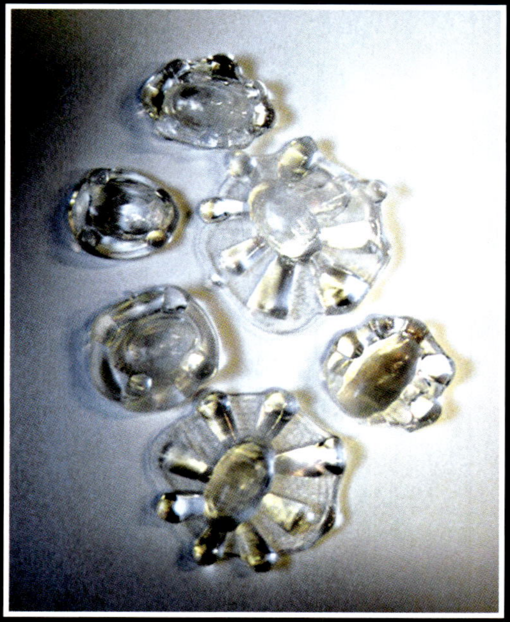

Another type of calcium-rich glass implants.
Photo: Paddy Hartley.

A medical use which exploits the characteristics of a solution. A research team at Guy's Hospital in London, in a rare collaboration between art and science, are producing casts that are rich in calcium. They are used as implants to replace bone, to which the existing bone can bond.

allows the body to lay down its own calcium on top, and by this means to completely absorb the implant.[1]

The third example is one in which a glass artist literally invents a new glass process, whereby glass characteristics that have been known about since the Mesopotamian era – in this case the fact that hot glass can be poured in a stream – are used as a source from which to create objects of unique character and beauty.

These are just three examples of the implications of the special nature

[1] Dr Ian Thompson & Paddy Hartley at Guy's Hospital, London. See website: Project Façade.

of glass; and the fact that new glasses are being designed at an enormous rate to perform totally diverse, highly specific functions shows that the opportunities exist for each maker to customise their individual use of glass. This can be at a much lower level of technical manipulation than the examples cited, yet may still rely on the special nature of glass as a solution: by additions to the glass while casting, or through the use of ceramic oxides, powdered metals, wires (see the photos on p. 201), or traces of materials that are perhaps conventionally thought of as contaminants. Diana Hobson, famously and radically, introduced brick dust, powdered shells and small stones into her delicate pâte-de-verre vessels.

The growth in recent years of globally available, off-the-shelf glasses in ranges of compatible colours, and in a range of formats – from grain to sheet, rod and ingot – has made the production of professional-looking work much easier to achieve. However, this has come at the cost of personal experiment, and has perhaps resulted in a certain sameness in colour, glass type and texture. In this regard, it is interesting to note the lengths to which some artists will still go to avoid this standardisation. For example, Linda MacNeil in her jewellery (see photo on p. 88) creates a personal vocabulary of colour by painstakingly bonding slivers of stained-glass sheet to the base of clear cast sections, and backing each sliver with a mirrored surface.

The search for a distinctive, recognisable approach to glass involves a personal cocktail of ingredients, one of which often involves a particular way of interpreting both process and material. This has become more important in such a competitive world, and at the same time more difficult, as information becomes easier to access and the production of more and more sophisticated work spreads across the globe.

This increase in range and quality is not to be regretted when it brings with it a greater emphasis on personal imagery and intent at the expense of mere technical novelty.

Only a few decades ago, just being able to cast glass was enough to excite interest, and questions that involved deeper creative motives were somewhat overshadowed in the headlong search for novel ways of merely shaping the material. We are now a couple of generations down the line from those heady, exciting and naive days, though most of the pioneers of the studio movement are, happily, still with us.

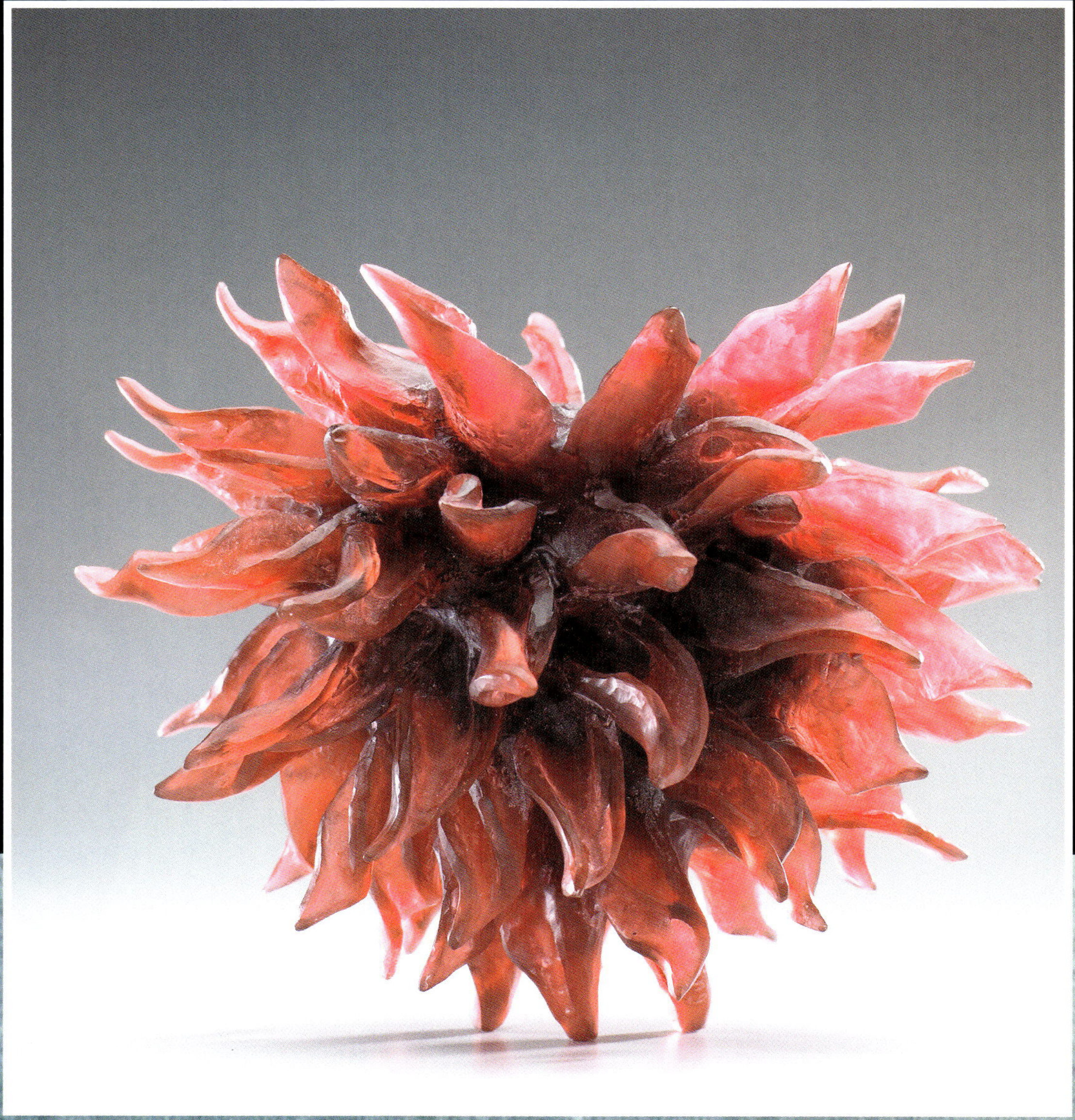

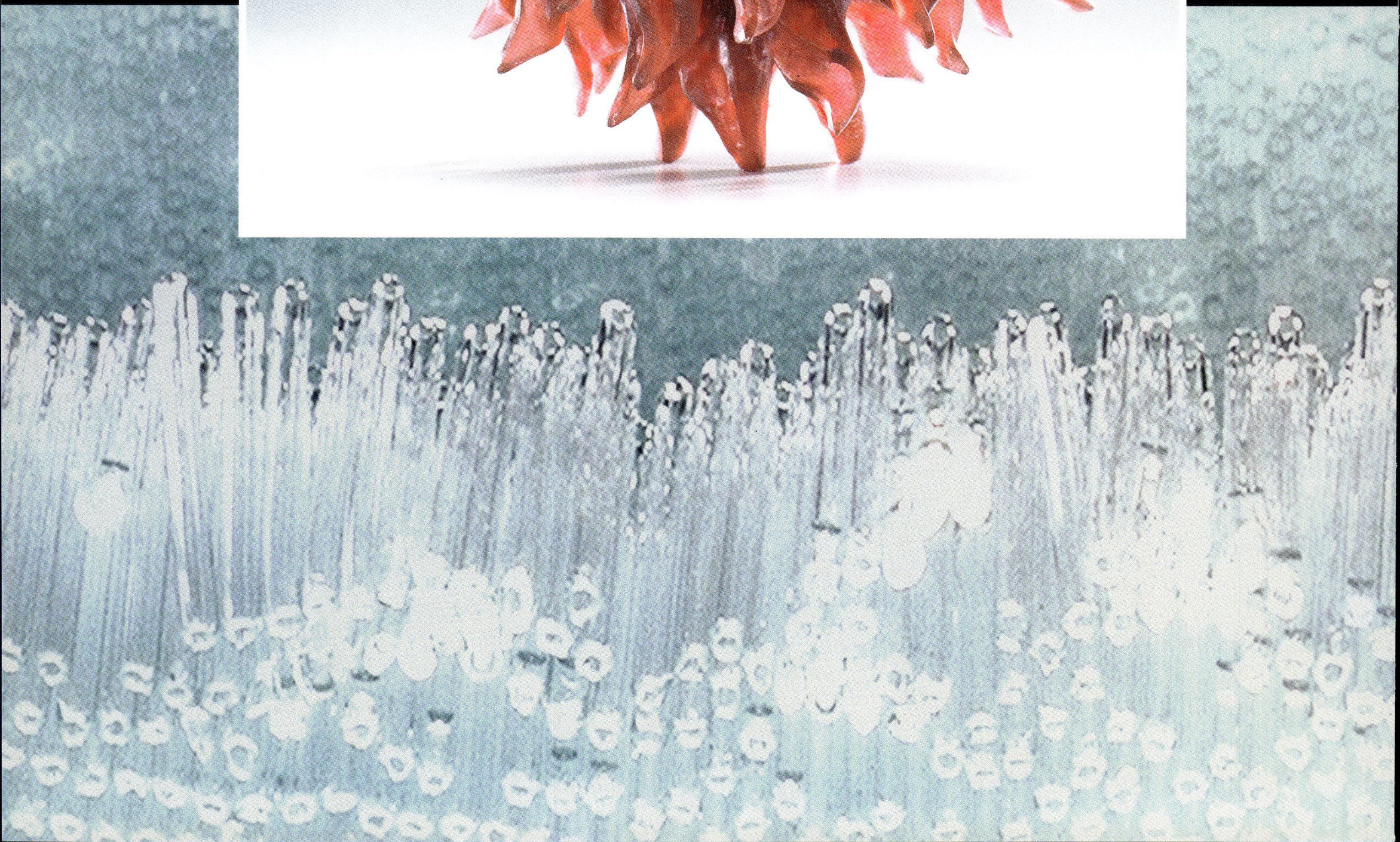

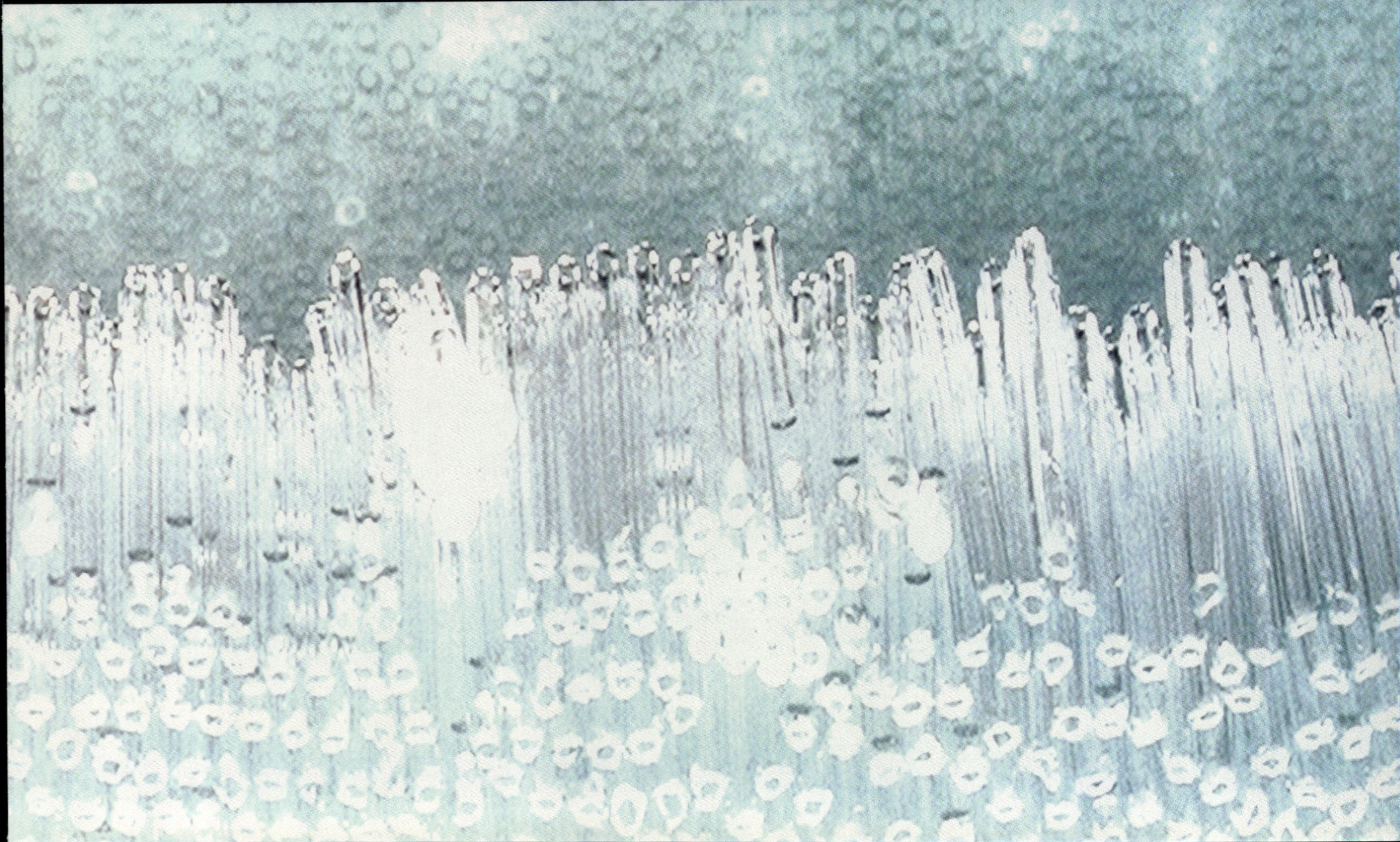

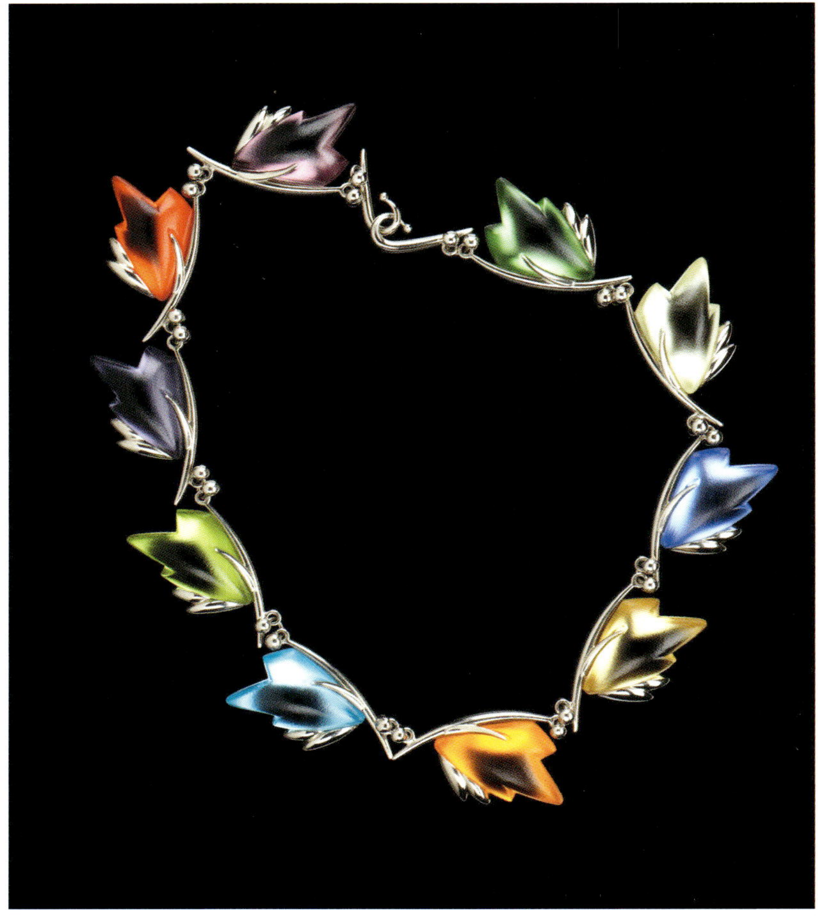

In choosing who to approach with a request for material for this book, I established a number of aims. The first was to restrict myself to practitioners who, in my estimation, produced work of the highest quality, independent of their age or reputation. With this proviso met, I have tried to ensure that the work featured covered the full range of kiln-forming methods, as well as an equally full range of object types, scales and contexts. The artists vary greatly in age: from well-known figures who have played major roles in the studio movement, to relatively young makers who are just emerging into the spotlight. The artists also represent a wide range of countries: from major centres that have figured strongly in the studio movement from the beginning, to relative newcomers.

I have chosen to present each artist separately, and have decided to use the temperature range of kiln-forming, from low to high, to determine the order of their presentation. I will start, therefore, with those artists who use glass as a surface, either printing or painting on enamels, to slumping, stretching, fusing or casting.

I could have chosen to present the artists alphabetically, but I believe that, in a book driven predominantly by the discussion of method, this way enables the most effective presentation and understanding of the range of kiln-forming activity at large today. It is worth reiterating that more kiln-forming is being undertaken now than at any time in its 5000-year history. Although most of the techniques being practised are prefigured elsewhere in the long history of glass-forming, their range, variety and sophistication place them firmly in the 21st century.

I have invited each artist to give me a personal statement that reflects their motivation and, where possible, offers some insight into their creative and material methods. I have been surprised by the generosity and openness of the majority of makers, particularly when a hard-won technique is described in detail.

I have attempted, wherever possible, to present artists' statements in their entirety, to preserve the insights they give into the individuals concerned as well as their creative and presentation of themselves to the public through artists' statements and websites. However, it has occasionally been necessary to edit statements, and where this has happened I have attempted to remain true to the original. My motives for writing this volume are threefold: to present a picture of contemporary kiln-forming; to stimulate, inform and perhaps influence the next generation

PREVIOUS PAGE

Anja Isphording, *# 107*, 2006. H. 19 cm (7½ in.), D. 20 cm (8 in.).
Photo: Ken Mayer.

Anja Isphording's forms are truly three-dimensional in the sense that they do not pay lip service to notions of the container but rather, following the natural patterns of growth that inspire her, radiate from their centre like flowers themselves. (See also p. 122.)

◄ *Bouquet* from the *Floral* series, Linda MacNeil, 2006. Acid-polished multi-coloured transparent glass laminated to mirrored glass; polished 18 carat white gold. D. 15 cm (6 in.).
Photo: Bill Truslow.

Linda MacNeil's attention to detail is seen in this necklace, where she laminates clear lost-wax casts to thin slivers of colour and mirror to achieve precisely the range of colour and quality of reflection she envisaged. (See also p.129.)

of makers; and, I hope, to contribute to the debate about the issues that underlie and ultimately give meaning to its outcomes.

The works themselves provide eloquent examples of the range and quality of contemporary practice, and give indications of the technical expertise and procedures involved. Where the artist has provided images and/or explanations, these are included, and where appropriate I have added my own comments and suggestions.

I have banded artists together within loose groups that share kiln-forming procedures carried out at similar temperatures. This is to highlight the activity in this area, and to allow the images and information to reinforce one another. I have finished with a group that extend their kiln-forming practice by combining it with other materials, or by using more than one method of glass-forming in the same object. I have often argued that glass moves forward creatively when it is confronted with the challenges that come with operating within a wide material and cultural context, and the example set by this group illustrates that point. Their willingness to move beyond the limits of one method or one material provides proof, if it were needed, that despite the fact that kiln-formed glass has never been as varied, widely spread or vibrant as it is now, it is far from reaching its limits as a creative vehicle.

Surface Imagery

The first group of artists use different ways of exploiting glass as a surface on which to fuse, draw, or paint images in glass powders or enamels.

Dr Kevin Petrie

The main focus of Kevin Petrie's research has been the development of new approaches to applying imagery to ceramics and glass, and the dissemination of these approaches in a usable format. His book *Glass and Print*, also published by A&C Black, presents the results of this research, which is drawn from two separate strands of creative activity: glass and printmaking.

Petrie's imagery is drawn from landscape, with recent work exploring how direct drawing can be fixed into permanent form via his unique kiln-forming method. Integrated glass printing is his new process, combining industrial print technology with kiln-forming to enable the creation of pieces where the printed image and the glass are fully integrated. This offers a subtly different aesthetic to more conventional approaches, where

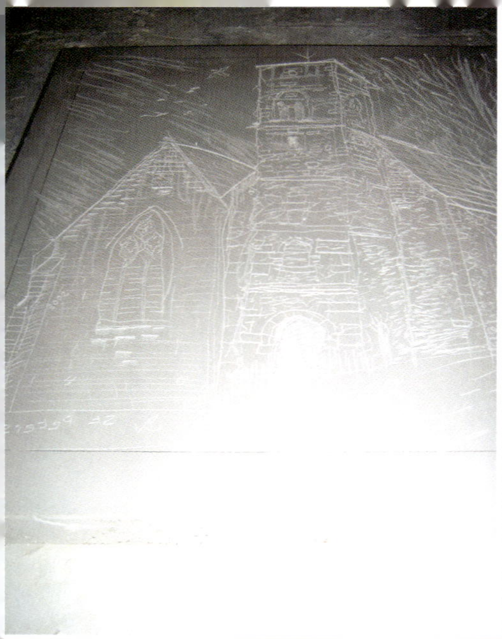

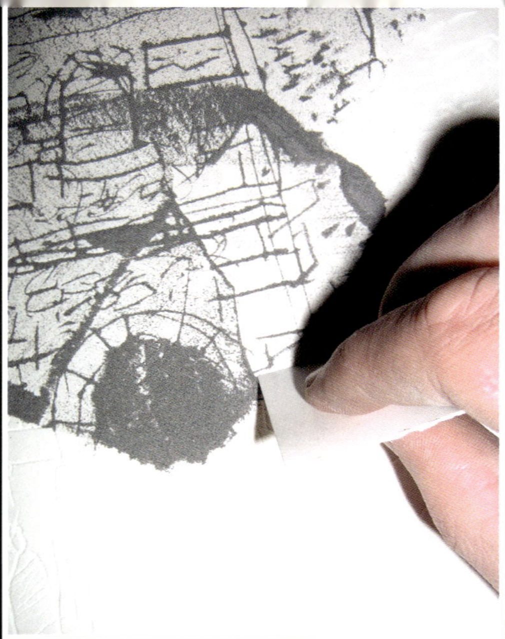

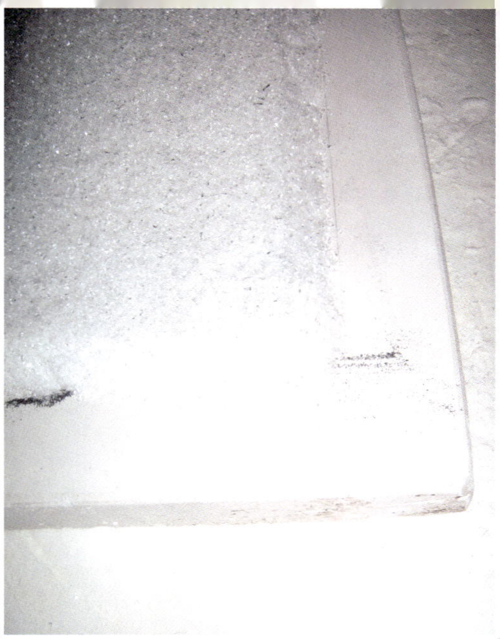

▲ A plaster/molochite batt is cast onto a sheet of glass.
Photo: courtesy of the artist.
This is drawn into with a sharp metal tool to create an intaglio image.

▲ Bullseye frit is applied to the drawn areas like applying ink to an etching plate. The glass frit can be manipulated with care to create areas of tone or texture to complement the fine intaglio lines.

▲ A form board is placed over the mould to create the perimeter of the piece. More frit is then sieved onto the drawn area. This can be clear, opaque or coloured. A coarser grade of frit is then added up to the level of the form board. This is smoothed with a straight edge to create an even finish, and the board is then removed. This causes the edge of the drawing to collapse, the effect being rather like the irregular or deckled edge on handmade paper. The piece is fired to 720°C (1328°F), after which it is carefully removed from the mould and cleaned.

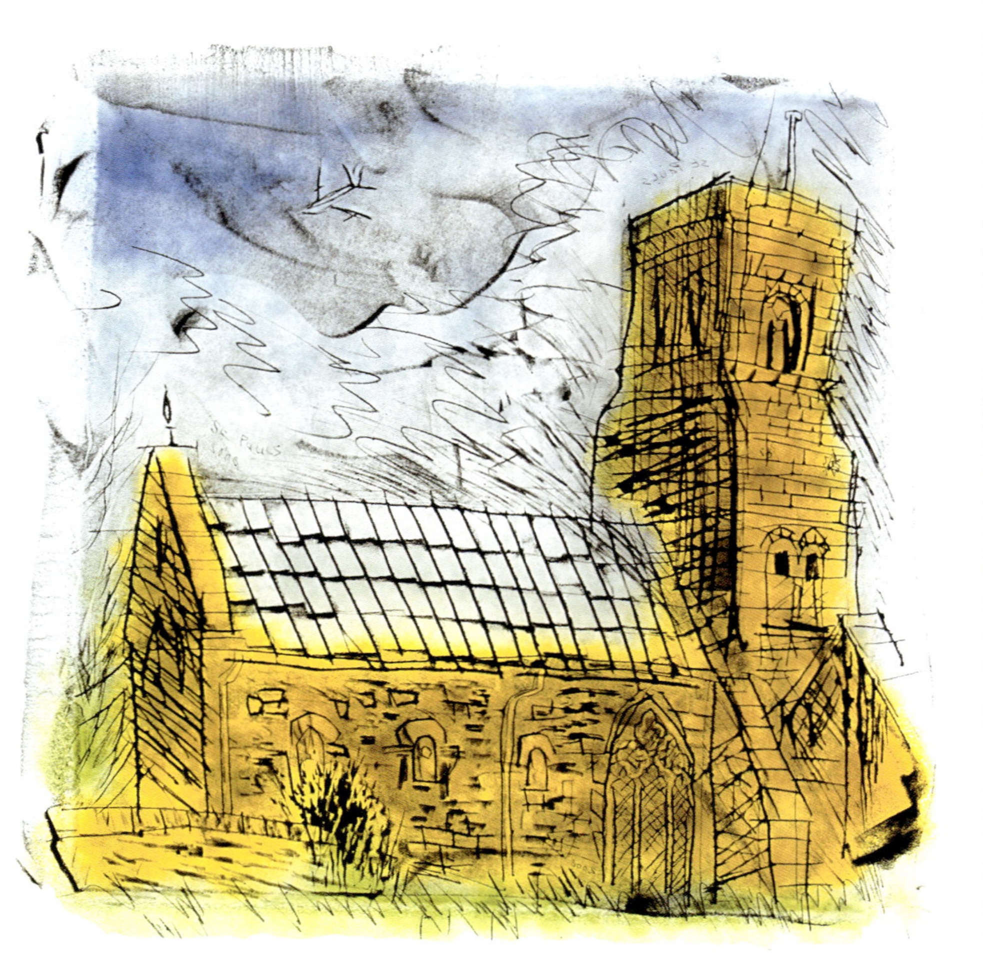

◄ *St Paul's Church – Jarrow 2*, Dr Kevin Petrie, 2008. Integrated glass drawing, 53 cm x 54 cm x 0.5 cm (20⅞ x 21¼ x ¼ in.).
Photo: David Williams.

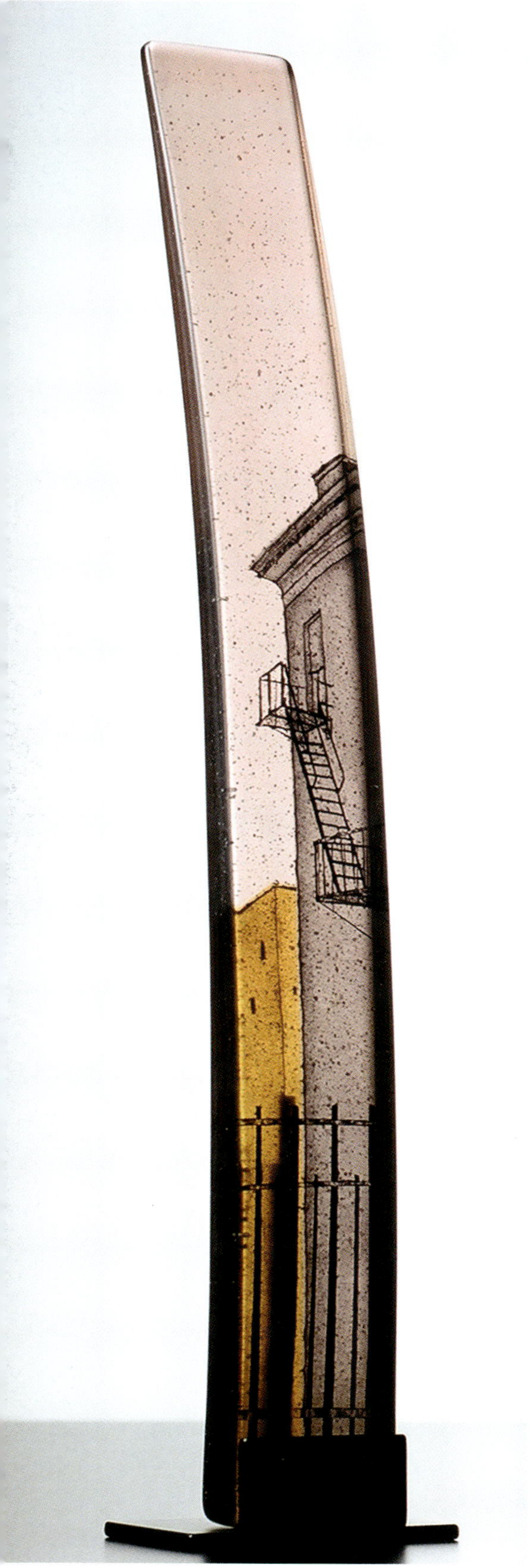

the print 'sits' on the surface of the glass.

His working methods involve the translation of direct drawing from nature into glass, while leaving as little evidence as possible of the intervening process, so as not to dilute the immediacy of the initial experience in the field. Large-scale drawings are produced directly in the landscape, using the experience of the moment to produce spontaneous images that record the feeling rather than produce a literal representation. These drawings form the basis of his glass images, and the original glass process allows them to retain their original qualities intact.

Jeremy Lepisto

There are definite similarities between the approach of Jeremy Lepisto and that of Kevin Petrie. They both value the hand-generated response to their subject, and rely on techniques derived from printmaking; Lepisto studied printmaking before moving to glass.

Artist statement

I look to make works that highlight the complex in the common. I find inspiration in my relationships. I feel that we are the result of our choices. I also find inspiration in my environment. I find it in objects or structures that are typically peripheral to everyday scenes and items. I create new images from my environment and give them a hint of familiarity without suggesting any place in particular.

By hand-rendering the images in my work I am able to easily pull from a vocabulary of qualities without any specialised equipment or preparation, and the work also retains a handmade quality.

Technical process

My pieces are technically referred to as being kiln-formed glass. They are fused and formed in the kiln through a combination of time, temperature and hopefully a bit of talent. Each piece is constructed from a combination of a number of separate sheets of compatible coloured sheet cut to form,

◄ *Built to Leave (Tower series)*, Jeremy Lepisto, 2006. H. 65 cm (25½ in.), W. 13 cm (5⅛ in.), D. 7 cm (2¾ in.).
Photo: Paul Foster.

A sculptural form produced from fused layers of glass with hand-applied enamel decoration.

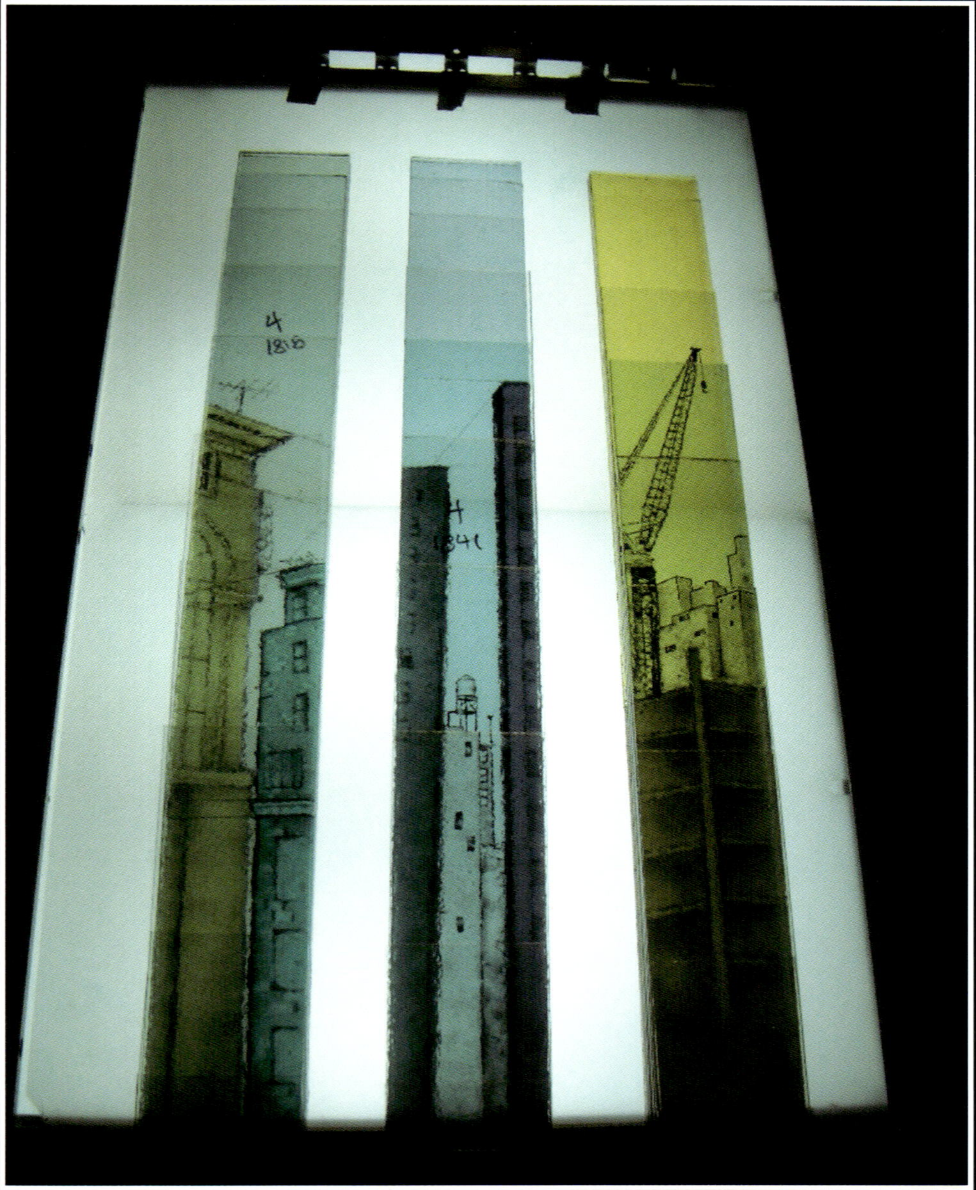

◄ Jeremy Lepisto.
The creation of the linear detail.

► Jeremy Lepisto.
The application of the enamel.

▼ Jeremy Lepisto.
Fired detail.

Jeremy Lepisto's complex multilayered images are painstakingly built with layers of applied and fired detail fused into single forms. Firing is carried out with great care to prevent distortion of either the imagery or the outside profile of the glass sheet. This involves an accurate control of temperature and the buttressing of the stacked sheets with ceramic batts.

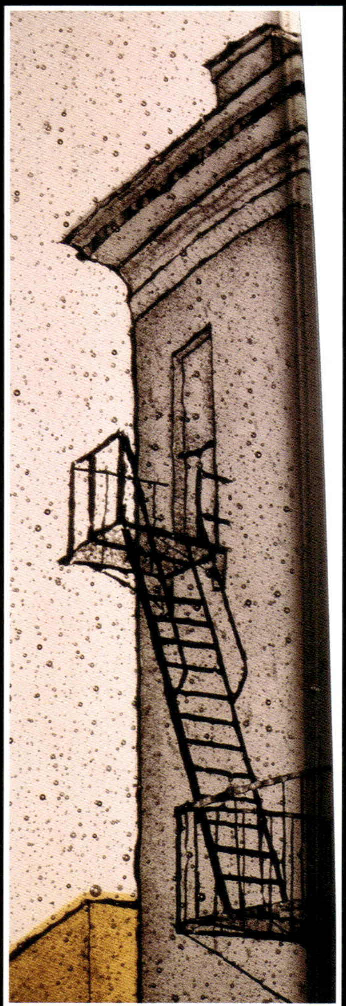

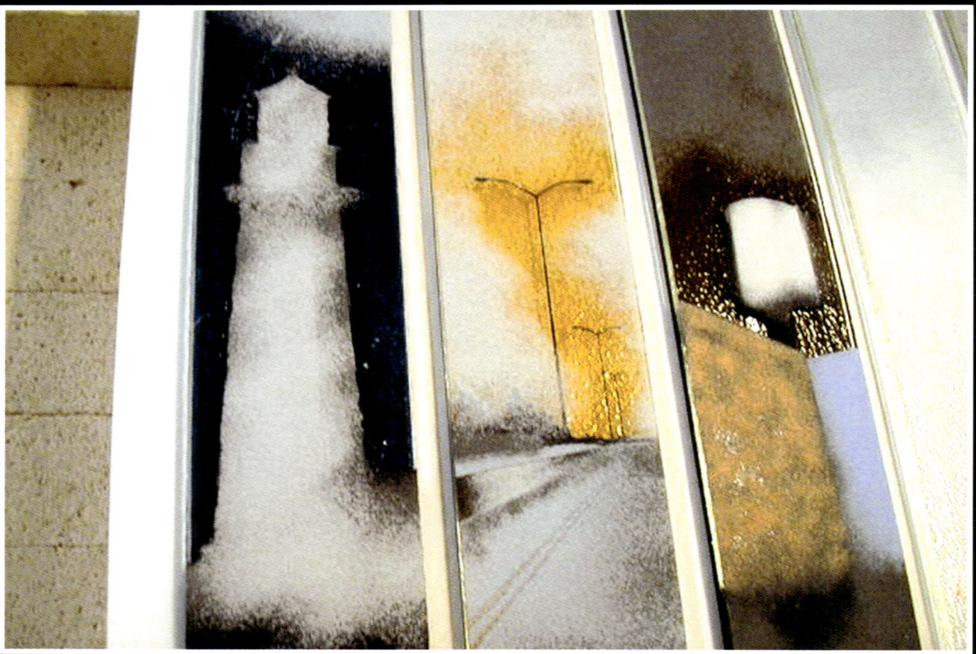

and fused together in a kiln. The standard thickness of each sheet is 3 mm (⅛ in.), and finished pieces can comprise anything up to 26 layers. On one or many of these layers, hand-rendered images are created using high-fired enamel paints to make the fine hard lines.

This process is one that I have developed using basic printmaking skills. I put clear contact paper on the glass sheets to get imagery, draw and register what I want on the paper, cut off the drawn lines with a sharp blade, wipe 'Paradise Paint' (a brand of pre-mixed enamel) over the now exposed areas with a palette knife, and remove the excess paper. After the hard lines have been rendered, black powdered glass is then sifted over and pushed around to achieve tone and greyscale. Each layer is sometimes pre-fired in a kiln to make certain that the density is correct and that the images will stay put when stacked with other pieces. This process ensures that each image is my own, and that each piece is unique.

The sheets are then stacked up and placed in a kiln. The edges are 'dammed up' to preserve the cut contour by preventing the glass from flowing. A controlled ramp brings them up to 800°C (1472°F) and then back down, fusing the separate sheets into one thick piece. This will take anything from one to two weeks in the kiln. The piece is then removed from the kiln and extensively cold-worked, using machine-applied abrasives to carve and smooth the glass.

Amber Hiscott and David Pearl

The partnership of Hiscott and Pearl extends the techniques of enamelling and slumping to the design, production and installation of dramatic architectural features. The hand manipulation of the glass and its decoration are balanced by, and contrasted with the construction, which in its pristine engineering acts as a brilliant foil to the glass.

Combining Amber Hiscott's orientation to painting with the formal and material interests of David Pearl, their work displays technical innovation and the expressive use of bold abstract hand applied enamel.

Razor Shells is 4.1 metres (13 ft 6 in.) tall and made from 30 panels of silkscreen-printed, kiln-shaped, toughened and laminated 20 mm (¾ in.) glass. The 50 square metres (538 sq. ft) of glass is supported by two interlinked 'trees' of polished stainless-steel tube.

Artist statement

'We are primarily site-specific artists working in the public realm for sculpture and architecture. Although our work is rooted in hands-on studio practice, large commissions for projects as varied as The Royal

Razor Shells (Callaghan Square, Cardiff), David Pearl & Amber Hiscott, 2008. H. 4.1 m (13 ft 6 in.), W. 2.75 m (9 ft). ➤

Photo: courtesy of the artist.

A free-standing architectural feature constructed from enamelled and slumped sheets of flat glass on a stainless-steel frame. The apparent simplicity of the basic process belies the skill required to apply it to such a large project. The free application of the enamel creates rich imagery, which contrasts with the overall form and the engineering of the structure.

David Pearl & Amber Hiscott, detail of *Razor Shells*. ➤➤

Photo: courtesy of the artist.

The accuracy of the metal armature complements the enamel imagery.

David Pearl & Amber Hiscott, *Razor Shells* (process). ➤

Photo: courtesy of the artist.

The individual pieces of flat glass set out on the studio floor prior to slumping, which will also fire the enamels. The organisation of the shaping and process had to be exceptional to ensure the level of accuracy required for the overall sharpness of form. The free application of the enamel is noteworthy, as it leaves the creative decision-making in the hands of the artist.

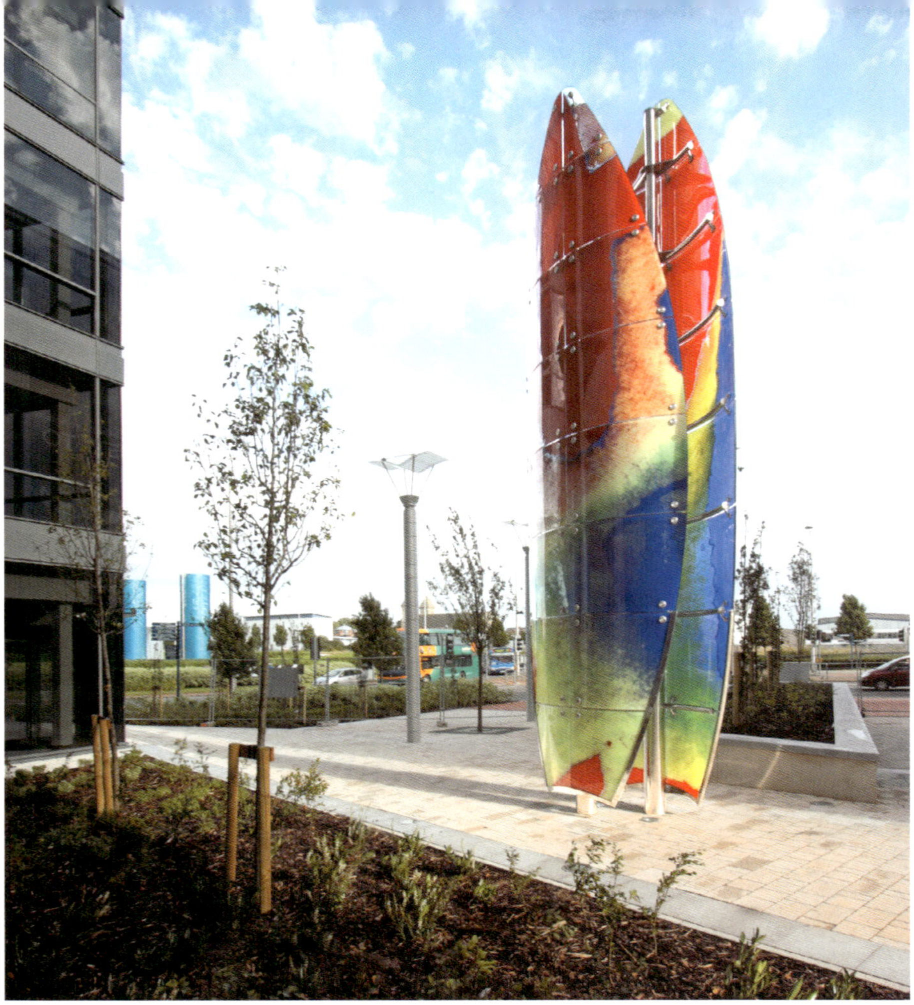

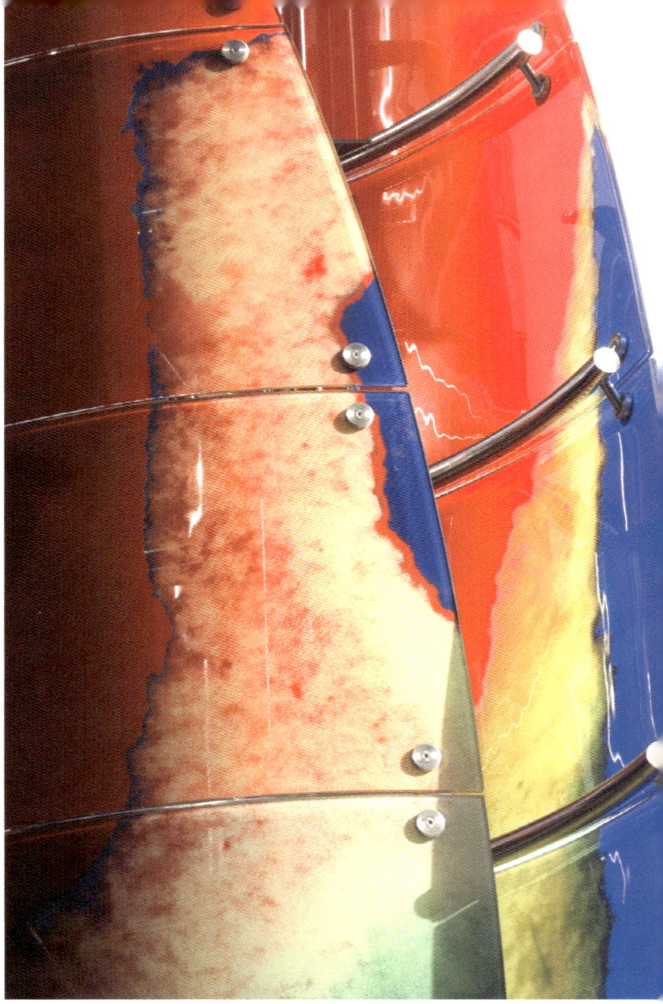

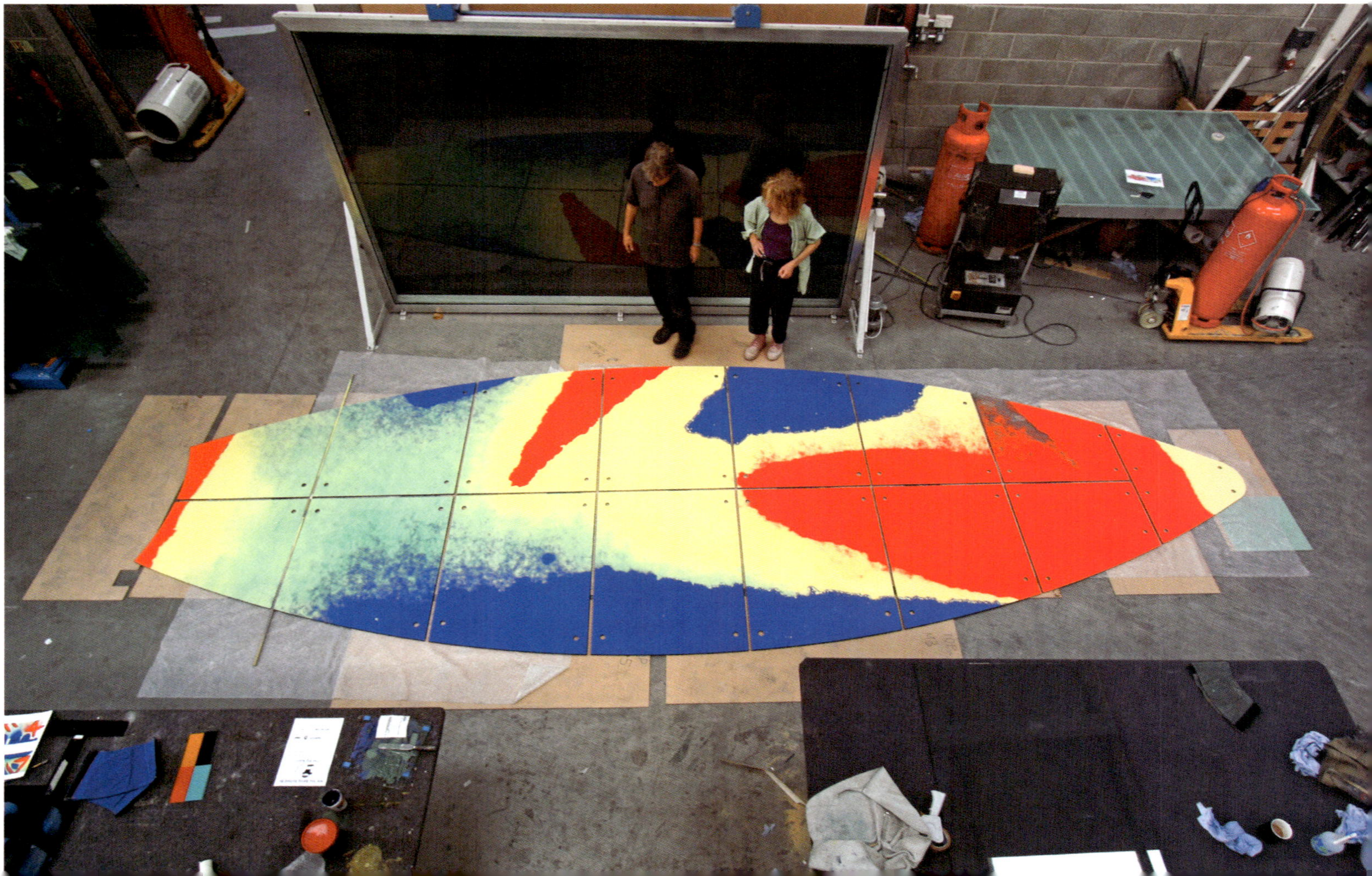

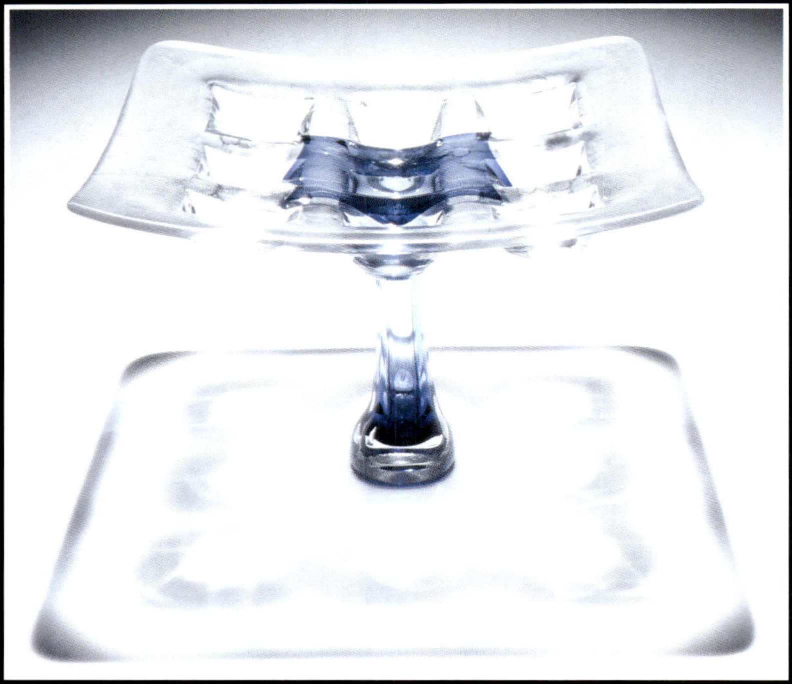

▲ *Upright Grid*, Louise Watson, 2007. Slumped-glass form, W. 28 cm (11 in.), D. 28 cm (11 in.), H. 19 cm (7½ in.).

Photo: Frank Thurston.

Slumping is unique among kiln-forming methods in that it starts with a two-dimensional form and ends with a fully three-dimensional one. The control is provided by the organisation of a moulding system that is only partial, and which relies on the original glass sheet retaining some of its formal integrity.

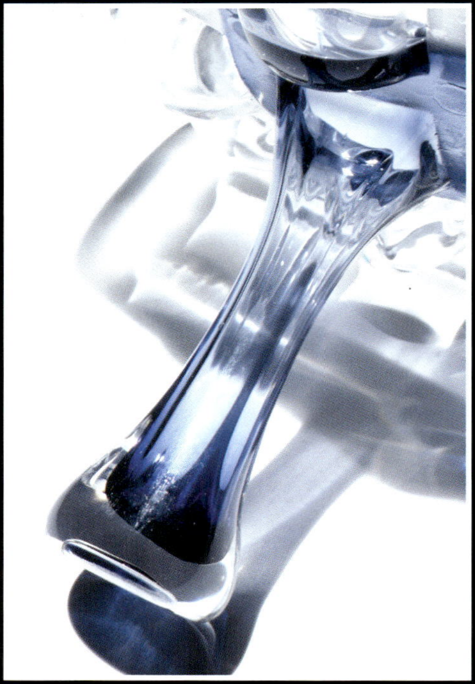

▲ Louise Watson, detail of *Upright Grid*.

Photo: courtesy of the artist.

In free-slumping a range of forms is possible depending on the precise temperature to which the arrangement of sheet and mould is taken. Here the glass has been allowed to slump through the apertures of the mould until it has reached a ceramic batt and been formed by the contact.

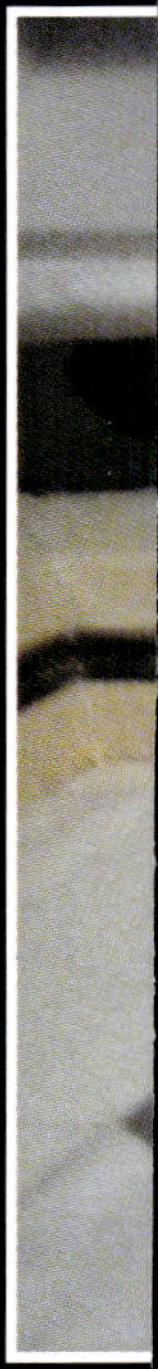

Exchange Theatre, Manchester, the Royal Scottish Academy of Music and Drama, Glasgow, Unilever Headquarters, London, and more recently the Wales Millennium Centre in Cardiff have required that we work closely with a small group of outside fabricators.

We find that working with specialist fabricators extends the range of what we can produce, but removes little of the stress involved; the constraints of time and budget apply a subtle pressure to limit experiment and innovation.

Nonetheless, having good working partnerships with fabricators, as we now do, gives us increased confidence in dealing with the increasing complications of being commissioned for the public realm. Also, working with the same fabricators means that personal and working relationships grow over the years, and your collaborators more readily understand where you are headed with your ideas when they are still at the experimental stage.

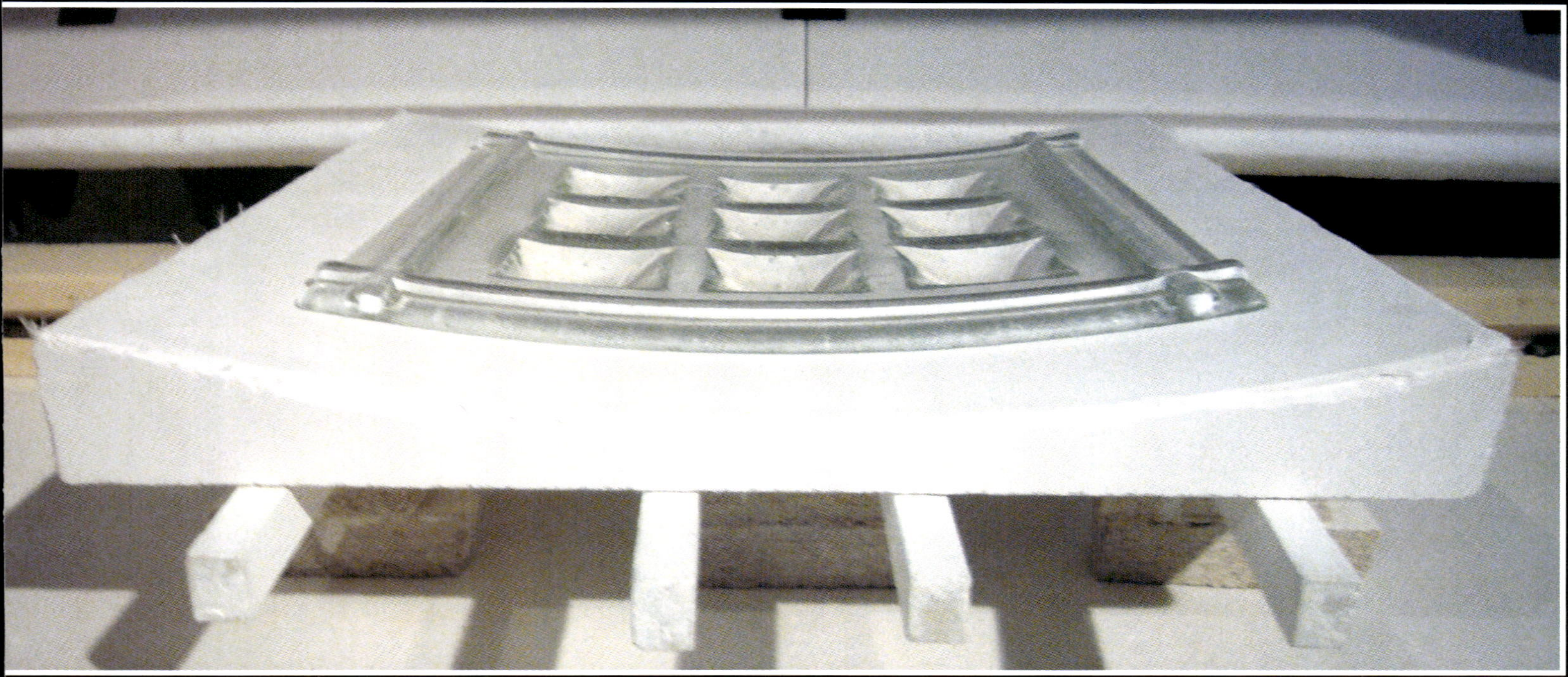

▲ Louise Watson. Slumping mould in position in the kiln.

Photo: courtesy of the artist.

The precision with which the artist designs and organises her moulds is evident in this illustration. Distances and levels are meticulously calibrated to ensure the desired outcome. This kind of kiln-forming requires patience, an eye for detail and constant control and observation during the process to achieve this level of success.

Slumping

The deformation of sheet glass by using a variety of systems, from fully three-dimensional moulds to apertures, suspension and partial supports for the softening glass, characterise this next group.

Louise Watson

Louise Watson starts with the simplest of elements – flat, standard sheets of glass – but, through a rigorous control and attention to detail using the behaviour of glass while slumping, transforms them into three-dimensional forms of originality and presence.

Artist statement

I am a glass artist working to commission in both public and private sectors. I use kiln-forming techniques to produce wall-hung, suspended or free-standing bespoke works for interior, exterior and architectural spaces. These are commissioned for site-specific locations or exhibited in galleries and exhibitions. In my work, whether commissioned or personal, I draw initial inspiration from the immediate surroundings – from architecture, the environment, space and colour – with the intention of exploring colour through light and form.

Through a process of slumping, a two-dimensional work takes on a three-dimensional form. In doing so, all the aspects that fascinate me about glass are accentuated. Where applied, colour becomes stretched, as does the form, and the tonal range and the range of shapes are increased. The effect of light and translucency are enhanced, reflecting off various angled planes, casting shadows, and projecting colour onto other surfaces. The result is an autonomous object creating a focal point in space.

Motivated by the endless possibilities of manipulating glass through kiln-forming, I am constantly excited by the physical changes that occur during the heating and cooling process. I thrive on the anticipation of not knowing exactly what might be found in the kiln hours after the firing commences.

Eeva Kasper

One of the shifts in practice that is evident in current kiln-forming is the rise of high-temperature activities and a corresponding reduction in low-temperature forming procedures like slumping and distortion. It is therefore good to see younger artists carrying out their personal search for form in this area.

Artist statement

I consider glass a source of infinite possibilities. I have not yet found an idea I could not express in glass. I am enchanted by the multiple options that glass offers me. I find it to be the material that enables me to reflect my surroundings in the best way, providing references to the past and contemplations on eternal as well as personal themes.

The glass pieces are produced by distorting sheet glass suspended in the kiln on wires that are looped through drilled holes. The exact form the distortion takes is determined by manipulation of temperature and observation. The way that these pieces are combined and photographed extends their impact into wider aesthetic territory.

Only in my Dreams, Eeva Kasper, 2007. Installation, slumped glass. Diameter of installation approx. 150 cm (59 in.). ➤

Photo: courtesy of the artist.

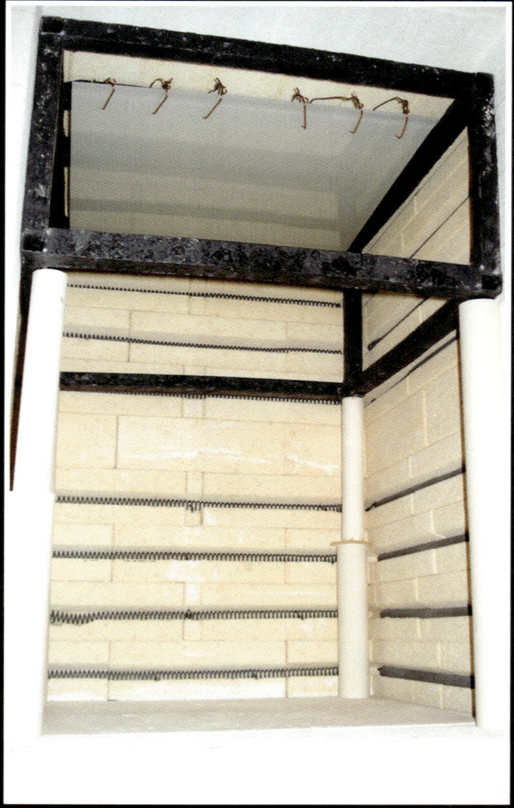

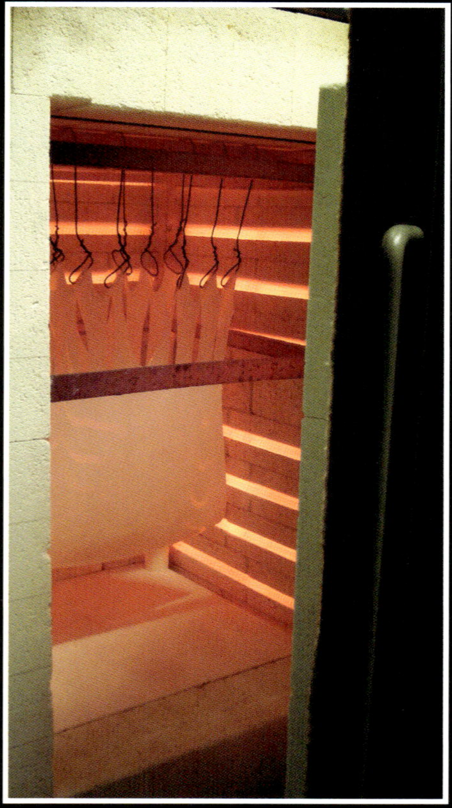

Eeva Kasper. The production of a section of *Only in My Dreams*.

Photo: courtesy of the artist.

A sheet of glass is placed in the kiln suspended on a metal frame by copper wire. The resultant slumped form will be dependent on the orchestration of the elements in the forming equation. Apparently, small details like the size of the drilled holes and the distance between them have the potential to affect the final form in quite dramatic ways.

Eeva Kasper. The glass sheet beginning to deform at 595°C (1103°F).

Photo: courtesy of the artist.

This kind of glass-forming is a dialogue between the forces involved, with the artist as the director. Visual access to the kiln is essential, with the line between success and failure being measured in tiny heat differences and as little as a few seconds.

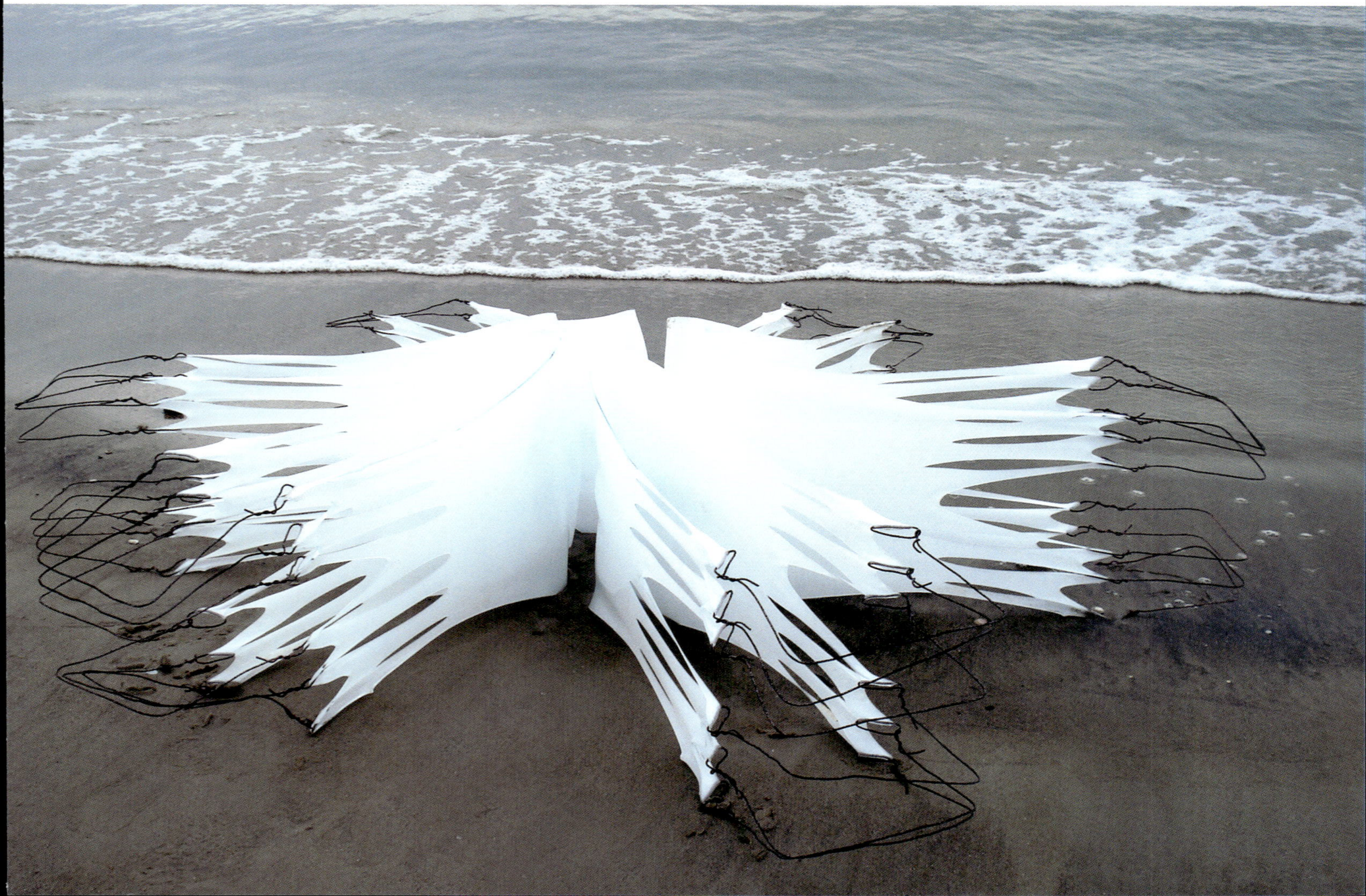

Rain-Curtain, Mary Shaffer, 2000. ➤
Cast from wax original. H. 182 cm (71⅝ in.).

Photo: Dan Merse.

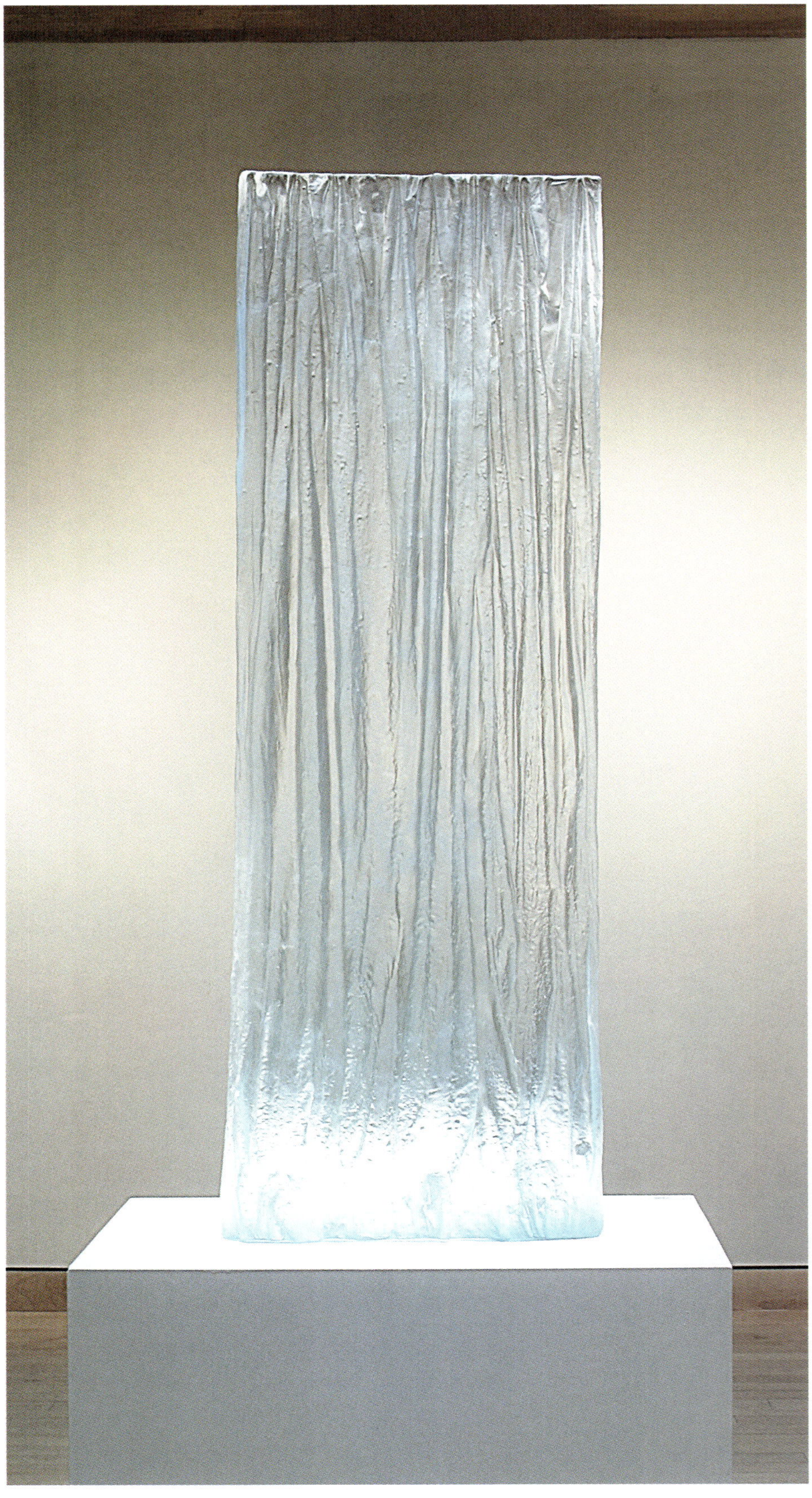

Made at Lhotsky Studios during a visit to the Czech Republic after working at a Symposium at Novy Bor. The work that originally established Mary Shaffer as an artist who used glass in an essentially painterly way was characterised by its hands-on approach; it sought to use glass to answer formal questions rather than merely to exploit its decorative qualities. This piece, produced by a commercial studio, used the facilities and expertise available to produce work that was more architectural in its ambition and scale.

Mary Shaffer

Mary Shaffer is known as an artist who uses glass in a painterly way, characterised by a random, 'mid-air' technique. She explores formal questions rather than merely exploiting the decorative qualities of glass. In *Rain-Curtain* she uses a hands-on approach, making the mould from clay and wax, exploring concepts of liquid versus solid and movement versus statis. The work appears to defy gravity by holding up that which is falling, and solidifying a liquid that looks like water.

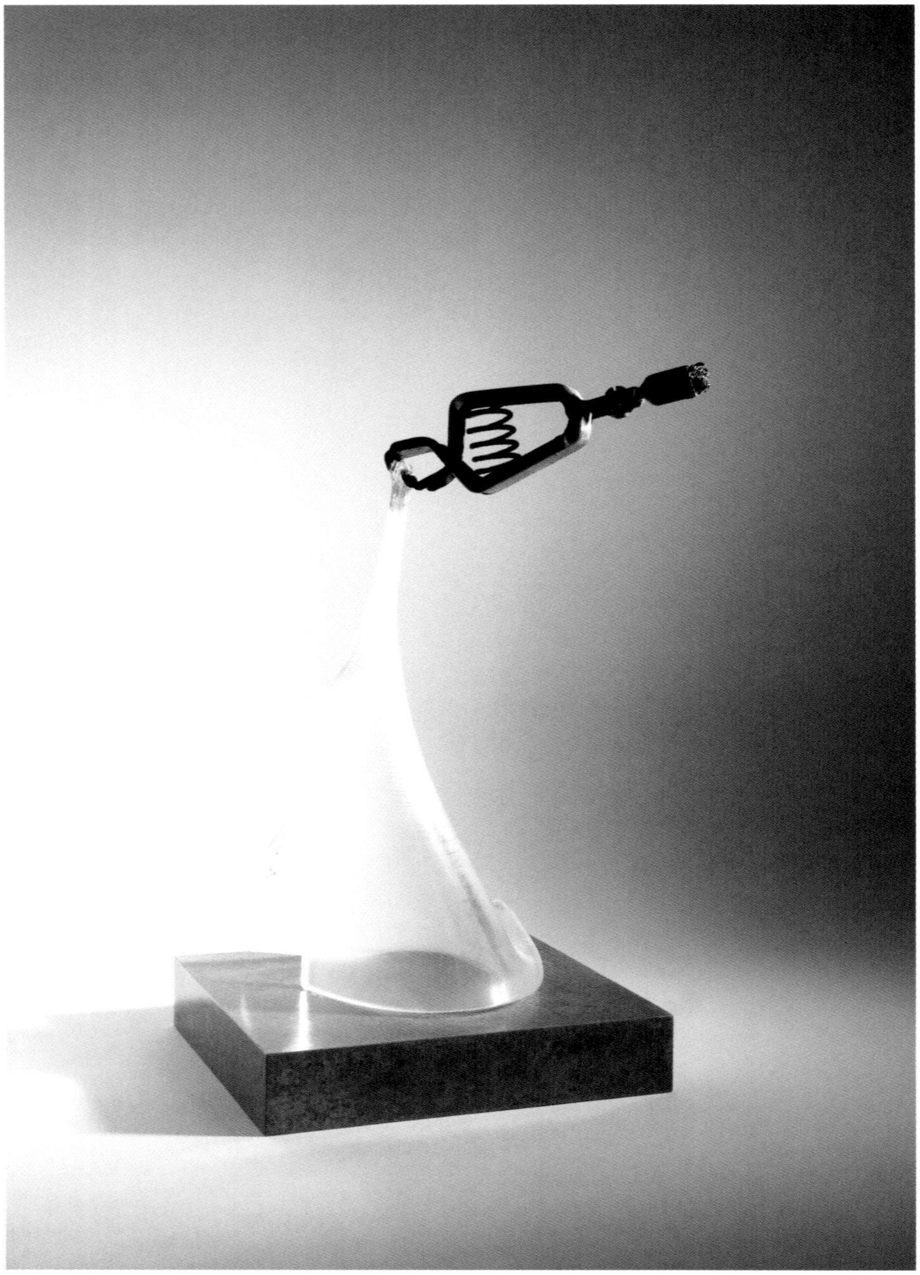

◄ *Sparked*, Mary Shaffer, 2003. Glass, bronze and metal, H. 36 cm (14 in.), W. 20 cm (8 in.), D. 18 cm (7 in.).

Photo: Kathleen Brennan.

In this piece Shaffer returned to an earlier theme, one which is particularly associated with her, the interaction between found objects and sheet glass in the kiln. As the artist explains, 'The hardware is part of an electrical attachment. I put it on a bronze wall-box. With this piece I super-cooled the glass to get the surface devitrification that I love.'

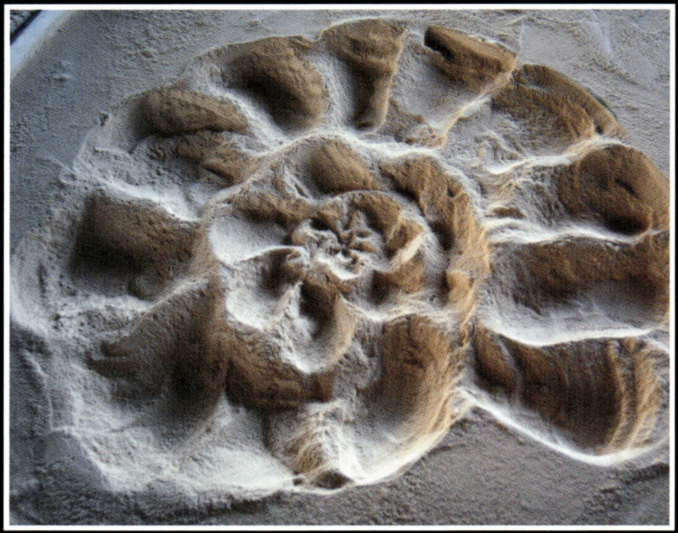

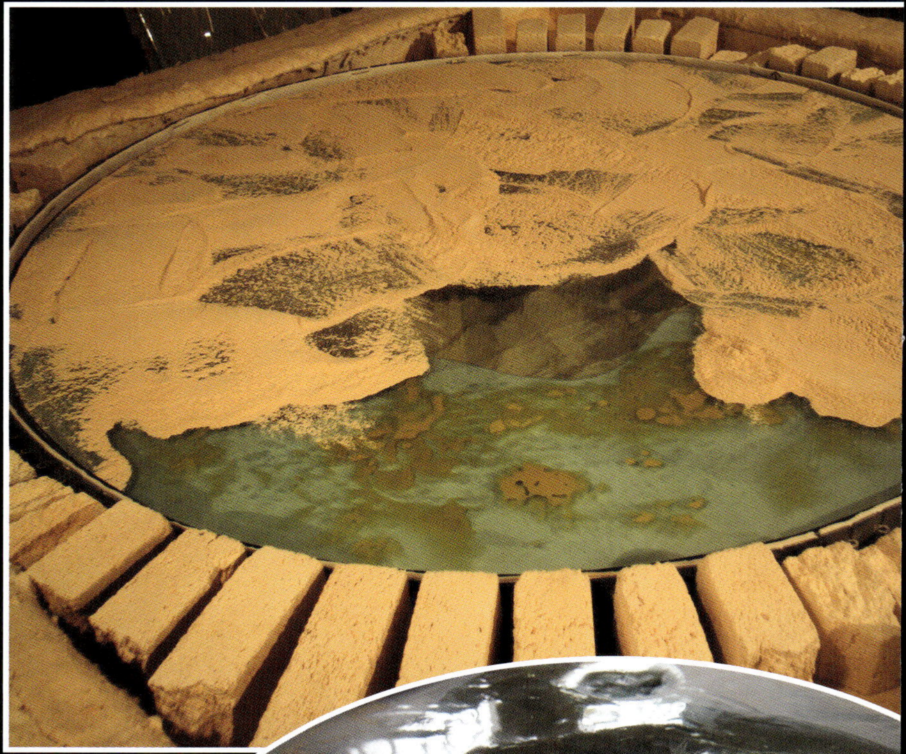

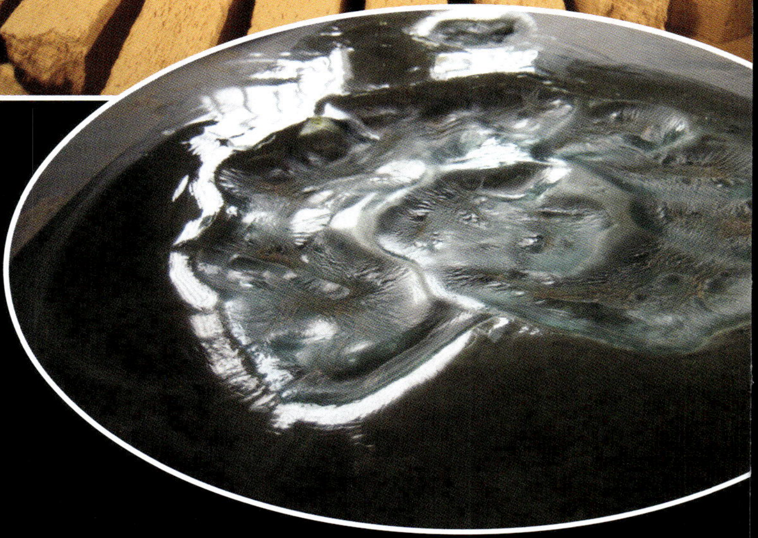

The mould is created by hand with a bricklaying mortar used in the steel industry. ▲

Painted with glaze (in places that are to be matt) or not (in places that are to be transparent), the layers of glass are built into the kiln. The top layer is painted by hand with paints containing silver oxide. While it is still completely wet, the next layer is put on, and so on, until all four layers are in place. Next the glass is covered with the bricklaying mortar. It is heated at 40°C (104°F) per hour up to 580°C (1076°F), then raised to 850°C (1562°F) in only 15 minutes, and held there for about 40 minutes. It is then dropped quickly to 630°C (1166°F), and then to 590°C (1094°F) over six hours; from there it is dropped at 25°C (77°F) per hour to ambient (room) temperature. ➤

Tomasz Urbanowicz

Tomasz specialises in slumping sheet glass into moulds on a massive scale, while at the same time colouring the forms and textures by a variety of original methods, which exploit the ability of softened glass to absorb colour both from locally placed oxides and from applied enamels. His combination of control and experiment is truly remarkable.

Artist statement

I am a lucky person to be able do what I like – to create glass. Glass is for architecture, because for me it makes no sense to be in galleries.

My desire to see how a project, which is a vision of my imagination,

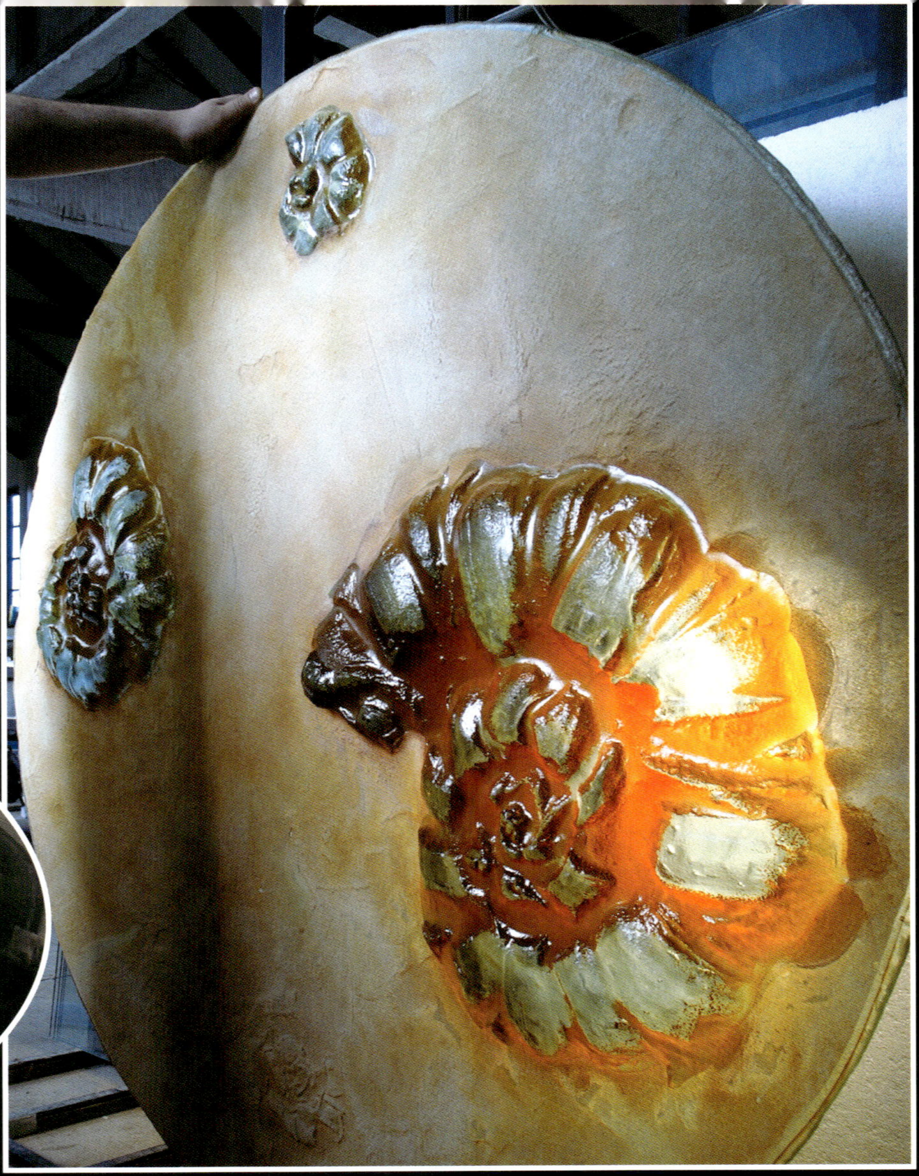

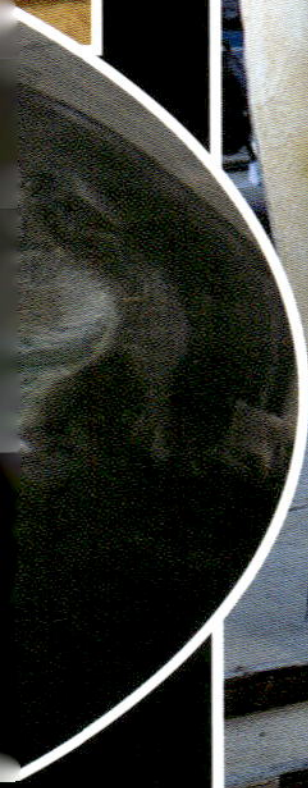

Ammonite feature panel, Tomasz Urbanowicz, 2008. D. 2 m (6.6 ft).

Photo: courtesy of the artist.

For Hotel Spa 'Centuria', Ogrodzieniec, Poland.

(Inset)
The glass is taken out and cleaned. It reveals a very special, shining top surface. After cleaning it is painted with low-temperature metallic oxides to achieve colour. These are applied in different ways for the background and the ammonites respectively, by spraying with a high-pressure gun, and painting horizontally to catch the relief.

becomes a real work is my biggest motivation to create. Because of its unpredictability light is very difficult to work with, and yet it plays an important part in making the vision come true. The major issues, while making projects for architecture, are the context of its specific site, its function and the client. When I see plans, or a place, the project appears immediately. I just know. The project I make is this one, and I am sure what the solution will be like.

The important aspects in designing are idea, vision and conversation. I don't really take technology into consideration, and whether or not it will be easy to make. Usually it depends on experiment, but it always works. If I have enough determination to see it through, all technical problems become minor and solvable. I know that large, thick sheets of glass do not accept many mistakes, and must be treated very professionally, but on the other hand I know that there is a lot of space for intuition born of experience, or maybe luck and coincidence, in the way that some solutions are achieved.

Technique

All of my knowledge has been gained by experiment. My technique varies according to the effect I want to achieve. Usually I create thick glass pieces (up to 50 mm/2 in.) using float glass, mainly because it is cheap and available in large sheets. I built my IR (infrared) kiln myself. Its dimensions are 3 x 2 x 1 m (9 x 6 x 3 ft).

I would like to describe the process for making glass for a hotel spa in Ogrodzieniec in Poland, which is in Jura Krakowska, an area widely known for ammonites. I designed three circles, each of 150 cm (59 in.) in diameter. The idea was to reveal colourful and transparent ammonites emerging from a frosted, stonelike surface. The surface detail reveals hidden colour when lit from below.

Janet Kelman

Kiln-forming is an essential stage in the production of Janet Kelman's pieces. In fact her beautiful forms only become fully three-dimensional through her use of the kiln. However, before they reach this final stage, they are shaped into flat discs by blowing, and then carefully sandblasted to create both their distinctive outline and their delicate, linear modelling. The sandblasting involves the selective masking of areas to create the patterns.

The discs are then deformed by stages, being heated first into a simple bowl form, and subsequently over an asymmetric former to generate their organic, final shape. This process is rigorous in its attention to detail, often involving multiple firings, and the re-sandblasting of areas that do not match her desire for perfection. The results speak for themselves, and incidentally illustrate the way in which kiln-forming can be enriched by the involvement of other ways of shaping and decorating glass.

Brilliant Green and Teal Seafan, Janet Kelman, after several firings. ➤

Photo: Leslie Patron.

Each firing is carefully organised to develop the different elements that give the final pieces their subtle changes of plane and movement. This is achieved by the use of ceramic fibre paper that holds some aspects of the form, while allowing others to move.

Brilliant Green and Teal Seafan, Janet Kelman, 2008. H. 27 cm (10⅝ in.), W. 54 cm (21¼ in.), D. 54 cm (21¼ in.). ➤

Photo: Leslie Patron.

Janet Kelman's pieces are the result of several distinct levels of activity. The initial disc is blown and spun, with the colour variations created at this stage.

Carved roundel before first firing. ➤➤

Photo: Leslie Patron.

The flat roundel is elaborately carved by selective sandblasting to create both the outside profile and the many delicate layers, before being slumped over a former. This basic form will be re-sandblasted to add more detail and shifts of texture before being slumped several further times to achieve the full, characteristic three-dimensional form.

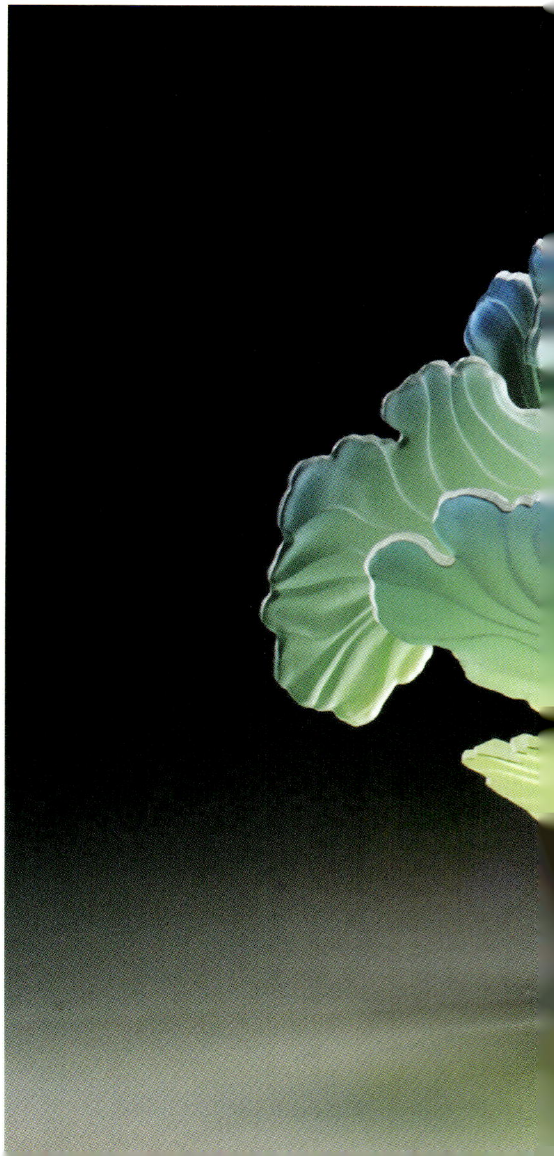

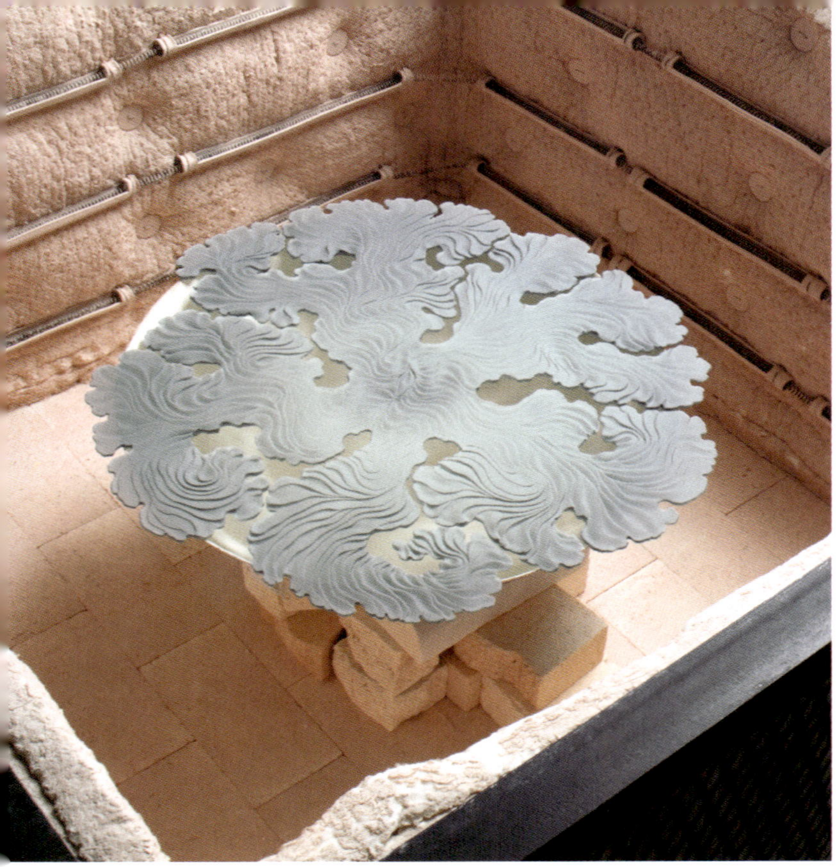
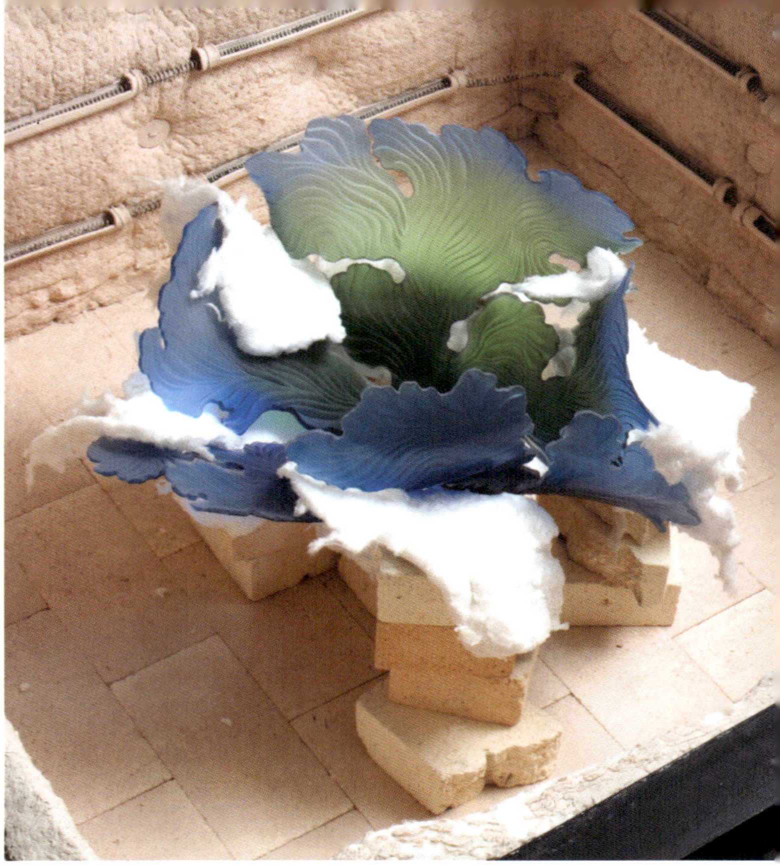
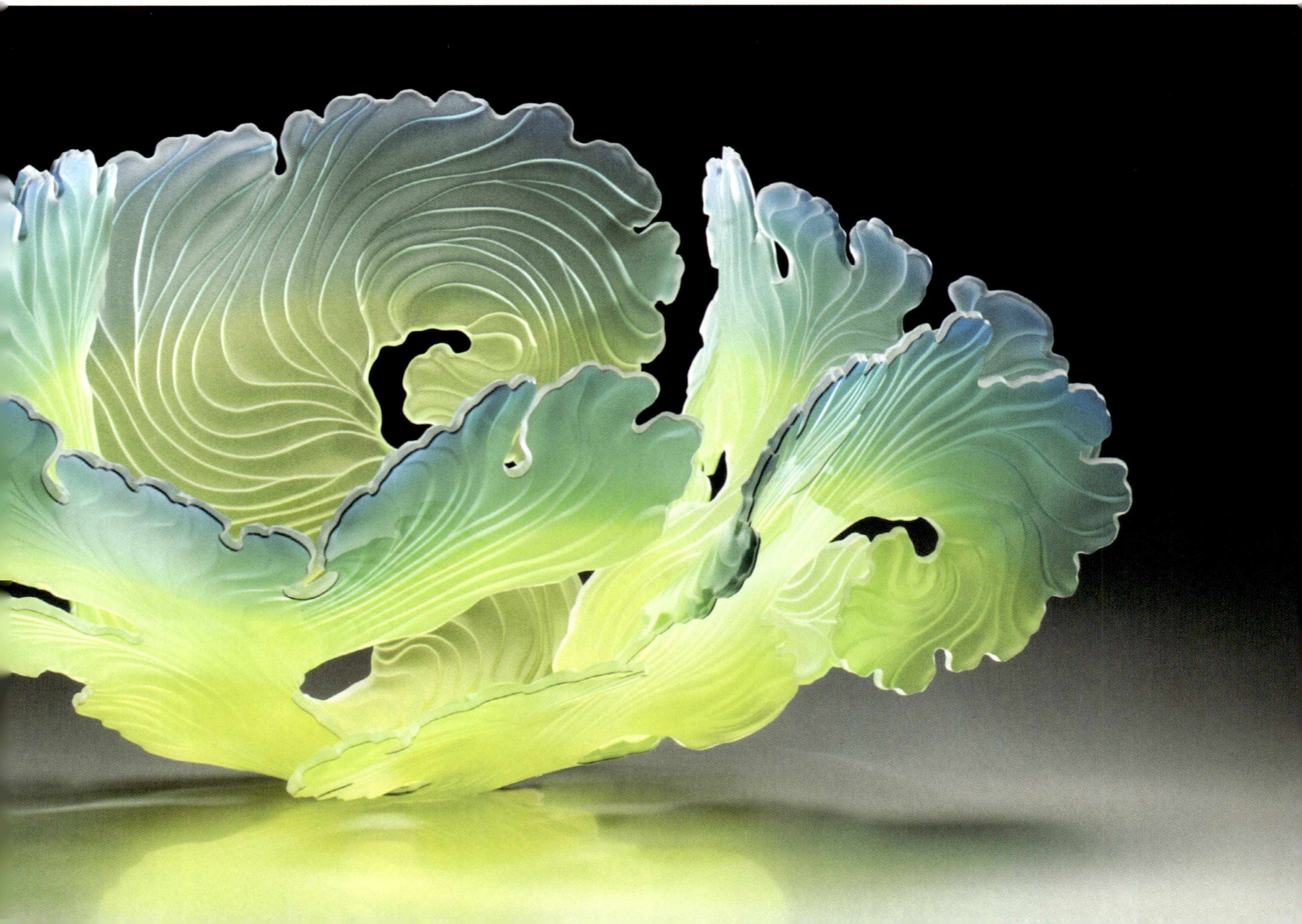

Lara Aldridge. Detail of laminated decoration in a fused and slumped platter.

Photo: Simon Bruntnell.

The subtle and varied effects that characterise the work of Lara Aldridge, created by metals in a variety of forms, trapped between the layers of glass during fusing and shaping.

Square platter by Lara Aldridge. 40 x 40cm (15¾ x 15¾ in.).

Photo: Simon Bruntnell.

The dish was created by simultaneously fusing and slumping two sheets of glass, and trapping between them a variety of metals in a number of configurations. The colours are caused by the reactions of the metals to heat and the various conditions that exist between the glass sheets, particularly in terms of the amount of oxygen, which, depending on the precise position of the metal within the sheets, creates different types of oxidisation conditions.

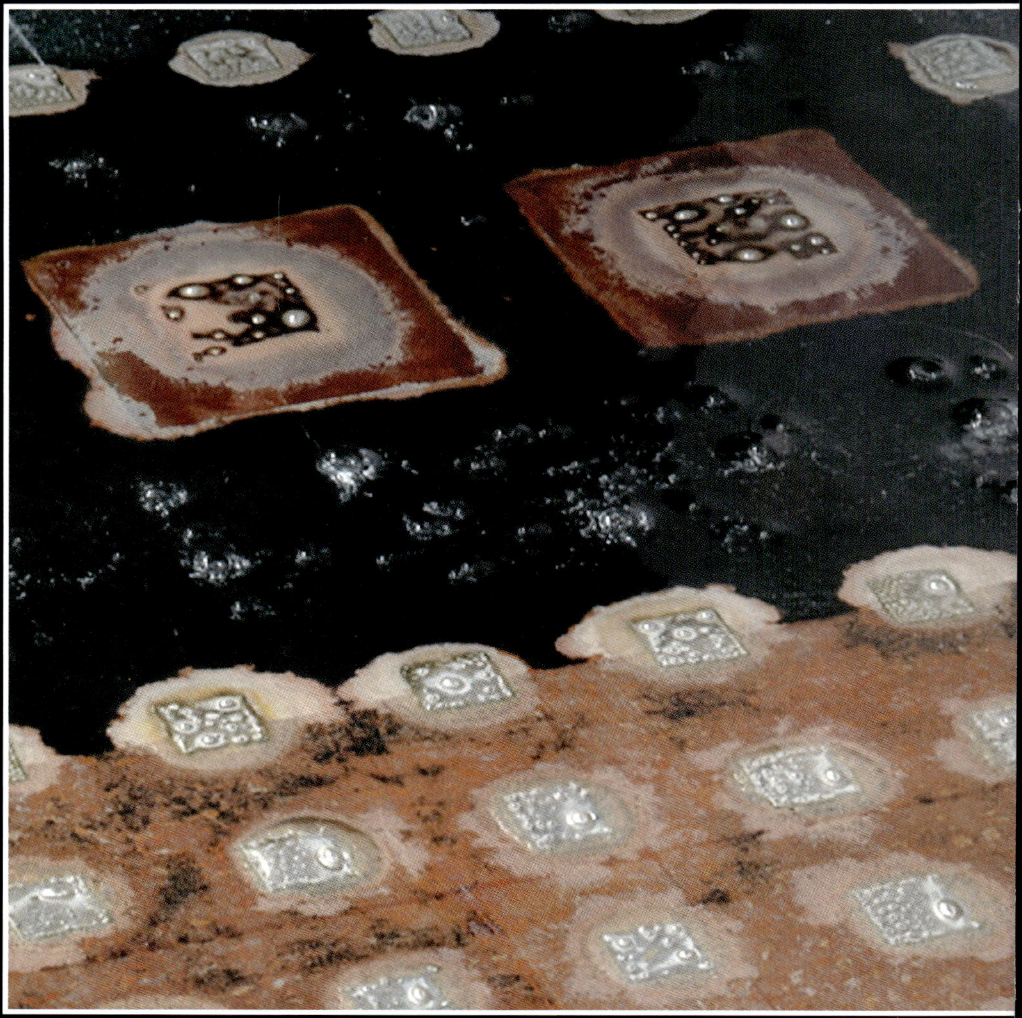

Artist statement

The *Seafans* combine my fascination with underwater images and a personal view of femininity. The glass is strong, although it appears delicate, as if it might break easily. The viewer may be intrigued but also a little fearful. As a container for treasure, the vessel shape protects something precious and beautiful. The flowing arms wave an invitation to peek inside and seek out the feminine self.

Lara Aldridge

The work of Lara Aldridge combines and exploits fusing and slumping. By using a total support for the form to mould her shallow dishes and architectural features she can employ higher temperatures than are possible when a partial support is used. This higher temperature allows two or more sheets of glass to be fused together as they slump, along with the trapping between these sheets of materials like enamels, metal foils, wires and weaves. These act

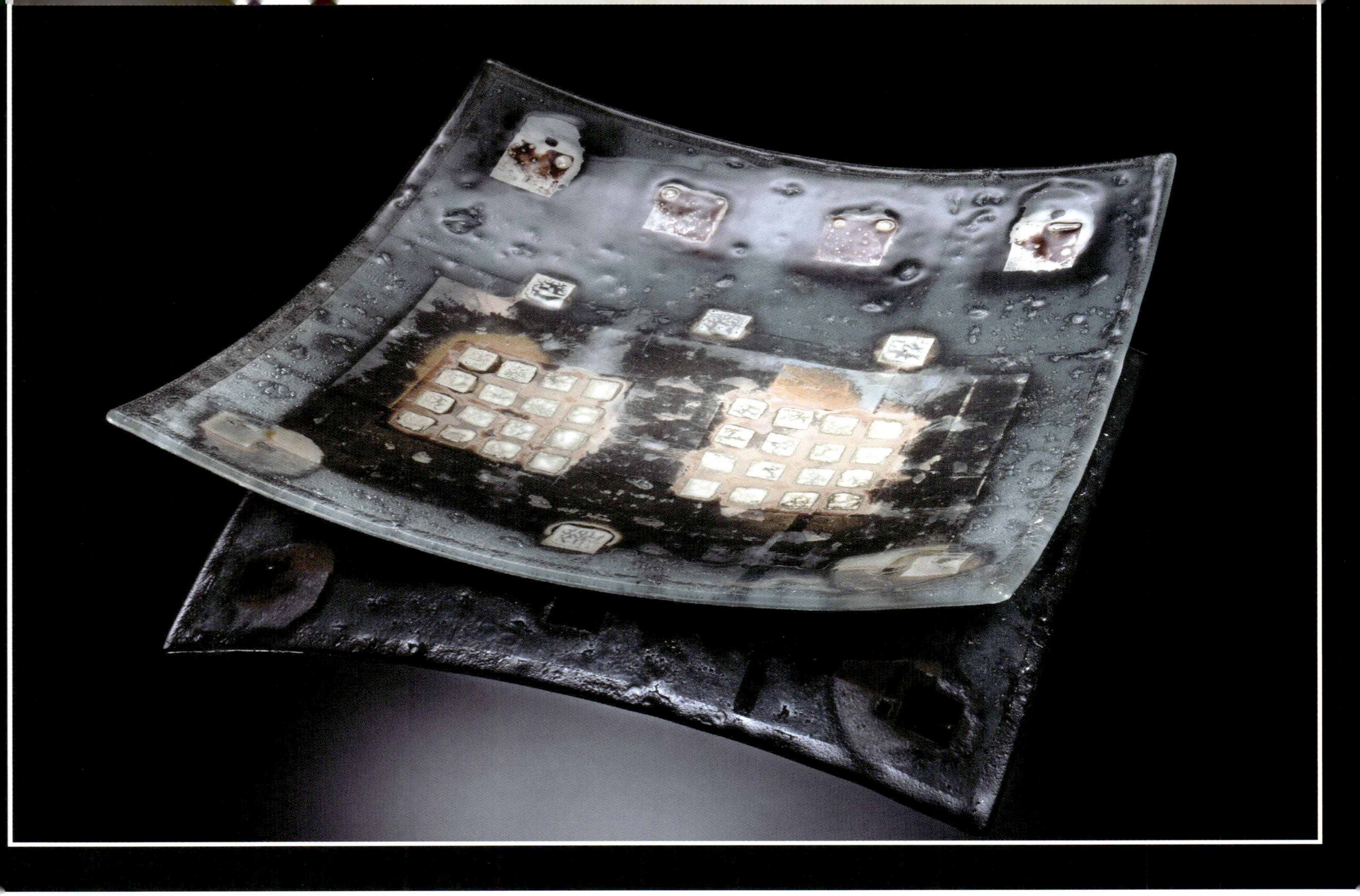

as decorative inclusions, and react, to both the heat and the decreasing amount of oxygen as they become trapped, by changing colour.

Fuse-casting

This technique involves different sections of glass being heated until they fuse together, but without losing their physical or visual identity. Fuse-cast works vary from loose agglomerations of glass pieces that retain much of their shape in the fused mass, to complete fusions, where the only evidence of the separate pieces lies in areas of defined colour within the mass of finished glass. Generally, these extremes lie at either end of the temperature range used in fuse-casting.

Julius Weiland

The use of glass in pulled rod and tube form as elements in the production of fused glass artefacts has a long history, going back at least as far as the Egyptians. The technique of mosaic glass has been used to create exquisite, jewel-like pieces at many periods during the history of glassmaking, with many of them in our own era, the work of Klaus Moje being a prime example. The fact that artists continue to find something new to say with this ancient way of shaping glass is testament both to its inherent appeal and the creativity of those who use it. Julius Weiland brings a new approach to certain elements of rod-fusing, namely scale and form. His choice of simple, standard borosilicate tubes allows him to exploit the hardness of this high-temperature glass in the production of large-scale fully three-dimensional sculptural forms.

Artist statement: Concepts in glass

I came to the medium of glass more by chance than by choice. I was introduced to it by Ann Wolff, my teacher during my time at art school. She encouraged me to use this material not just technically, but also conceptually.

I started to experiment with glass tubes, and developed a technique that was simple but effective, the tubes being stacked in a fireproof mould and heated in a kiln. When the softening point of the glass is reached, the heat is reduced by opening the kiln to freeze the form, prior to annealing. By refining this technique again and again I brought it to a level where I could control the process and realise bigger objects.

In works like *The Great Curve* series, I investigated the relationship between the material and the shape of the sculpture. While one is voluminous and made from larger tubes, the other is flat and consists of thousands of small tubes. Both pieces mark a change in my work towards a more conceptual approach.

The geometric circle is a key element in my work, so the choice of the tube is no coincidence. The regular circles that result from cutting the tubes crosswise relate them to the final overall shape of the piece. Beginning with the first circular vessels, nearly all of the ensuing shapes were also generated from combinations of circles. Out of this concept I have developed my own formal language, which now extends beyond glass to find expression in many diverse materials – bronze, aluminium and neon – in addition to cast glass. Though I have worked with these other materials for a number of years, the glass tubes retain their primary importance for me with their capacity for generating new sculptural concepts and ideas.

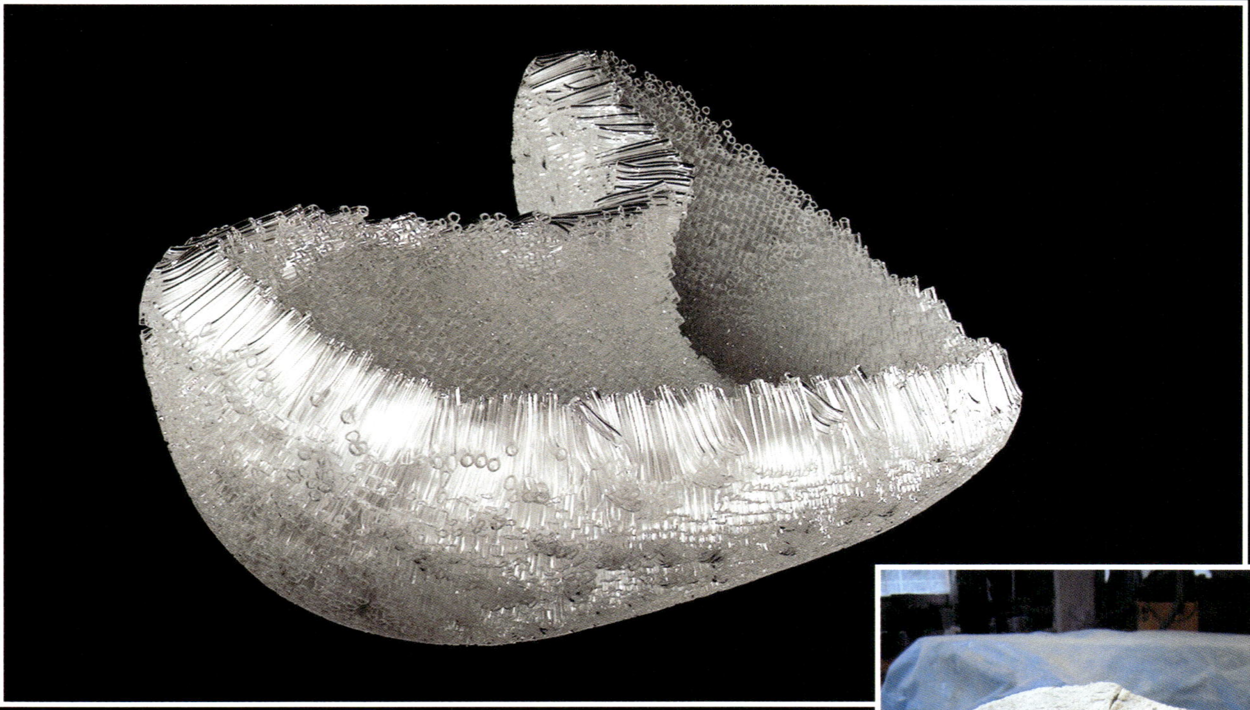

▲ Julius Weiland, *Cell*, 2006. Fused glass tubes, 78 x 48 cm x 21 cm (30¾ x 19 x 8¼ in.).

Photo: Stephen Falk.

Julius Weiland uses industrially produced tubes as his raw material, fusing them in sculptural high-temperature concrete moulds. His control of form is exercised through hand-modelled and carved moulds. He uses temperature to deform and fuse the tubes within the moulds, to achieve precisely the right balance between the exterior form and the individual glass elements.

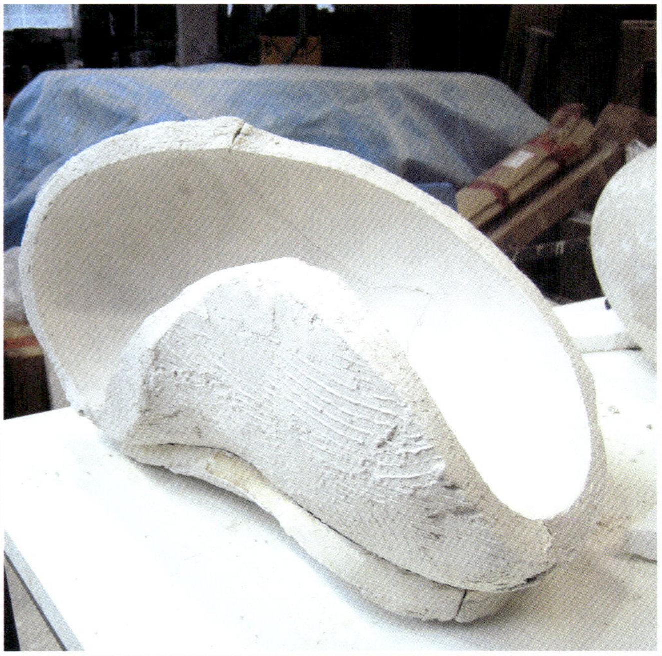

Julius Weiland. The outer mould for *Cell*, consisting of four parts locked with each other. ➤

Photo: Julius Weiland.

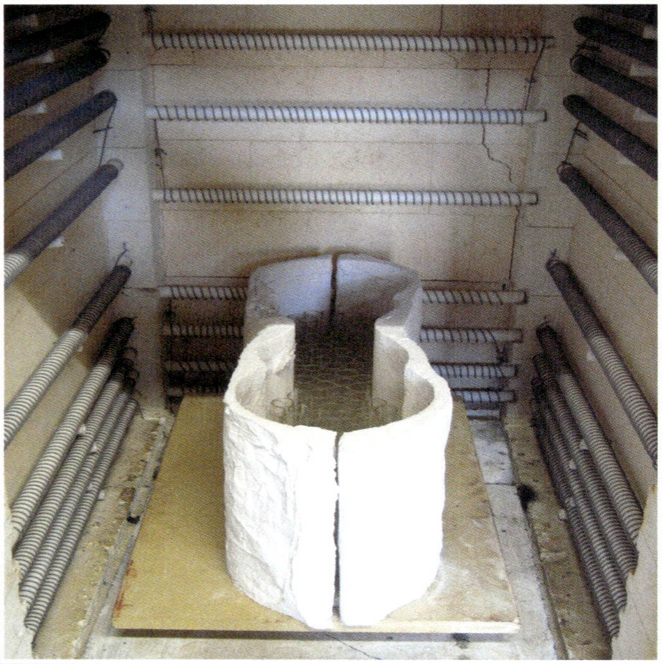

Julius Weiland. A simple two-part mould of fireproof concrete with stacked tubes in it. ➤

Photo: Julius Weiland.

The use of fireproof concrete is made possible by the hard glass of the tubes and the fact that the glass is fired to deformation and fusing temperature when the glass is not viscous enough to stick to the mould. As a result, such moulds can be used a number of times.

Sean Albert

On the face of it Sean Albert's pieces appear to be technically simple, despite their monumental presence and painterly shifts of colour that put one in mind of artists like Rothko and Cy Twombly. However, this apparent simplicity is both deceptive and hard-won. His pieces rely on a precise control over every aspect of his chosen method: the production of the canes, and the positioning and firing as well as the proportions and finishing of the three-dimensional forms.

Intentionally Random Line Study 7.1.06. (Red and Light Blue), Sean Albert, 2006. Kiln-formed glass, H. 34 cm (13⅜ in.), W. 28.5 cm (11¼ in.), D. 6 cm (2⅜ in.). ➤

Photo: Russell Johnson.

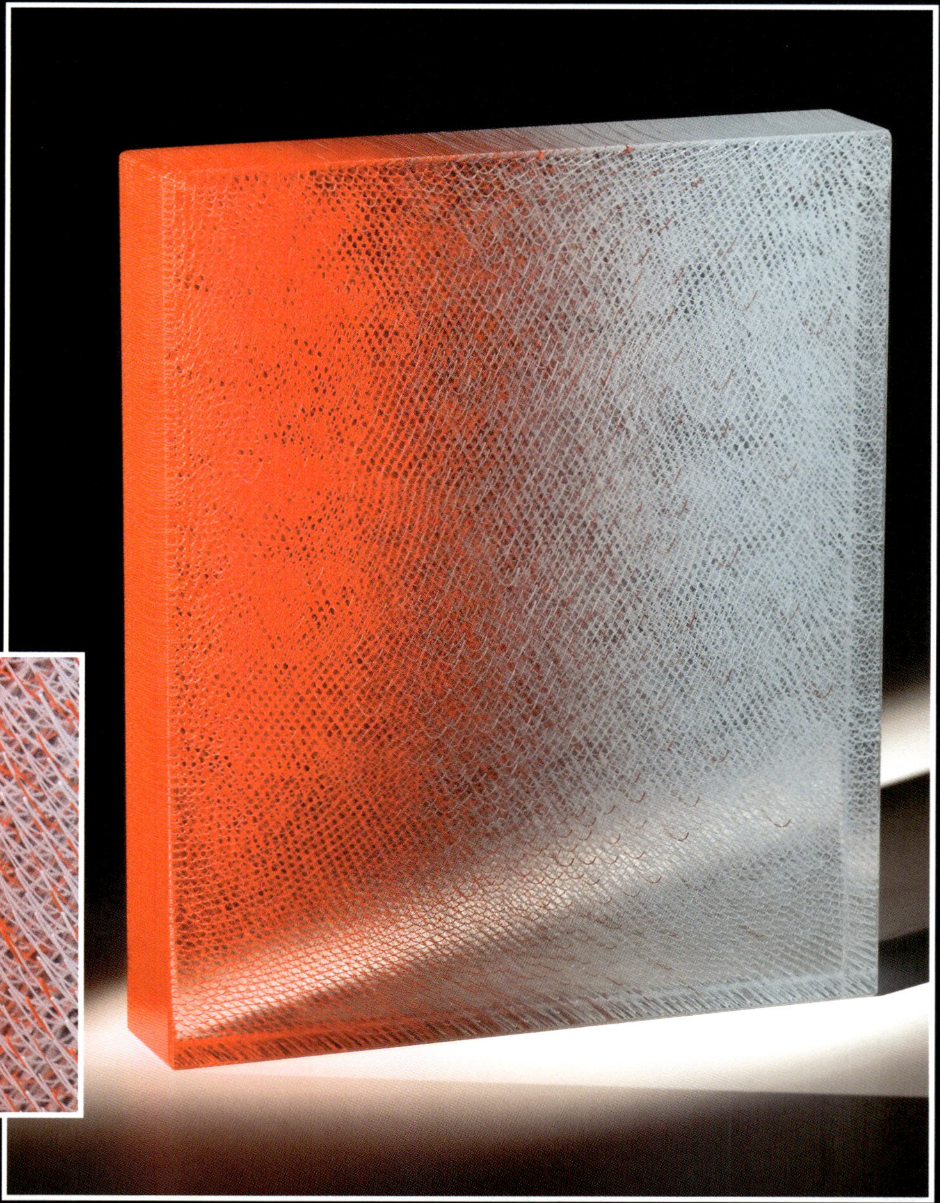

Sean Albert's immaculate pieces are the result of his meticulous preparation. Not only does he make the canes himself to ensure their consistency, he painstakingly places them one at a time into the mould prior to fusing. The resulting block is surface-ground and polished to bring out its subtle internal graphic structure and depth.

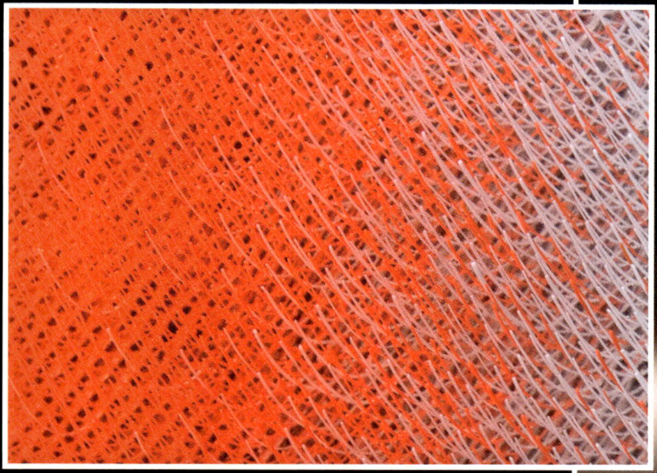

▲ Sean Albert, detail of *Intentionally Random Line Study.*

Artist statement

The inherent qualities of light, shadow, space, colour, line, transparency and pattern are a few of the most prominent foundations of my visual language. By taking advantage of naturally occurring, or by intentionally fabricating, juxtapositions of elements of this language, my minimalist sculptures, paintings and installations have the ability to convey a sense of movement, an illusory space within, and thereby to suggest the presence of subtle or even extraordinary phenomena.

Each *Intentionally Random Line Study* piece comprises 10,000 to 15,000 individual pieces of hand-pulled cane. The pieces are arranged into a desired composition by hand, one at a time, before firing takes place.

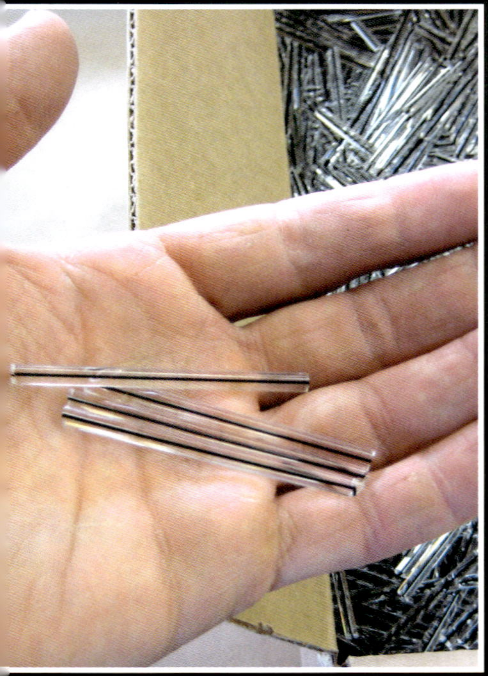

▲ Sean Albert. Individual cane sections.

Photo: courtesy of the artist.

Placing the individual cane sections into the mould to achieve the level of consistency needed requires great skill and patience.

Jane Bruce

Jane Bruce also produces sculptural pieces by fuse-casting, but instead of using small-scale glass elements like rods, she fuses together carefully cut and arranged sections of colour. The resulting artefacts use profile, light

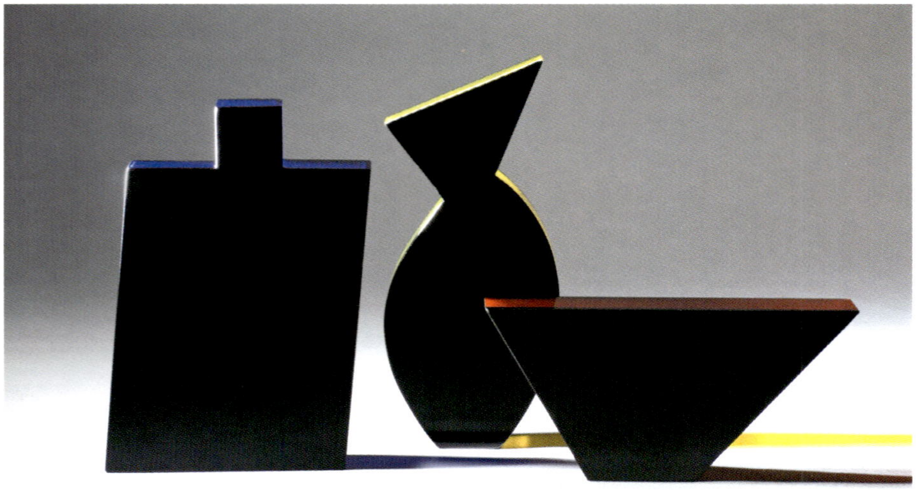

▲ *Black Vase, Bottle, Bowl*, Jane Bruce, 2008. Part of the *Vase, Bottle, Bowl* series (set of three). Vase: H. 33 cm (13 in.), W. 13.3 cm (5¼ in.), D. 3.8 cm (1½ in.); Bottle: H. 29.2 cm (11½ in.), W. 19 cm (7½ in.), D. 3.8 cm (1½ in.); Bowl: H. 13.5 cm (5¼ in.), W. 28 cm (11 in.), D: 3.8 cm (1½ in.). Kiln-formed, cold-worked Bullseye glass.

Photo: Paul Fuller.

Jane Bruce's sculptural works derive their inspiration from drawings that explore the nature of outline and identity. In glass these concerns are transformed by the interplay between shape and colour, shadow and light. The quality of the pieces depends on the precision of the original drawings and the way in which these are translated into glass. Attention to each detail of the cutting, fusing and polishing process ensures that the final piece achieves maximum impact.

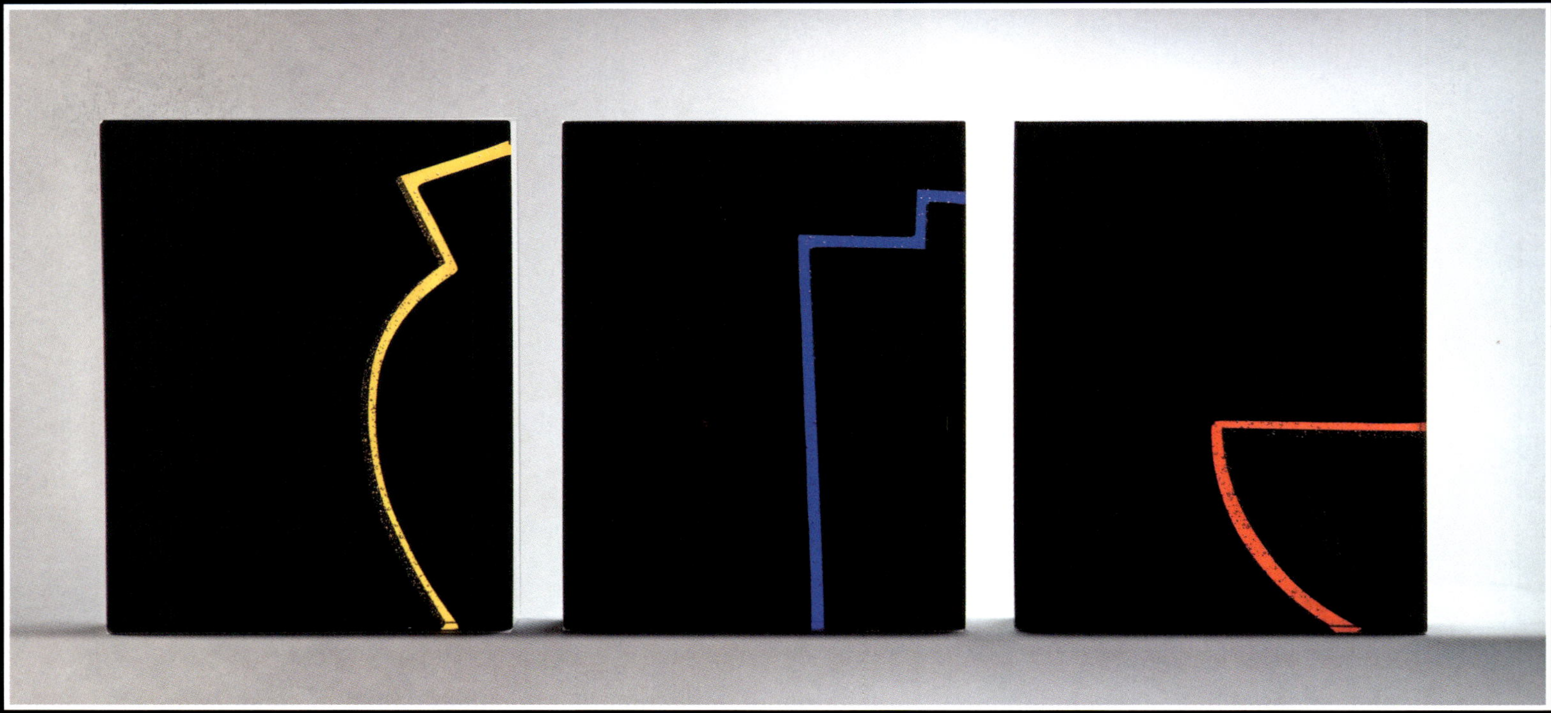

▲ *Light Lines*, Jane Bruce, 2006. *Vase. Bottle. Bowl* series.(set of three black blocks). Kiln-formed, cold-worked Bullseye glass. Each block. H. 28 cm (11 in.), W. 21.5 cm (8½ in.), D. 4.5 cm (1¾ in.).

Photo: Steven Barall.

and colour to explore the nature of the familiar outline, be it vase or house. Her drawings stand as parallel lines of enquiry rather than acting as preparations for her glass. Like many artists, she has moved from one glass technique to another as her themes have suggested it – a case of technique following idea rather than the other way round.

Artist statement

My work is deeply rooted in the history of the decorative or applied arts, particularly the vessel. If I were to pick an adjective to describe my work, it might be 'formal'. I am interested in how composition, light, colour, proportion and the juxtaposition of positive and negative space work within an object or group of objects. 'Formal' is a term rarely used in the context of the decorative or applied arts, but it is essential in painting and sculpture and is, I believe, equally essential to the object.

In 2005 the specific form of my work underwent a major shift away from blown work to kiln-formed and hot-cast forms, which, whilst also concerned with abstraction, light and transparency, continued my investigation into the vessel. At the same time I have been working on a series of house forms, which explore a more personal concern related

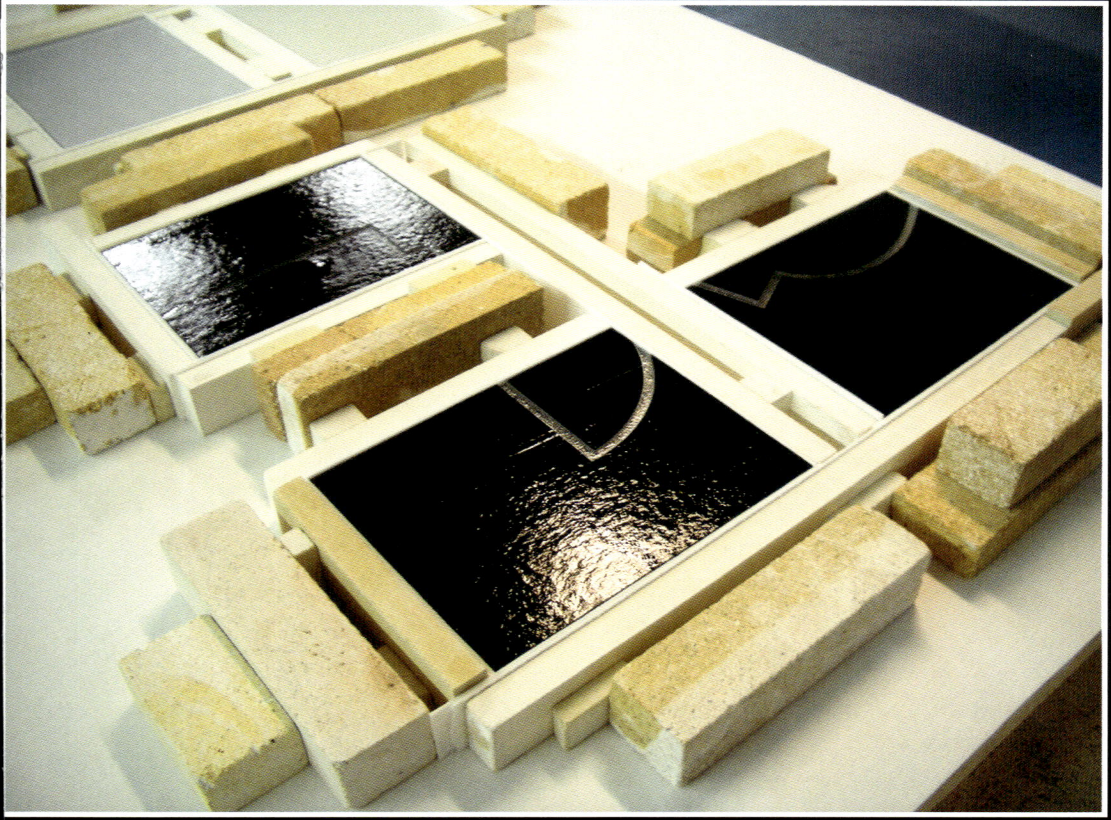

Light Lines, Jane Bruce. Kiln Shot.

Photo: courtesy of the artist.

The precision needed to achieve the refinement of the final image is evident in the care with which the pieces are arranged in the kiln prior to firing. The carefully cut pieces are dammed with ceramic walls to prevent movement or distortion during fusing.

to landscape and loss in a particular place, the far north-east of Scotland.

I am currently working with Studio Ramp, the fabrication studio in Portland, Oregon, to produce these pieces. This way of working has opened up new and unexpected directions in my work that were not previously possible. It has afforded me the opportunity to move from one process (blowing) to another (kiln-forming), enabling me to expand and develop ideas and content within a body of work, unrestricted by technique. It has also provided the time to move from one medium (glass) to another (drawing), permitting the development of works on paper that open up and complement the ideas produced in glass.

Kirstie Rea

Kirstie Rea uses fuse-casting to create shapes which contain separate colour areas within their boundaries. These are then placed on or against surfaces, which causes the colour to react to its background through reflection. The results are pieces that clearly transcend the individual glass form or forms; much more than merely the sum of their individual parts, they cohere into complete images that connect across space.

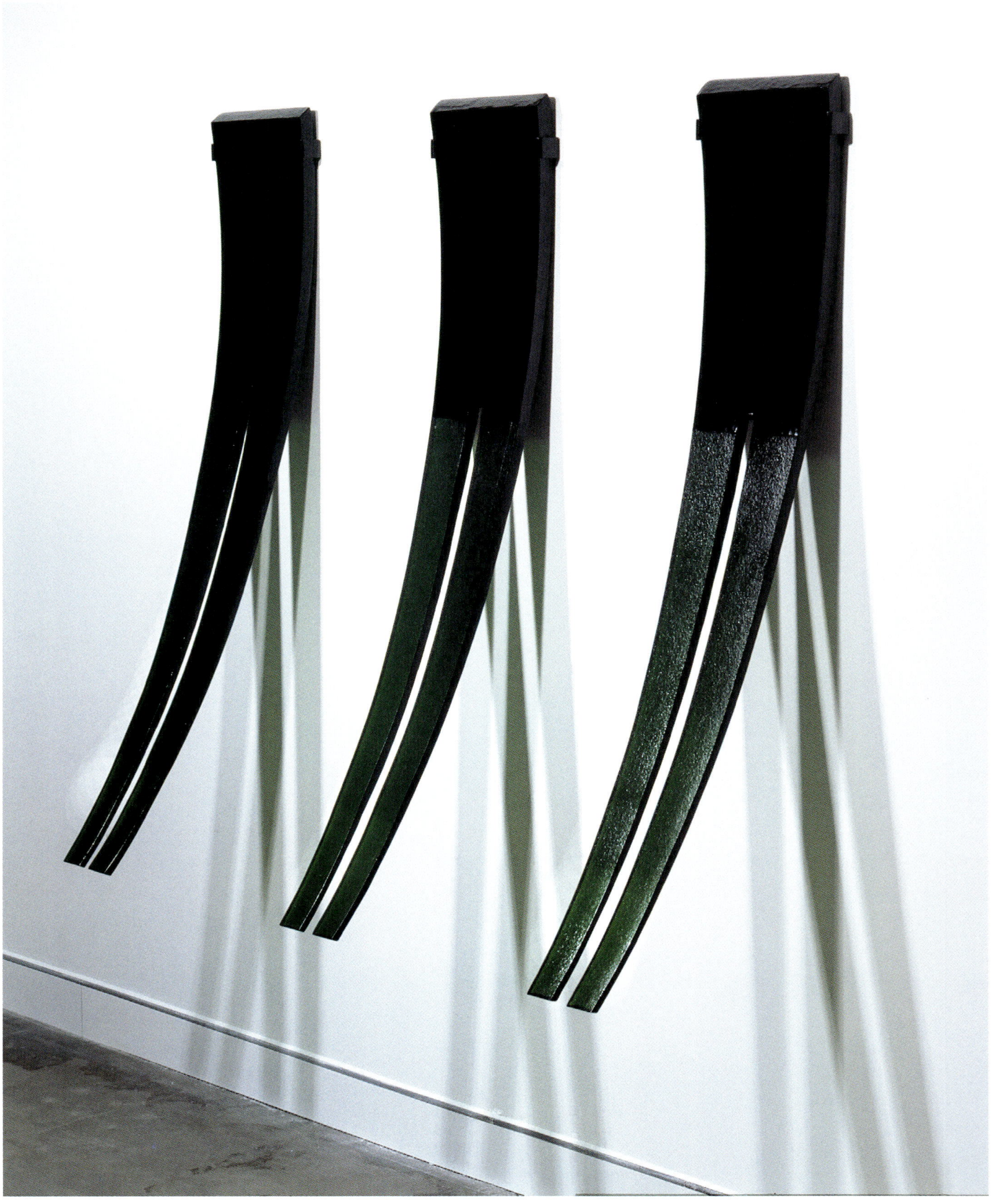

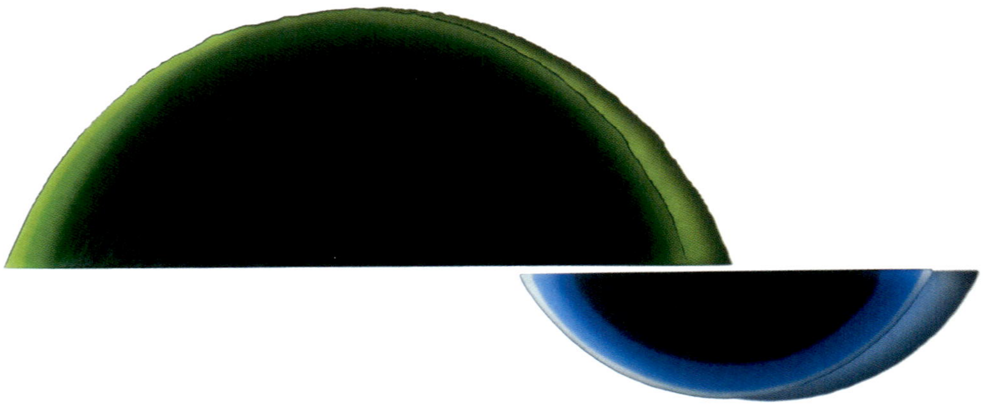

Broadening the Blades, Kirstie Rea, 2004. Kiln-formed, wall-mounted wheel-cut glass, H. 110 cm (43½ in.), W. 100 cm (39½ in.), D. 15 cm (6 in.).

Photo: Steven Murray.

Kirstie Rea's sculptural and painterly works push the scope of kiln-forming aesthetically and technically. To maintain control of colour, form and texture during the fusing and cold-work stages requires great skill.

Kirstie Rea, *The Lake*, 2006. Kiln-formed, wall-mounted wheel-cut glass, H. 29 cm (11⅜ in.), W. 65.5 cm (25¾ in.), D. 3.5 cm (1⅜ in.).

Photo: David Paterson.

Control over the processes ensures that the impact of the final pieces is not diluted by imperfections or distracting, telltale signs of manufacture. The results, like this monumental wall piece, are images of quiet power.

Artist statement

Being shown the values of space outside of the city whilst growing up has left an indelible mark on me. It has captured my imagination, my heart, eyes and spirit, which still have their focus beyond the city limits.

Out there things become clearer, freer. There is a sense of simplicity; all is pared back, reduced to the basics. The light smells and the air is full of colour. Understanding and establishing connections to the land seems possible. Clean dirt, new light. I'm intrigued by issues of land practice that impact on rural areas, wilderness and everything in between.

I am in awe of the power and resilience of these landscapes and environments, and their ability to heal what happens to them. Objects from these landscapes radiate energy and residual power as they recline near where they once made their mark. Times roll on, seasons change, and the landscape records and absorbs all. The more it is loved and cared for, the more it lets you in. These interior moments and stories are reflected in my works.

Udo Zembok

Udo Zembok's output ranges from the sculptural to the architectural, although it all stems from the same creative source and the same technical means of achieving it. The overwhelming impact of his work, and surely the key to his art, is suffused and all-pervading colour. This is achieved by fusing together up to seven sheets of industrially produced float glass with powdered colour trapped between each layer. At the same time the glass is given a texture which serves to intensify the effect of the colour. The free-standing sculptural pieces are also bent as they fuse, to give them stability.

The title of this series, *Colourfields*, clearly makes reference to the New York school of painting epitomised by Mark Rothko. However, Zembok's use and manipulation of colour through his highly personal techniques gives the original inspiration a new and surprising dimension. The colour in Udo's pieces is luminous and, perhaps because of the layering, appears to inhabit space rather than exist on a plane surface. His architectural use of this technique brings a special kind of colour to buildings.

Pâte de verre

This group of artists all describe their chosen technique as pâte de verre. At its most basic this involves the fusing together of fine glass granules supported by a mould, which gives the cast its form. The exact details

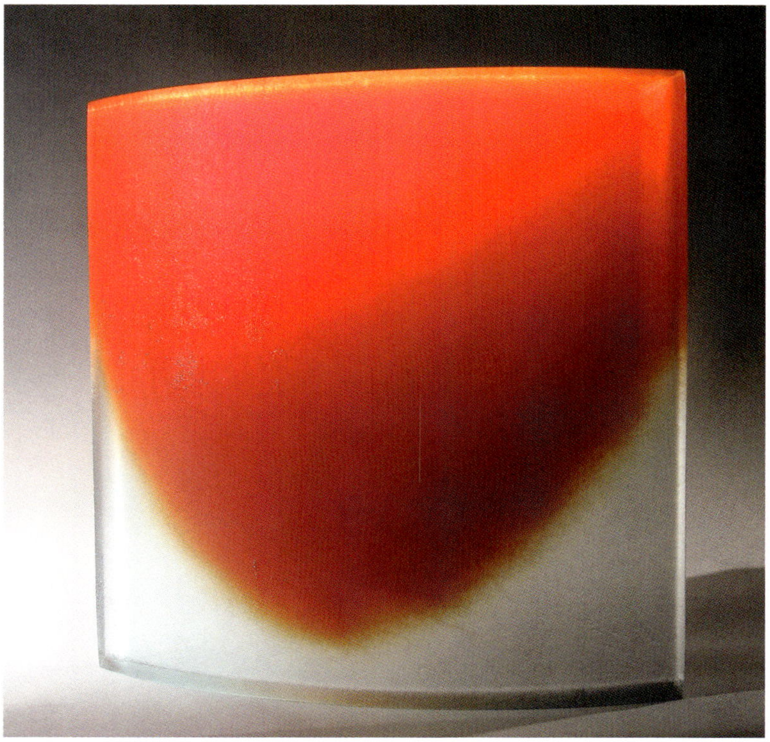

▲ *Colourfields 8*, Udo Zembok, 2007. 70 x 70 cm (27½ x 27½ in.).

Photo: courtesy of the artist.

Bent and fused sheet glass with enamel inclusions. Udo Zembok traps enamel and a variety of oxides in between multiple layers of fused and shaped glass sheets. The resulting build-up of luminosity floating within the glass interstices creates a sensation of saturated colour of great intensity.

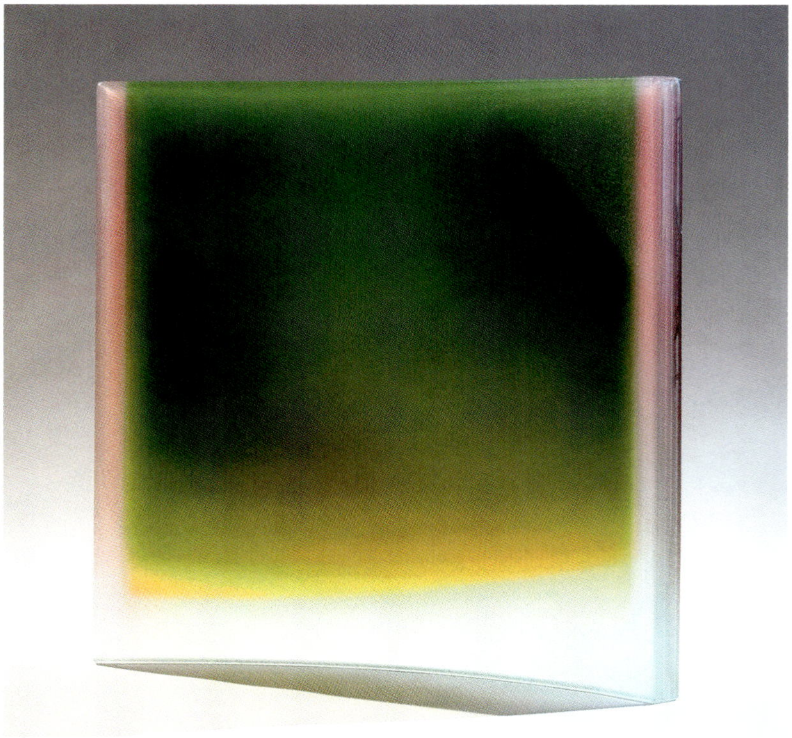

▲ *Colourfields 22*, Udo Zembok, 2005. 60 x 60 cm (23½ x 23½ in.).

Photo: courtesy of the artist.

Variations in the position of the enamel layers create soft veils of colour in addition to stronger areas.

of the technique can vary from artist to artist; in fact this has been a feature of the generic procedure since its development in the late 19th century, the reasons for these differences invariably dictated by each artist's aesthetic preference.

For example, the temperature at which the grains are fused together can be used to determine the texture of the finished piece; generally the higher the temperature the less visible the individual grains will be. There are also many other factors that each artist can manipulate to suit their particular vision – among which are grain size, application of the grains to the mould, design and manufacture of the mould and the wax original, and choice of glass type. One fact is common, however: pâte de verre is one of the most painstaking and delicate of glassmaking methods.

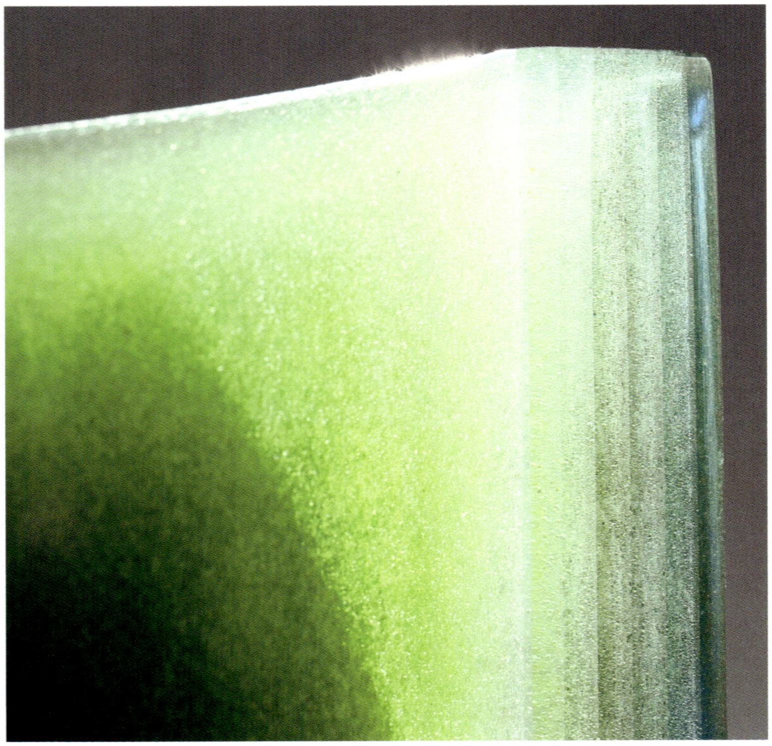

▲ Udo Zembok, *Colourfields* (detail).

Photo: courtesy of the artist.

The layers of glass (in this case six) carrying and separating the individual applications of colour. The thickness of the glass sheet between each layer allows the light to enter and contribute to the vibrancy of the final image.

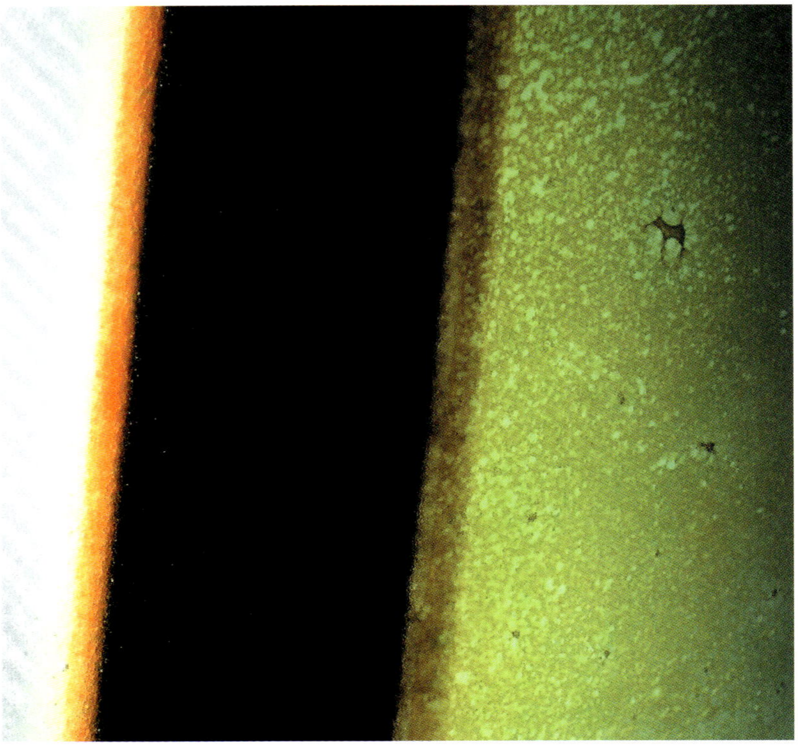

▲ Udo Zembok, sculpture project (detail).

Photo: courtesy of the artist.

Variations created by the use of stencils and selective applications of colour create a different range of qualities.

Penny Fuller

Penny Fuller's pieces are characterised by their open-textured, rich colour. The individual grains are lightly fused together to emphasise the impact each one makes, both as combinations to the overall texture and as individual areas of pigment. In her *Leaves* series the forms are produced by an unusual and individual method. The grains are applied to the outside of a convex former rather than fully enclosed inside a mould. This means that the shapes are created face down, the eventual inside of the leaf forms being the only areas in direct contact with the mould. This allows her to keep an open texture in her pieces, and, crucially, allows her to create the veining in relief through channels in the surface, which is such a feature of these delicate works.

▼ (Inset)
Penny Fuller, detail of *Leaves*.

This detail emphasises the range of different qualities achieved by the way the artist uses the support moulding system.

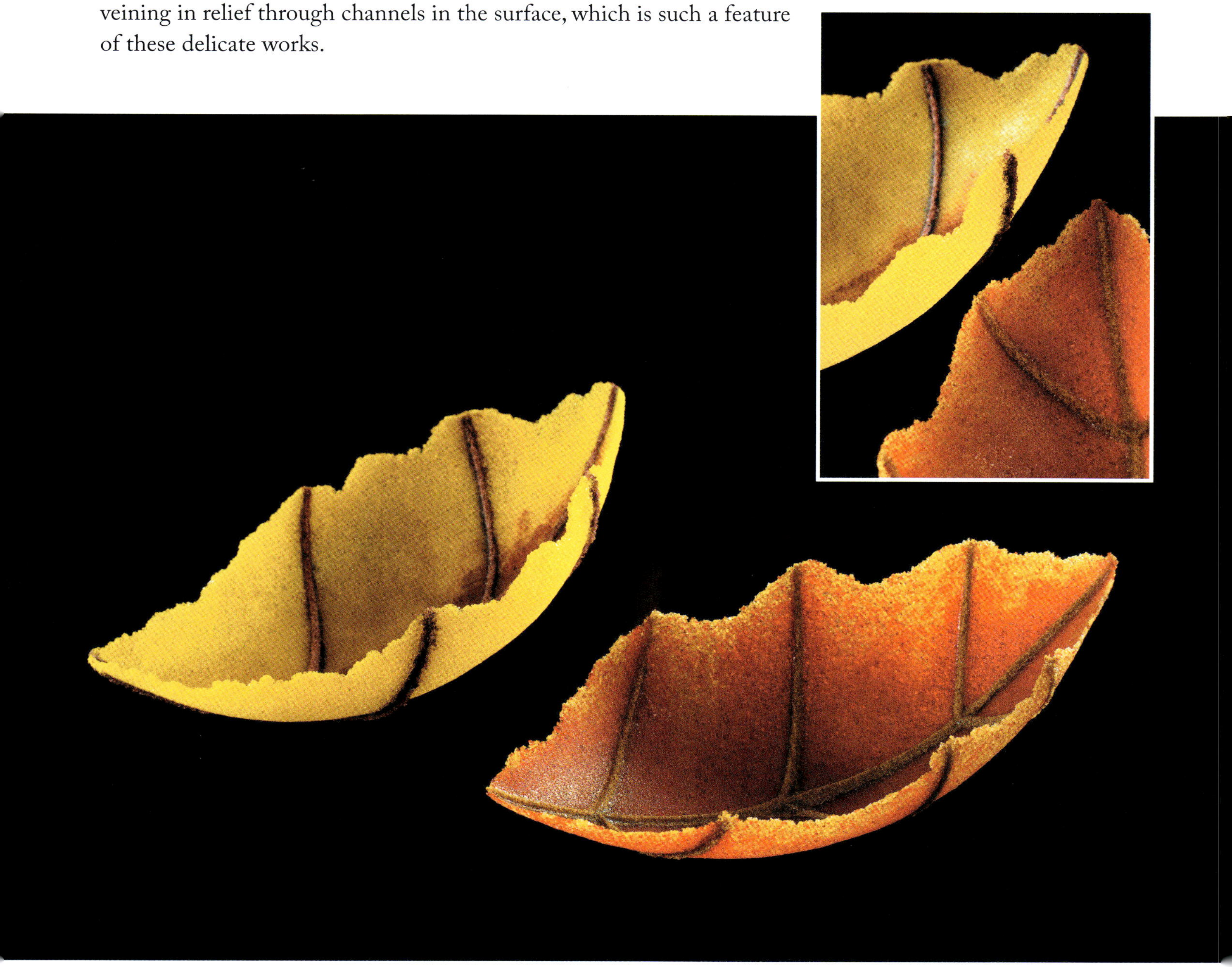

Artist statement

Each leaf tells the story of its journey through seasons of continual change. From intense summer greens to rich autumn reds and golds, the leaf slowly prepares for its final stages of transformation. In my work leaves are symbolic of the flow of life and the nature of impermanence in all things. Colour, pattern and texture express change and brevity, as the whole cycle of life unfolds into one fleeting glimpse of reality extending beyond the limits of human perception.

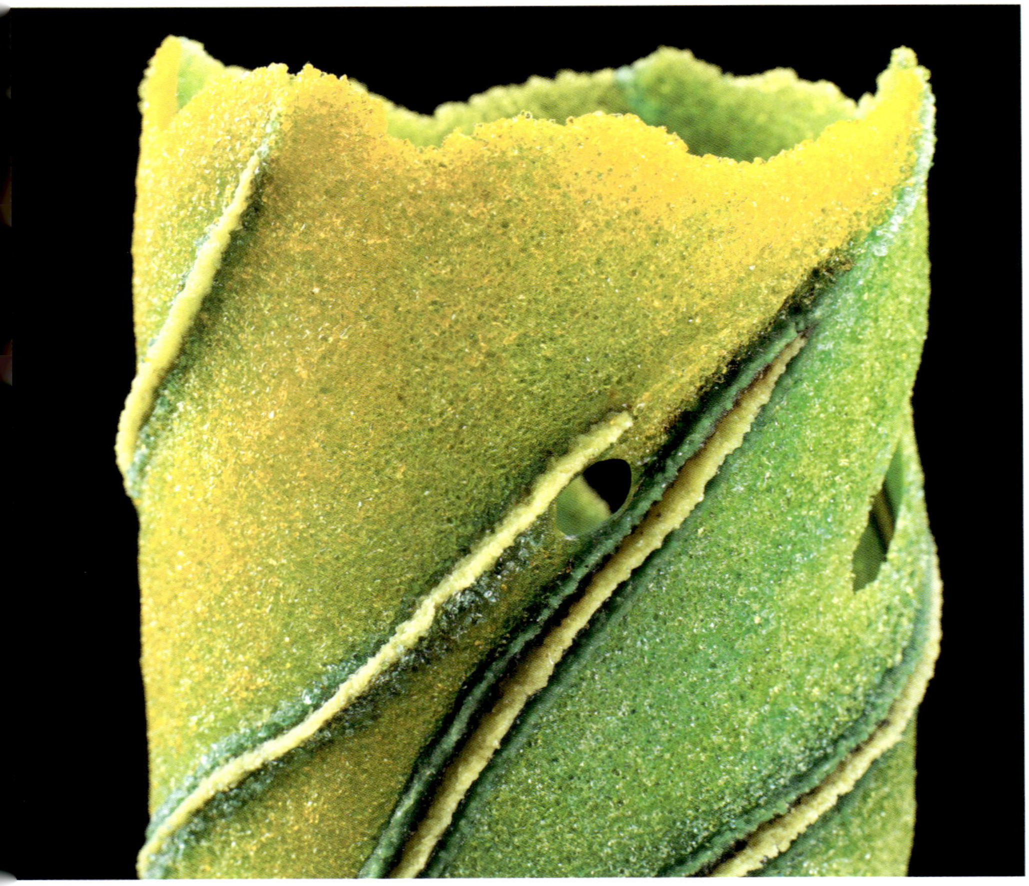

◄ Penny Fuller, *Green Palm*, 2004. H. 10 cm (4 in.), W. 13 cm (5⅛ in.), L. 27.5 cm (10¾ in.).

Photo: Grant Hancock.

This piece illustrates another benefit of Penny Fuller's looser way of forming glass granules. Because she has greater visual and physical access to her moulding surfaces she also has greater control over the disposition and depth of the glass layers prior to firing. The juxtaposition of voids and solids is an example of this.

◄ *Leaves – Autumn Series*, Penny Fuller, 2004. Yellow: H. 5 cm (2 in.), W. 11.5 cm (4½ in.), L. 20 cm (8 in.); orange: H. 4 cm (1½ in.), W. 10.5 cm (4⅛ in.), L. 19.5 cm (7⅝ in.).

Photo: Grant Hancock.

Penny Fuller's pâte-de-verre casts use a highly personal variation of the conventional moulding system. These pieces are the result of granular glass placed over a support rather than inside a total mould. This means that the inside of the container form is created by the support, along with the raised veins of the leaves, while the edge and back are allowed to form more freely.

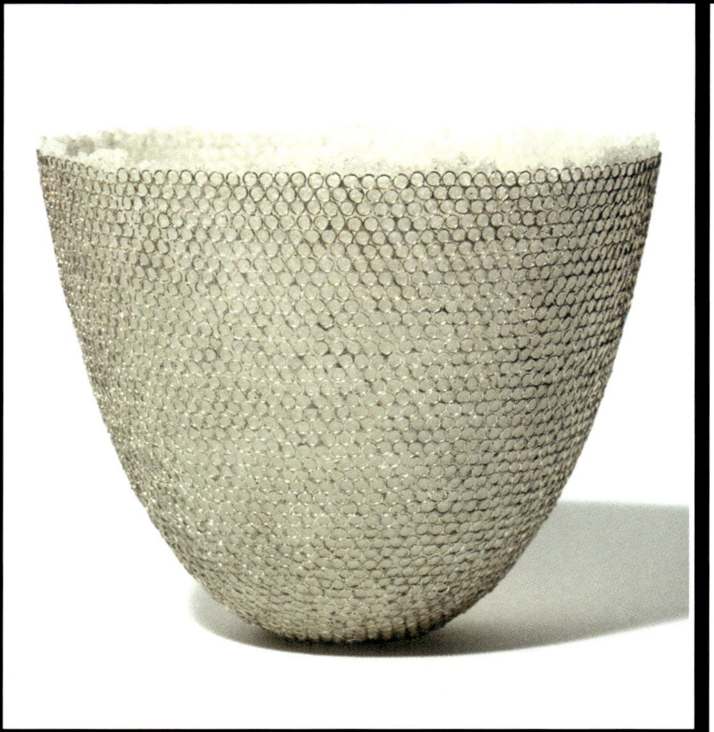

▲ Untitled (vessel), Sylvie Vandenhouke, 1999. Pâte de verre and soldered silver. H. 10 cm (4 in.).

Photo: courtesy of the artist.

A delicate, thin-walled pâte-de-verre vessel cast inside a silver cage.

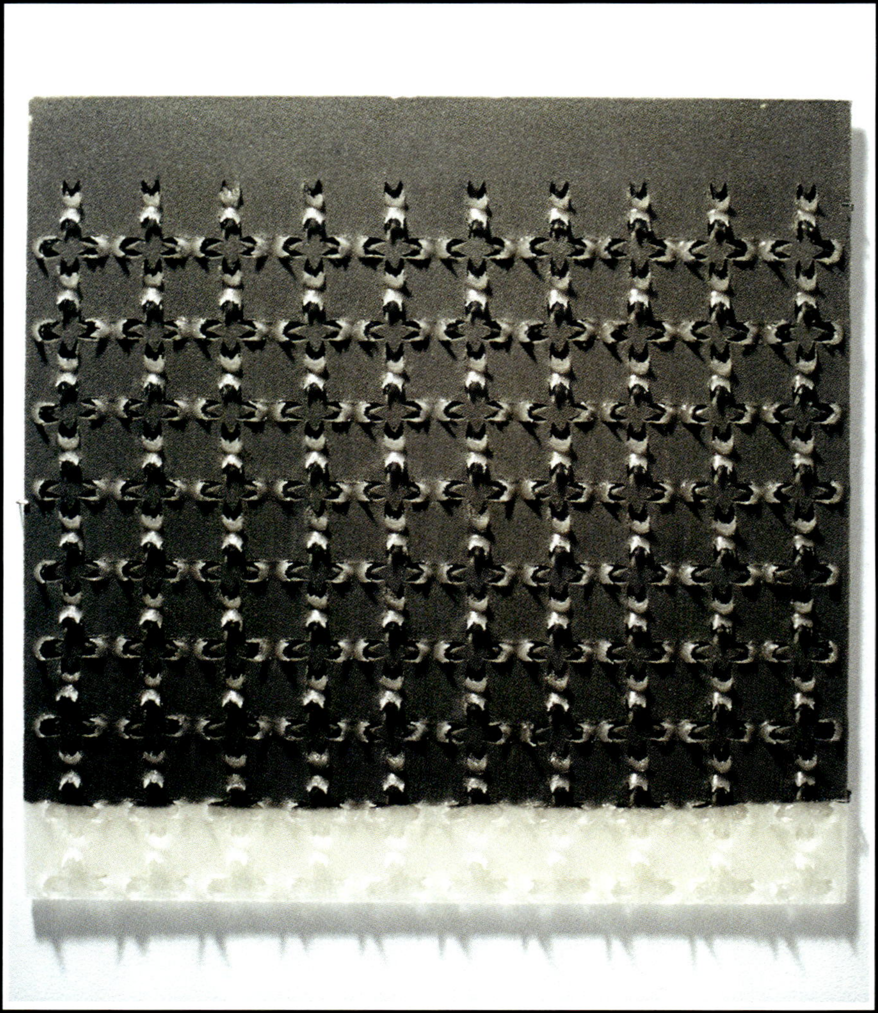

Sylvie Vandenhoucke

As an artist and researcher, Sylvie Vandenhoucke works with a diverse range of materials, including metal, paper and carpet in addition to glass. Her work builds on and around a core of intense interest in glass, especially pâte de verre. She has, for example, investigated in depth how colour can be generated directly in a clear-glass batch during the shaping process of pâte-de-verre casting, and how the decomposition of metal oxides can be used as a shaping tool in the making of an art work. The results are intriguing, with sometimes ambiguous substances raising issues of colour, surface texture, density, solution and dispersion.

In her work she uses this personally developed palette of colours and qualities to create delicately structured artefacts with subtle surfaces, which invite inspection and appreciation at close quarters, where their shifts of form and texture fully reveal themselves. Many of her pieces are developed from a single, flat surface, like paintings, and indeed are presented as wall-hung art works.

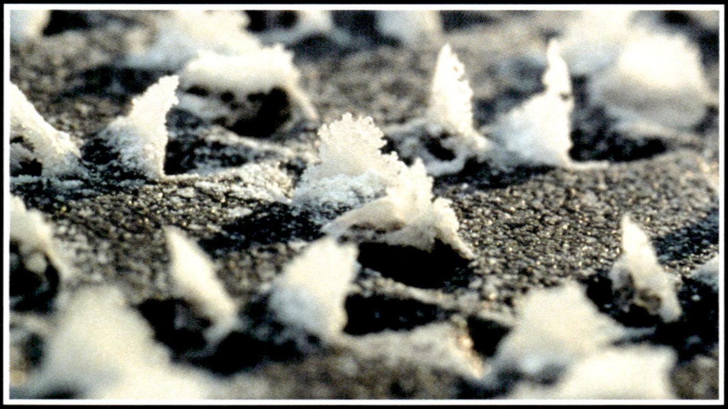

Latitude 90.04, Sylvie Vandenhoucke, 2005. Wall piece, 27 x 27 x 0.8 cm (10½ x 10½ x ⅜in.).

Photo: courtesy of the artist.

In an unusual shift of emphasis, Sylvie Vandenhoucke has used the delicate nature of fine-grain pâte de verre in the production of wall pieces that have the qualities of paintings. Using extremely fine granules and exerting great control over moulds and temperatures, the projecting surface details of the pieces play with light and shadow to create actual and illusory patterns.

Sylvie Vandenhoucke, details from *Latitude 90.04*, wall piece.

Photo: courtesy of the artist.

Showing the control achieved over both the shape and the depth of the three-dimensional details.

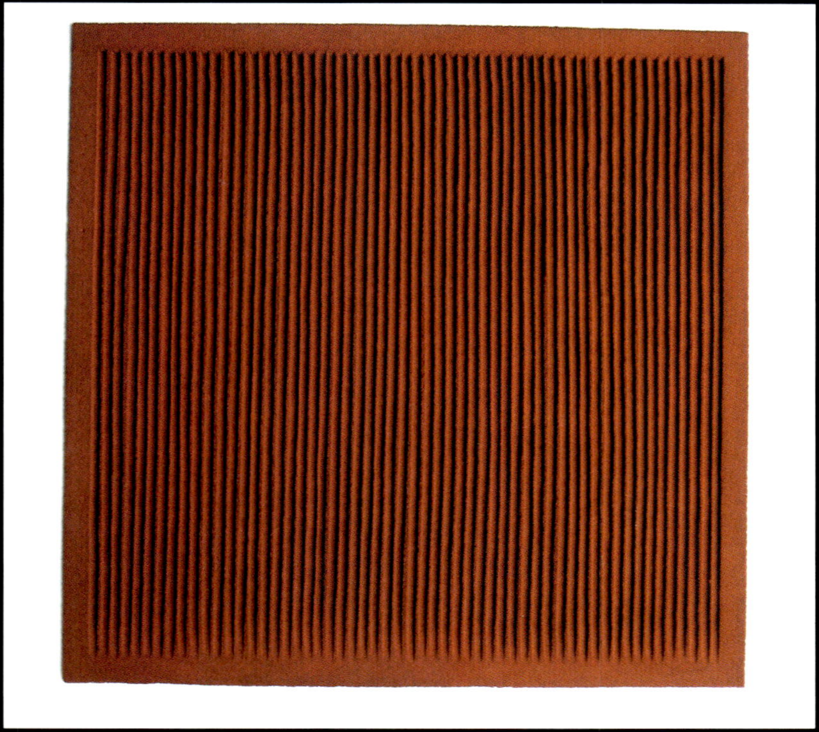

Aeroplano (Red), Sylvie Vandenhouke, 2007. Pâte-de-verre wall piece. 35 x 35 x 0.8 cm (13¾ x 13¾ x ⅜ in.).

Photo: courtesy of the artist.

A larger wall piece of great subtlety, which relies on the qualities of the colour and texture of the glass for much of its impact and presence.

Artist statement

My work contemplates the dwelling between heaven and earth, the transcendental experience, the sublime; how to make the invisible visible, how to dematerialise matter. The work reveals a non-physical or inner space, trapped in between the layers of the miniature landscape. One's understanding of the work alters radically with viewing distance and angle. Orderly patterns slide into chaos; snowlike softness sharpens into angled fins; superficial marks deepen into vents; changing light through a window unmasks lengthening patches of colour as shadows. The unfolding of the infinitesimal in the whole silently discloses this invisible nucleus of the work.

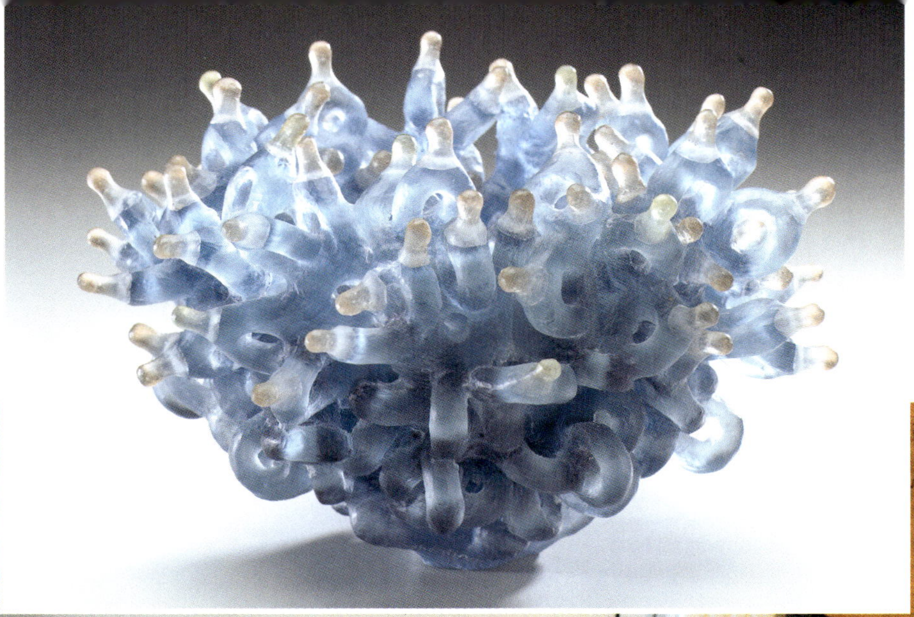

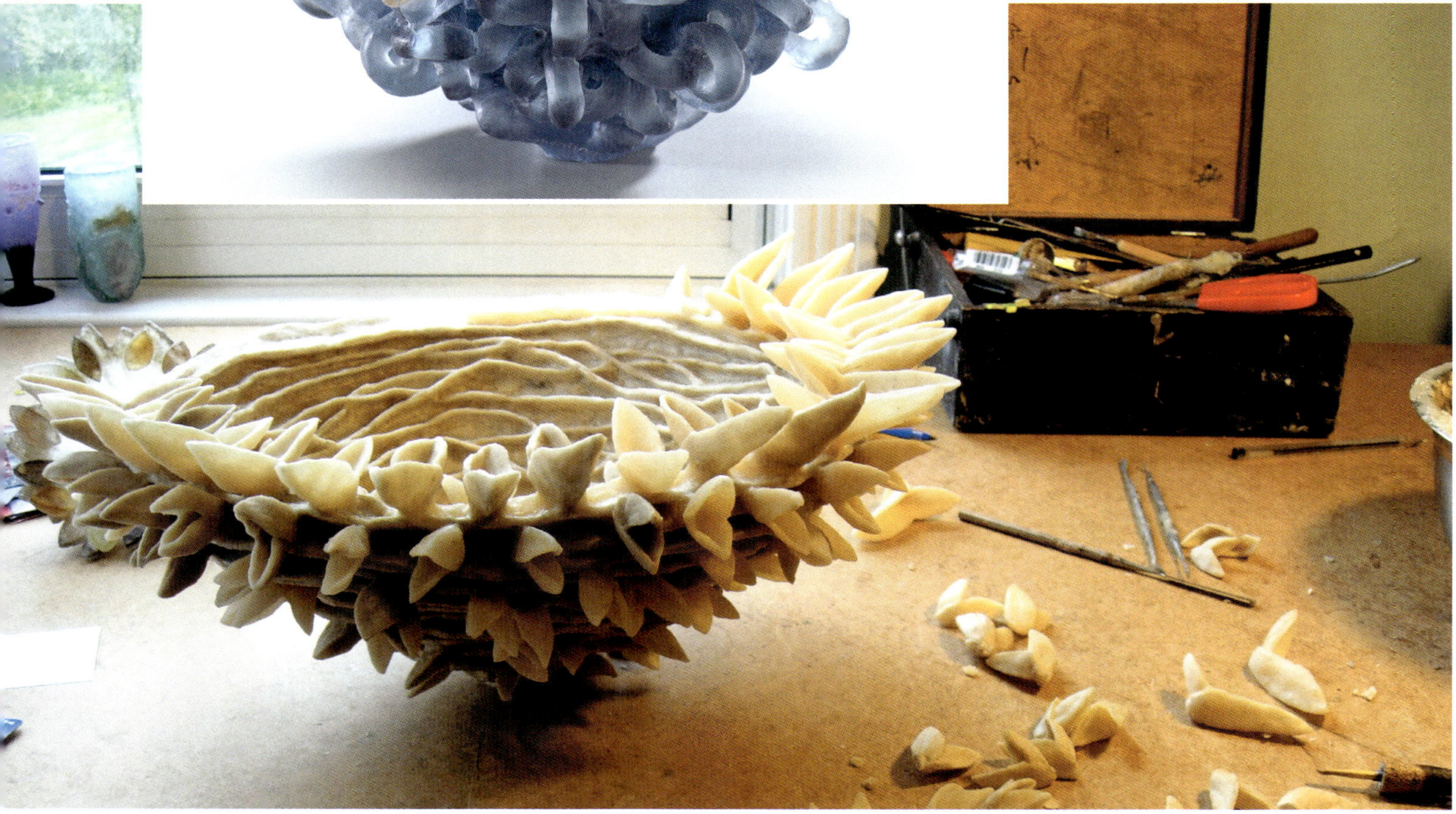

▲ Anja Isphording, wax model.

Photo: courtesy of the artist.

The use of beeswax as her modelling material of choice means that Anja Isphording extends control over her organic-inspired forms by allowing the hand production of soft, open forms which derive from detailed observational drawings.

▲ (Inset)
Anja Isphording, *# 106*, 2006.
H. 17 cm (6⅝ in.), D. 24 cm (9½ in.).
(See also image on p.86).

Anja Isphording

Anja Isphording decided not to provide a statement to support her works, preferring to let the pieces speak for themselves, which they do, eloquently. She also chooses to identify her pieces by the use of numbers rather than names.

Her pieces derive their organic forms from observational drawings, which are developed three-dimensionally in hand-modelled beeswax prior to being cast in glass. In her finished works she avoids the connotations of the vessel by relating her forms to the open structures of the flower forms that inspire her. The resulting pieces, with their delicate lacework of jewel-like colours, are both distinctive and original.

Nancy Klimley

The current work of Nancy Klimley explores the three-dimensional possibilities of traditional pattern forms. Her frank statement reveals much about her creative process, and is refreshingly open about issues like series production and the need to profit from one's endeavours.

Artist statement

The concept

The direction of my current work started with a challenge to myself: could I add depth to traditional patterns? My previous work had been using vessels as surfaces to embellish, but I realised that patterns were what really interested me. My goal was to explore their visual possibilities and to elevate patterns into sculptures in their own right. Historical architecture, textiles and industrial design, as well as nature, have become sources of inspiration for me. I am already finding that the patterns are affected when subject to different kinds of lighting, different-coloured backgrounds and different viewing angles, and I am very excited about the many possibilities this concept presents.

The creative process

When I am developing a new concept I ask myself three questions.

1 Is the concept unique.?
2 Can the concept be developed into multiple series?
3 Based on the amount of time and money needed to realise the new concept, can I sell it at a profit?

***The Intersecting Rings* series**

When I started working with this pattern I was surprised to find that it had been used throughout history to represent many different subjects. The Egyptians used the pattern to symbolise lotus leaves, while the same pattern in traditional American quilts is called 'double wedding rings'. The pattern takes on a whole new appearance when depth is added. By eliminating colour in this series, I have placed the emphasis on shape and form through the contrast between light and shadow. As the viewer moves around the sculpture, the pattern changes continuously, from balanced to asymmetrical, and the piece becomes animated.

The technique

After experimenting with numerous techniques for firing my delicate pierced panels, I have found the most successful results come from firing

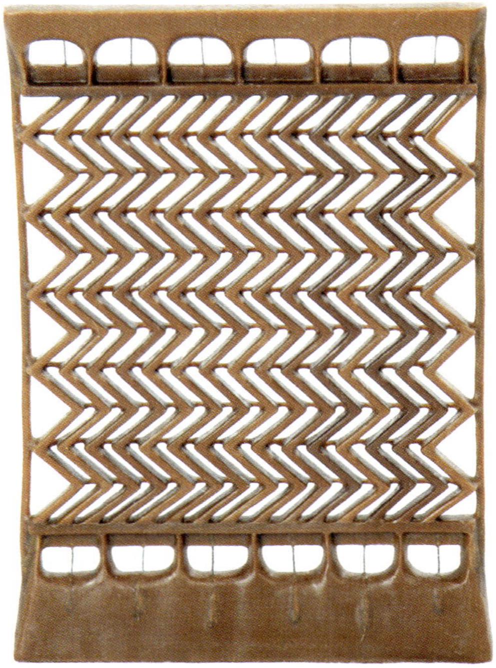

▲ Nancy Klimley, Wax model.
Photo: courtesy of the artist.

Nancy Klimley's lacelike glass structures push the accepted boundaries of both wax and glass in their creation. The wax structures are built on armatures of wire which are removed at the steaming stage, and the openwork lattice has solid areas top and bottom to aid both steaming and glass access during casting.

the structures upright. The wax is supported internally with additional wires that are removed after steaming. The biggest issue has been how to steam such a detailed pattern. The wax photograph shows how I leave the mould open at the top and bottom to allow the steam to reach as much wax as possible. After steaming, I close one end with mould mix and attach a custom reservoir with more mix at the other end. Because steaming takes so long, I usually end up with flashing across some areas of the open work, but it is very thin and is easily removed by cold working. I use a foredoom (or flexidrive) for this purpose, to remove the sprues and to avoid putting too much stress on the structure of the piece.

I think that the most important part of technique is to be open to new ideas, so what I have described here will certainly change.

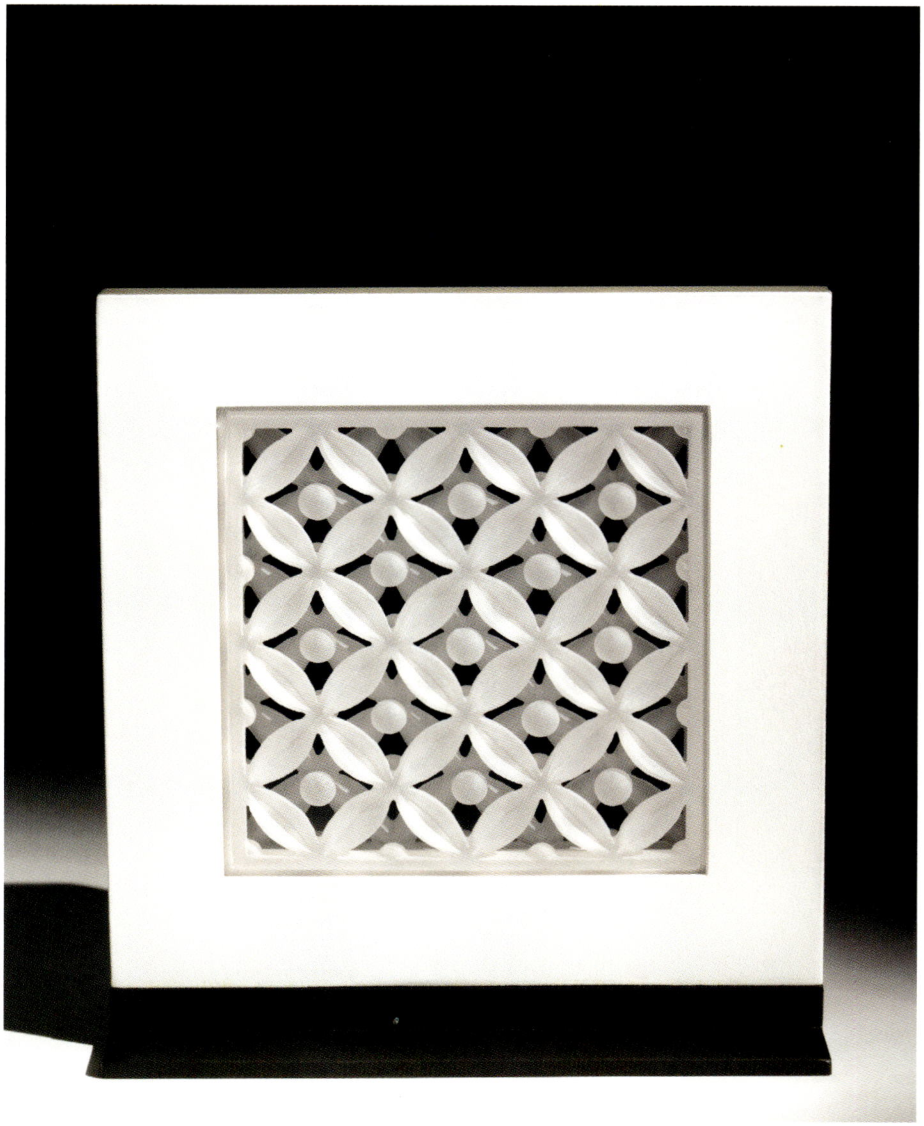

Nancy Klimley, *Intersecting Rings series*. H. 130.5 cm (51 ⅜ in.), W. 30.5 cm (12 in.), D. 4 cm (1½ in.). Base depth: 13 cm (5⅛ in.). Cast Gaffer glass with wood frame/two panels with glued dots.

The complex open-work nature of the structure creates barriers to the movement of glass during casting. These are overcome by long casting times and the use of pure, fine glass granules. Because of the prolonged high temperature some flashing occurs across details, which has to be removed.

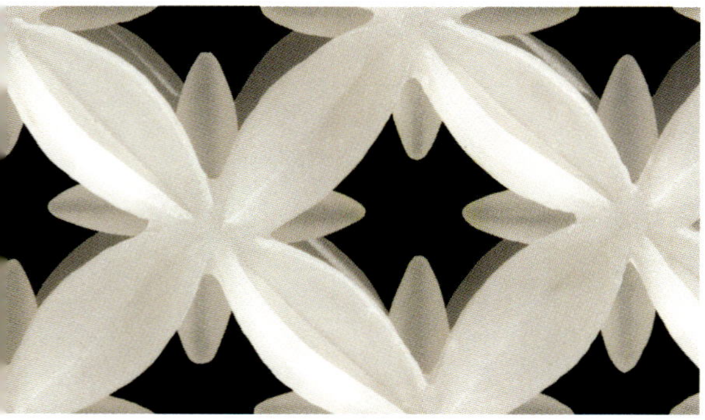

Nancy Klimley. Detail of an *Intersecting Rings* series.

Photo: Russell Johnson.

The image relies on the accurate nature and control exercised by the artist at every stage of the modelling, moulding and casting stages. This is a different pattern from the *Rings* series.

Karen Akester

Karen Akester uses pâte-de-verre casting to capture the subtleties of delicate fabrics with uncanny accuracy. As a result, her sculptural pieces carry echoes of the previous use of these fabrics and the eras in which they were produced.

Artist statement

In trying to capture remnants of the past I am dealing with a fragile material, attempting to replace an idea with something tangible. By working through memories of a personal and collective nature, I have been trying to understand how we visualise memories, and how imagery influences our view of our past. I have been collecting memorabilia, old clothes, shoes and photographs, all in various states of disrepair. They each have their own memories, conveying a story that is both personal and universal. However, I have no personal connection to these source materials, so although they evoke in me strong feelings, I can still enjoy the sense of anonymity.

Exploiting the rich textures and decaying materials, and with an element of the half-remembered, I can narrate my own stories, transforming these discarded objects into meaningful and coherent ideas, faded remnants of a childhood past. I would like my work to be seen as a celebration, a study of loss, fragility and childhood.

Process

My initial step is to take impressions from the clothes I have collected, so I might replicate them in glass using the pâte-de-verre process. This allows me to cast very fine pieces of glass, producing ghostly, brittle interpretations, the fragile delicacy of which I believe captures the fragmented nature of old memories, and creates an illusion of decaying, almost forgotten relics.

I begin by taking clay impressions of the original garments, as this allows me to reposition folds and creases in the fabric until I have an imprint I am happy with. From this I take a Gelflex rubber copy, which provides me with a flexible master copy that I can fold and shape to make a sculptural print. From this I take a refractory mould in plaster and flint. Once this has dried out I can apply the glass paste – a mixture of glass powders, water and, depending on the mould's contours, a glue binder such as methylcellulose. I spray the mould surface with water until surface damp, and, mixing the glass paste to a gluey consistency, paint it onto the surface of the mould, building up thin layers of paste which must be allowed to dry between each application. It's a repetitive process that I find meditative, and it gives me time to control exactly

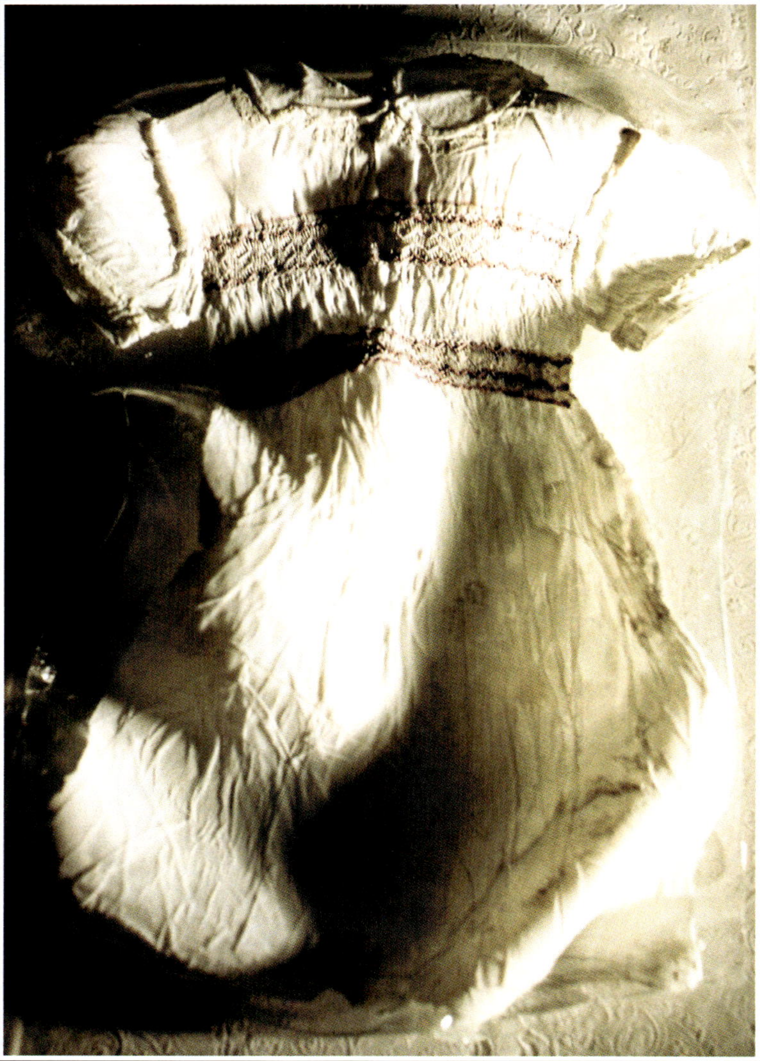

▲ *Smock Dress* (full length), Karen Akester, 2007. L. 61 cm (24 in.), W. 41 cm (16 ⅛ in.).

Photo: courtesy of the artist.

Pâte-de-verre smock dress fused and slumped, attached to pâte-de-verre wallpaper panel. The amazing accuracy of Karen Akester's casts is achieved through a carefully controlled sequence of stages, from the impressions taken from the original fabric to the transference of these to the mould and the pâte-de-verre casts themselves.

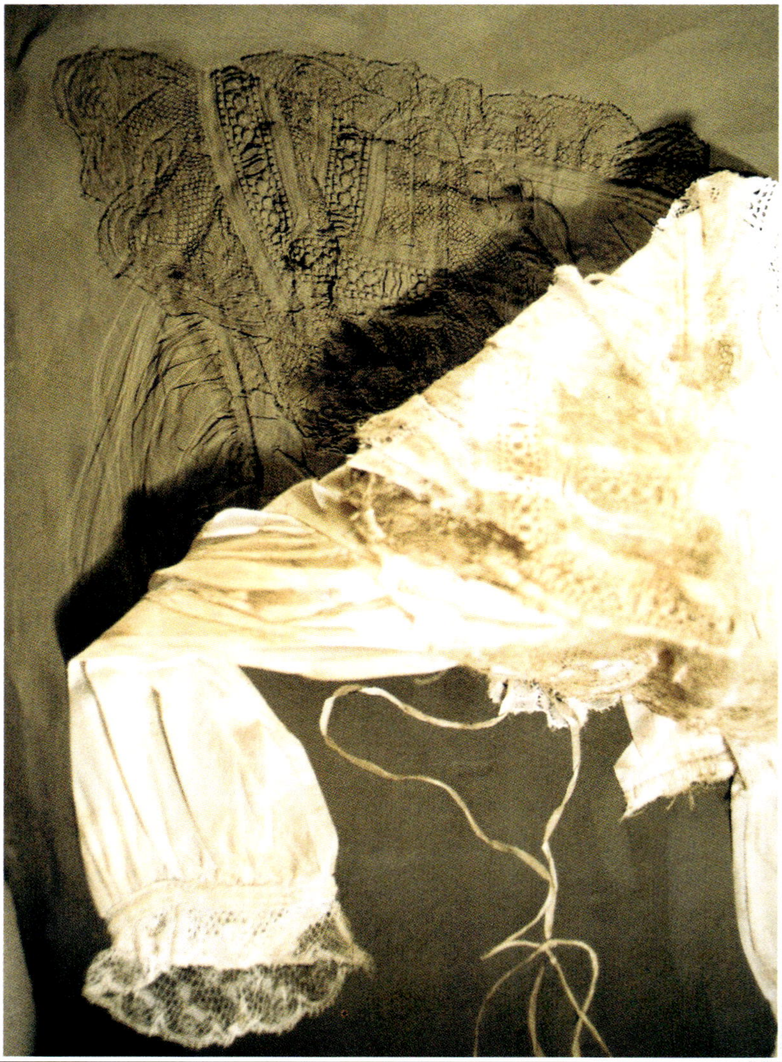

▲ Karen Akester. Clay press mould.

Photo: courtesy of the artist.

Working with soft clay enables the artist to place the garment in exactly the right position before taking an impression, and to capture the full range of the fabric's qualities.

where I want the colours and glass to be. Once the final layer has dried, and the paste is about 5 mm (¼ in.) deep, I load it into the kiln. The glass powder, compacted to the surface of the mould, picks up the finest detail, its opaqueness creating a true imitation of the original garment.

The pieces are fired several times, with further layers of paste added in areas that during the firing cycle have developed imperfections. It is now that

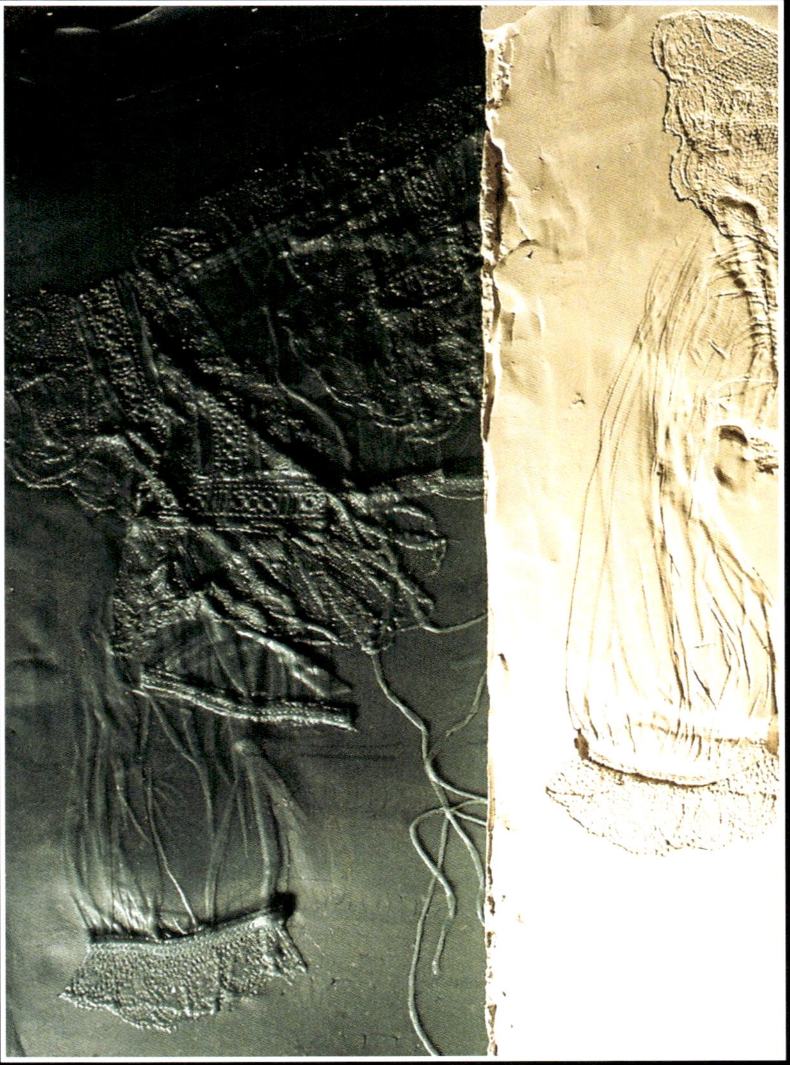

Karen Akester. Clay and Gelflex mould.

Photo: courtesy of the artist.

The original clay impression is used to take a flexible rubber master which can then be used in a number of ways to create refractory casting moulds.

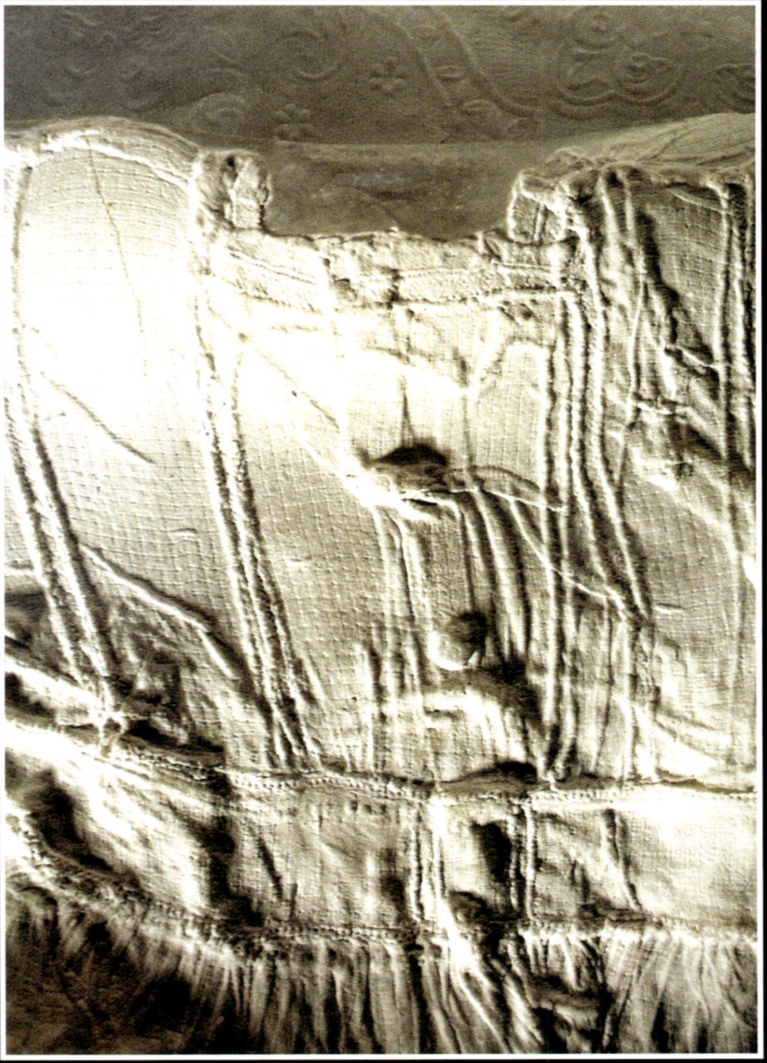

Karen Akester. *Folded Dress* (button detail), 2007. L. 36 cm (14⅛ in.), W. 32 cm (12⅝ in.). Pâte de verre folded short-sleeved dress, fused and slumped with separate pâte-de-verre wall-paper panel.

This detail illustrates the accuracy achieved by Karen through her meticulous control of the process.

the glass takes over – stretching, curling and distorting over the contours of the mould – and I concede control to the heat of the kiln. In such a controlled procedure, it is a rare moment of letting go, where a happy accident or slight surface imperfection can give new life to a piece of work. The final firing is the fusing and slumping of the sheet glass to the reverse of the garment. Only then can the piece be removed from the mould.

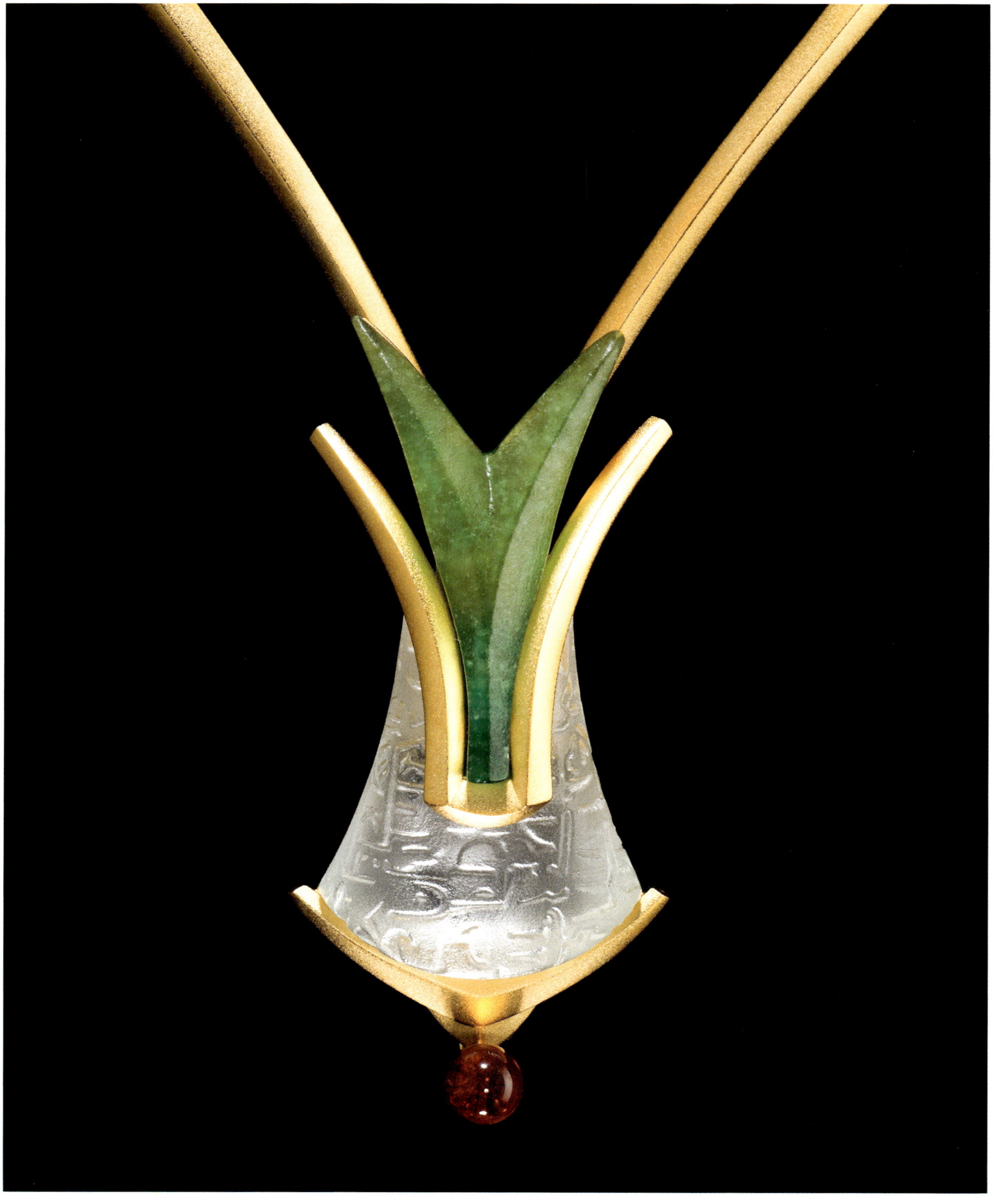

Linda MacNeil

Linda MacNeil has been a major figure in world glass for many years. Her work continues a tradition of glass use that is among the most ancient, that of using it as a fully fledged material in the production of jewellery. While the Egyptians valued glass as a precious stone in its own right, it has taken artists of the standing of Lalique to raise what is nowadays regarded as a more prosaic material to a similar status in our own era. Linda MacNeil emulates this achievement through a mixture of high-quality individual artistry and a painstaking technique.

The glass jewels (shown on p.88) were cast by lost wax in colourless glass; their colour is achieved by grinding their bases flat and attaching thin sheets of coloured glass to the bases, then covering them with a reflective surface of pure gold. This gives a range of colours which is not dependent on standard glass ranges, and imparts a magical quality to the way the colour illuminates each glass jewel. The use of 18 carat gold to mount and form the glass casts into a necklace reinforces the perception of glass as the equal of precious stones.

In *Egyptian Reed* Linda employs coloured pâte de verre to produce the shape and surface modelling of the pieces that make up the pendant. It is interesting that her title makes a self-conscious reference to a period in history which regarded glass as being worthy of jewellery.

◄ *Egyptian Reed* from the *Floral* series, Linda MacNeil, 2003. Pâte de verre (green); acid-polished amber glass, 24-carat gold-plated brass. Pendant 8 cm (3⅛ in.).

Photo: Bill Truslow.

Despite the fact that the Egyptians used and valued glass as a precious material, very few contemporary artists have chosen to do so. Linda MacNeil is one exception, combining a variety of cast glass with metals in the creation of her distinctive pieces.

Dan Dailey

A major figure in international glass for over three decades, Dan Dailey has never allowed himself to become limited in his use of material, glass type or technique, preferring to use and to master a wide range of methods to fully realise his rich and complex imagery. The exceptions to this eclecticism in his output are the editions of pâte de verre sculptures that he has designed for Daum over the years.

These two pieces of Dan's illustrate his use of a wide vocabulary of forms and qualities. His use of pâte de verre is highly selective, and all the more effective for it.

Artist statement

I began working with pâte de verre at Crystallerie Daum in 1976, and the company has produced nine editions of my cast glass sculptures since then. In my own studio, beginning in about 1993, we have produced numerous elements in pâte de verre for chandeliers, sconces, tables, vases and sculpture, incorporating the casting with other types of glass, and supporting it with metal frameworks.

Dan Dailey, detail of *Chanteuse*, from the *Circus series*, 2000. Blown glass. Fabricated, patinated, gold- and nickel-plated bronze. Pâte-de-verre details. H. 84 cm (33 in.), W. 45 cm (17¾ in.), D. 26 cm (10¼ in.).

Photo: Bill Truslow.

Dan Dailey has always worked across a wide range of glass types and processes to realise his personal vision. In this complex glass- and metal-constructed piece he reserves the use of pâte de verre for the production of crucial details.

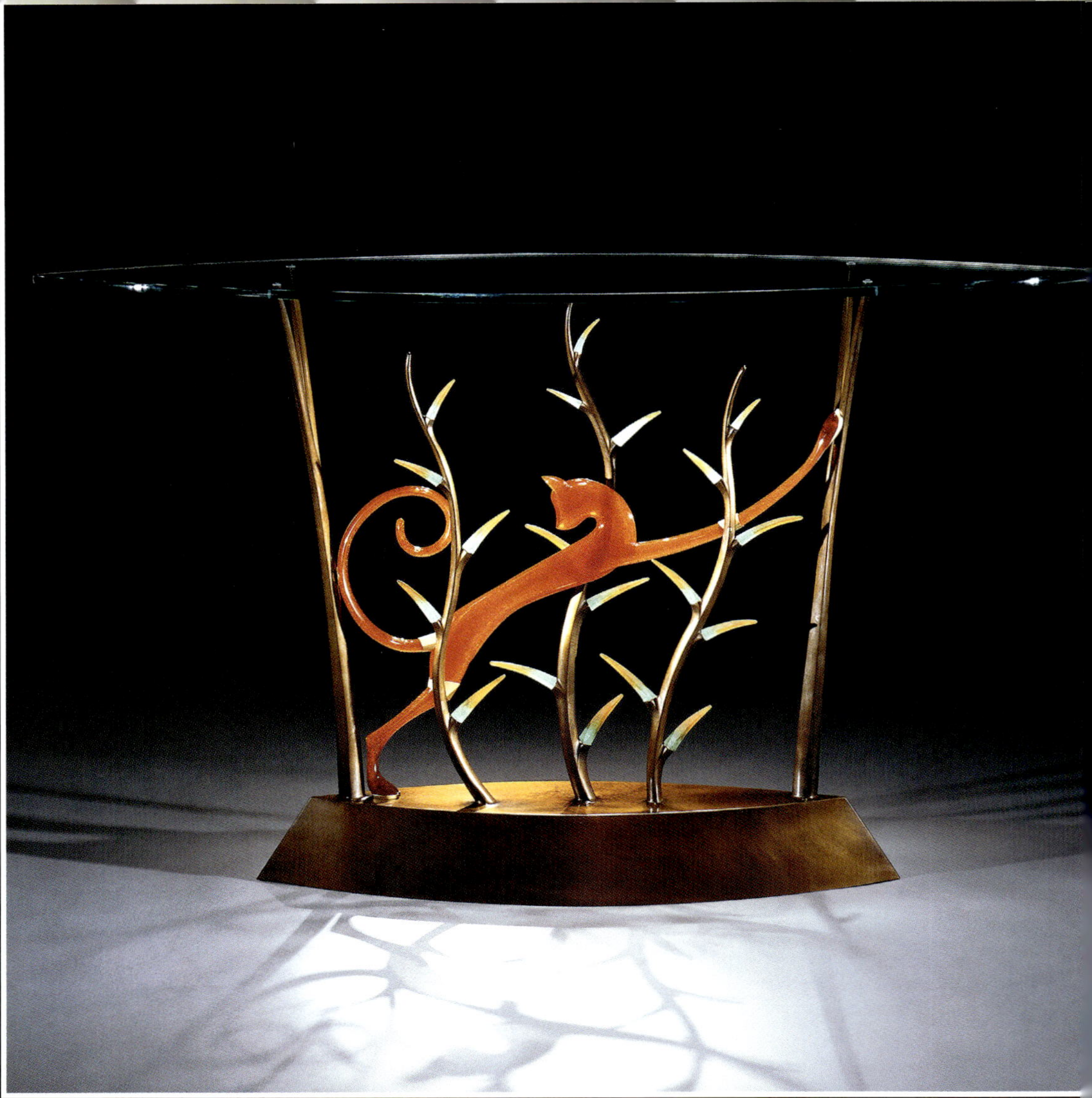

Ratteau's Puma (limited edition sculpture), Dan Dailey, 2000. Pâte de verre, plate glass, patinated cast bronze, 90 x 160 x 56 cm (35½ x 63 x 22 in.).

Photo: Noel Allum.

A large-scale bravura piece that extends the scale and application of pâte de verre into new areas, through its combination with plate glass and metals.

The Flower of Mediation Speaks the Truth of Dharma, Loretta Hui-shan Yang, 2004. L. 380 cm (12 ft 6 in.) x W. 78 cm (30¾ in.) x H. 18 cm (7 in.).
Loretta Hui-shan Yang makes reference to both Chinese philosophy and traditional art forms in her immaculately produced casts.

Similar to sandblasted and acid-polished glass, pâte de verre has a quality of capturing light and defining form. The ability to create colour blends in slabs of glass that can then be cut and fitted for incorporation into assembled sculpture has extended my palette greatly. Glass castings, in contrast to the look of blown, lamp-worked, cut and polished, or slumped glass, adds a variable method of creating shapes and colours. The diverse possibilities of glass provide me with endless ways to realise my ideas.

Loretta Hui-shan Yang

After a highly successful career as an actress, in 1987 Loretta Yang turned her attention to glass. She has since become China's best-known contemporary glass artist, and runs her own company producing pâte-de-verre casts of amazing quality.

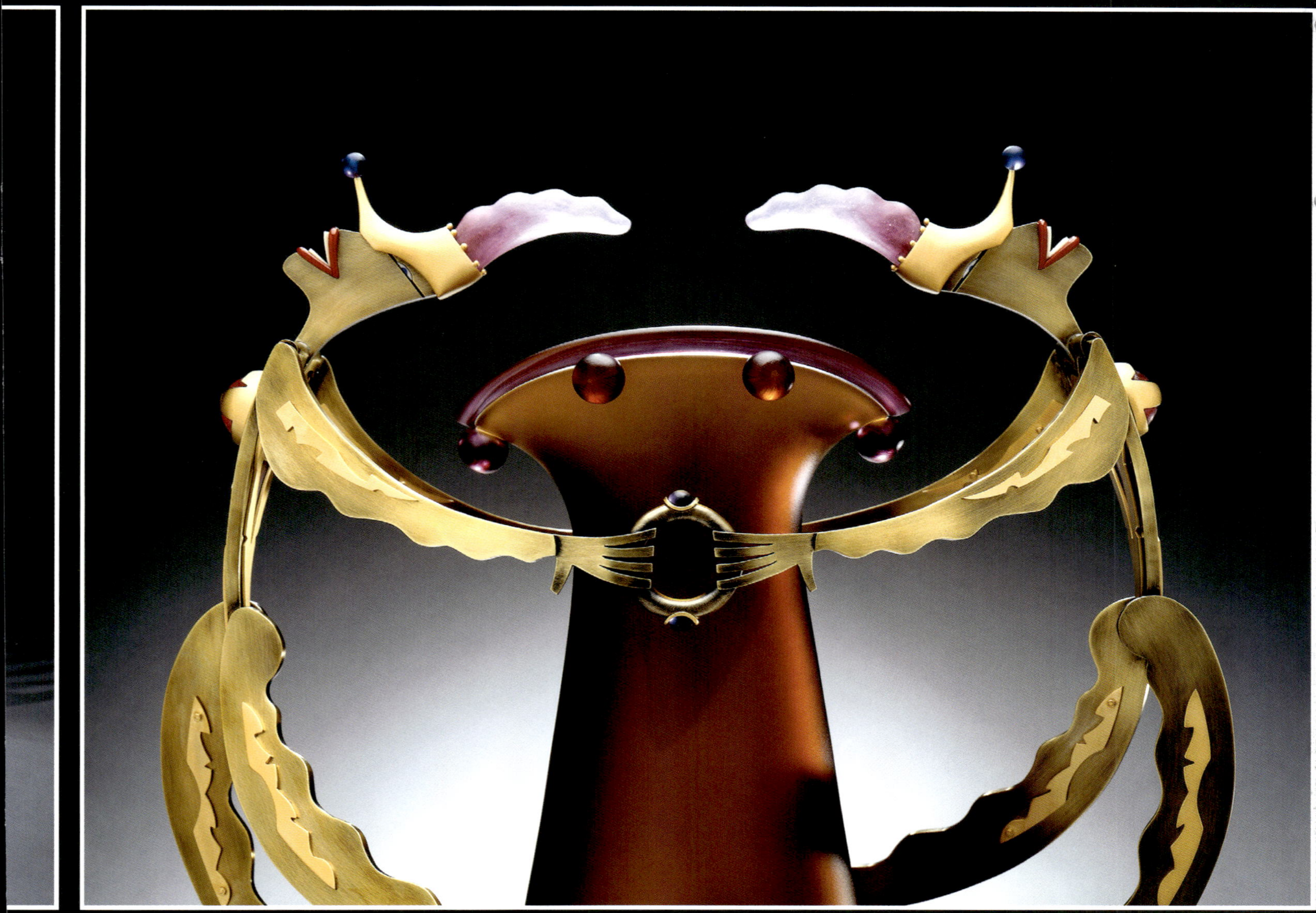

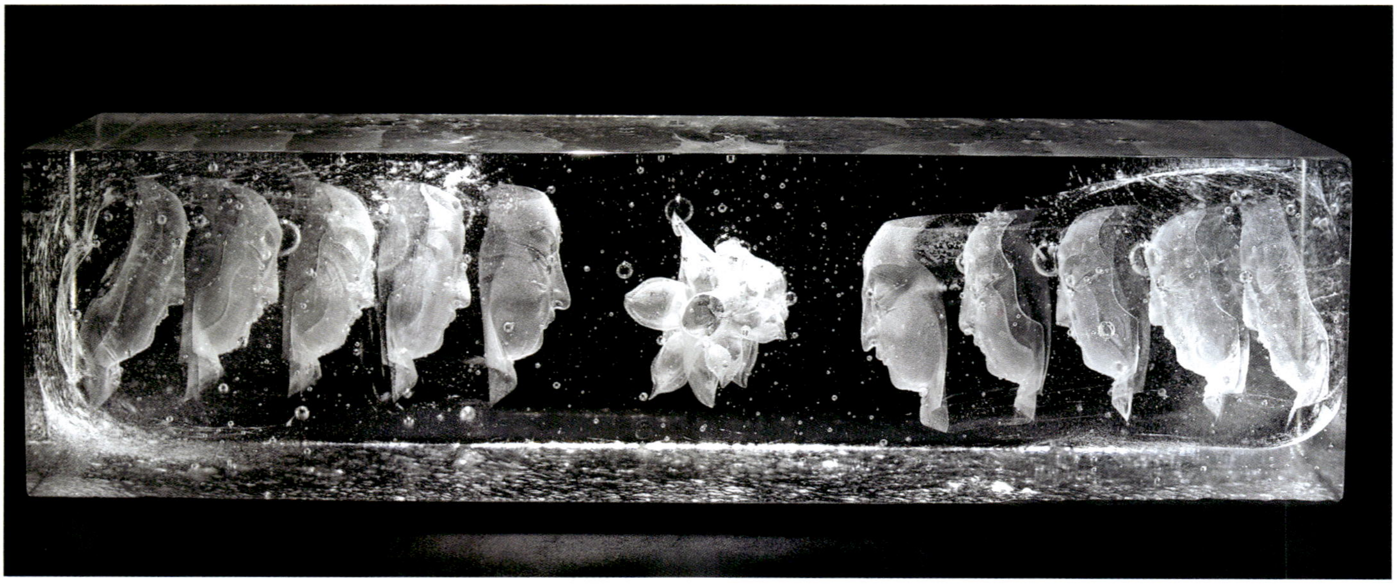

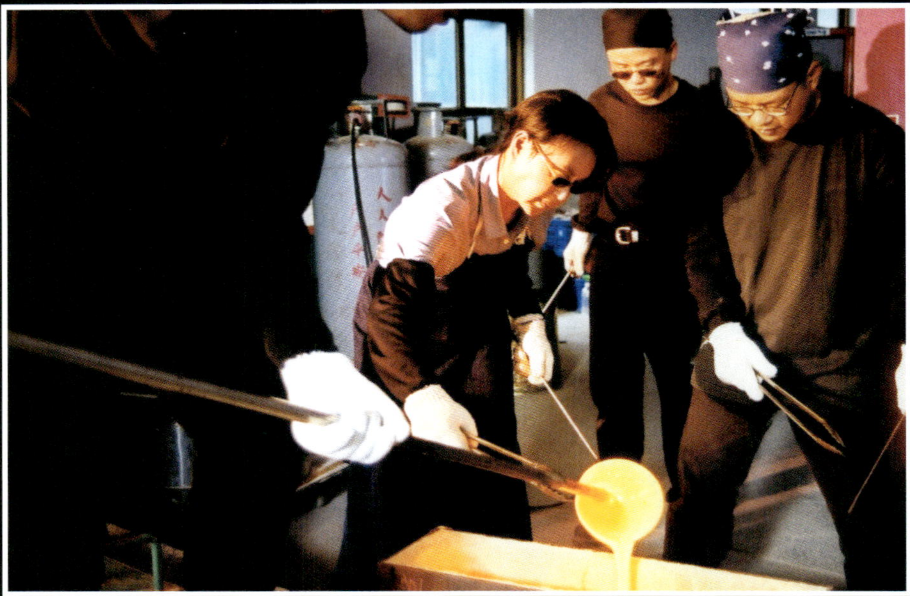

◄ Loretta Hui-shan Yang.

Photo: courtesy of the artist.

Pour-casting a single-colour sculpture. In common with an increasing number of artists Loretta Yang employs a number of different techniques to produce her work. Where single-colour quality is needed she casts directly from a furnace rather than inside a kiln. This increases control and limits the potential damage to the mould detail.

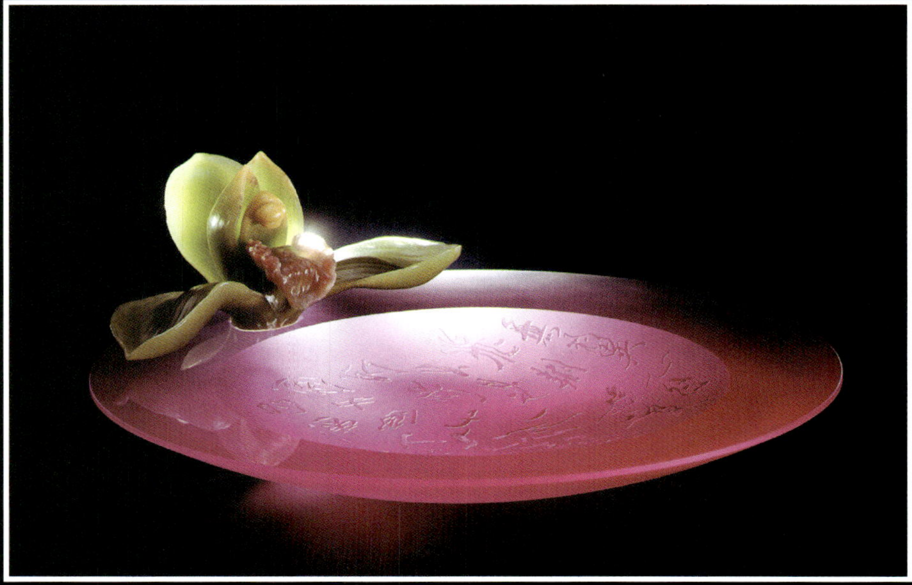

◄ *Reflection of the heart*, Loretta Hui-shan Yang, 2004. L.60 cm (23½ in.) x W. 65 cm (25½ in.) x H. 30 cm (11¾ in.).

This pâte-de-verre and cast molten-glass sculpture displays to great effect a control of texture and colour in the relationship between the lotus flower and the oval dish form. In common with bronze art forms these pieces are often produced as limited editions of around 12.

Artist statement

I began my pursuit of contemporary Liuli (glass) art in 1987, and in the process revived China's art of pâte de verre, a technique that flourished in China in the 4th century BC. For me, Liuli is an everyday art form. It is a meaningful creation exploring the brevity and bitterness in life, and the illusion of existence. Because it is fragile, and because of the games it plays with light, unique emotions are readily evoked.

Liuli serves to remind us of the concept behind 'impermanence'; our lives are at once beautiful and weak, infinite and impermanent; I have always believed that within the truth of Liuli lies the people's history and a seldom-seen possibility. Once it is endowed with humanistic qualities, this substance abounds with intrigue, satisfying me and filling me with joy.

Multi-process multimedia construction

This group of artists have one thing in common that prompts me to group them together: the fact that they all cross material or process boundaries. Despite the fact that I have been for most of my life associated with kiln-forming as a method of shaping glass, I have nevertheless always stressed the importance of cross-fertilisation, and the dangers of relying on a single material or process. All of these artists cross boundaries in their individual creative enquiries, and as a result produce work that could not have been achieved by kiln-forming alone. Some achieve this by combining glass forms and techniques, others by including other materials in their constructions. Most see themselves as artists who use glass rather than glass artists, and this is reflected in their personal statements.

Elizabeth Swinburne

Elizabeth Swinburne has never been content to work solely through any one glass method, preferring to let her creative enquiry find expression through a variety of materials and processes. As a result her output has been varied and consistent in its originality.

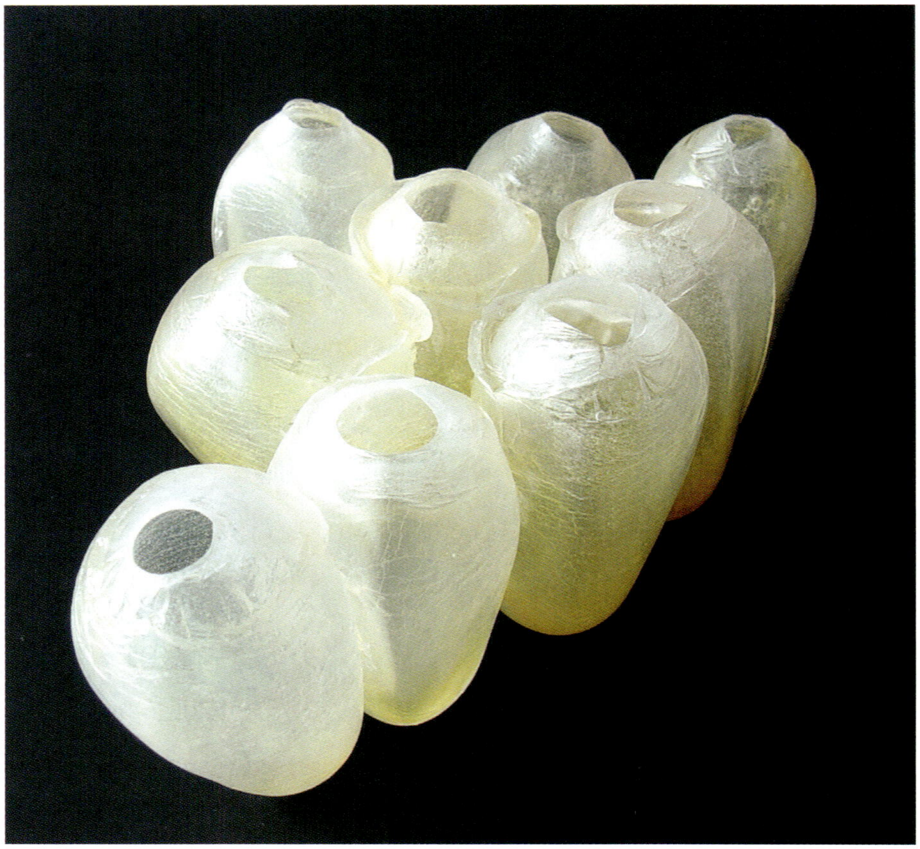

Golden Seeds, Elizabeth Swinburne, 2005. H. 11 cm (4⅜ in.), W. 33 cm (13 in.), D. 19 cm (7½ in.).

Photo: the artist.

Elizabeth Swinburne's current work illustrates an interesting trend, in which artists not only move between glass processes but are prepared to cross the barriers between them by using stages within different techniques in combination. The *Seeds* series is produced by fusing blown forms into groups in a kiln, their collapse being prevented by packing them internally and externally with powdered kiln mix. The resulting forms, while retaining their original blown shapes, gain beautiful distortions of their skins in addition to coalescing into a single piece.

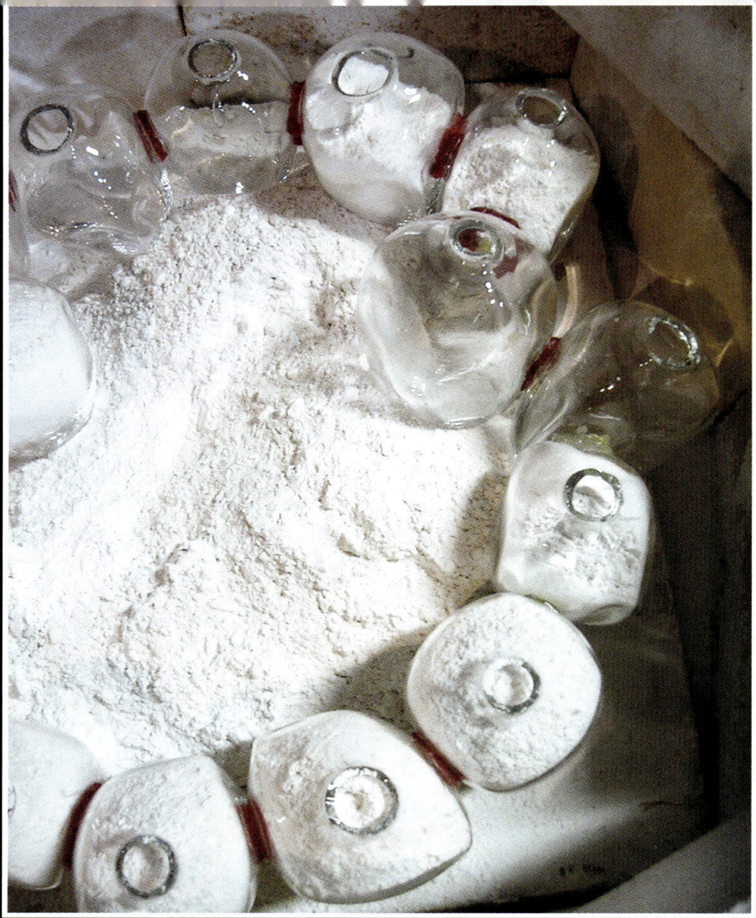

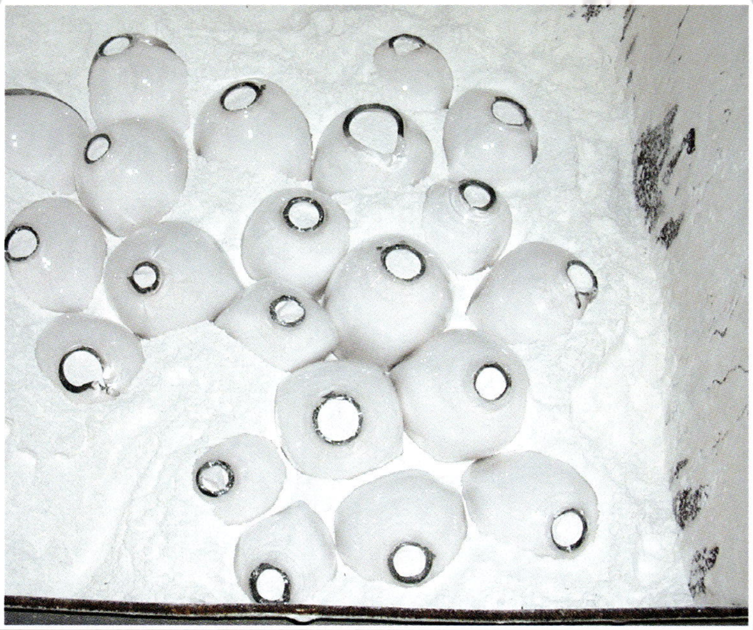

◀ Elizabeth Swinburne.
A piece in the kiln before firing, showing the individual blown-glass elements waxed together and part-filled with mould mix.
Photo: courtesy of the artist.

▲ A piece in the kiln completely packed with powdered kiln mix. After firing, the kiln-mix is removed to reveal the sculpture.
Photo: courtesy of the artist.

Artist statement

My most recent body of work explores ideas of subtle progression, growth and absence. It is important that the viewer has a sense of recognition rather than one of exclusion. With their first look they might see seeds or eggs, and from that starting point can begin a journey in their own imaginations. The objects are familiar, reminding one perhaps of the eggs of caterpillars discovered on the underside of a leaf, or the empty cocoon of a butterfly. Yet the works raise as many questions as they answer. What has emerged from these waxy shells of fragile glass? Was it ugly or beautiful, benign or harmful? Of course the 'thing' that has escaped or hatched from the work is my breath.

As in earlier works it is the surface or 'skin' that is important. In the past my interest has been in heightening the awareness of both the physical and metaphoric moment when we meet and touch. Today it is fragility, vulnerability and a sense of age that fascinates me.

Technical description

The objects that I am currently making use a combination of free-blown and kiln-formed casting techniques. Elements are first blown at the

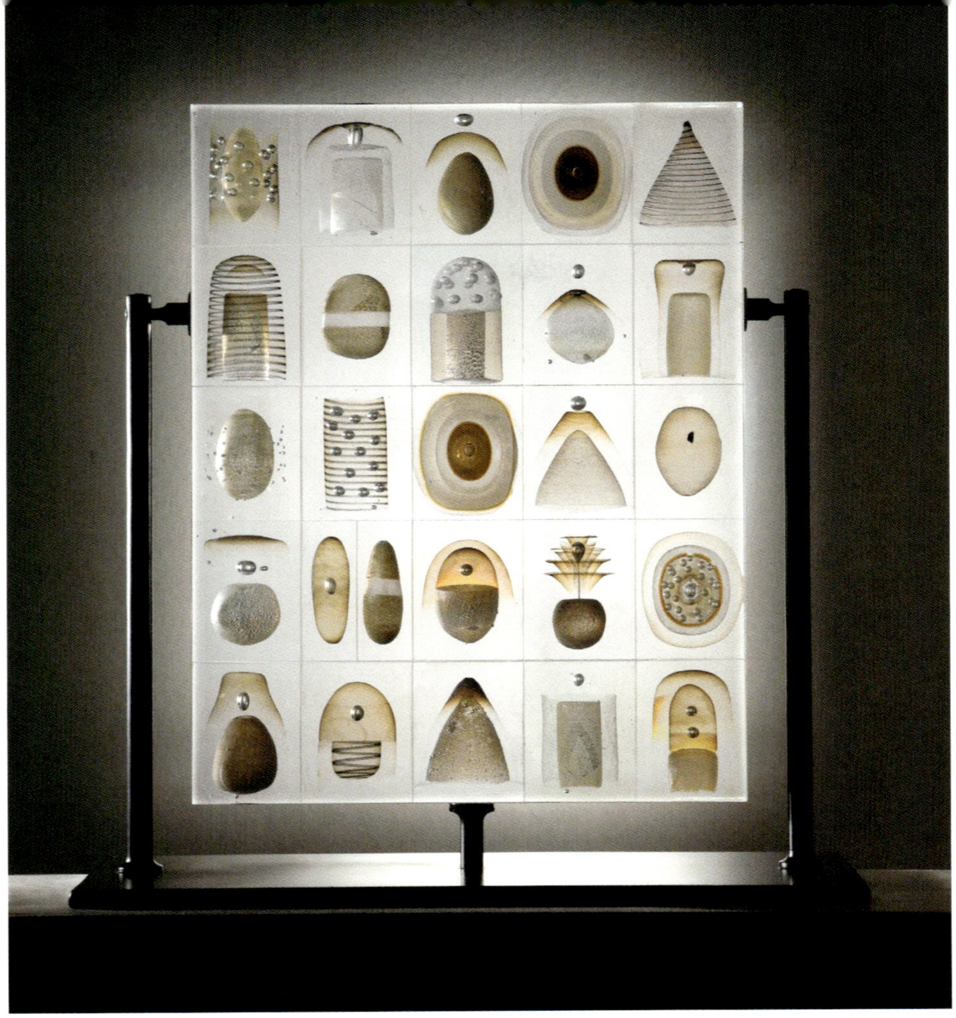

Specimen Panel, Steffen Dam, 2007. H. 50 cm (19¾ in.).

Photo: Steffen Dam.

Steffen describes his process as follows: 'Hot-worked objects are made in several layers divided by silver foil, carbon, glass powder or mineral powders. The object is dipped into the furnace to gather layers of clear glass around the object, enough to form a blocklike shape. After cooling they are ground to very exact measurements and angles. Groups of between 9 and 35 blocks are placed next to each other in the kiln, supported on all sides and very gently fused together. All surfaces are machine- and hand-ground and polished.' The way in which Steffen combines blowing, hot manipulation, kiln-forming and cold-working results in works which have many layers of rich textural and formal quality.

furnace, then once annealed they are assembled in a kiln and fired to a high casting temperature of just under 900°C (1652°F). A dry mould mix is used, enabling the delicate blown forms to survive the casting process while at the same time fusing together. The interiors are packed with dry mould mix to ensure that they retain their original forms.

It is this combination of glassmaking processes that gives the final objects their fluidity and 'glassiness', qualities which are usually only associated with molten glass.

Steffen Dam

Many artists who are renowned for their glass work started their creative lives studying through other media or disciplines. Steffen Dam belongs to this group, but is unusual in that he was trained initially as a toolmaker. However, after a number of years working in the metal industry, he changed his life by opening a studio to explore the material properties of ceramic and glass. In this sense he is largely self-taught; but surely echoes of his previous life inform his highly original glass pieces, not least in their exquisite precision, achieved by skill and a search for perfection. His

Steffen Dam cold-finishing a piece. ➤

The use of handheld grinders and polishers enables the artist to bring the device to a static piece of glass rather than bringing the glass to the machine. This allows for flexibility, and is invaluable for working on awkward-shaped and heavy forms.

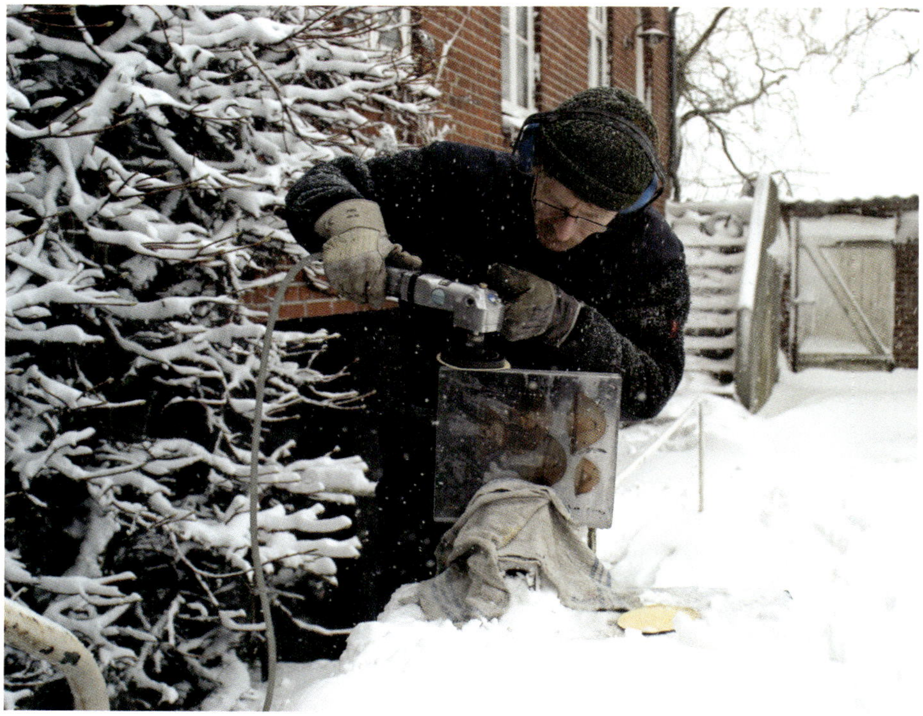

Black Perforated Bowl, Steffen Dam, 2006. D. 54 cm (21¼ in.). ➤

Photo: courtesy of the artist.

Steffen describes the making of this piece: 'This piece is made from sheet glass slumped into the desired shape. The idea is to drill away the plate, leaving only a structure describing the shape. Since the drilling is done with something that looks like an ordinary drill press, and the glass is handheld while doing so, there is a limit to the closeness of the holes if one wants a reasonable chance of the piece surviving. There are up to 750 holes in some pieces.'

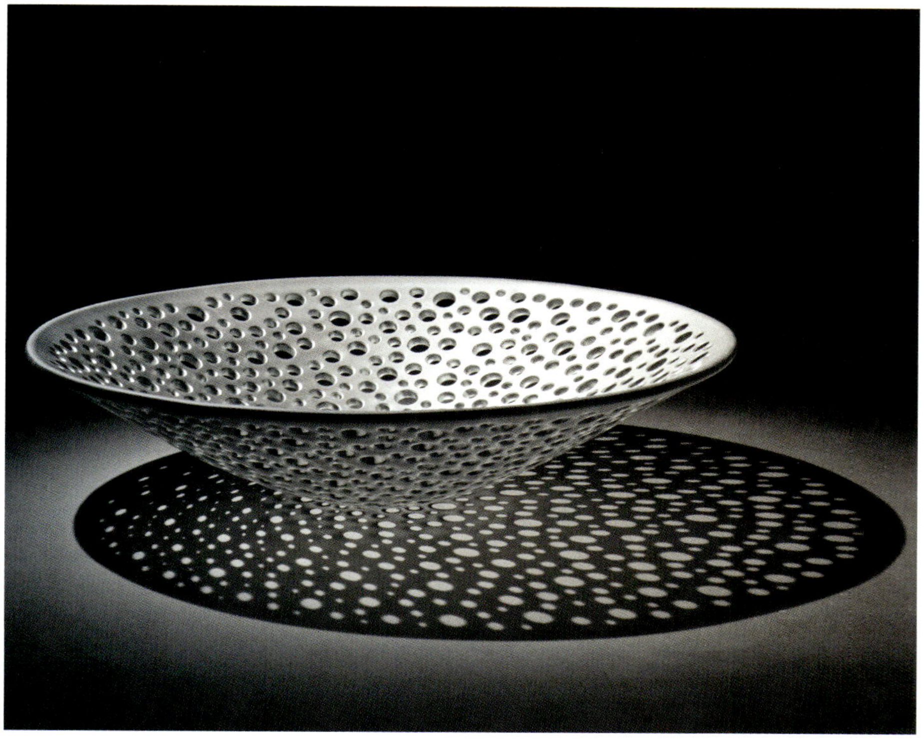

combinations of blown and hot-glass forms, by encapsulation in fused panels, painstakingly cut and polished, are highly unusual and personal. The drilled and slumped dishes also display something of the engineer's aesthetic in their combination of solid and void.

Artist statement

I originally trained as a toolmaker and worked for some years as such before I realised that my curiosity spanned more than that which is simply measurable. In glass I found these qualities. The uncompromising nature of this material exactly fitted the precise and analytic way of thinking that I was taught in constructing industrial tools.

During my first ten years of glassmaking I was practising and experimenting with all of the different techniques to become a good craftsman. While doing so, I discovered a new kind of beauty in the fringes of the well-crafted glass I was making. In the area of faults and mistakes – the unwanted air bubbles, ash marks, soot, cracks and crookedness – I found something that could not be predicted or sketched beforehand. I set the established and traditional techniques to one side, and started making glass 'all wrong' in an attempt to capture the good in the bad. Out of these experiments came the 'Fossils', 'Plants' and other objects, like frozen extracts of chaos to be watched undisturbed.

The other side of my work is exploring the fundamental qualities of glass: transparency and the ability to accumulate and bend the light. At present, this has resulted in the bowls and plates with drilled holes. As these have progressed, the objects have become more air than glass. These two sides of my work, the accurate and the freely expressed, could be interpreted as a contradiction, but they are not. Each side feeds off the other; the accurate work is the foundation for free expression, and vice versa.

Gerhard Ribka

Gerhard Ribka, like many of the artists in this group, uses glass very much as a fine-art medium. While the line between the decorative and fine arts is becoming ever more blurred, and to some extent unimportant, there are extremes at either end of the sliding scale that extends from one to the other. This is generally reflected in the statements that have been provided by the artists, with the use of medium to express a philosophic, poetic or moral standpoint indicating a more mainstream, fine-art approach. However, I feel that this is a horizontal rather than a vertical line, with the perceived differences between one extreme and the other being a matter of type rather than hierarchy. In any case, once objects exist and take their place in the public domain, they have a habit of redefining themselves many times over, according to their cultural context and the time that has passed since their manufacture.

This does not mean, of course, that artists' statements are irrelevant or

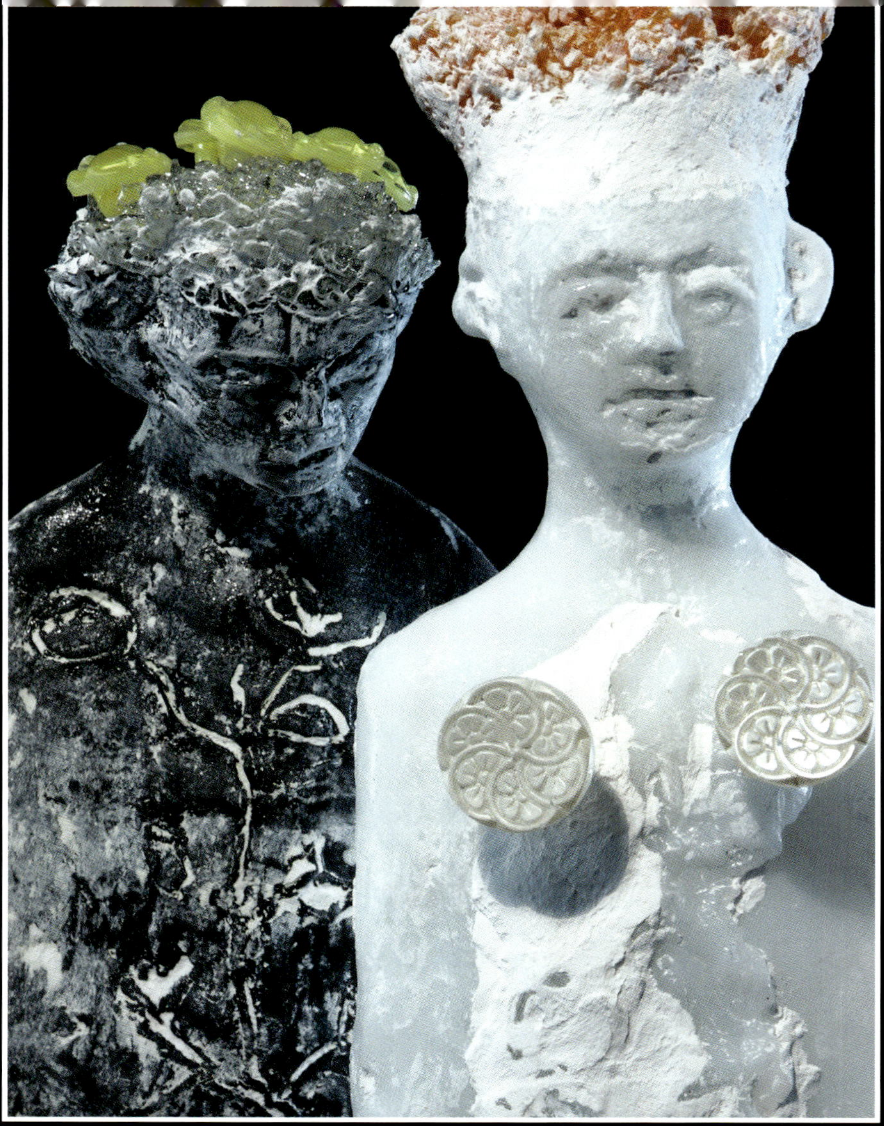

Behind You, Gerhard Ribka, 2005. ➤
Kiln-cast glass, refractory, glass button, H. 16 cm (6¼ in.) (tallest).

Photo: courtesy of the artist.

Gerhard Ribka's attitude to every aspect of his work is determined by the sculptural atmosphere he wishes to create. 'Finish' for him can mean leaving parts of the refractory mould as an essential part of the finished work. He combines a range of materials with glass to both extend and challenge conventional expectations.

Doubts But, Gerhard Ribka, 2007. ➤➤
Kiln-cast glass, brass, oil paint, lead. H. 26 cm (10¼ in.), W. 14 cm (5½ in.), D. 14 cm (5½ in.).

The enigmatic qualities of Gerhard's pieces are the result of his painterly approach to making, combining and finishing his sculptures. Kiln-formed glass is the essential, dominant factor, but its free association with an uusual variety of materials adds much to their power.

misleading, merely that they reveal the spirit and motivation that brought them into being rather than fixing their categorisation for all time. Read in this spirit they are both interesting and enlightening.

Artist statement

For my sculptural work I employ the lost-wax process. As a refractory mould material I use Luminar Mix. The glass is mostly Kugler granules, which are like fine sugar, though I sometimes use other glass, like Poschinger (Bavarian Forest) cullet, with pieces up to 4 cm (1½ in.) thick.

The models I make mostly in wax, though sometimes in clay which is then recast in wax via a cold-set silicone rubber. The models are handmade using images as inspiration or as a starting point, e.g. Greek terracotta figures or ancient Turkish figurative sculpture. Recently, I have started using found objects like dolls or doll parts, which are also cast in wax via silicone.

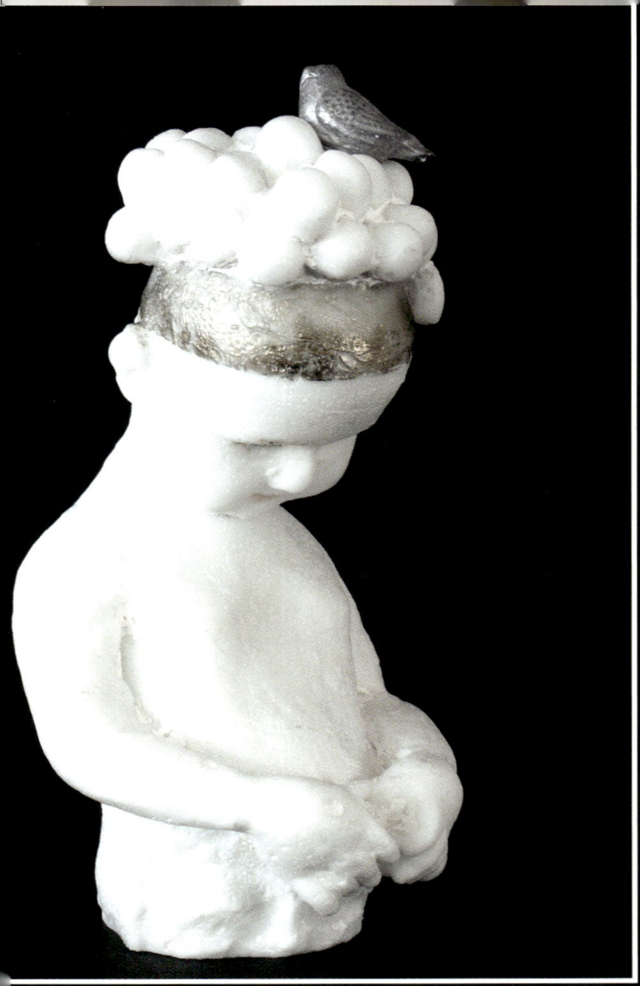

Bait, Gerhard Ribka, 2006. Kiln-cast and kiln-formed glass, sandblasted, stained, wire, silicone, H. 23 cm (9 in.) ➤

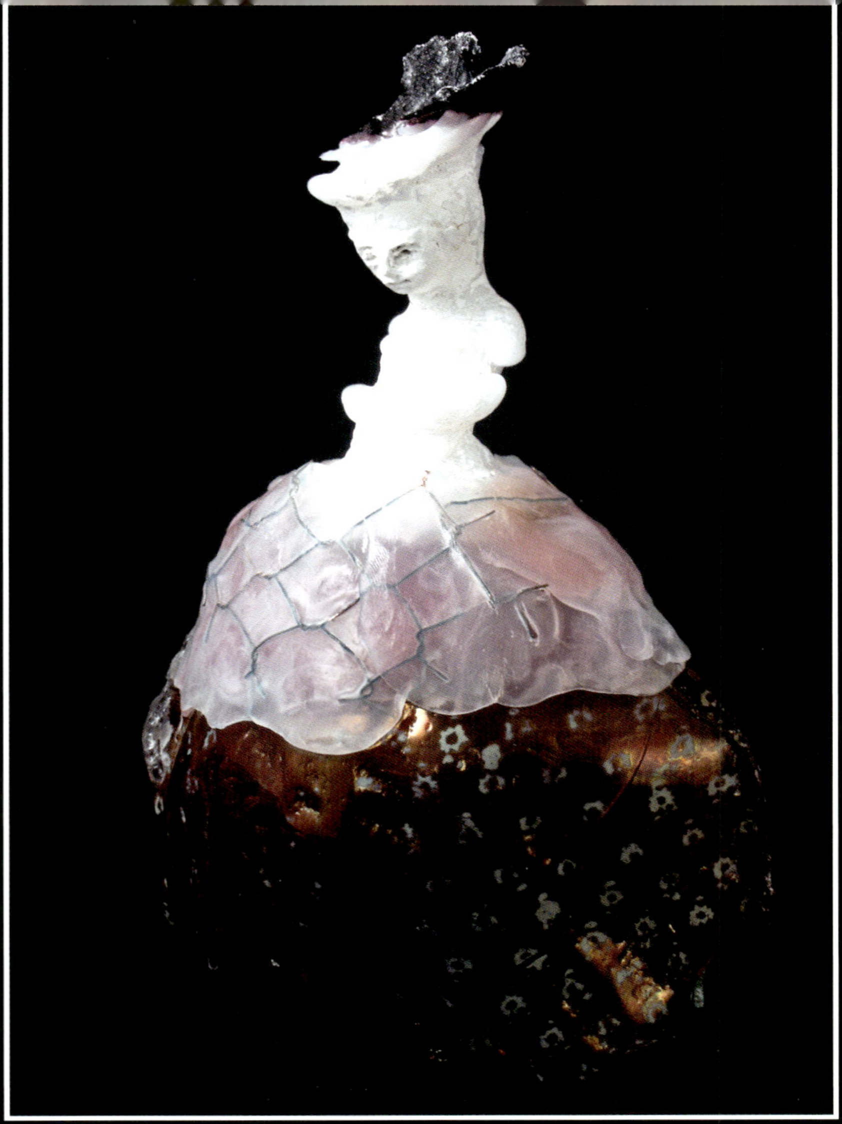

The process of working on the cast glass is very important to me. Each one of the following may be used to develop the image from its raw, as cast, state:

1 Removing only parts of the refractory mould.
2 Applying pigment, metal leaf/coatings or wax.
3 Combining smooth and coarse areas of the glass surface using different firing temperatures.
4 Using an opaque glass, which is etched to create a more stone-like character, or playing with the transparency/translucency of clear glass.
5 Combining with other materials like paper, papier mâché, metal or silicone.
6 Adding detail with oil paint.

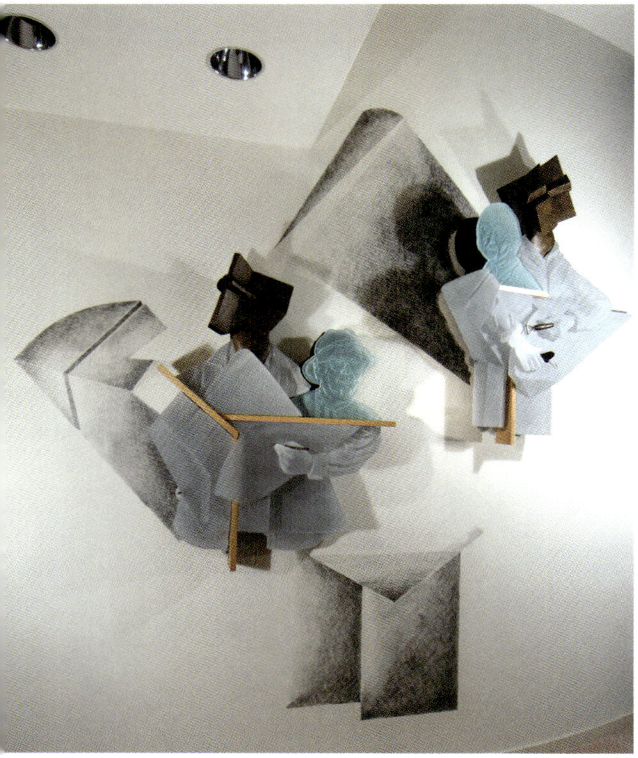

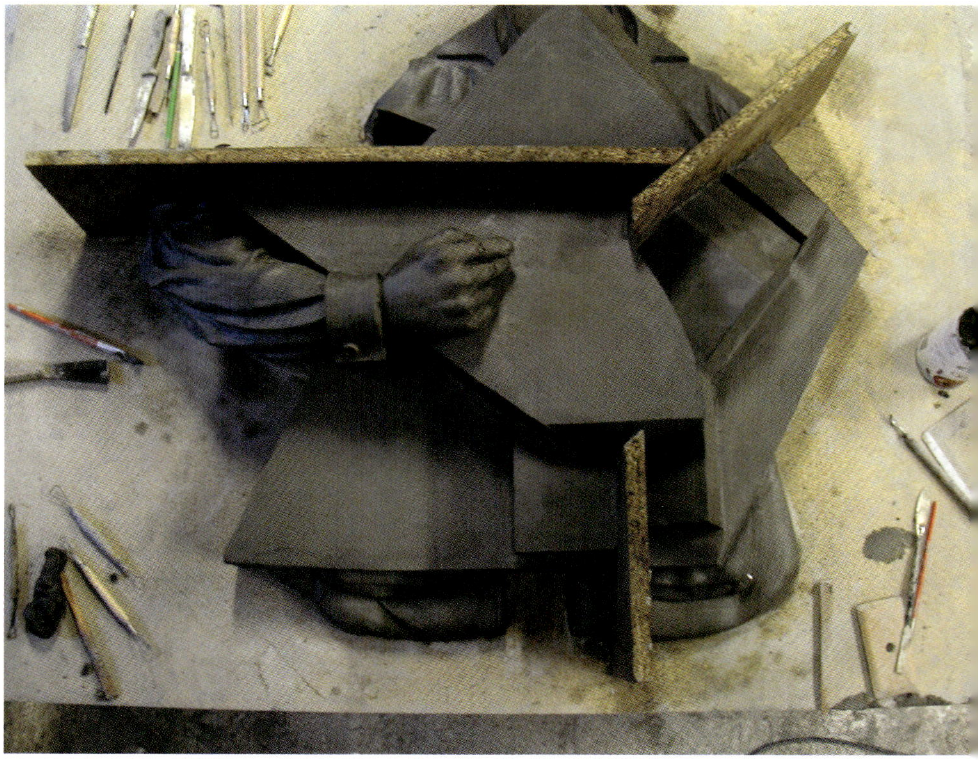

▲ *Libensky-Brychtová*, Steve Linn, 2004.
H. 351 cm (11 ft 6 in.), W. 305 cm (10 ft),
D. 30 cm (12 in.).

Photo: Mark Haiman.

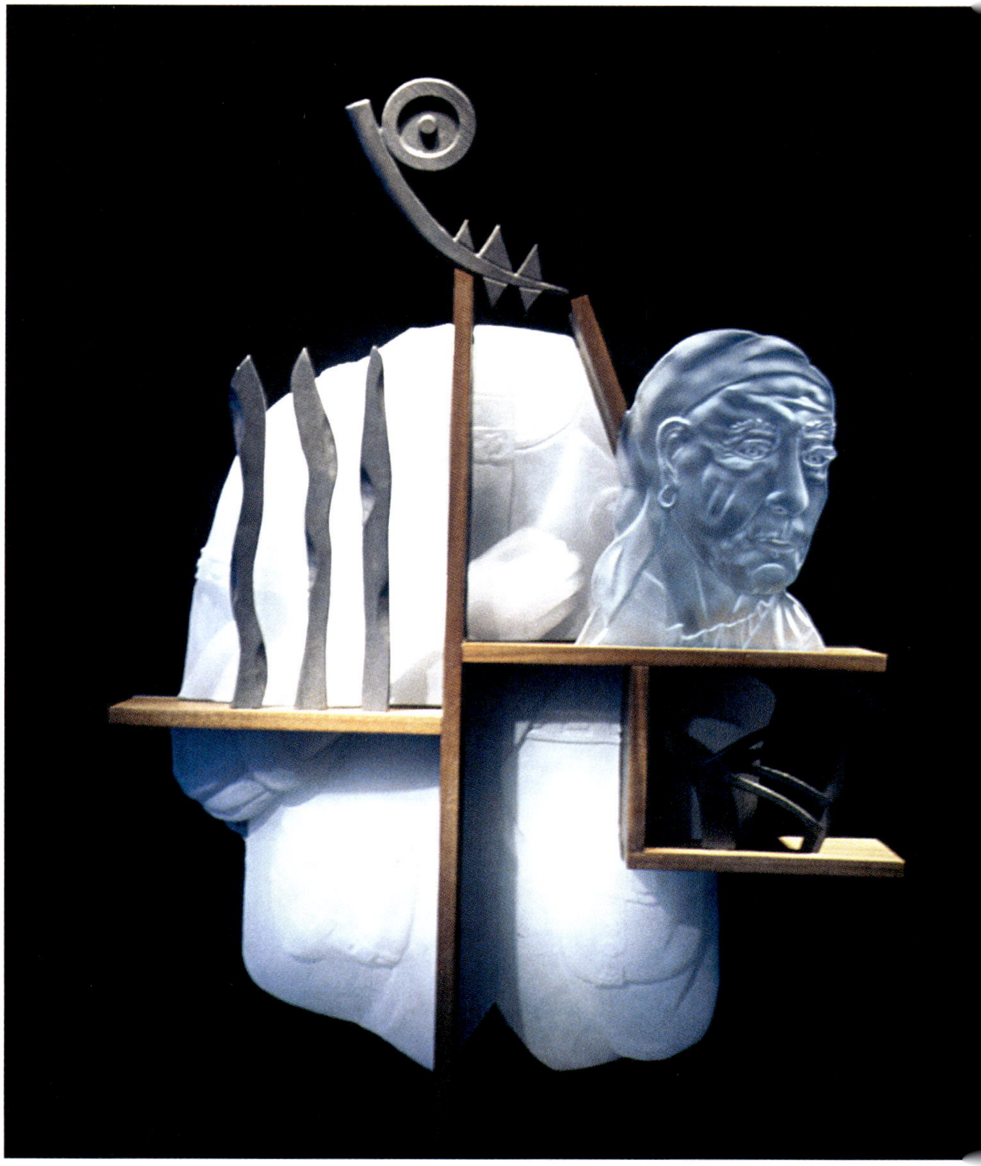

Steve Linn describes himself as 'a documentary sculptor, usually working in a large format, telling stories of peoples lives'. His use of glass, employing many forms and techniques, in combination with wood and bronze (among many other materials), means that his commitment is to the integrity of the final piece. His approach is in refreshing contrast to much derivative, craft-based sculpture; he is an example of someone who uses glass in his work but is not dependent on its inherent qualities for the effectiveness of that work. His works are perhaps best described in his own words: '*Libensky-Brychtová* attempts to show the dynamics of the working relationship between this extraordinary couple that collaborated in creating their spectacular and revolutionary work. Starting, as they did, with a Libensky drawing, I began this portrait with a very large-scale drawing directly on the wall.'

There are solitary figures, more geometric in form. Sometimes, however, these figures form groups. They are either solid glass or parts of them are hollow, being made from wire mesh or slumped float glass instead of being cast. The more recent solitary figures have acquired a partner, smaller in size and made of a different material.

In parallel to my sculptural work I produce written texts. For some texts I use fairy tales as a starting point, mainly their storyline, as a catalyst or guideline. For others I use found photographs, just as I use images of ancient sculpture as starting points for my three-dimensional work.

◄ Steve Linn.
Clay model for *Libensky-Brychtová*, demonstrating intensive development of the idea prior to the use of glass.

Photo: courtesy of the artist.

Steve Linn

Artist statement

In the realm of art, which for me is about ideas and the artist's ability to communicate them, I have carved out a small space for myself that is occupied by few others. I am a documentary sculptor, usually working in a large format, telling stories of other people's lives, some well-known, others not. By using a three-dimensional picture plane filled with visual information and objects, I attempt to develop the histories surrounding the characters that I depict. Yes, there is usually an image of my subject, but that is only a part of the whole piece. It is the rest that makes these portraits unique.

◄ *Boxes of Dreams*, Steve Linn, 2003. Multimedia wall piece, H. 110 cm (43¼ in.), W. 76 cm (30 in.), D. 17 cm (6¾ in.).

Photo: the artist.

Lots of research and reading, along with kiln-formed glass, sandblasted flat glass, cast bronze and carved wood, are brought together to define each sculpture intellectually and visually. In the two pieces chosen to be represented in this book, the first, *Libensky-Brychtová*, attempts to show the dynamics of the working relationship between this extraordinary couple, who collaborated in creating their spectacular and revolutionary work.

Starting, as they did, with a Libensky drawing, I began this portrait with a very large-scale drawing directly on the wall, done as a background. Next there is an interpretation of the drawing as the rest of the piece emerges, showing both their separate and collective work. To define the subject, I used as a basis for this sculpture the concept and construction of their piece entitled *Bird*, dating from 1985.

The other selection, *Boxes of Dreams*, is about Louise Nevelson, and goes to the heart of the personality and force of this grande dame of sculpture. She is featured as part of the stacked boxes of assembled found shapes, which she acquired as scraps from woodshops and then built into monumental walls of controlled power and elegance. Fashion-conscious to the end, I saw her often in the street in Soho, New York, where we both lived for many years.

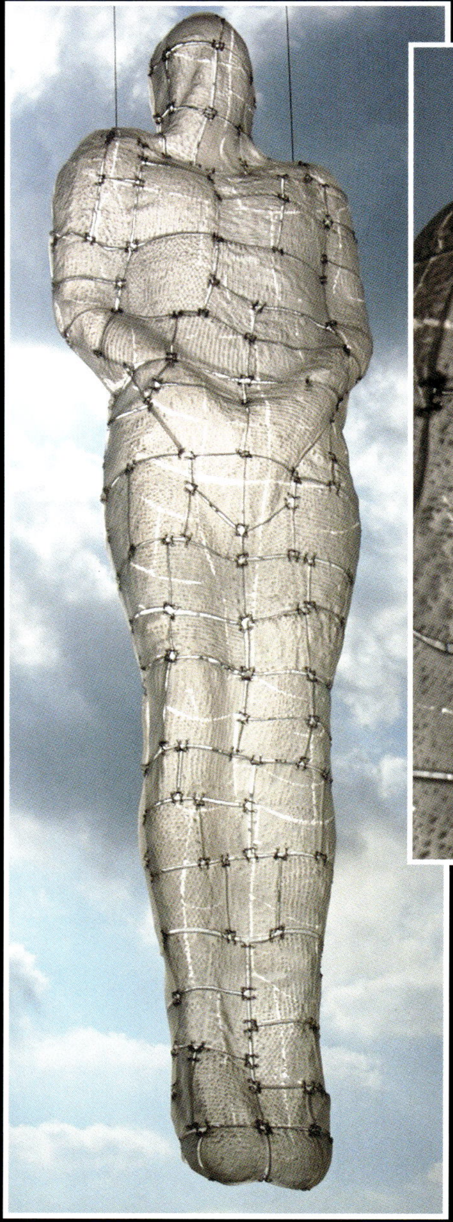

Albion, Max Jacquard, 2004. Fused and slumped Artista glass and bronze wire. H. 180 cm (71 in.) W. 58 cm (23 in.) D. 30 cm (12 in.).

Photo: the artist.

A monumental life-size piece made from a large number of slumped pieces. Each piece carries a separate part of the profile; and the entire form is cleverly constructed. The production of large-scale sculptures from glass usually carries with it penalties in terms of weight and fragility. Max Jacquard sidesteps these problems with his creative construction methods and his use of suspension to present this work.

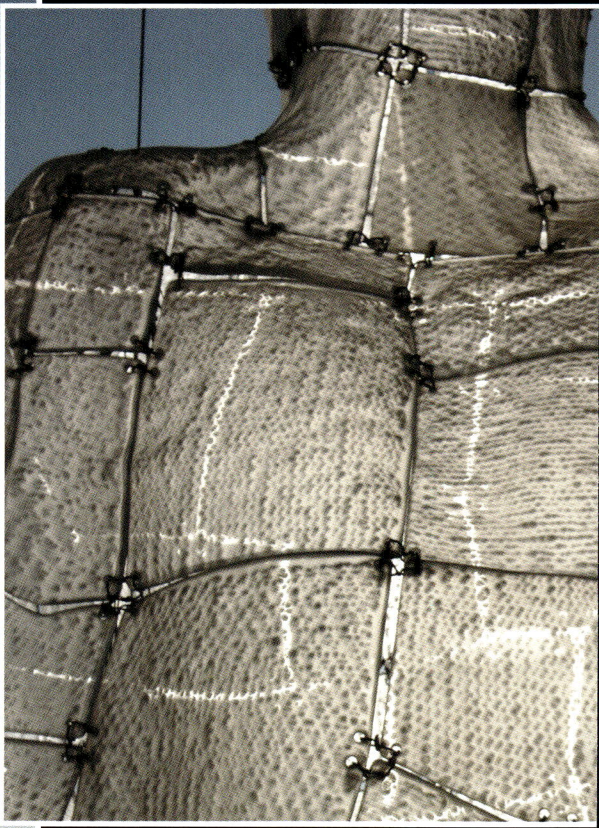

Max Jacquard (detail).

Photo: courtesy of the artist.

Max Jacquard

Max Jacquard's work is characterised by its range and diversity, both in terms of his use of glass and in the themes that he tackles in his work. He is not constrained by any single material (although glass is his main medium) or by any single formal vocabulary. It is therefore not possible to present any example that is typical of his output as a whole, so I have chosen instead to show only one small area. I have selected one of his constructions which, in keeping with the aims of this book, shows an area of glass use that is unusual and, I hope, of interest to artists and students because of the possibilities it seems to suggest.

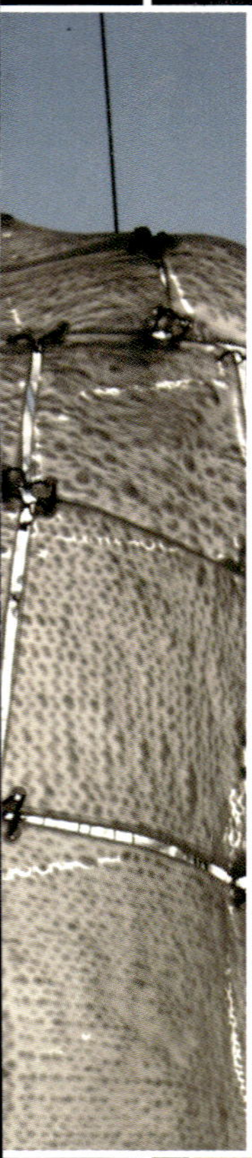

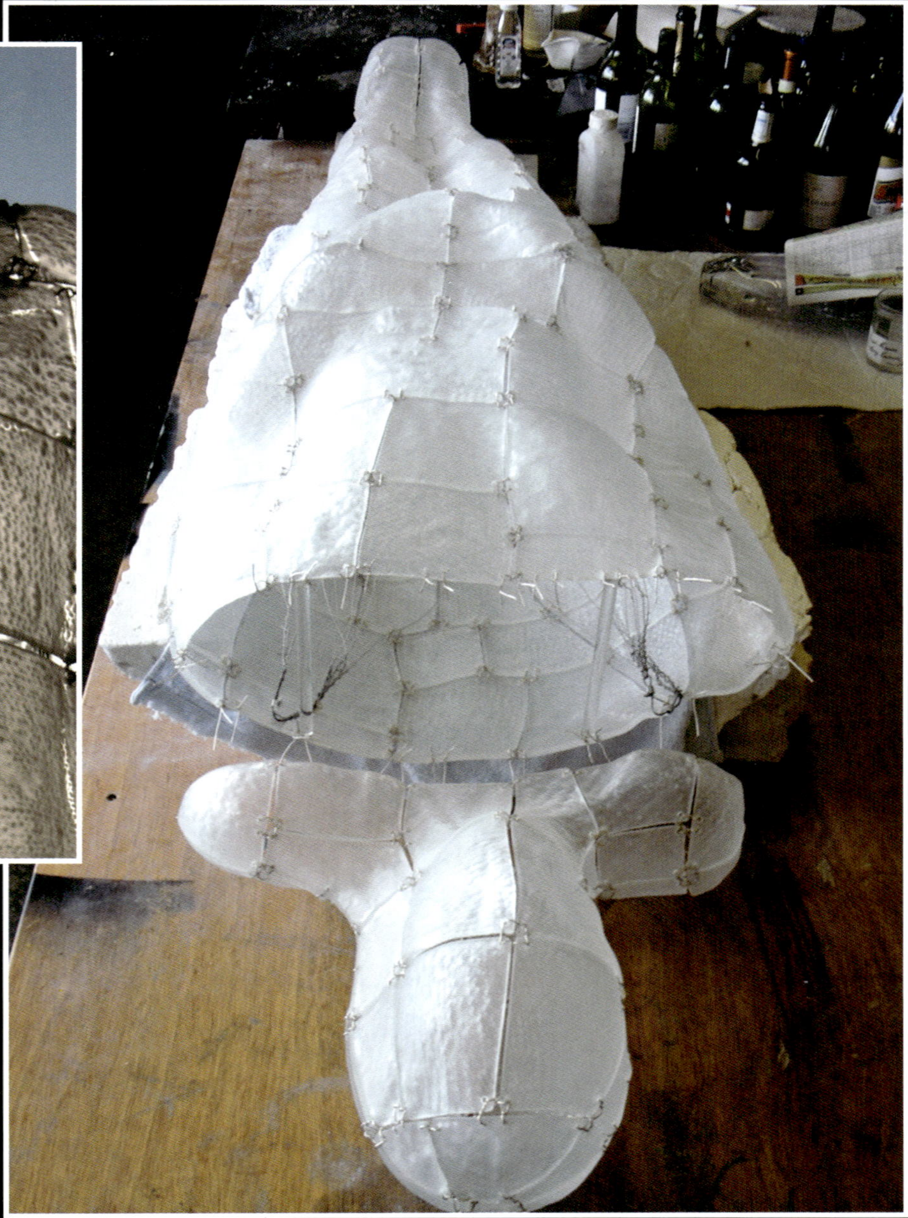

Max Jacquard (detail of construction).

Photo: courtesy of the artist.

The apparent looseness of construction brings with it great advantages. The large-scale form can be dismantled and reassembled for transportation, and damaged sections can be replaced.

Artist statement

My work contains narratives that are forged, knitted together and layered. Personal memories and associations interweave with aspects of archaeology, mythology, folk traditions and human relationships with nature.

Glass is used metaphorically – not just for its contemporary, tactile qualities, but the history and alchemy of its transformation. The simultaneous presence of internal/external elements, the contrast of strength and durability with brittleness and fragility, the play of light and shade – all make reference to the corporeal and ethereal worlds in which we exist.

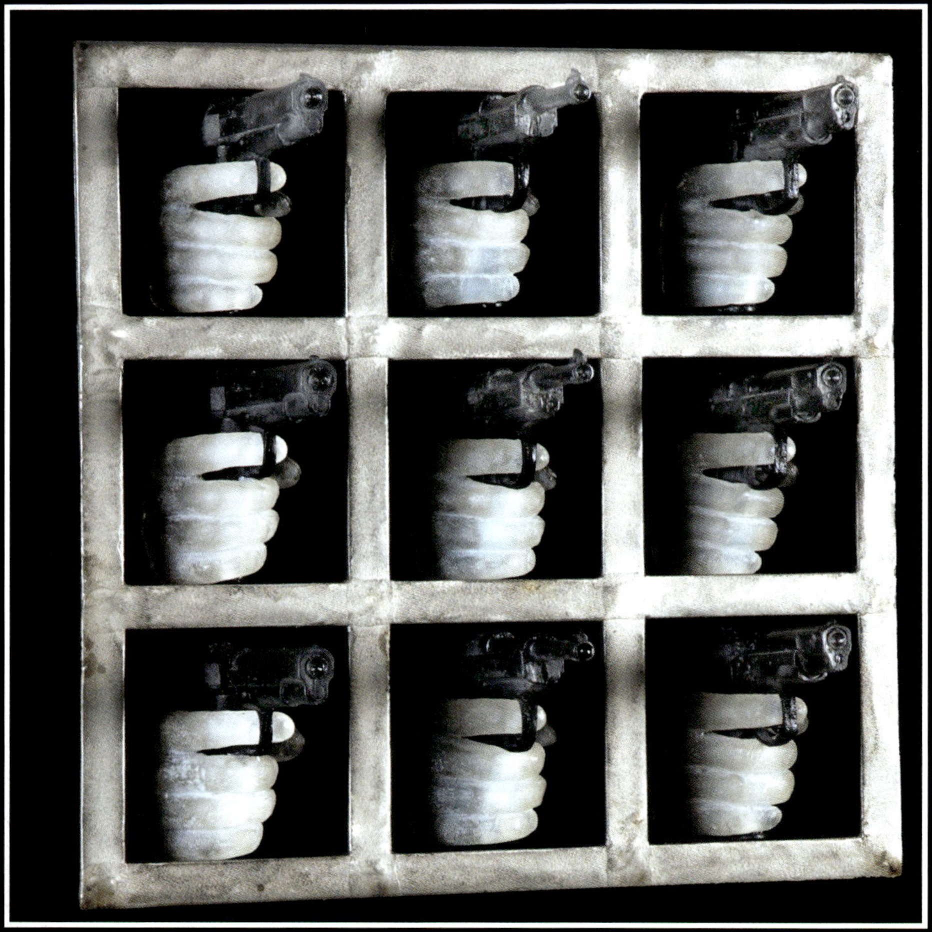

Armed Men, Janusz Walentynowicz, 2002. Kiln-cast glass, welded steel. Flame-sprayed stainless steel. H. 53 cm (21 in.), W. 53 cm (21 in.), D. 20 cm (8 in.).
Photo: courtesy of the artist.

An artist who is not afraid to confront major issues in his work, Walentynowicz's approach to material and technique is equally bold. He uses a variety of materials in combination with glass; he always reserves glass for elements that exploit its special qualities to the full. The guns and arms in this piece are cast by lost wax and assembled in the metal frame.

Rage Aid, Janusz Walentynowicz, 2002. Kiln and sand-cast glass, 38.5 x 24 x 20 cm (15⅛ x 9½ x 8 in.).
Photo: courtesy of the artist.

The gun was kiln-cast by lost wax, then enamelled, heated and set into molten glass ladled from the furnace into a pressed sand mould. The frame is welded steel. In common with the other artists in this group Janusz demonstrates how the artificial barriers between glass techniques can be fruitfully broken down.

Janusz Walentinowicz

Janusz Walentinowicz uses glass, arguably one of the most beautiful and decorative of materials, to tackle issues of life and death. His design sense and craftsmanship are used to produce works of great visual quality that, like a Trojan horse, release their serious message only after they have captured our attention and admiration.

Artist statement

The subject matter in this body of work is somewhat at the far periphery of what I normally deal with in my work, but as almost on a daily basis I have to drive by the slogans of the Guns Save Life organisation, posted as 'roadside poetry', they eventually caused a reaction.

'Guns Save Life,' the slogans state, referring to the hypothetical number of lives saved by families protecting themselves with firearms against

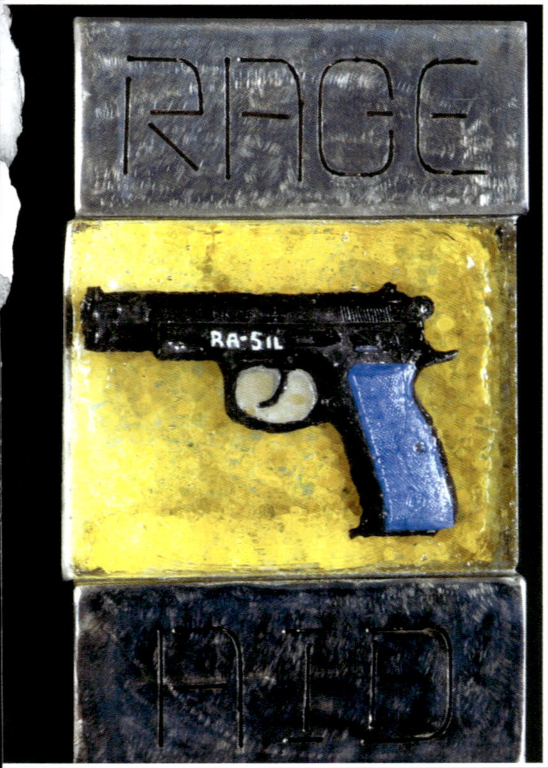

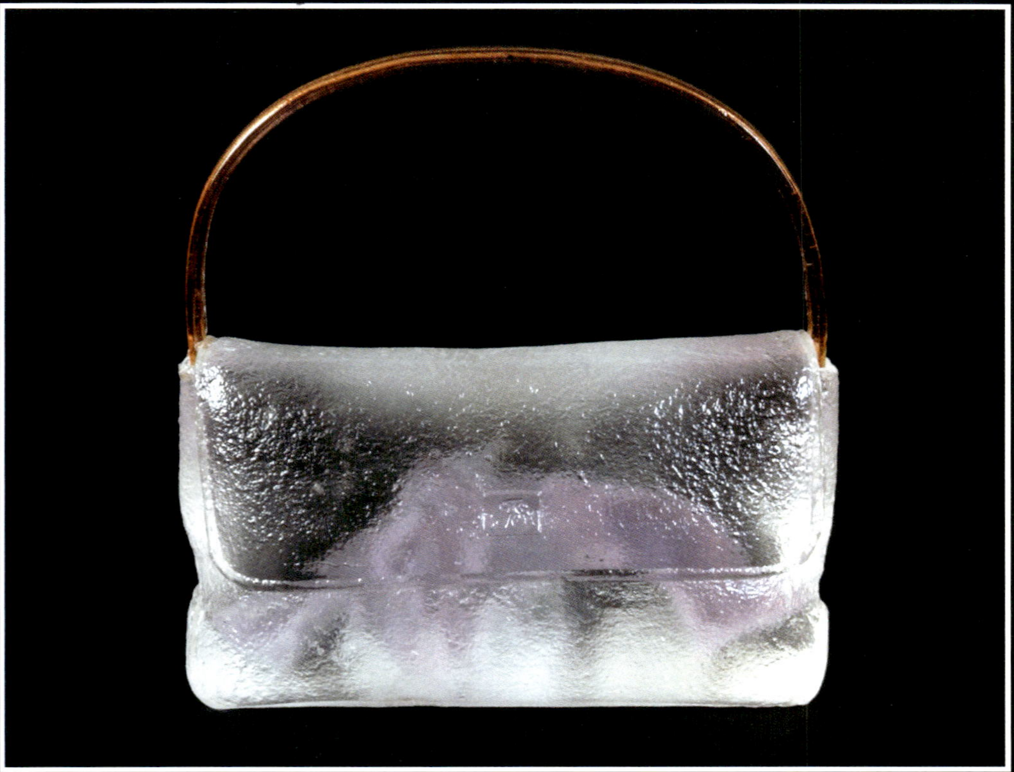

Purse with Gun, Janusz Walentynowicz, 2002. 23 x 23 x 9 cm (9 x 9 x 3½ in.).
Photo: courtesy of the artist.

Janusz describes the making of the sculpture: 'The gun was kiln-cast by lost wax. A refractory shell was made from a wax of the purse. After the shell was fired it was placed inside a metal box, which was filled with resin-bonded sand and baked; this was to enable the mould to withstand the pressure of the hot glass. The purse mould was then ladled into with hot glass, and the gun, again heated to about 510°C (950°F), was picked up and pushed into the molten glass from the bottom of the purse, which was the top of the mould. The handle was produced from a strip of Bullseye sheet by flattening and slumping.'

intruders; but the many lives lost due to tragic accidents and mistakes, where unfortunately kids are often the innocent victims, are not accounted for. To be effective in home defence, guns must be within reach and either loaded or with ammunition nearby, where in turn kids might find them and cause the tragedies we know all too well from the news. On the other hand, an intruder will often be a teenage kid making the misjudgement of his life by breaking into a home, very likely unarmed, and paying with his life for a mindless mistake.

Are we really honest when claiming that the gun we have is for self-defence? Or is the truth more that we want to take revenge on any intruder on our personal space? How can we argue that more and easier access to hand weapons will lead to greater safety?

Masayo Odahashi

Masayo Odahashi produces figures that are cast in glass through the lost-wax process. Lost wax, also known as *cire perdue*, was developed in Greece and China over 2,000 years ago to produce bronzes. It has only been adapted for glass-casting in the modern era, starting with artists like Frederick Carder. Masayo's use of glass enables her to both cast and colour the figures by selective use of enamels, which are painted onto the cast and re-fired, achieving the enigmatic and ethereal qualities that she seeks.

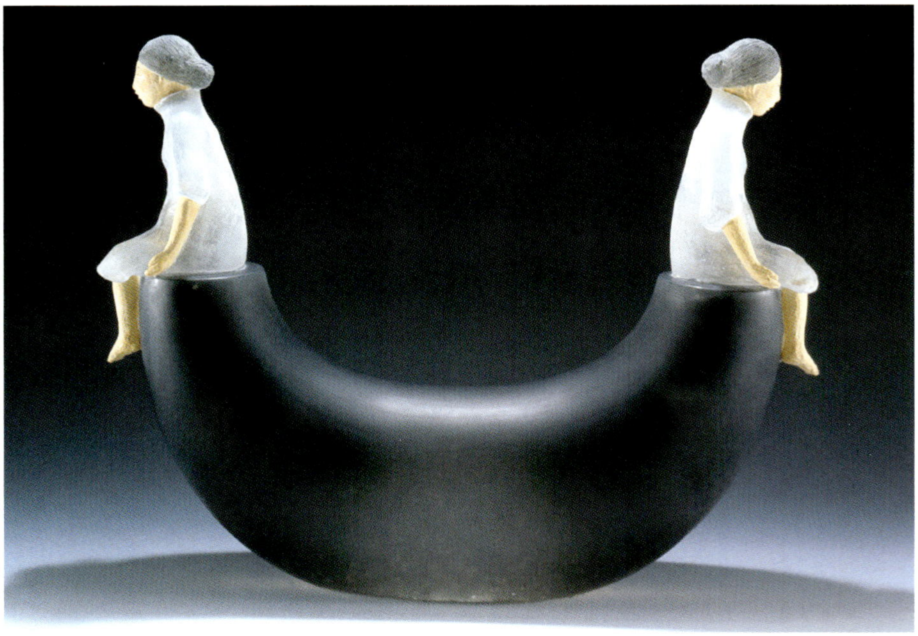

Balance, Masayo Odahashi, 2007. W. 57 cm (22¼ in.), H. 40 cm (15¾ in.) D. 14 cm (5½ in.).

Courtesy of Morgan Contemporary Glass Gallery, Pittsburg, PA, USA.

In the creation of her enigmatic figures Masayo Odahashi extends the range of kiln-casting to give her a wider vocabulary of qualities to draw on. Her figures are kiln-cast in fine frits, but are then removed from the mould and selectively painted with high-fired enamels. They are then reinvested and re-fired, to fix the enamels and retain the precision of the original. Selective finishing, including polishing, adds more range and subtlety to the final piece.

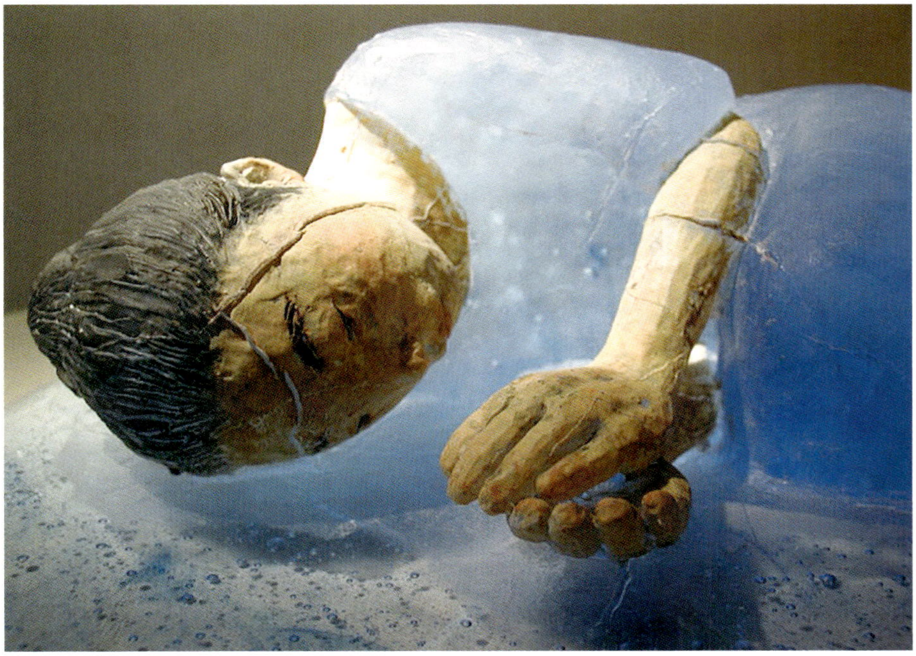

Deep Sleep III (detail), Masayo Odahashi, 2007. H. 36 cm (14 in.), D. 13 cm (5 in.).

Courtesy of Morgan Contemporary Glass Gallery, Pittsburg, PA, USA.

This detail shows the controlled, multilayered qualities that the artist achieves through her original combination of kiln techniques.

Artist statement

I am interested in the things we all share, but which do not show up so clearly: emotional changes arising from the process of living, or shared experiences, or memories that are acquired day by day. I am creating compositions to make people aware once more of these inchoate things we all have in common. I also see these creations as a way to share my world view; they are a way of getting my ideas across. You will find glass that fills the vessel of the body, and which faintly shines, as if to indicate what exists within.

Si Cheng

China has only recently included glass as a university subject. Most of its lecturers have been trained in the West, and the departments set up since 2000 have tended to follow the use of glass as a medium for personal

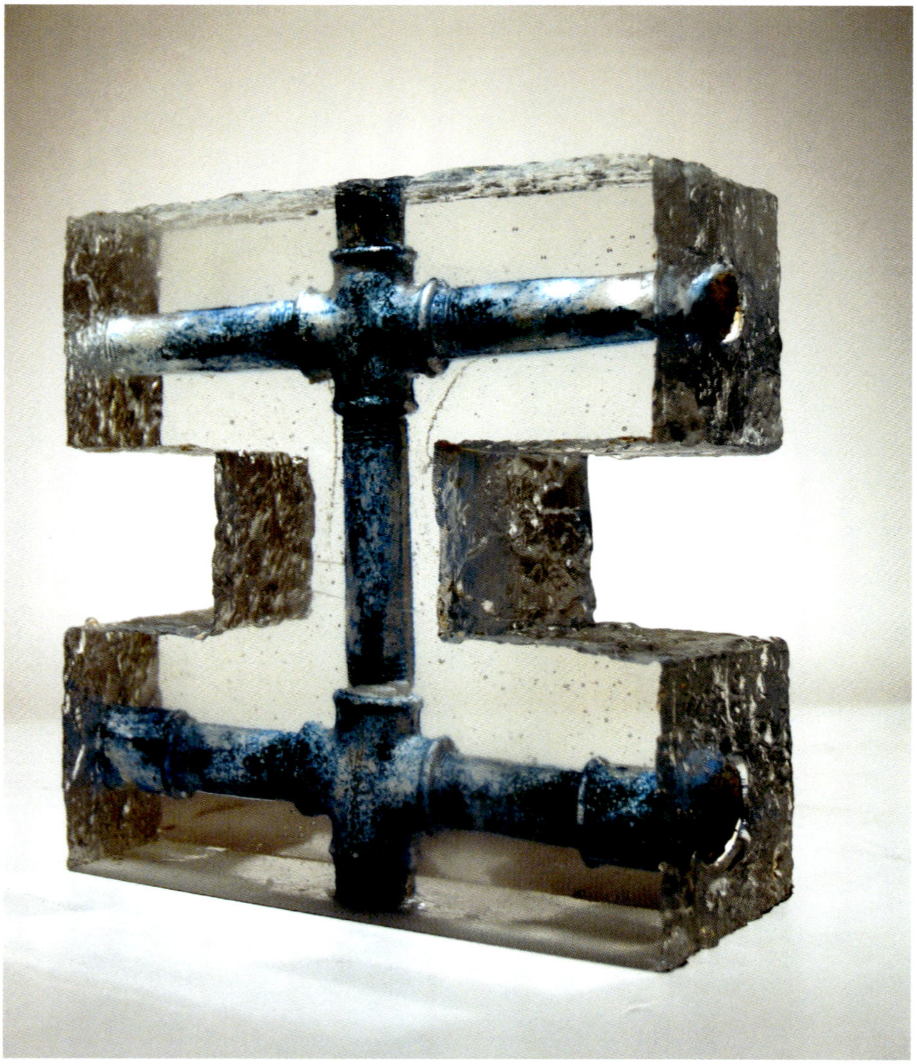

◀ *Chinese Character*, Si Cheng, 2007. 20 x 20.5 x 8.5 cm (7⅞ x 8⅛ x 3⅜ in.). Photo: courtesy of the artist.

Si Cheng is one of the new generation of artists working in glass in China, itself a newcomer to the global studio-glass movement. In this piece Si Cheng shows not only that he is looking to his own culture for inspiration (the piece is based on a Chinese symbol), but also that he is seeking to extend the accepted limits of kiln-casting. The piece is cast with a refractory core in place which is removed after firing, giving the glass mass a hollow illusory form running through it.

expression, with kiln-forming as the main method of choice. It is interesting to see that both Si Cheng and Dong Hai Guan have chosen to reflect their own history and culture in their work, and in doing so have, at the same time, pushed the boundaries of established casting techniques.

Artist statement

This piece is one of my *Chinese Characters* series. The outline of the piece is of a Chinese character, while the internal void, on which colour is scattered, is in the shape of a pipe, which runs through the entire work. This can be seen through the transparent glass that makes up the form.

This series expresses my attitude to my cultural heritage. The use of language to express ideas is symbolised by the letter as an outline. The pipe is used to represent the real, physical world; the two depend on each other, but are also independent.

Keith Cummings

As one of the oldest (living) artists in this volume, my involvement with glass stretches back almost half a century. In common with many of my contemporaries my art education did not initially include any glass. This was simply because it was not available, even as a component on courses, let alone as a subject in its own right, when I began my art education.

The birth and growth of the global studio-glass movement had at its core the attempt to master the diverse range of techniques that can be applied to the material, and to harness them for personal studio use. The pioneering Wisconsin workshops of Harvey Littleton, for example, had

Blush, Keith Cummings, 2008. H. 22 cm (8⅝ in.), W. 18 cm (7 in.), D. 7 cm (2¾ in.). ➤
Photo: Simon Bruntnell.

The base of this piece is a lost-wax cast in finely crushed soda glass. The colour is kiln-oxidised copper and silver wire, and the striations are the deliberate result of topping up the mould as the glass settled. Holes were cast in the base to act as anchors for the fabricated metal vertical bars. The oval piece was achieved by drilling a hole in one piece of glass and substituting another colour to fill the hole. These two pieces were then fused and slumped into a curved mould to create the distortion. The piece was then selectively cold-finished.

Keith Cummings, detail of *Blush*. ➤➤
Photo: Simon Bruntnell.

The movement of the coloured insert during slumping into a convex mould can clearly be seen.

Keith Cummings. Wax model with wire inserts. ➤
Photo: Simon Bruntnell.

This wax model, which provided the form for *Leonardo's Mountain*, was built onto a constructed card base, which minimised the amount of wax to be steamed from the mould. Silver-plated copper wires have been laid into the surface of the wax to create colour, texture and linear detail in the final cast. Copper dust has also been brushed onto the high surfaces to become absorbed into the mould surface.

Leonardo's Mountain, Keith Cummings, 2008. H. 19 cm (7½ in.), W. 17 cm (6¾ in.), D. 17 cm (6¾ in.). ➤➤
Photo: Simon Bruntnell.

The cast, in standard soda glass, has picked up the wires and powders and oxidised them. All of the colour in an otherwise colourless glass has been created by the impact of the metals on the softened glass during firing. The insert was created from a cold-set rubber cast of the declivity, and a mould produced from this was used to cast the glass 'pool'. The 'Mona Lisa' image is an enamelled oval placed into the concavity prior to the rubber cast, and which fits into the base of the glass pool.

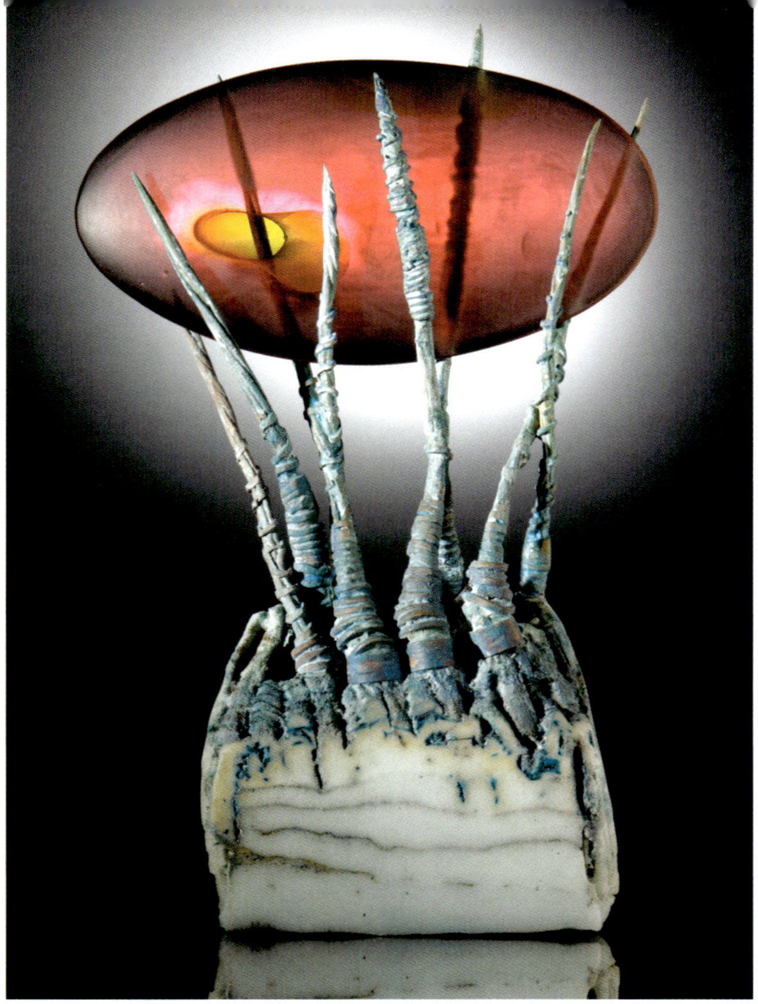
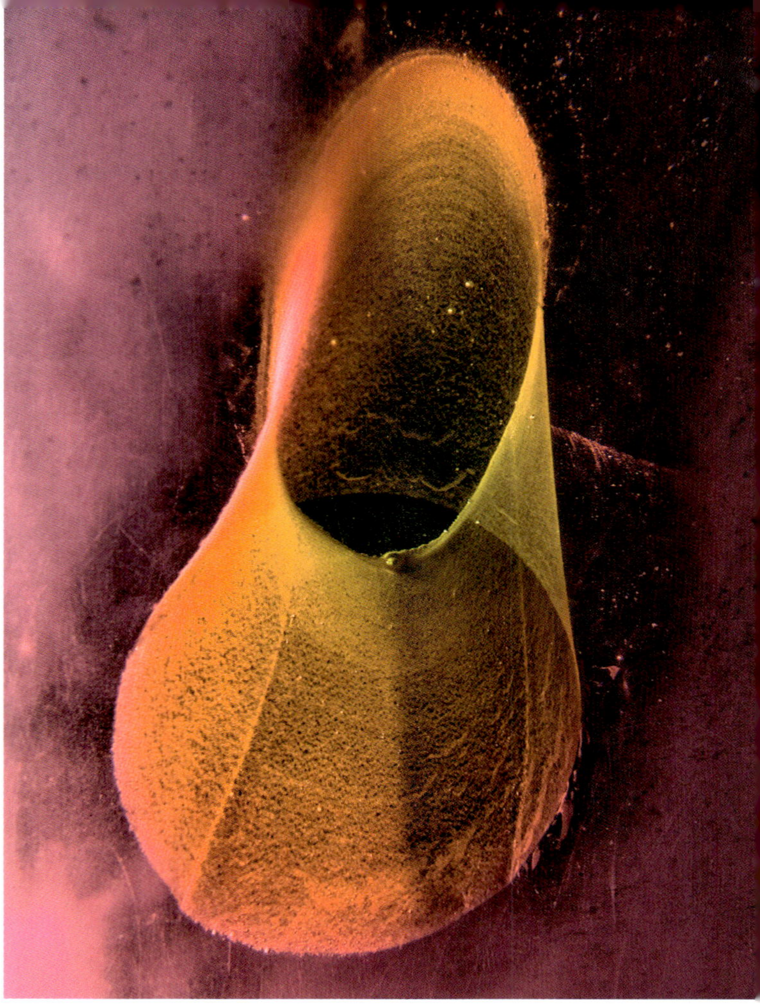
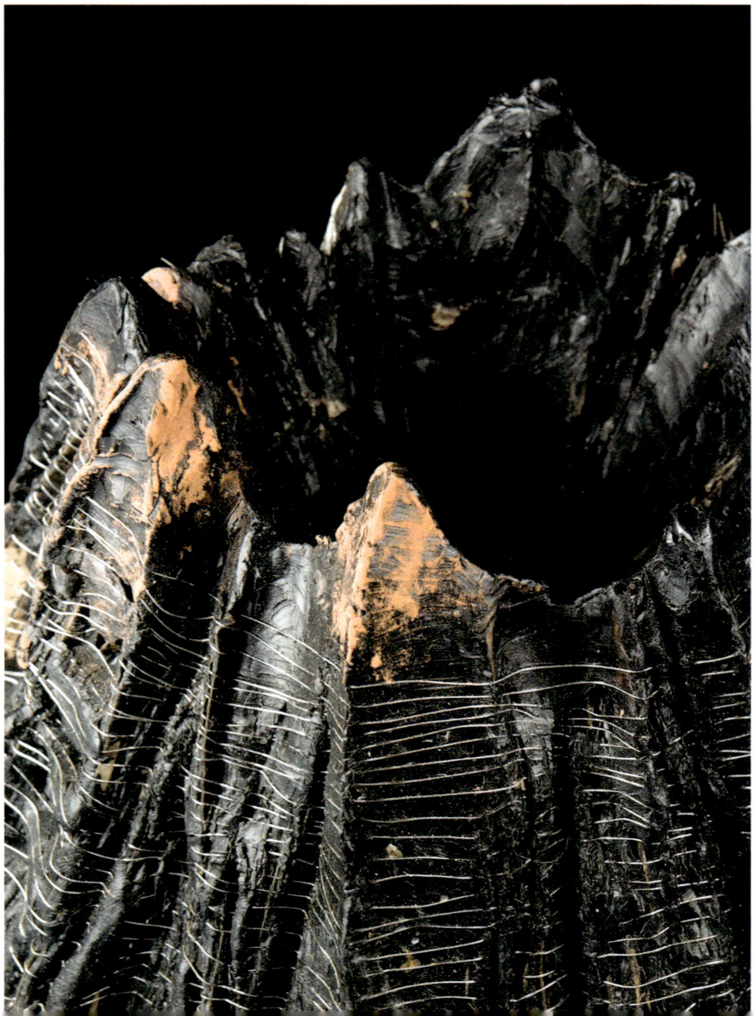
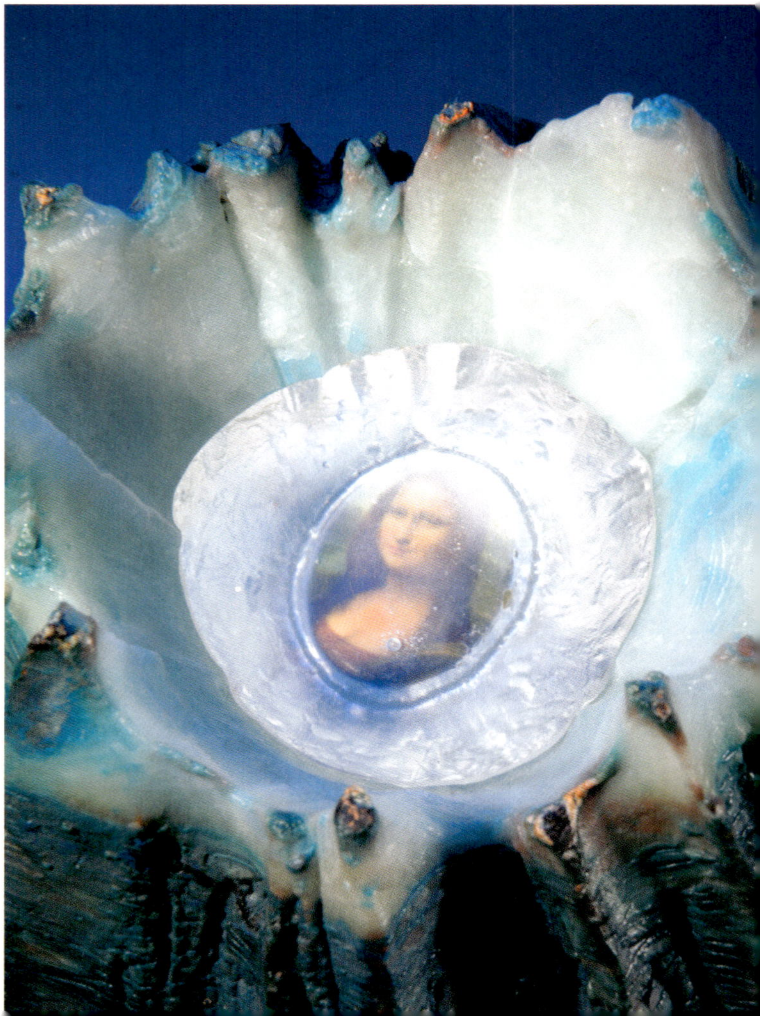

as their central aim the adaptation of hot-glass technology and the physical manipulation of glass so as to place it at the service of the creative individual within the studio, rather than the factory production line. Kiln-forming, on the other hand, took longer to find its place as a major component of the movement; for in doing so it had to struggle to resurrect ancient methods, as well as invent new ones from scratch.

Because of my background I still approach glass through drawing, painting and construction. Making in glass and metal is an extension of this activity, and I take full advantage of the staged nature of kiln-forming to evolve my pieces rather than make them to a design drawing. The drawings and paintings that I make explore forms, images and colours that sometimes take years to reappear in my three-dimensional objects.

Any contributions I have made to the process vocabulary of kiln-forming through my teaching and writing have had as their aim the expansion of its formal and expressive ranges. My pieces emerge from a creative dialogue between natural form, the material qualities and behaviour of glass, and my need to make and communicate.

Process

Not surprisingly, I employ a wide variety of kiln techniques in my use of glass as an artistic medium. However, a major theme of more recent and current practice has been the fusion of metals into glass while it casts, to achieve variations of line and colour both in and on the surface of the glass.

Ann Wolff

Ann Wolff's work is driven by her need to express the graphic themes revealed by her drawings, which are the central powerhouse that has sustained her output in glass for over forty years. In terms of glass she has constantly searched for fresh means of expression, and this has led her to range across glass techniques, avoiding narrowness in favour of creative freedom.

Much of her output has been characterised by her use of surfaces as destinations for her characteristic and original drawings. Her use of etching, engraving and painting on glass allows her to retain the natural gestural spontaneity of her drawings and paintings. Since the 1990s, however, there has been a shift toward the realisation of her forms into three dimensions, often on a monumental scale.

Despite her success and renown as an artist who uses glass as a major medium, Wolff has always maintained her creative independence from it. She has, through the example of her work and through a famous lecture

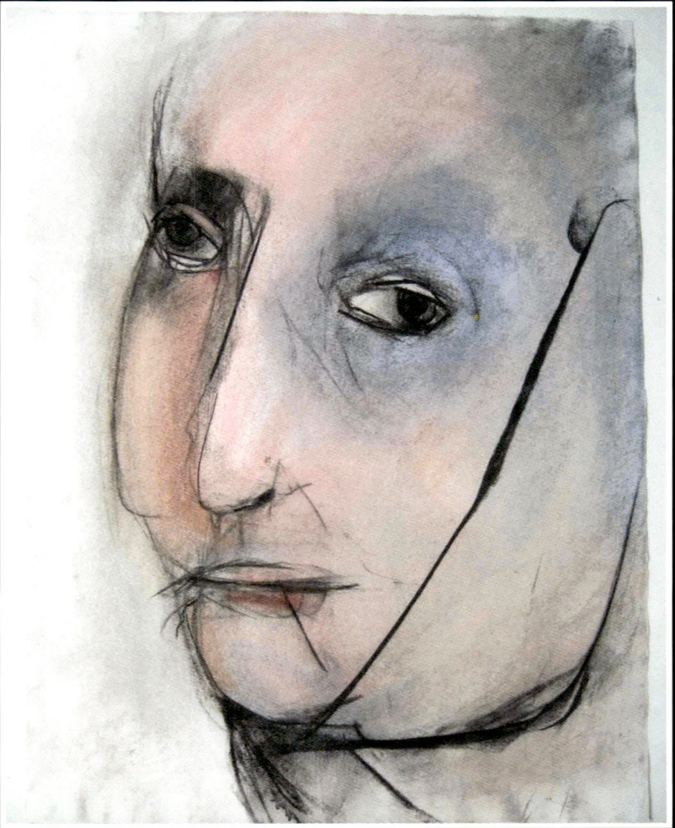

Head, Ann Wolff, 2007. Pastel drawing, 60 x 40 cm (23½ x 15¾ in.)

Ann Wolff's artistic development spans four decades, and has continued to evolve, driven by drawing. A constant theme within the variety of her expression has been the individuality of the human form.

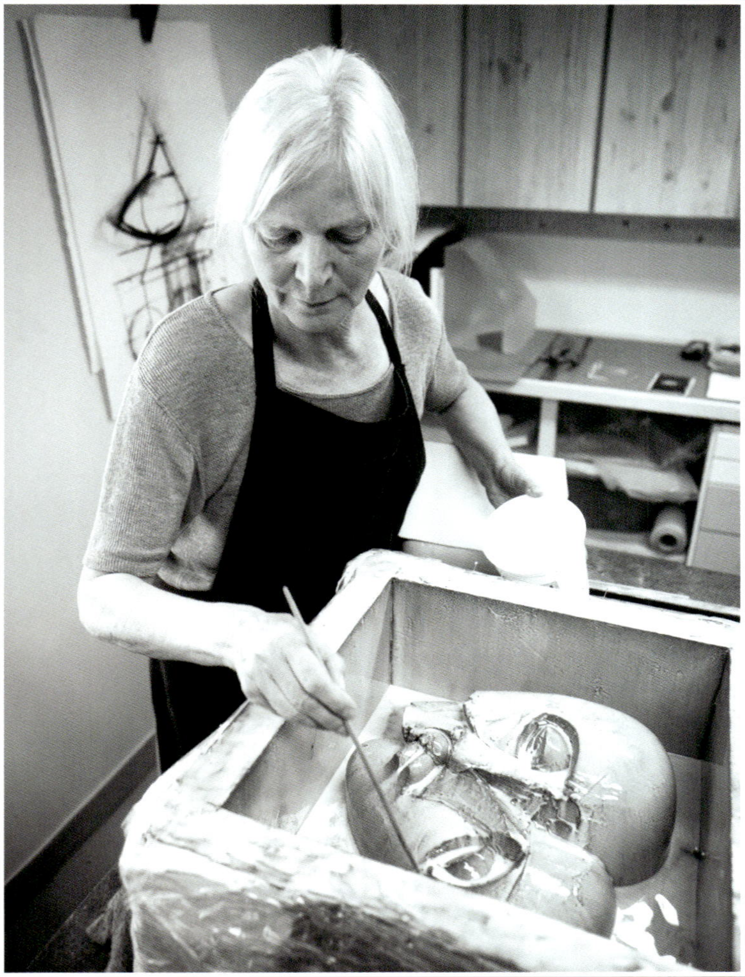

Ann Wolff working in her studio, 2005.

The theme of the human head finds its expression in three dimensions. These solid models will become hollows within a monumental glass cast.

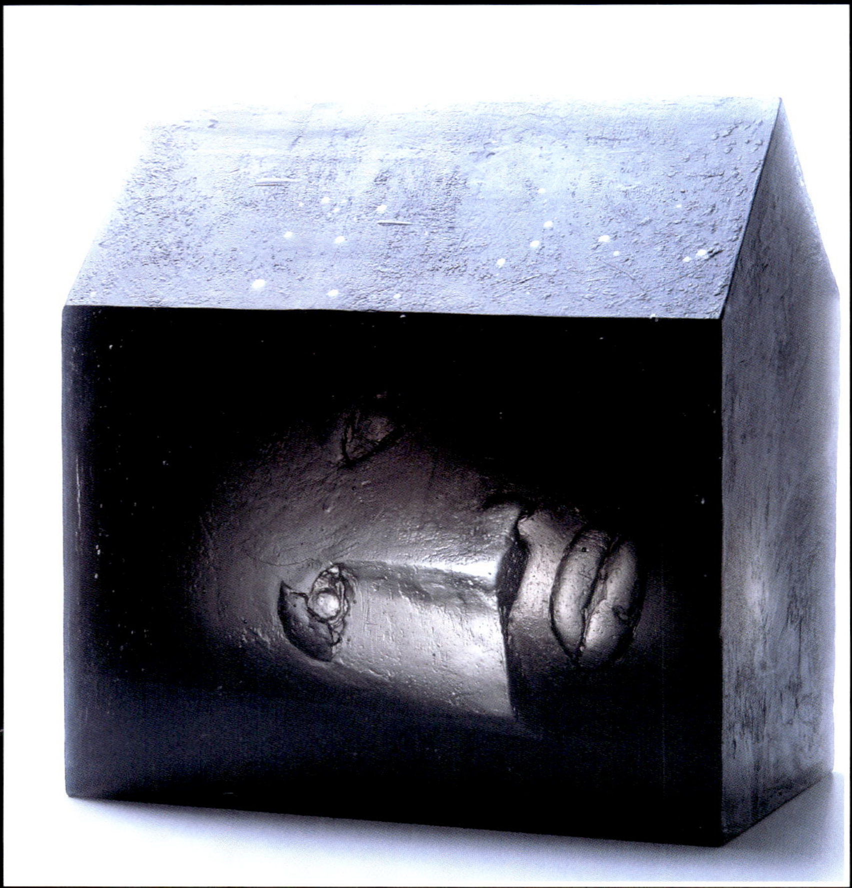

Domus, Ann Wolff, 2005. H. 37 cm (14½ in.), W. 35 cm (13¾ in.), D. 22.5 cm (8⅞ in.).
Photo: Ludger Paffrath.

A single-colour cast sculpture that contrasts the solid rectilinear house form against the hollow heads within, described in terms of modulations in the single colour of the glass.

delivered at Stockholm in 1990, expressed the need for artists who use glass to avoid the pitfalls associated with it – namely, the risk of relying on the magical nature of glass to cover up or enliven an unoriginal idea. This message is perhaps even more relevant today, when glass is so often taught in isolation from mainstream, bedrock art skills and thinking.

Martin Hlubuček

Martin Hlubuček is a designer and sculptor in the Czech tradition, producing monumental sculptural glass casts of great purity and precision. Each aspect of his pieces is crucial to their overall effect, and each stage of their production is geared to this end. His works are produced in series, and draw on elements of pure form allied to the object's potential function within architectural spaces.

Artist statement

Functional and technical aspects are interwoven in forms of design, but also within the arts and crafts, which at the same time make references to the fine arts. It is precisely this position that interests me greatly. My work is an illustrative example of the often open boundary between design work and original artistic creation. Creations using mould-melted glass work with the magic provided by the material – the shine of light through the hollows sunk within the mighty sheet of glass. Although it is certainly possible to use the work functionally, it nevertheless significantly crosses the boundary of function towards the status of a work of art. Its character of mysterious and elegant 'altar' artefact with inner light allows it to enter the architectural area of an interior not as an accessory, but as a fundamental element that attracts attention and creates an atmosphere for the place.

Process

My production procedure is as follows:

a) First of all the shape is modelled with special reference to its construction, with close attention paid to detail. Refined proportion is a prominent feature in my own style of glassmaking.
b) A wax model is created to serve as the core for the mould. Once the wax form is embedded in the refractory mould material, the wax is steamed out completely.
c) The glass is either put into the mould void in solid form prior to firing, or dribble-cast from a ceramic reservoir placed over the mould. This method is particularly good for eliminating bubbles.

Circles, Martin Hlubuček, 2006. ➤
H. 7 cm (2¾ in.), W. 40 cm (15¾ in.), D. 40 cm (15¾ in.).
Photo: Jaroslav Kvitz.

Martin Hlubuček casts pieces which need absolute control over all the aspects of making and casting to guarantee an unblemished stillness of form. His monumental single-colour casts play with shadows within the form created by variation in the surface – such as the circles in this piece, glimpsed through the bulk of the glass.

Martin Hlubuček, melting. ➤
Photo: courtesy of the artist.

Martin casts his pieces himself, placing the glass ingots directly into the mould or, as in this case, in ceramic pots with holes in. These are placed over apertures in the mould, and the glass melts into the aperture. The advantages of this method are twofold: the glass is kept mobile as it melts, reducing the likelihood of devitrification, and imperfections like bubbles are also less likely.

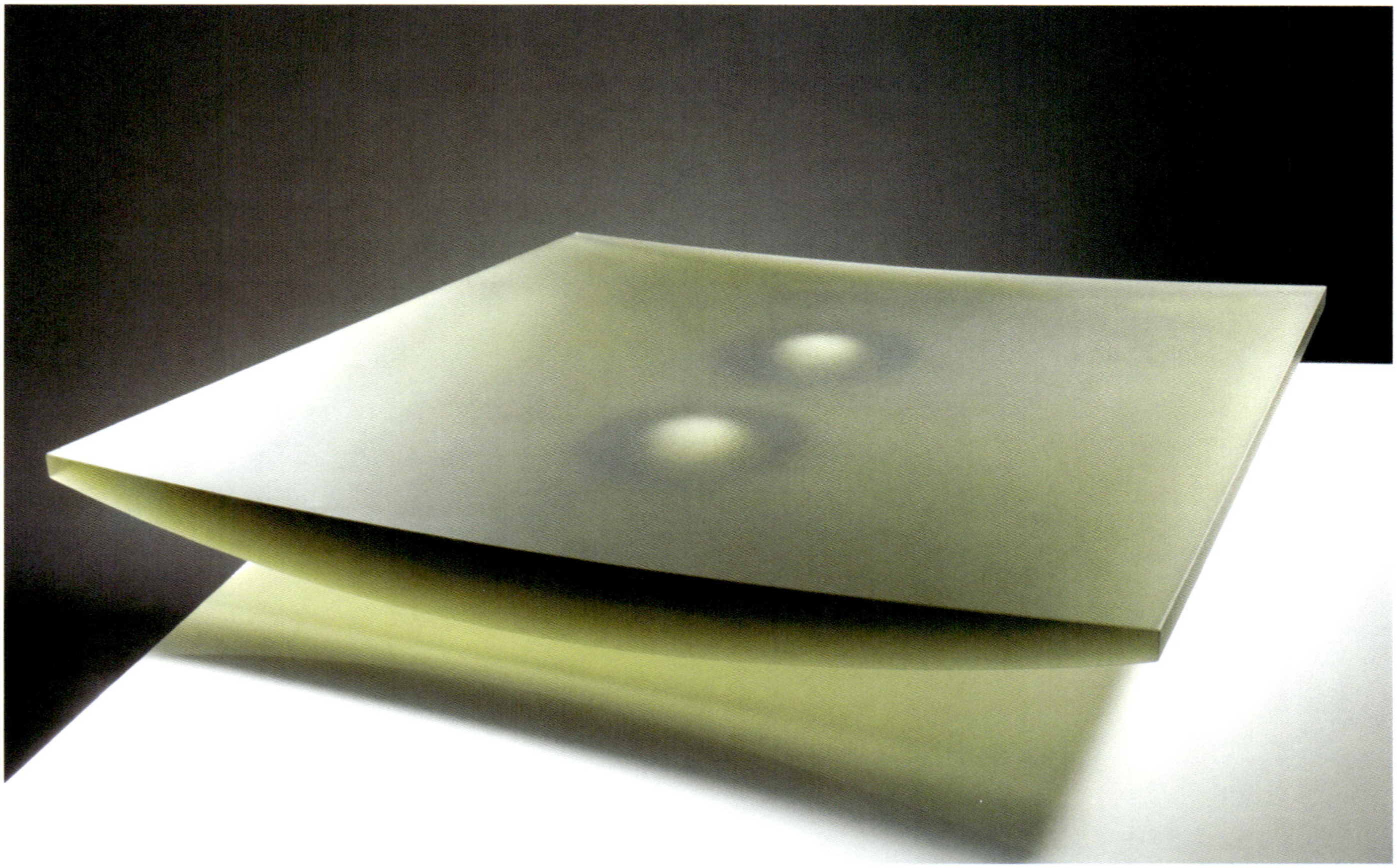

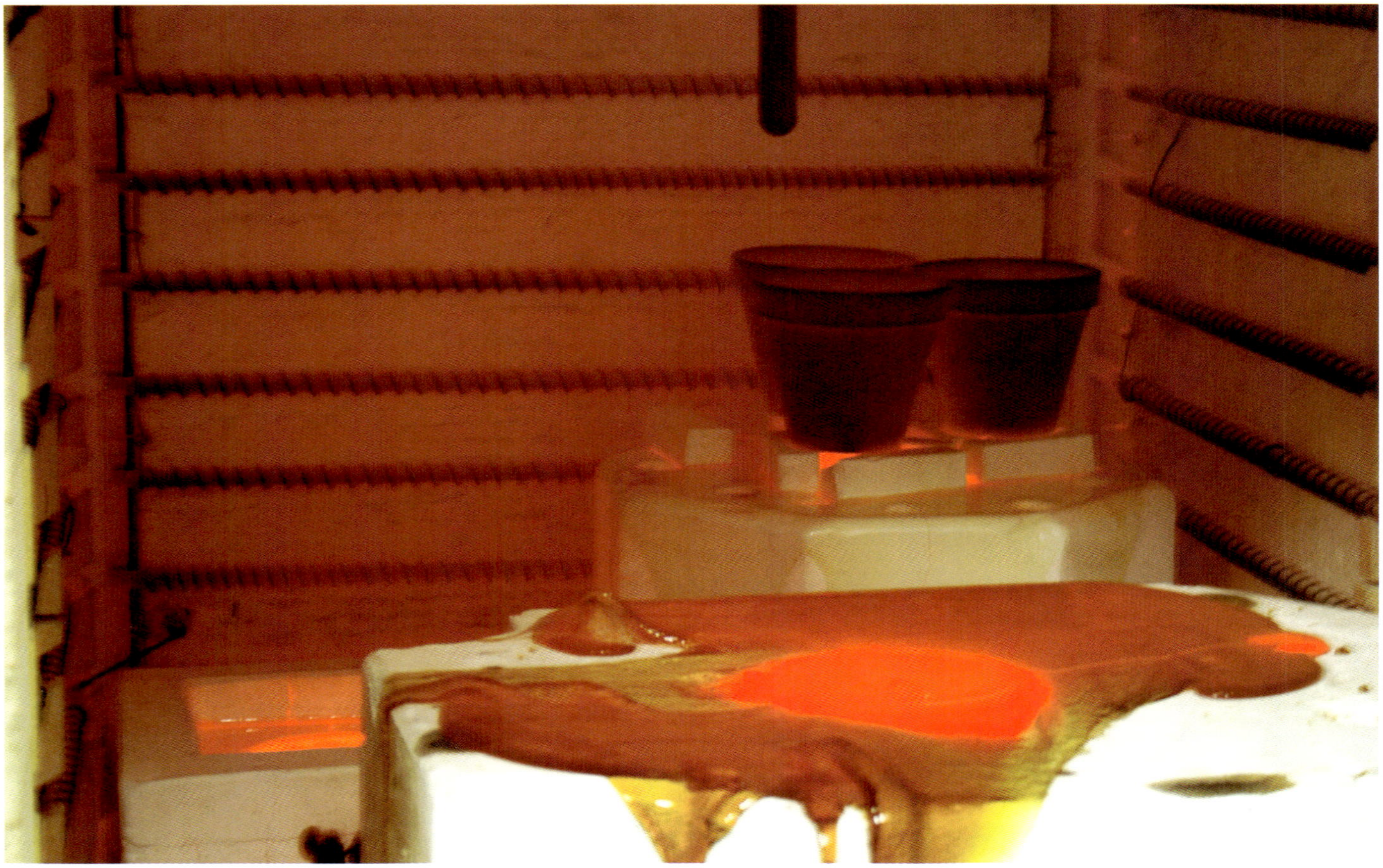

Cone Inversion, Brian Glassar, 2004. ➤ H. 38 cm (15 in.), W. 54 cm (21¼ in.), D. 23 cm (9 in.). Collection: Dan Klein.

This piece was cast in lead crystal at the Lhotsky studio. All the frames into which the glass is set are aluminium, held together by magnets. To ensure that the cast-glass sections fit perfectly into the metal frames, the original models from which the metal and glass were cast are highly engineered; the ability to do this derives in no small part from the artist's lifetime's experience as a jeweller.

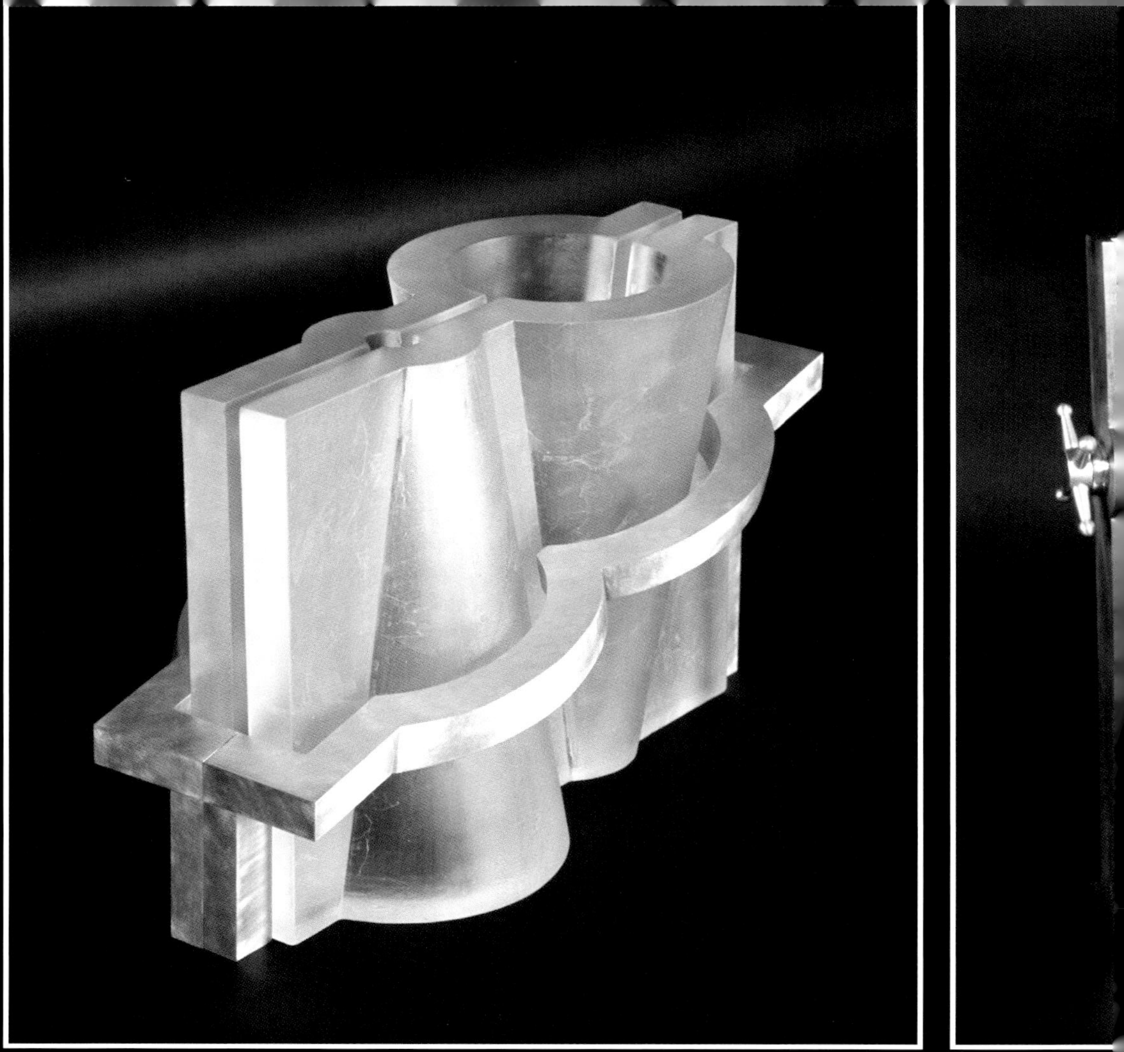

d) After removal from the mould the glass form is cold-processed. I use the services of a skilled, professional glasscutter. I oversee every aspect of the process to ensure an accurate realisation of my predetermined shape. I am not interested in making changes during manufacture; this is the essence of my method. In addition to refined proportion and the construction of shape, an essential goal is the achievement of perfect surface quality.

Brian Glassar

Brian Glassar was trained as a jeweller and only turned his attention to glass in mid-career. But his former experience has influenced the way he uses glass, by bringing to it both a sensitivity to the material and a range of skills that had been honed by the precise demands of fine jewellery design and manufacture. The resulting glass pieces are surprising in many ways, in particular their sculptural monumentality and their concern with

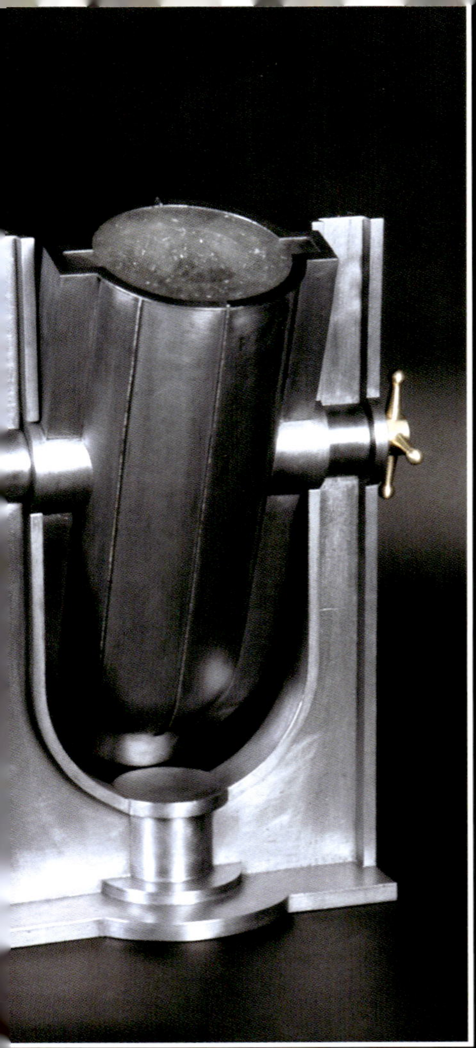

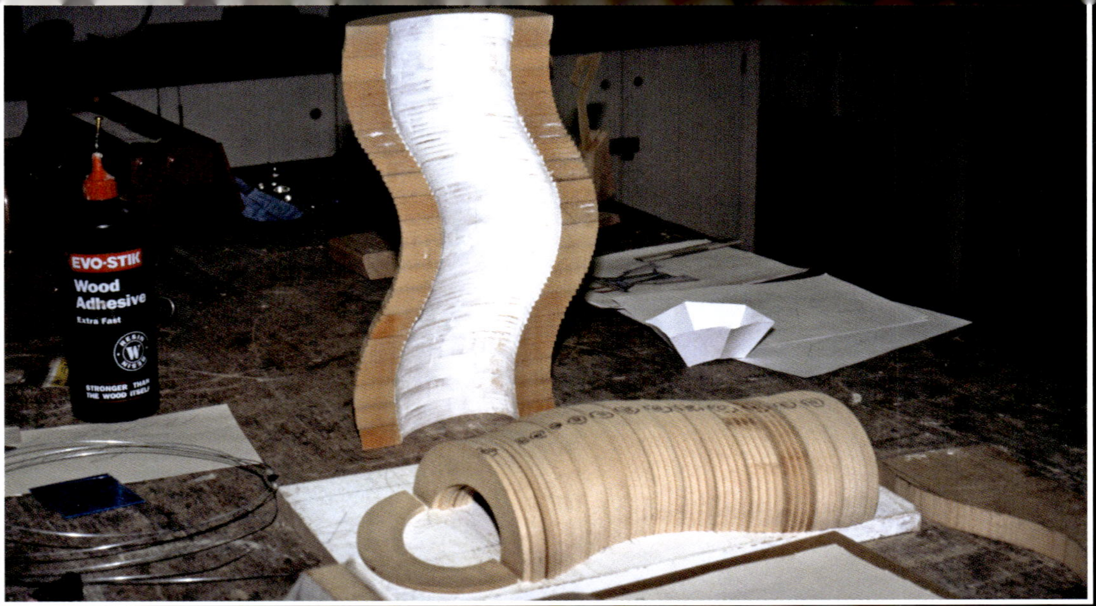

◄ *Belljar*, Brian Glassar, 2004. H. 50 cm (20 in.) W. 30 cm (12 in.), D. 18 cm (7 in.).
The glass form, sheathed in lead, is multi-positional within a fabricated aluminium framework which is also lead-covered. The industrial imagery, and the hiding of the glass within machine-like forms, represents an original approach to, and reaction to, the natural and somewhat overused attractive nature of glass.

▲ *Three Ellipses* (form development), Brian Glassar, 2003.
An insight into Brian's working methods.
Photo: courtesy of the artist.

Cutting and gluing together 60 identical pieces of MDF to create the basic form of one half of a master pattern for the glass castings in this series of pieces.

form and movement rather than with mere decoration. What is not surprising is the elegant way in which the glass casts are related to the cast metal housings that act as their settings.

Like an increasing number of contemporary artists, Glassar has his glass forms cast commercially (by Lhotsky). The perfect nature of these casts serves his vision exactly, but requires the prior manufacture of the prototypes of the glass forms in another material. This approach, of course, removes any possibility of the happy accident or any opportunity for revision during the making process. It is seen in the work of a number of artists in this volume, and represents a different aesthetic and creative attitude to the journey from concept to form, where the creative process is allowed full reign throughout. One could not imagine the works of either Glassar or Peter Bremers (see pp. 160–62), for example, being produced by any but this method, such is their need for certainty.

Artist statement

Movement and the possibilities for change within an object, combined with ambiguity of function, have always been key aspects of my work. For many years I was concerned with making work for the body, utilising its energy to make the 'worn' object spin, slide, pivot – to change and to question. Gradually, the concerns of size, weight and comfort became too restrictive, and my focus changed.

Since attending an inspirational masterclass with Bertil Vallien in 1997, I have been working on a larger scale using kiln-cast glass. This is frequently in conjunction with other materials, those I feel have a natural and historical affinity with glass, cast iron, lead and rubber.

The three-dimensional objects I make often make reference to our industrial past, and raise questions of function/non-function, fine art/design.

Colin Reid

Colin Reid needs no introduction. He has been making significant work by kiln-forming for the best part of thirty years. Although the majority of his output is in cast glass there has been a constant evolution in his vocabulary and in his use of the material. From his early interest in the creation of internal structure and colour in his pieces, he has gradually turned his attention to the relationship between the external skin of the glass mass and the refractive qualities of the glass itself. To this end, he has more recently shifted to the use of high-quality optical blocks for his casts, for the internal purity of their glass; by this means he creates ambiguous reflections across the form.

Reid is unusual in the sense that he is as equally at home working sculpturally as he is working to site-specific commissions.

Colin Reid, Loading the optical glass for *Cypher Stone*. ➤
Photo: courtesy of the artist.

The use of single glass ingots for casting means that the mould must be open enough to allow the glass to be placed directly into the mould's aperture, and the cast is slump-cast gently into the form. The weight of the glass is so great that hoists have to be used to position it. Annealing is a lengthy process with such large pieces, but is made slightly easier by the fact that the precise annealing and strain points can be obtained from the suppliers, and the form is a coherent volume with no great contrasts of thickness.

Artist statement

A trip to Japan earlier this year provided the starting point for several new works. I was teaching a workshop there, and took my group to the coast to see what material we could find for casting. It was a rather desolate spot, but I found some wonderful rocks, which have inspired a new series of pieces. This is typical of how my work comes about. I never start with a blank piece of paper. I hunt for forms and textures that interest me, and either cast them in situ or bring them to the studio to use as a starting point. In this case I used silicone to make an impression of the rocks, and then, by a process of lost-wax casting, made the forms I wanted to create in glass.

Transparency is one of the defining qualities of glass, and one which I

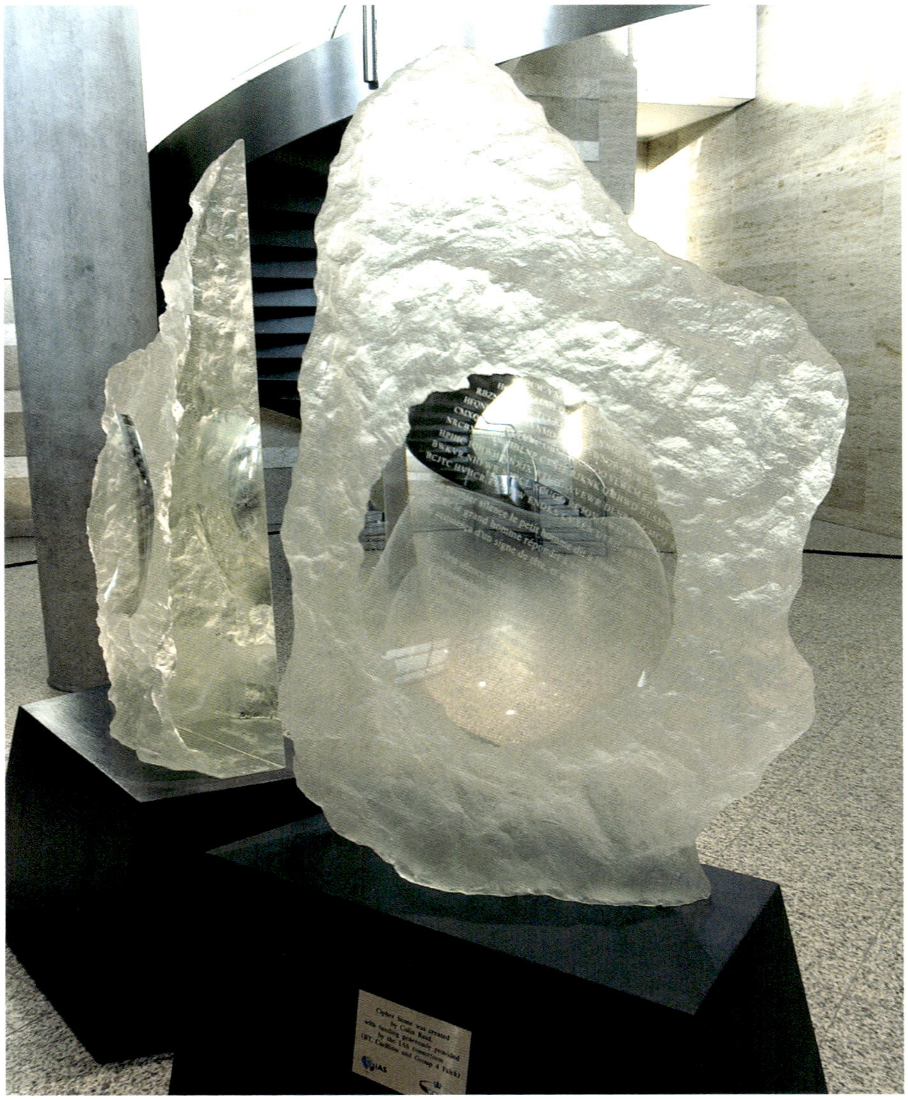

Cipher Stone, landmark artwork for UK Government agency HQ, Colin Reid, 2004. H. 200 cm (79 in.).
Photo: courtesy of the artist.

Colin Reid uses solid optical blanks to cast his massive sculptural forms. This ensures that the casts are water-clear and that cutting on and into the surface affords maximum refraction.

Untitled, Colin Reid, 2003. H. 20 cm (7⅞ in.), W. 22 cm (8⅝ in.), D. 19 cm (7½ in.).
Photo: courtesy of the artist.
Private collection.

Cast from weathered stonework from Gloucester Cathedral. The contrast between the textured and the clear areas has been achieved by polishing some faces and leaving others as cast. The colour is the result of copper compounds placed on the mould's surface to react with the glass during firing.

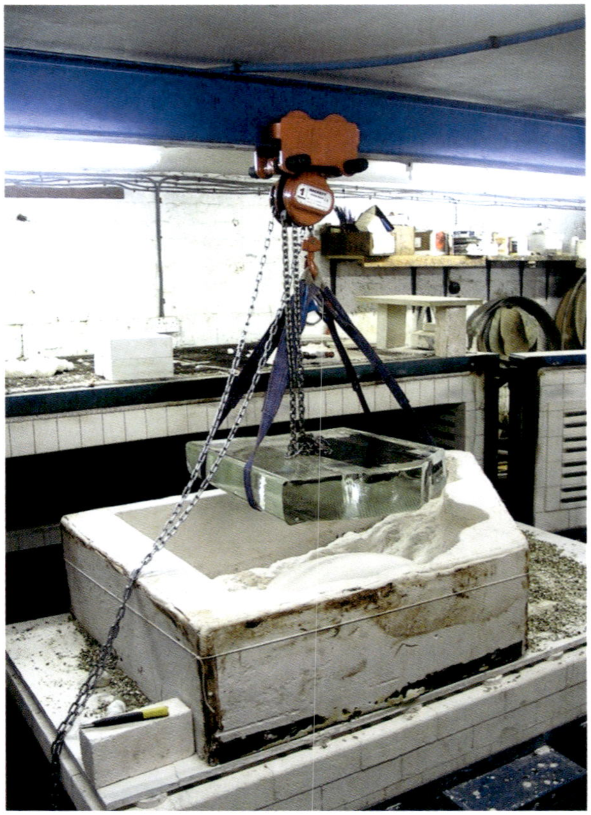

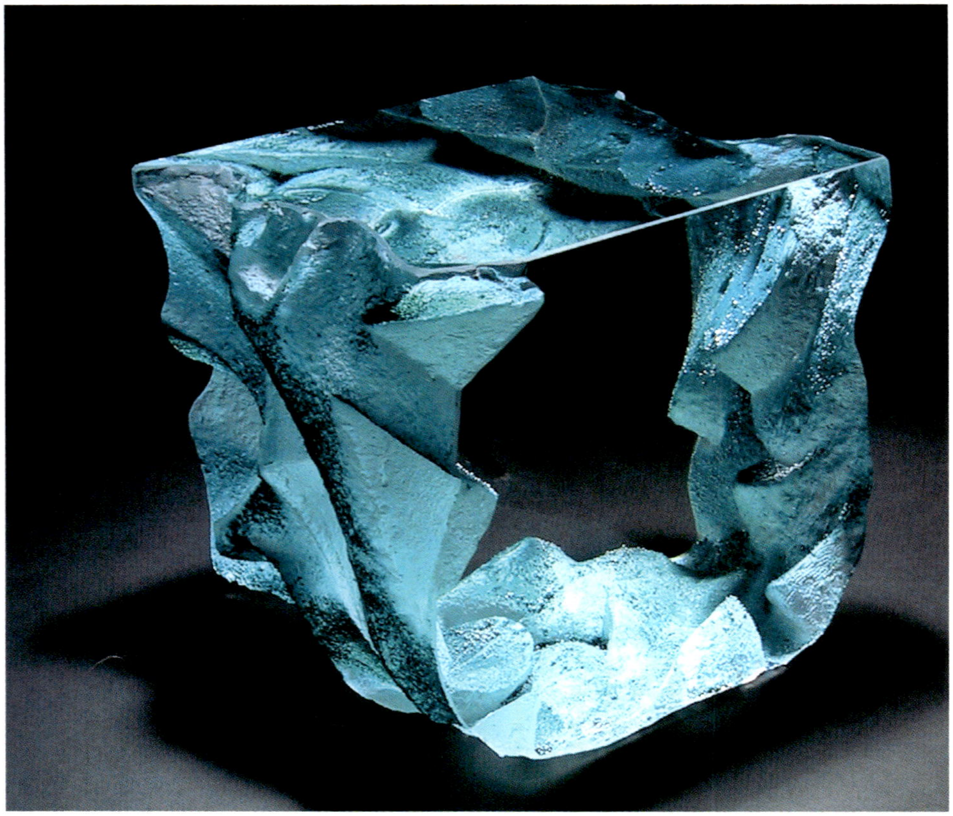

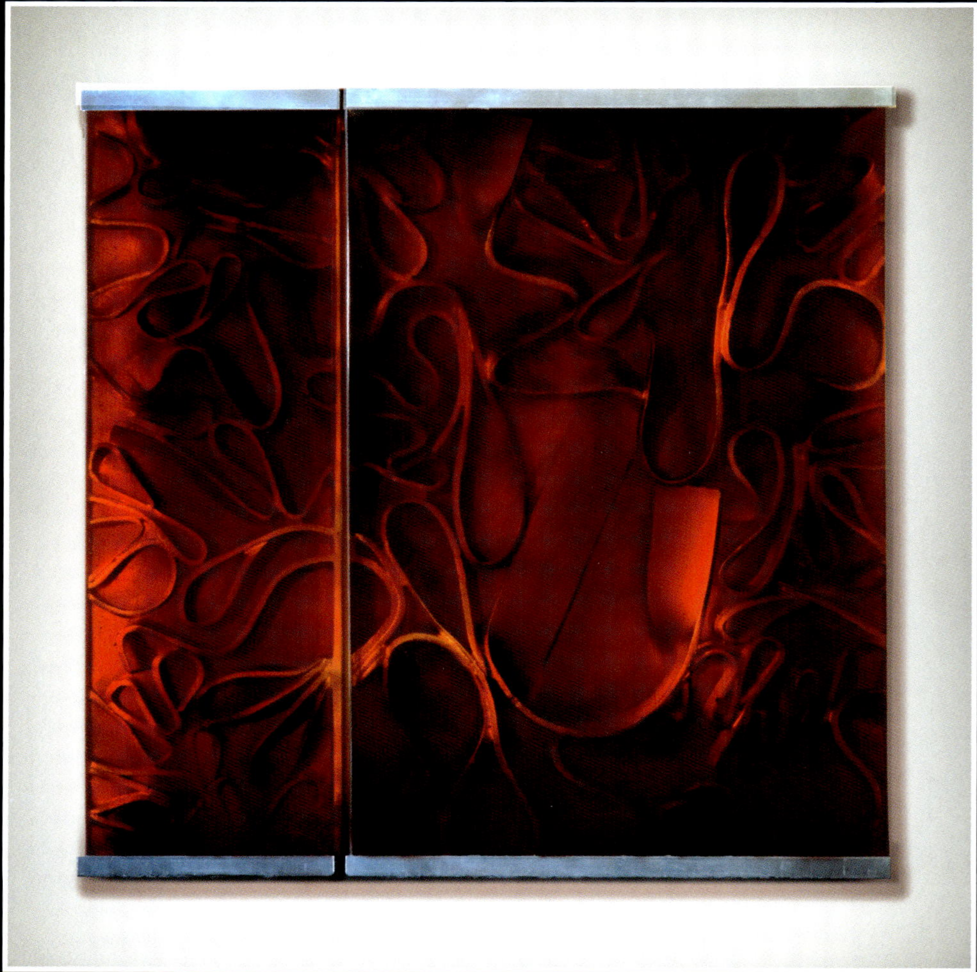

Arabesque 2, Daniela Turrin, 2008. Two panels, each H. 55 cm (21⅝ in.), W. 18 cm (7 in.) D. 6 cm (2⅜ in.). Photo: Franca Turrin.

The quality of colour and depth in Daniela Turrin`s painterly wall pieces is a classic example of the dictum, 'The whole is greater than the sum of its parts.' The apparent simplicity is actually the result of the creative exploitation of the qualities of the glass set against the immaculate mould-making and casting. The surface of the glass cast is polished painstakingly by hand to ensure a flawless surface through which the modelling of the cast surface can be seen.

work with a great deal. With most materials one sees only the outer surface of the object; one cannot see inside. With glass the inner space and volume of the form are also visible. My work explores the relationship between the external shape and the inside of the form. Thus a familiar form may be cast in reverse so that it appears to be quite abstract at first sight. When viewed through the glass we can read the form, and it makes sense.

Daniela Turrin

Daniela Turrin uses kiln-cast glass to create what are, in effect, paintings. She uses the subtle variations in thickness and texture to model shifts of colour within what appears to be a flat surface. The results are wall-hung and can be read as pure image; and the qualities of the glass and the process she uses are harnessed to achieving this end. Technically, this is achieved by casting the coloured glass onto a deeply modelled and subtly variegated mould. The top surface of the cast glass is then painstakingly flattened and polished so that the modelling and texture are seen through

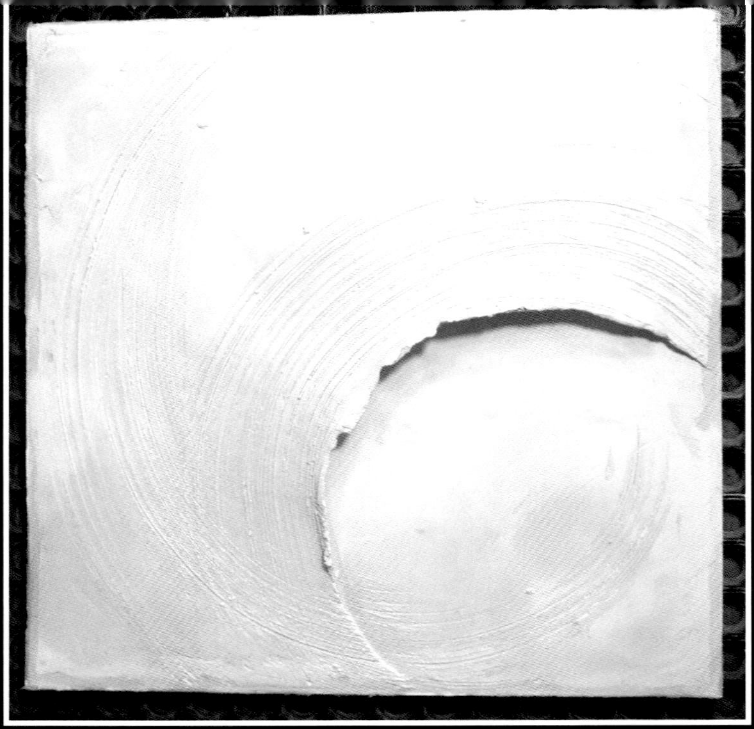

▲ Daniela Turrin, mould. Daniela's moulds are masterpieces of control. The crisp forms and textures are designed to create precisely the desired qualities in the cast surface.
Photo: courtesy of the artist.

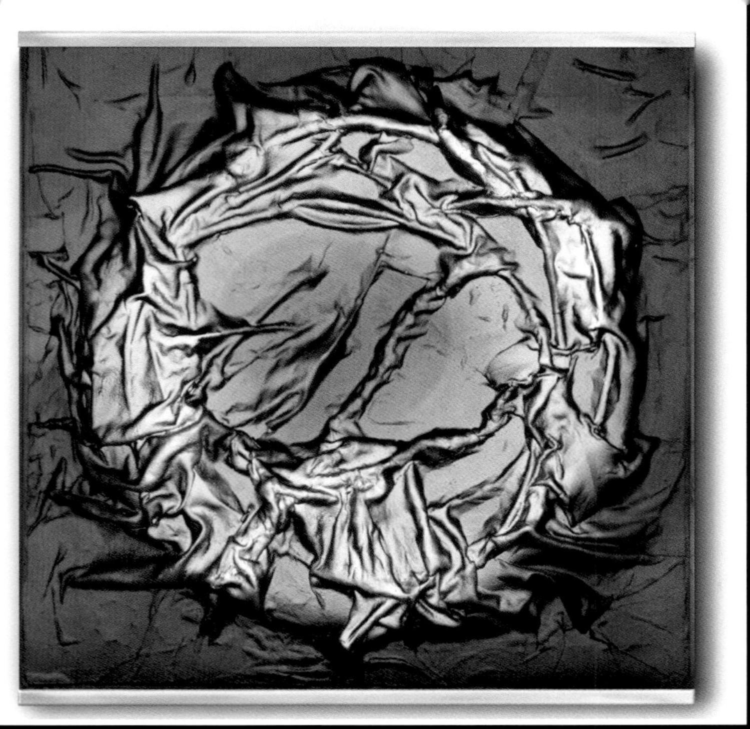

▲ *Aureolo 2*, Daniela Turrin, 2007. W. 40 cm (15¾ in.), H. 40 cm (15¾ in.), D. 6 cm (2⅜ in.).
Photo: Franca Turrin.

The use of a vibrant single colour in Daniela's powerful, painterly wall pieces presents the perfect foil for the hollows and textures revealed by the polished top surface.

it. The modulations of colour caused by the differences in depth add to this illusion.

Artist statement: Concepts and practices

Central to my practice is staying true to the medium I have chosen to work with. In its ability to allow the interior and exterior to be experienced simultaneously, glass offers the artist the unique potential to explore the sublime dividing line between the real and the imagined. For this reason, I have chosen to work with negative spaces within the material. Forms apparently captured within my glass panels in truth only exist as voids drawing their deceptive substance from the play of light within the material. These 'paintings' investigate the three-dimensional space through a planar surface – paradoxically, a classical painterly strategy, but here achieved through a sculptural technique.

The process involved in achieving this end result interestingly mirrors the concept behind the work, as I follow through a series of positive and negative reincarnations of the object. I begin with a positive form in fabric, clay, wax, paper, etc., then take a negative impression in silicone rubber. This in turn becomes a positive investment mould, which is cast as a negative in the rear of the glass panel. Sometimes this process can be punctuated by a number of intervening positive and negative forms. With each step I explore the same form from a different perspective, in a different material – and with each step I marvel at the sublime borderline between what is and what is not; that thin skin separating the exterior and interior of the form.

Peter Bremers, iceberg, Greenland.
Photo: courtesy of the artist.

In 2001 Peter Bremers undertook a voyage in a sailing ship to the Antarctic. The resulting journey dramatically affected his creative sources. Since then he has worked in blown glass, and more recently in the production of large-scale cast sculpture. The shapes, colours and textures encountered in the Antarctic have provided a rich store of inspiration. The importance of seeking constantly to find new additions to personal aesthetic vocabularies outside of the narrow confines of the material itself is underlined by his example.

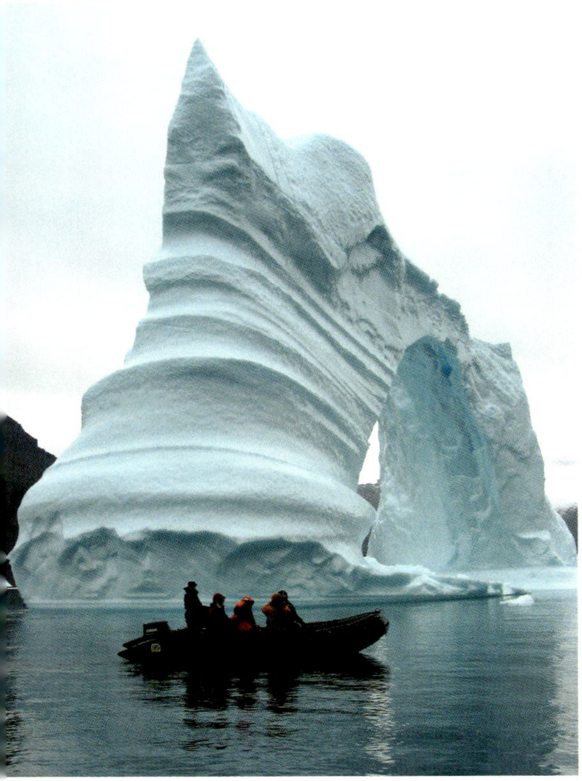

Peter Bremers

Peter Bremers has throughout his career to date used a variety of glass processes to produce his sculptures, each one resulting in glass forms which display a different facet of his creativity. His blown work is extremely organic, using a highly personal interpretation of the Graal technique to impart pattern to the body and shape of the free-blown pieces.

His more recent cast glass, by contrast, is based on first-hand experience of icebergs, the result of a voyage to the Antarctic. The way in which this journey inspired him is evident in the body of work that it has generated, and in the directness of the formal language, which makes the works, though ostensibly abstract, some of the most literal interpretations of source material in modern glass. This is something he acknowledges in his book *Icebergs*, in which he often places images of ice features next to the glass that resulted from it. What comes out of this is a kind of analogy drawn between frozen water and glass, and a tribute to both. It is an object lesson in the way that a new body of work can emerge from a deliberate move away from the limitations of glass and its attractive, but rather obvious charms as a material.

The route to the interpretation and realisation of this work led Peter to develop a new (for him) method of working. He chose to produce the models himself with great precision, taking the natural ice structures and shaping their essences rather than their portraits. Once the individual models were complete, he had them cast in glass by a commercial studio (Lhotsky), and one can appreciate why. The pristine nature of the large-scale single-colour casts is exactly right for the subject. After casting, Peter directed the selective polishing and finishing of the glass to give life to the pieces through variations in their surface texture.

Artist statement

In many non-western cultures it is customary to perform small daily rituals to pay homage to nature, ensure good harvests, propitiate the weather gods, pacify the ocean or give thanks to Mother Earth through music and dance. In the western world, it would appear that our sense of intimacy

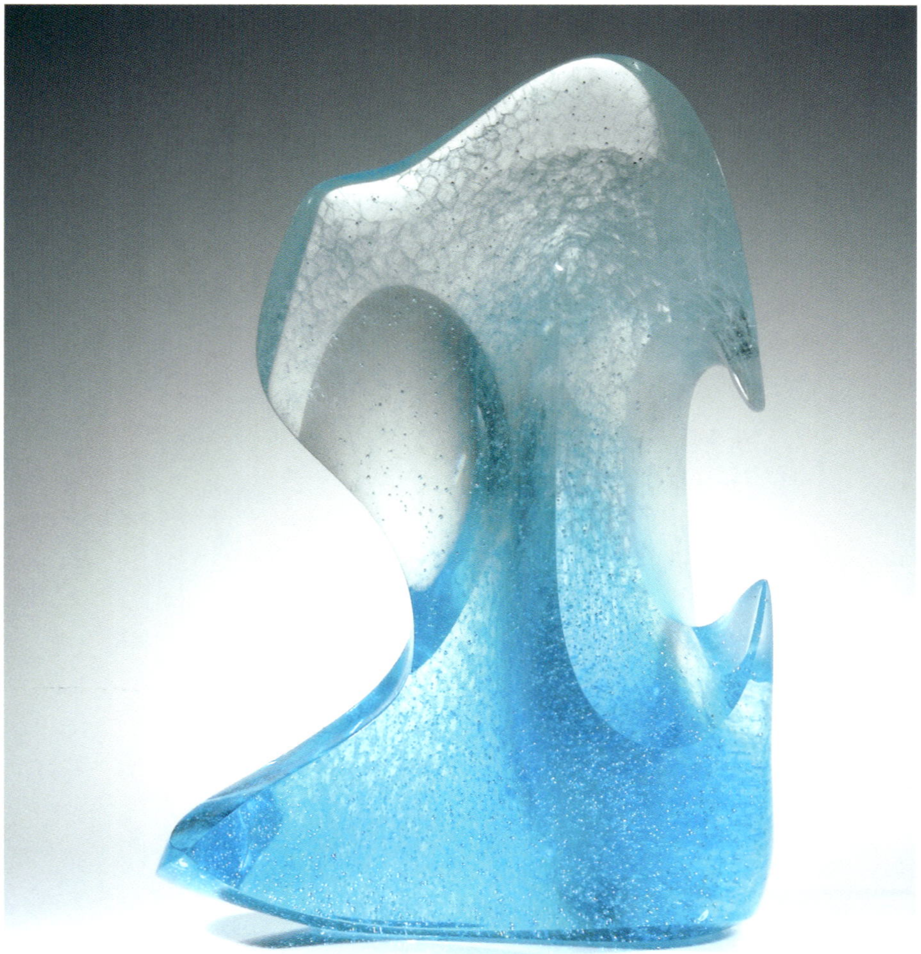

I&P07, Peter Bremers, 2007. H. 51 cm (20 in.), W. 35 cm (13¾ in.), D. 28 cm (11 in.); weight 38 kg (84 lb).
Photo: courtesy of the artist.

Cast by Lhotsky Studio from models made by the artist, this piece captures the structure and colour of ice in its internal structure. It was created by the selective filling of the mould with small pieces of differently coloured glass.

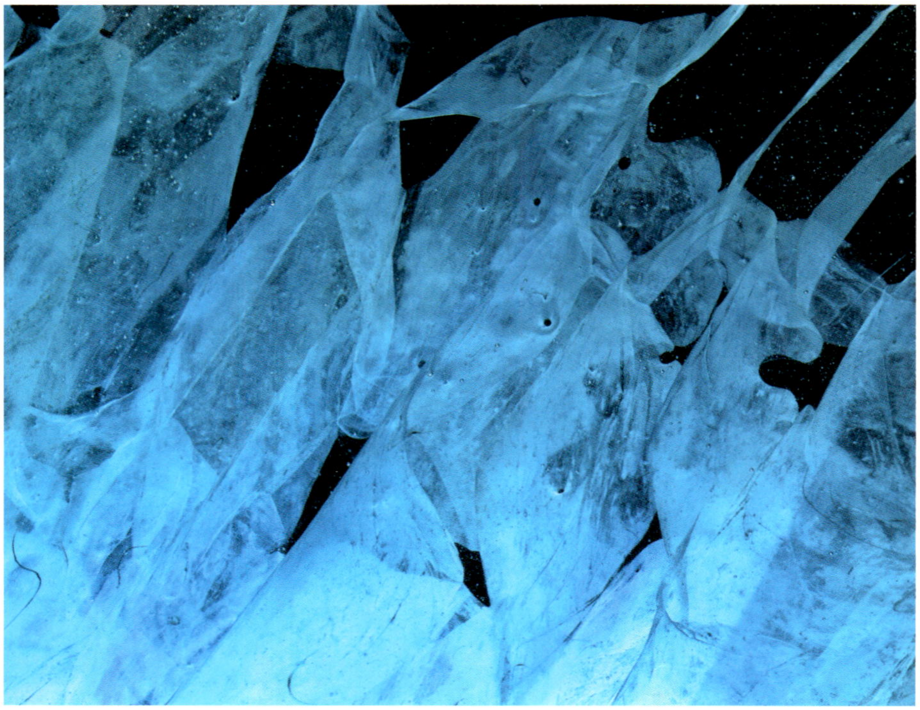

Peter Bremers, *I&P07* (detail), 2007.
Photo: courtesy of the artist.

This detail of a sculpture by Peter Bremers, which weighs 38 kg (84 lb), shows the internal structure created by the fuse lines between each separate piece of glass.

with nature, and our wonder at its beauty, is being submerged amid mounting anxiety about global warming and the dramatic impact of possible future climate change. We see the natural world as something separate from ourselves, exploit its gifts without restraint for economic gain, and by doing so turn it from an age-old friend to a hostile force. We show little trace of gratitude, and seem to forget that we ourselves are part of nature.

I can only say that, for me, the overwhelming emotion I felt when a mother whale with her calf swam alongside our boat and looked me long and hard in the eye, was a life-changing experience; as was my sense of insignificance in the face of the savage energy of the oceans; as was my delight at the sight of yet another majestic sunrise over a flawless, snow-covered landscape.

How can I express my gratitude for this inexhaustible source of inspiration other than by trying to depict the awesome power and majesty of nature in my sculpture? Not by aiming to imitate or equal it, but simply by expressing my sense of wonder as a human being and an artist.

Siblings, Sibylle Peretti, 2008. ➤
H. 56 cm (22 in.), W. 38 cm (15 in.).
Photo: Mike Smith.

As a sculptor first and foremost, Sibylle Peretti uses glass as a material of choice from which to cast her enigmatic figures, because of the natural mystery that the material brings to her creations. Her original models are made in slipcast porcelain, and provide the forms from which the glass-casting moulds are made. Finishes to the casts include delicate additions, engraving and painting. As an artist who also works in ceramic, Sibylle Peretti is very much an artist who uses glass rather than a glass artist.

High-temperature casting

The next three artists cast their pieces in a slightly different way to the slump-casters, who use large, often single ingots which are melted into their moulds to create forms in bright glass with the minimum of variation or visual disturbance in the glass mass. This is an aesthetic choice, but one that is made possible by the shapes of the sculpture and their open moulds.

To choose to cast at a higher temperature makes for two changes to the overall equation. Smaller pieces of glass can be used, and the forms that can be made may also be less open and more complex, with greater variations in thickness. There is also an aesthetic dimension: glass that is fired higher and in smaller pieces is denser and subject to internal ghosting and, on occasions, devitrification, qualities that can be actively sought by practitioners.

Children of the Sea (detail), Sibylle Peretti, 2006. Full sculpture dimensions: H. 60 cm (23⅝ in.), W. 60 cm (23⅝ in.), D. 40 cm (15¾ in.). ➤
Photo: Mike Smith.

The quality of the modelling is complemented by the subtle finishes and the colour of the glass.

Sibylle Peretti

Sibylle Peretti uses glass in the same way that another artist might use bronze – as a material best suited to realising her clay-modelled forms. Her use of clay to shape her figures and heads prior to their realisation in glass, via accurate moulds taken directly from the clay, displays the true origins of her creativity. The sculptures are modelled directly from life,

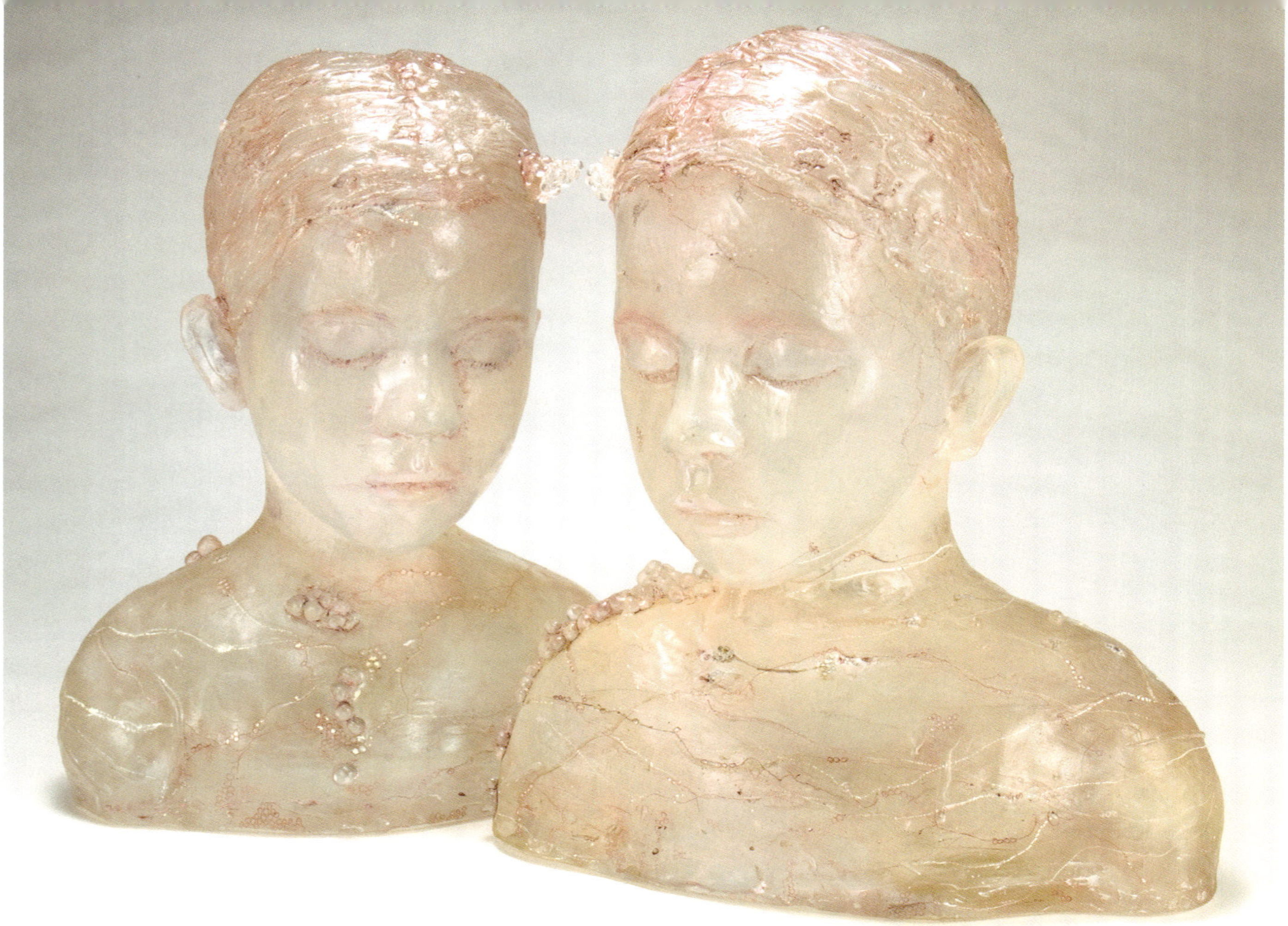

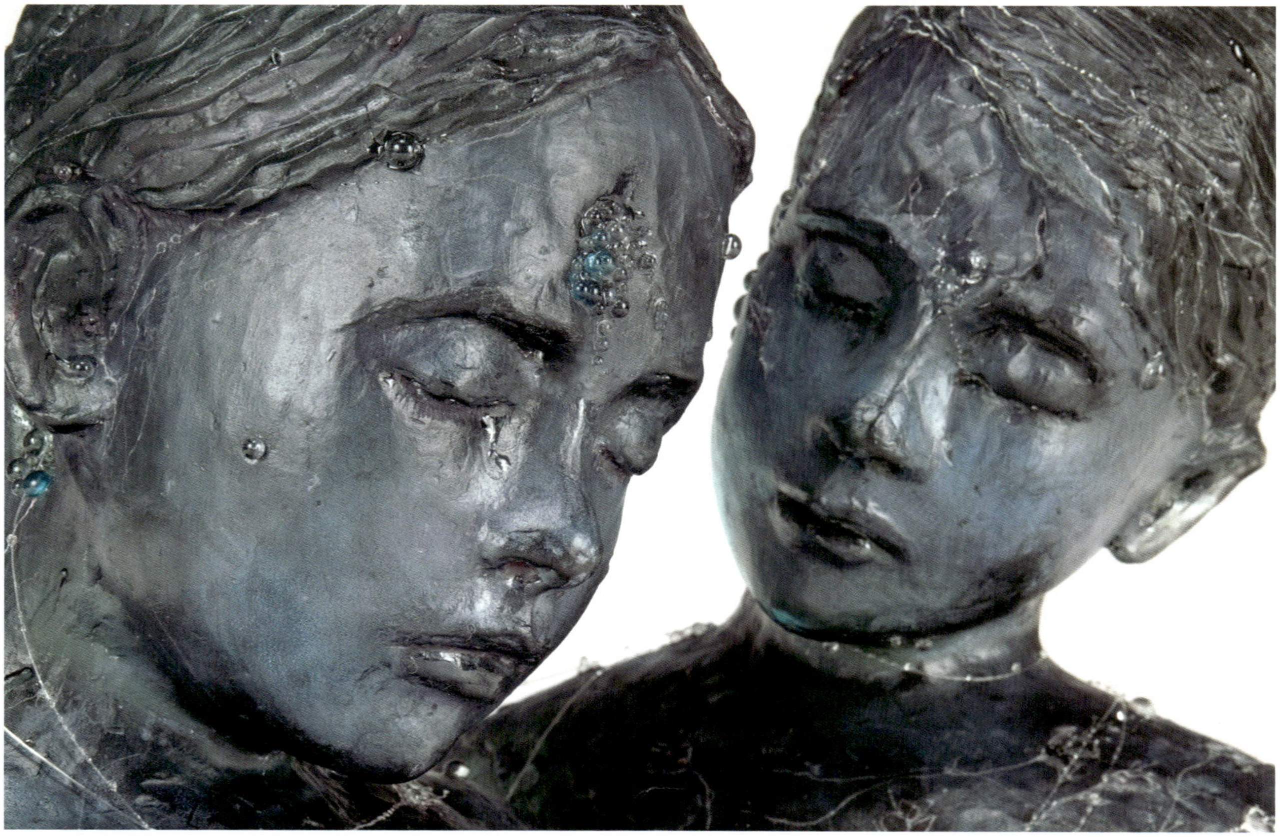

and in this sense are portraits in the accepted sense of the word, even if they do not necessarily function as such. Her choice of glass for the final interpretation of her work is made surely for the qualities that cast glass can bring to her forms, namely colour and texture. The impact of her enigmatic pieces is enhanced by the timeless quality of glass and the cast quality of the glass surface, which make the forms look as if they have always existed.

Zora Palova and Stepan Pala

A husband and wife who are leaders of the second generation of Slovak glass artists, Palova and Pala both studied under Vaclav Cigler but have converted his optical monumentalism to their own different, expressive ends. Each achieves highly personal variations of the vocabulary of large-scale cast and polished glass sculptures and architectural installations through subtle uses of form and texture. As Dan Klein says in his book *Zora Palova & Stepan Pala*, 'They use the inner structure of the glass mass, surface structures, or the contrast between smooth and rough surfaces. The modelling of surface with gesture, imprints of real structures, and painting on glass also appear.'

Although both Palova and Pala are important pioneers in the use of glass as an expressive medium, their paths from inspiration to form spring from their different personalities. Palova has said, 'My instincts are to the gestural', and the truth and influence of this statement can be seen in the gradual move in her work towards the organic, and in her confident use of her hand-formed building textures, which remain as evidence of the original clay forms from which the glass is cast. The way in which her forms evolve from the general to the particular, becoming specific in their single identities is akin to the way signatures turn generic letters into unique inscriptions each time they are written. As Palova herself puts it, 'I felt myself to be first and foremost a sculptor, and learnt about sculpture long before learning about glass.'

Pala, while naturally sharing Palova's technique and crucial Czech artistic heritage, has found his expressive outlets through the language of mathematics and geometry. His formal preferences are for regular forms and their repetition, using a meticulous, cold-working precision to articulate light. The resulting pieces, whether single casts or constructions, define the space around them, so it is not surprising that some of his best-known pieces have been made for specific locations.

Like Palova, much of his creativity is developed away from glass. He uses drawing as a means of creating and exploring structure. The linear

Blue Wing, Zora Palova, 2005. ➤
H. 110 cm (43¼ in.), W. 60 cm (23⅝ in.), D. 14 cm (5½ in.).
Photo: courtesy of the artist.

Zora Palova develops her forms from the model to the final finish. Her choice of clay rather than wax as her modelling material allows her to impart her hand movements and gestures to the mould surfaces. Once cast the glass is very selectively finished to create a series of contrasts between the human touch and its removal by grinding and polishing.

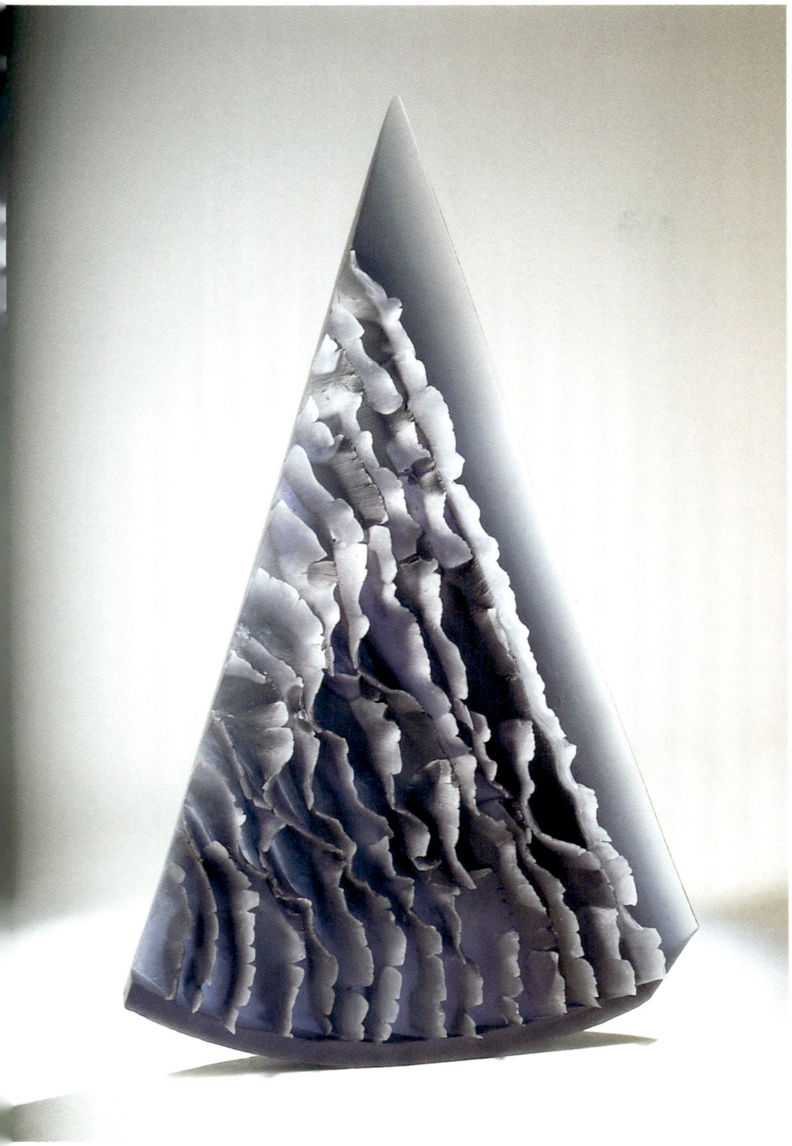

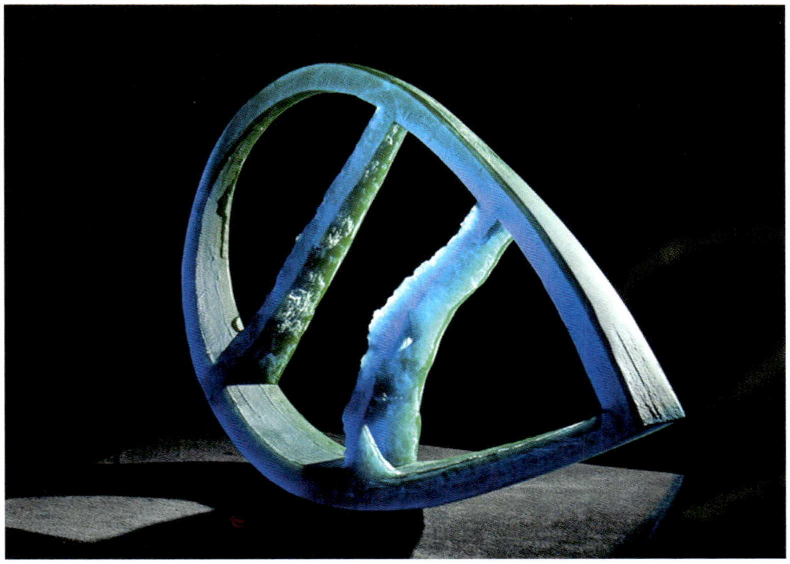

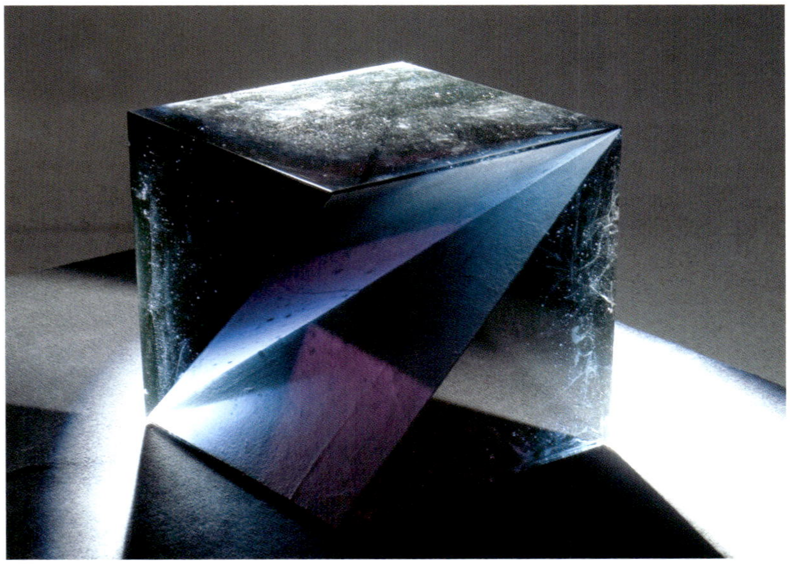

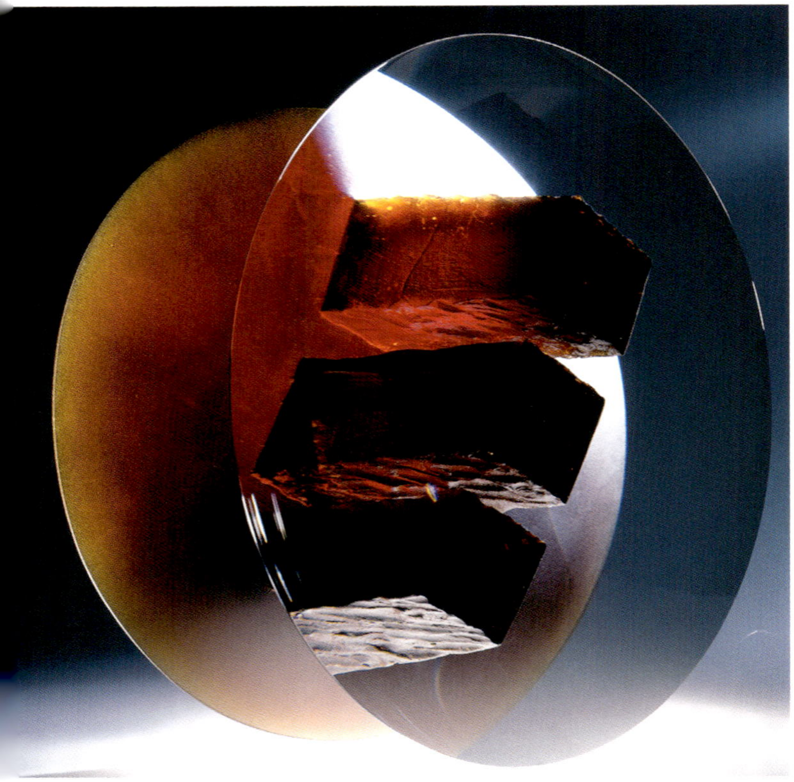

➤ *Drop*, Zora Palova, 2005. H. 70 cm (27½ in.), W. 110 cm (43¼ in.), D. 12 cm (4¾ in.).
Photo: courtesy of the artist.

The influences of natural organic growth are evident in this large-scale cast, which plays off positive against negative space, and texture against polished surfaces.

➤ *Cube 2*, Stepan Pala, 2007. 30 x 30 x 30 cm (11¾ x 11¾ x 11¾ in.).
Photo: courtesy of the artist.

Although his work sits within the tradition of Czech glass, Stepan Pala extends its range and repertoire through his use of strong colour and texture.

➤ *Red Space*, Stepan Pala, 2003. D. 60 cm (23⅝ in.), W. 35 cm (13¾ in.).
The combination of kiln-cast colour with austere, polished optical glass creates ambiguities of space and form.

webs of his drawings seek to define the mass of his glass works through their edges, and it is not surprising that he feels that his way of working has some affinity with musical composition. The drawings are sometimes the precursors of wooden structures which are used to explore the space, describing poles and blocks for the graphic lines.

In his recent work he has begun to explore the possibilities of laser-cutting controlled by computer technology, a move which is like an accomplished musician using a new instrument.

Both Palova and Pala are supreme examples of artists who use glass in the service of their personal visions, but do not rely on its natural beauty or mystery to achieve their aims.

Multicolour casting

The last group of artists share an important technical characteristic: their different works all display a control over the disposition of colour within them, albeit achieved by a number of variations. As colour is one of the more difficult elements to control, I felt that it would be instructive to look at these artists as a group.

At the most fundamental level, any attempt to introduce controlled local colour into a cast must do so in the same way as the various glass elements are introduced and packed into the mould. Within this basic premise, however, there are a number of possible variables, each leading to a different set of qualities. Finely ground glass offers a range of possibilities, from the ultimate control of Walter, with his glass 'paint', to packing the glass grains carefully into predetermined areas. Marie-Aimée Grimaldi falls into this latter category, as well as under the pâte-de-verre heading.

Another way of controlling local detail and colour is to introduce precast details into the firing. This allows for two distinct outcomes: firstly an area of highly controlled colour and form within, or emerging from, a differently coloured (or clear) glass; this can be seen in Antoine Leperlier's pieces.

Secondly, by burying the precast section(s) separately into the mould with the wax, the final cast can be made to comprise a number of interlocking but distinct pieces; this is seen in the works of Dong Hai Guan and again in the work of Marie-Aimée Grimaldi.

An interesting variation can be seen in the work of Steven Weinberg, where the clear glass is given a multicoloured surface by coatings which are then patinated. It is clear that this is an area of development that is well worth personal research.

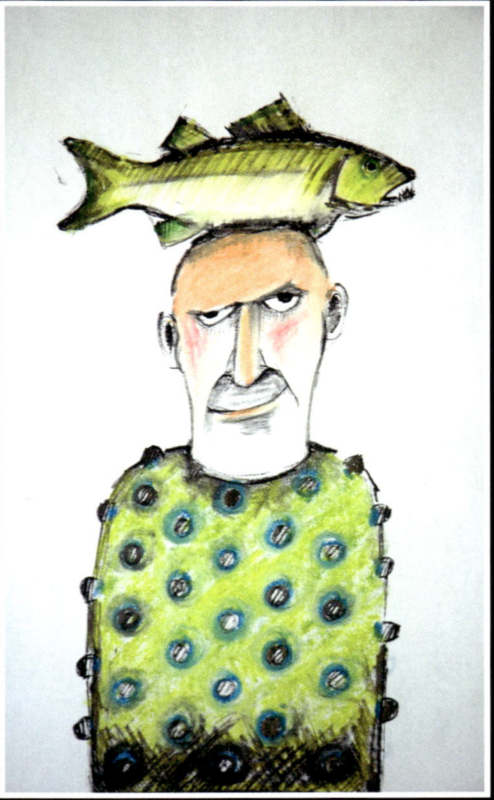

Fruits of the Sea, David Reekie, 2006. Drawing in mixed media, H. 30 cm (11¾ in.), W. 20 cm (7⅞ in.).

As the first stage in the production of a piece this drawing is remarkable for the way it accurately describes the eventual sculpture. This is by no means universal; many artists allow the journey from inspiration to form to help in the creative process. Perhaps the graphic nature of David Reekie's work and his many years of experience have made their contribution to his personal working method.

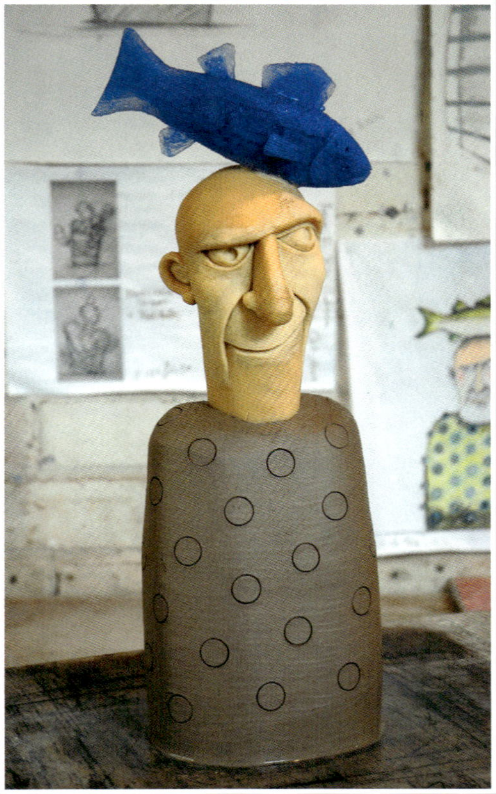

David Reekie, *Fruits of the Sea* (process shot).

This image tells us much about David's methods. The fish has been precast in glass and will become embedded in the mould material. This will ensure that the fish is complete in colour and does not have to be filled through the head during casting. The head is wax, whose qualities as a superb modelling material capable of expressing detail are ones that David exploits. The body is clay, so as to make removal from the mould a simple task, and also reflecting both the simple nature of the body and the need for a different texture from the head.

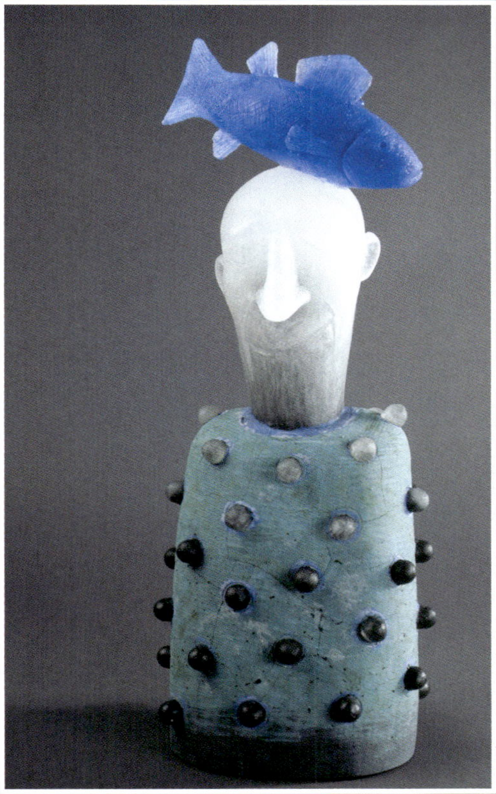

Fruits of the Sea, David Reekie, 2006. Cast glass, H. 41 cm (16⅛ in.), W. 18 cm (7 in.), D. 13 cm (5⅛ in.).

The finished sculpture.

David Reekie

David Reekie is extremely well-known, having been an important presence on the international glass scene for over thirty years. However, a number of comments are worth making, for their example to students and younger artists. David has sustained his career through a highly personal and consistent repertoire of imagery, generated and driven from a base of drawing. This has been used as the driving force behind his work for over three decades of development. The works remain totally recognisable, but are never allowed to become repetitive – always a danger when success can encourage an artist simply to produce more of the same. On the

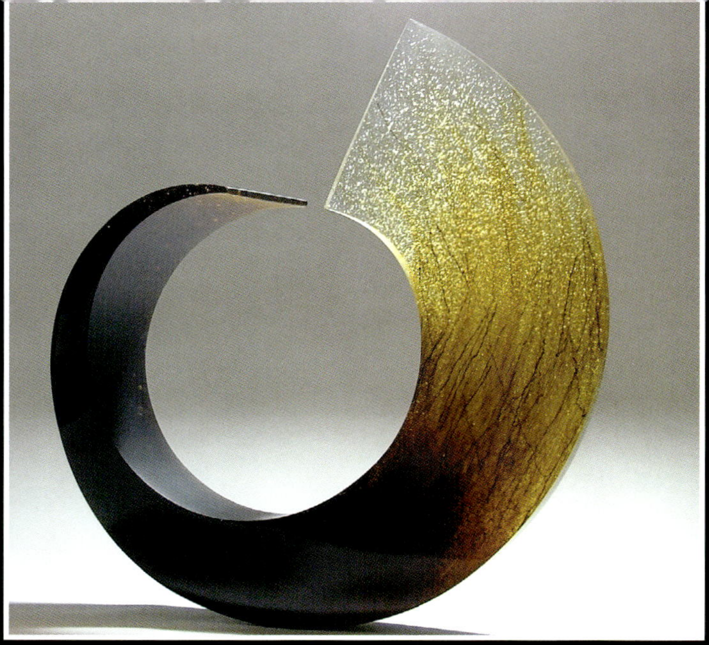

Sundowner 12, Galia Amsel, 2007. W. 60 cm (23⅝ in.), H. 54 cm (21¼ in.), D. 15 cm (6 in.).
Photo: the artist.

Dramatic forms inspired by a move to the Southern Hemisphere; Galia Amsel's pieces use variations in their colour to emphasise the movement and change in her sculptures. A sophisticated mould-making system learned from New Zealand artist Ann Robinson is of great interest for its efficient use of both material and energy.

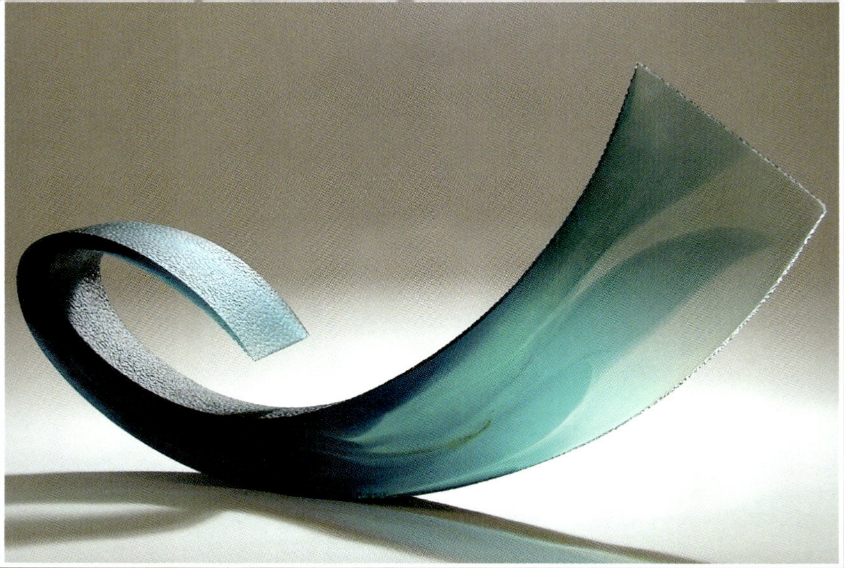

South Pacific Drift, Galia Amsel, 2007. W. 89 cm (35 in.), H. 48 cm (19 in.), D. 15 cm (6 in.).
Photo: the artist.

The mould has been selectively filled with variations in colour and grain size to achieve the modulations that are such a feature of her work. Cold-working includes sandblasting, acid-etching, hand-smoothing and polishing to create varied surfaces.

contrary, his technical vocabulary has kept pace with his aesthetic evolution: he is one of the few glass practitioners who are not afraid to combine glass with a range of other materials and objects, depending on the needs of the sculpture itself.

Artist statement

Although glass is my main medium I use other materials and found objects in my work. I am driven by a desire to make things, and during this making process I have the effects and qualities that glass can give me at the back of my mind.

Politics and how society affects our lives is always a constant influence. I combine all of these influences in my drawings, and they eventually filter through into the work.

I work in a very sculptural way, and this can be traced right back to my time at Stourbridge College of Art, where the influence of artists and teachers such as Harry Seager and Keith Cummings was a strong guiding force in the development of my work.

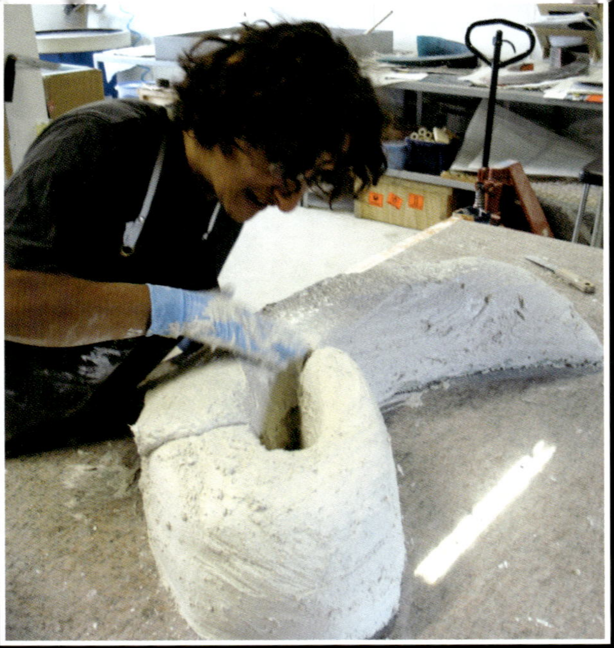

Galia Amsel, mould-making.
Photo: courtesy of the artist.

Building the layers of mould mix, reinforced with grog to produce a mould that has an efficient, even profile.

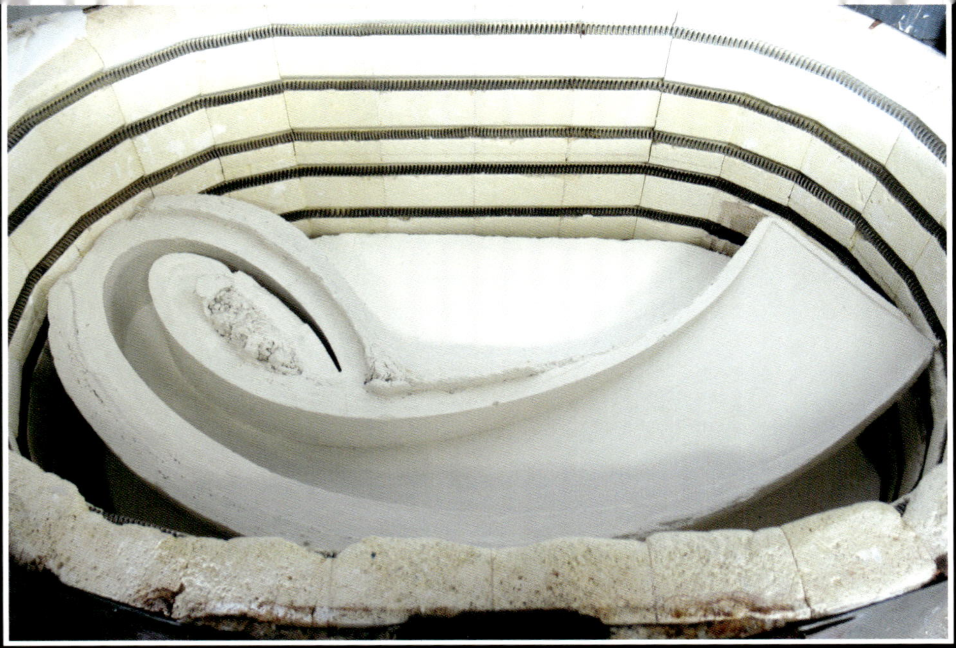

Galia Amsel, mould in the kiln.
Photo: courtesy of the artist.

These forms are cast from one long open side, and must therefore be set up in the kiln with great care to ensure that the top surface is absolutely level.

Galia Amsel

Galia Amsel has developed her current work over a career that has lasted almost twenty years. Formally, her work has moved increasingly towards monumentality and singularity of profile. Her move from England to New Zealand also provided her with a new set of visual and environmental stimuli.

The impact of her sculptures derives from the interplay between outline, mass, colour shifts and finish. All of these elements are subject to a painstaking control, from the construction of the mould to the details of the hand-polishing. The results, with their careful exploitation of reflected and transmitted light, seem to inhabit a realm somewhere between sculpture and painting.

Artist statement

My ideas are based around capturing moments in movement and rhythm, and exploring tension and balance. By working the surface textures and manipulating the use of colour, glass becomes the perfect medium for bringing my forms to life through the variety of ways it can capture and transmit light.

I find that my natural environment increasingly inspires me in the resolution of my sculptures.

Process

I learnt this mould-making process from Ann Robinson here in New Zealand. It is a process which builds up the mould in layers. The benefits include using less mould material, but also getting a more even thickness of mould around an uneven form, which then allows it to anneal more evenly after the glass has melted. The grog in the mixture makes the moulds quite strong, and they end up by being much lighter than poured ones. Moulds which have been built from a number of layers can be as little as 10 cm (4 in.) thick and yet can cope with the pressures of casting heavy pieces of 30 to 40 kilos (66 to 88 lb).

Bruno Romanelli

Now that the studio-glass movement is in its third generation, it is increasingly common for established artists to accept aspiring ones as studio assistants. This has a profound effect on those lucky enough to benefit from such an experience. It is a far cry from the early days, when very little information was available and the little that did exist had to be gained by constant experiment.

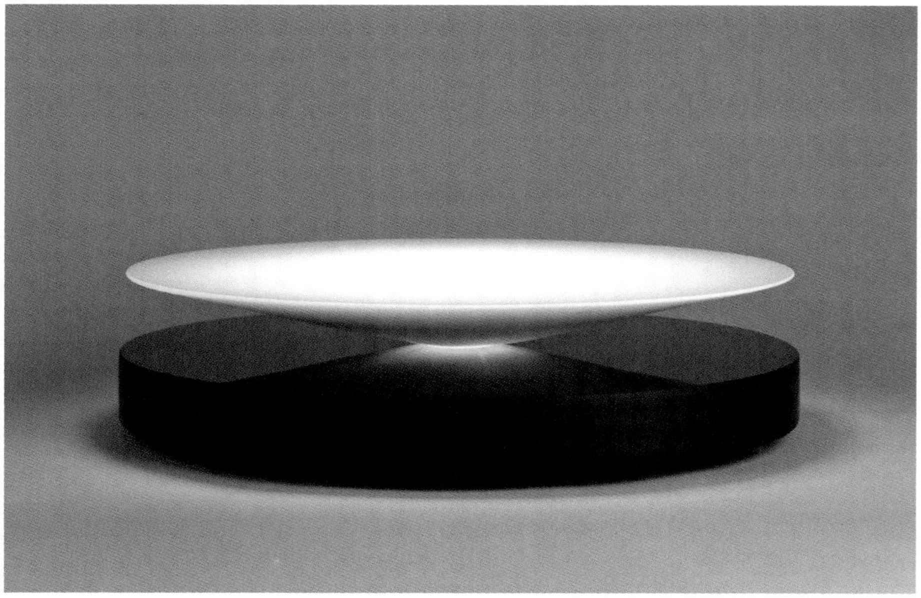

Vega, Bruno Romanelli, 2007. Cast and polished glass, W. 34 cm (13⅜ in.), D. 12 cm (4¾ in.). Photo: Alan Tabor.

Precision is a major characteristic of Bruno Romanelli's sculptures, involving total control of all aspects of the process stages – wax, mould, firing and finishing – to achieve the perfection needed. Bruno is one of a number of artists who passed through Colin Reid's studio and, despite learning much from working there, has gone on to produce original, individual work.

Bruno Romanelli benefited, like a number of others, from working as Colin Reid's assistant, and it is easy to see the influences in Bruno's mature pieces. However, although the technical control of large-scale casting is evident, the uses to which Bruno puts this are every inch his own. Bruno works with a limited range of geometric forms, with limited colour, and a precision of surface that means he relies on the complete control of each element to achieve the austere monumentality of his pieces. His control is absolute, allowing no room for accident or random effects.

Artist statement

Glassmaking for me is like a journey. Although I use the lost-wax process to cast the glass, each piece undergoes many different processes and stages, which also require a deep understanding of many other materials and techniques besides glass and casting. These processes give the piece 'history' and life as it is gradually revealed over a period of anything between three weeks and three months, depending on its complexity.

All my current works begin life from the same shape, a circle, the most basic and universal of forms. For me, the circle symbolises the continuum of life. Each piece is grown out of this one single shape to become a complex form constructed from many parts.

Geometry, symmetry, balance, precision and harmony are all words I would use to describe my work. The control of light and colour is also central, as is the relationship and balance of the individual formal components. It is this combination of light, colour, form, and their interrelationships, that creates harmony and energy within the work.

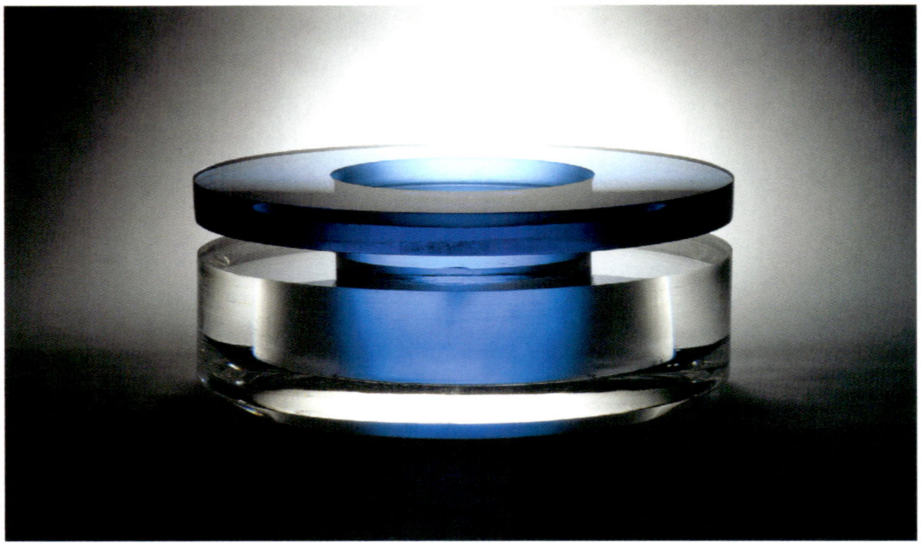

◄ *Regor*, Bruno Romanelli, 2007. Cast and polished glass, H. 28 cm (11 in.) D. 14 cm (5½ in.).
Photo: Alan Tabor.

Balance, symmetry and great stillness are the hallmarks of this particular piece. Unlike many artists Bruno does not find his inspiration from organic growth, but instead seeks to achieve contemplative calm in his forms.

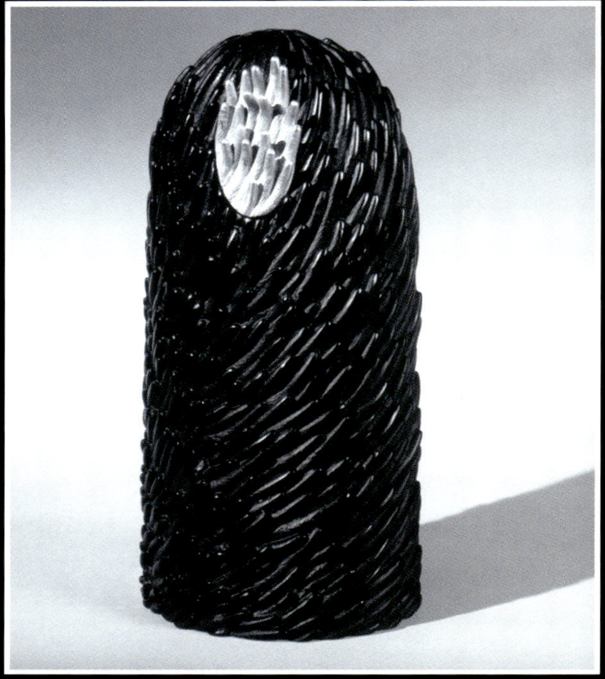

▲ *Nap*, Angela Jarman, 2007. Cast glass, H. 33 cm (13 in.) W. 15 cm (6 in.).
Photo: Alan Tabor.

Angela Jarman not only avoids any reference to the container form in her sculptures, but also prefers to use opaque, muted colours, or in this case black and white. This concentrates attention on the purity of form and surface.

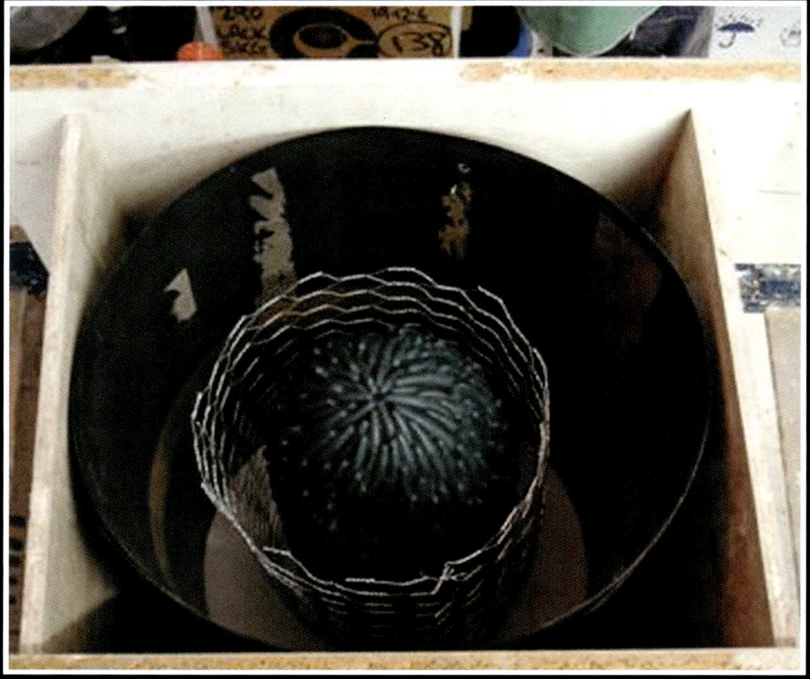

▲ Angela Jarman. *Nap* ready to pour. The use of a wire mesh is necessary to provide strength during casting, particularly when solid, heavy forms are cast, so as to prevent the weight of the glass mass from cracking the mould.

Angela Jarman

Angela Jarman's more recent work is the intensification of a characteristic that has been evident since she began exhibiting. It is also an interesting comment on an important aspect of kiln-formed glass. In Angela's case this has manifested itself as a shift to the use of opaque glass – mainly black and white – as her major material, an extreme version of her always muted palette. In terms of kiln-forming in general this illustrates a characteristic of the output of many practitioners, a choice of qualities of glass that do not match the conventional expectations of the material.

I am sure many kiln-formers have been confronted by the criticism that our works do not look like glass. While this is of no great importance on one level, it is worth consideration on another. Within glass as a material there are an infinite number of qualities. This is hardly surprising in a synthetic material with no 'natural' properties, and the fact that kiln-formers seek to interpret glass in a different way to, say, hot-glass work says much about the material's attractiveness for artists who are not afraid to challenge conventional preconceptions about the nature of the material.

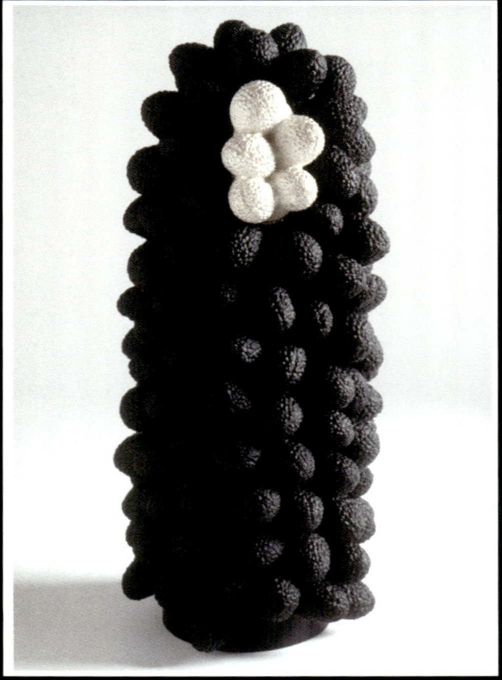

Pablo, Angela Jarman, 2006. Kiln-cast glass, H. 36 cm (14¼ in.), W. 13 cm (5⅛ in.).
Photo: courtesy of the artist.

The better the casting procedure, the less finishing has to be done. This shows how accurate a cast can be produced if the modelling, mould construction and firing is done with attention to detail.

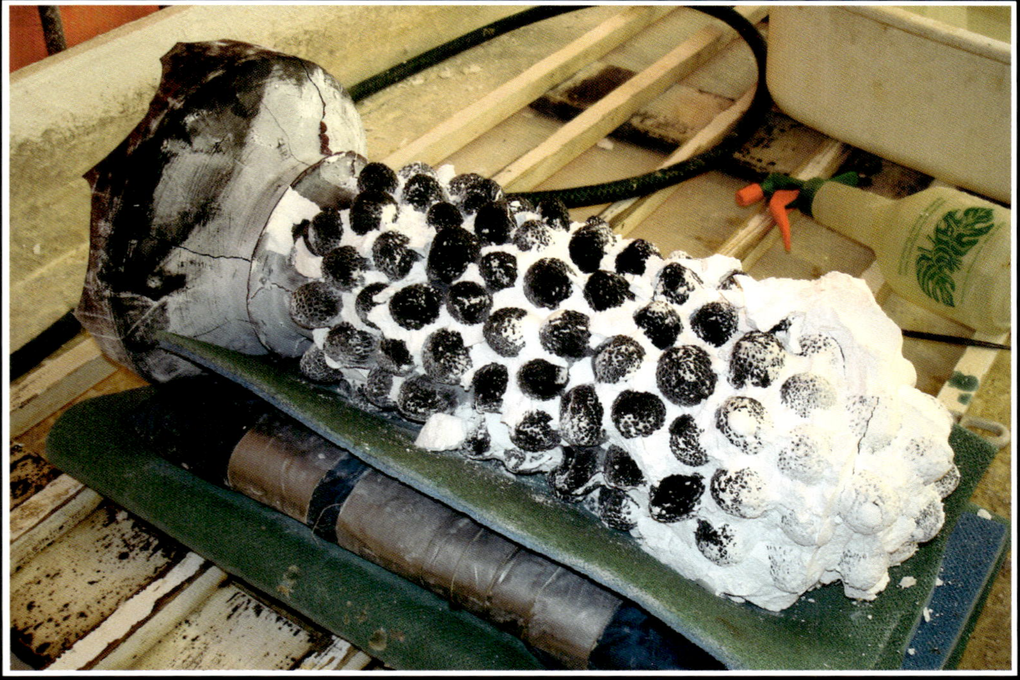

Angela Jarman. De-moulding *Pablo*.
Photo: courtesy of the artist.

Washing the mould mix from the glass surface.

Artist statement

The ideas for my work stem from a long interest I have had in biology and the natural world. I look to many sources for inspiration – animal, vegetable or mineral – but particularly aspects of growth, reproduction and multiplication, all the while trying to retain a sense of ambiguity. I want my work to refer to nature but to appear 'unnatural', and to carry a sense of the uncanny and sinister through subtle references. I've built up my own themes with a vocabulary of my own that I use by repeating and duplicating a specific part or by creating form on the inside through the use of a textured core.

By using only colourless glass for its transparency, and colours such as aluminium and silver for their neutrality, I hope to draw attention away from the glitzy aspect of glass, and to focus on the form, structure and texture of a piece. For the past few years, I've been using a lot of black glass, because of the way it seems to suck in the light and appear so dense and un-glasslike, and also because of its barren and sinister quality. But working with this glass has also proved to be quite problematic, as I have found it a much more temperamental material to work with than clear glass, and more prone to

Cage Head, Dong Hai Guan, 2007. ➤
H. 26.5 cm (10½ in.), W. 20 cm (7⅞ in.), D. 21 cm (8¼ in.).
Photo: the artist.

One of the leaders of China's emerging cohort of studio-glass artists, Dong Hai, although trained in the West, has rapidly developed an approach to kiln-forming that reflects the culture of his own country, while at the same time stretching the technical limits of the medium. This piece refers to ancient punishments, and places a cast head in a cast box independently of one another, an extremely difficult technical feat.

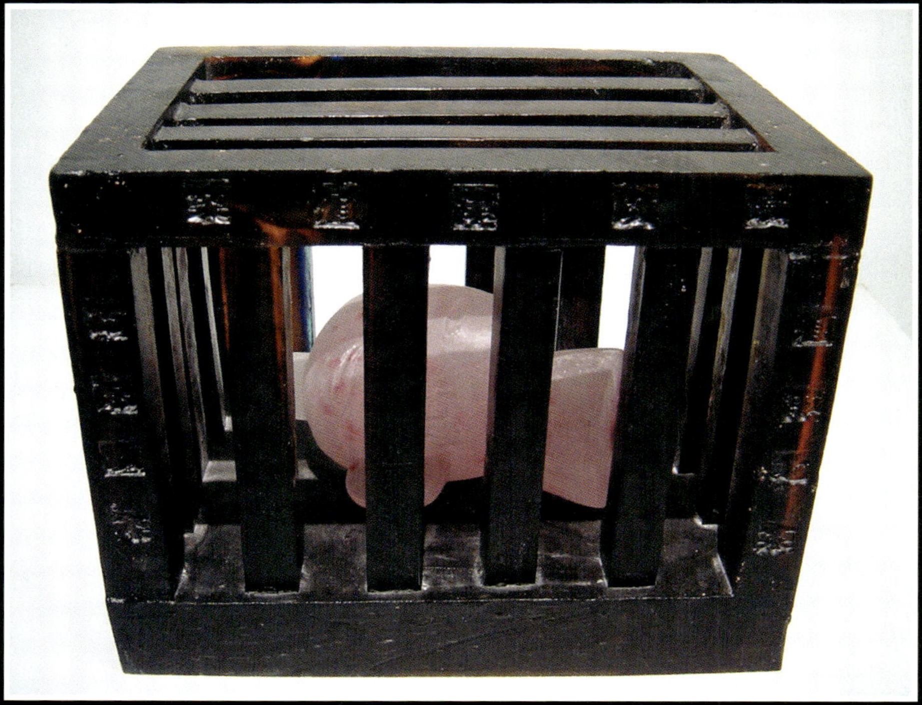

Link, Dong Hai Guan, 2007. W. 56 cm (22 in.) H. 13 cm (5⅛ in.), D. 13 cm (5⅛ in.). ➤
Photo: courtesy of the artist.

In this piece Dong Hai extends the technique of joining sections together by combining a traditional Chinese metal weight with a linked version of itself in glass.

failure. During casting, things frequently go wrong, and my success rate from each firing has been noticeably lower: for each piece that works, there has been at least one that has failed; either the glass did not move down into the mould properly, and I ended up with only half an object, or it took such a long time to cast that the mould lost its strength and burst.

Dong Hai Guan

Dong Hai typifies the new wave of Chinese artists. He studied glass in England and is now head of a university department of glass in Beijing, and a teacher, designer and maker of growing reputation. Despite taking many of the established techniques and values of western examples as their starting points, Dong Hai, his students and fellow practitioners have, in less than a decade, given creative glass a distinctively Chinese voice.

Kiln-forming is their preferred way of making glass, and artists like Dong Hai have shaped it to reflect their cultural context and aesthetic heritage. These examples of his work demonstrate an ability to contribute to the technical vocabulary of kiln-forming that bodes well for the future.

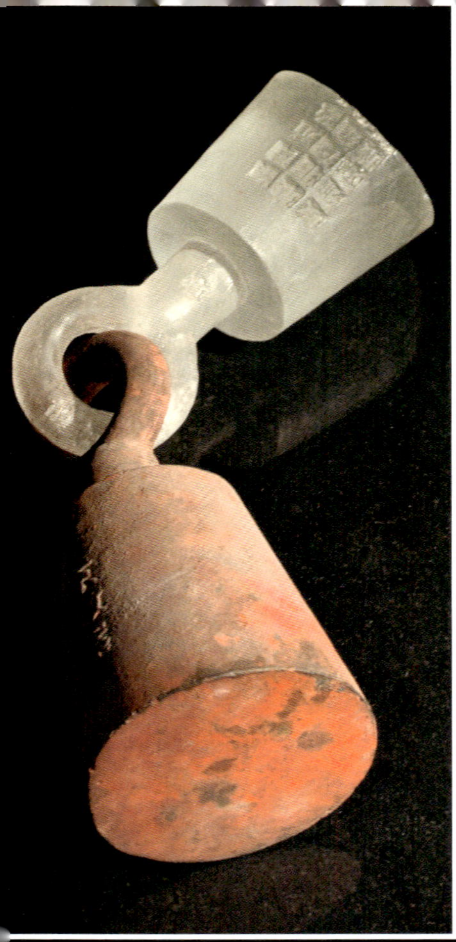

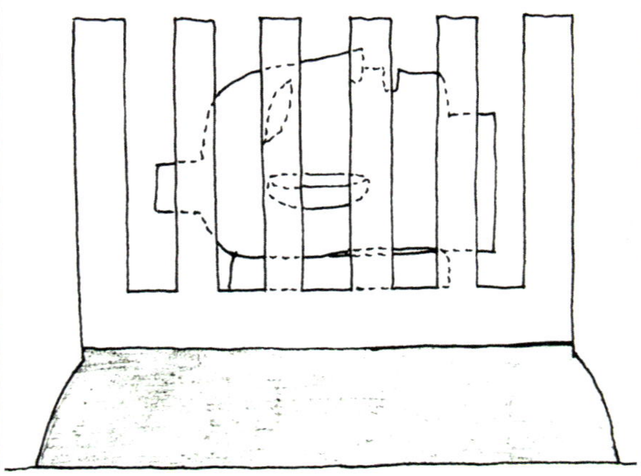

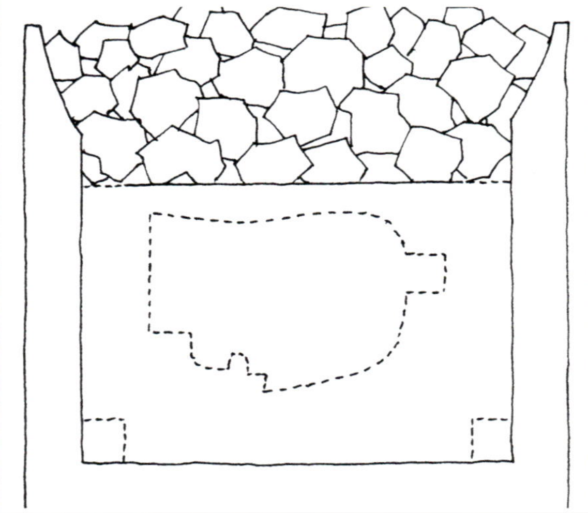

Dong Hai, process drawing.
Photo: courtesy of the artist.

Although this drawing by Dong Hai relates to the casting of *Box*, the principle is the same as for *Link*. The head is cast first, and placed inside the wax box on a small pad of kiln mix. The whole is invested (enveloped) in refractory mix and the wax box steamed out.

Dong Hai, process drawing.
The mould, containing the embedded glass head and the void of the box, is fired in the kiln with a reservoir of glass to cast the box. After firing, the mould mix is carefully removed to reveal the two elements of the sculpture. In the case of *Link* the iron weight was embedded in the mould mix in the same way as the glass head, with no part of it touching the other part.

The history of glass has seen the movement of glassmaking from culture to culture throughout its five millennia of existence. Each such move has resulted in a new approach to the material and its forming methodology. China, with its recent rise in global prominence, is the latest staging post in this repeating journey.

Artist statement

In ancient China punishments were extremely severe and cruel. One of the main examples was the exhibition of an executed criminal's head in a cage on the gate of the city. This cage symbolised the repression of the people's mental and physical freedom. To use this as the basis for a sculpture I had to devise a technique that allowed me to cast a head inside a cage. The apparent impossibility of this adds to the theme of control.

Process

I like the challenge of developing new techniques and stretching old ones. Success in this is allied to the expression of my ideas, the one supporting the other. Sometimes the magic is achieved by comparatively simple means.

First I cast a glass head, and then I make a wax cage with the top open. A clay base is made on which the glass head is placed on a piece of cast kiln mix. This brings the head into the centre of the glass cage when it is placed over it. The clay base acts as the reservoir when the whole is set in refractory kiln mix and the wax melted out. The whole mould with the empty cage sections is filled with glass and fired. The head remains untouched during firing as it is firmly embedded in the mould mix.

Irene Frolic

Irene Frolic has been creating her highly personal kiln-cast sculpture from her studio in Toronto for twenty years. Her early reputation was based on her interest in the crust of the glass cast, and the way in which

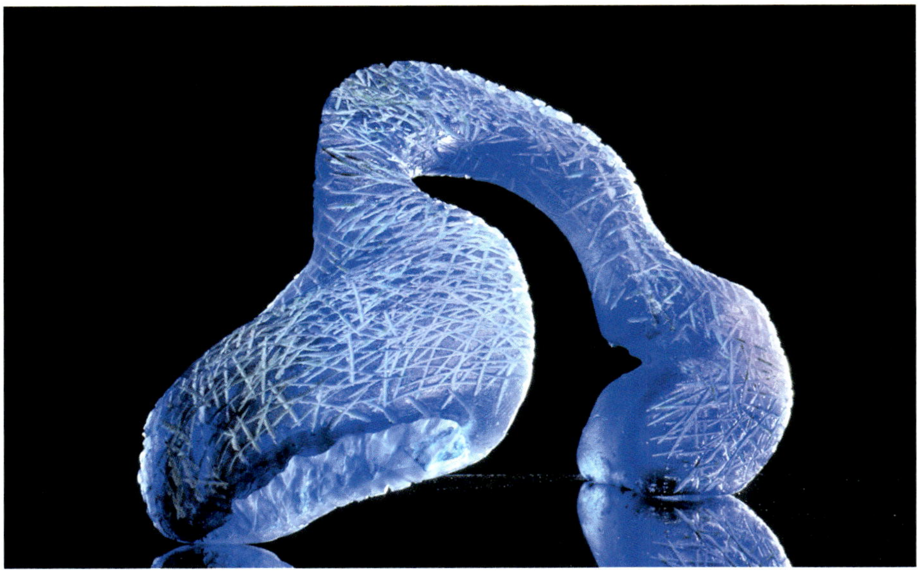

Blue Sprout, Irene Frolic, 2001. Kiln-cast using the lost wax process, H. 39 cm (15⅜ in.), W. 46 cm (18 in.), D. 30 cm (11¾ in.).
Photo: courtesy of the artist.

A characteristic common to artists who have consistently been at the forefront of kiln-forming for many decades is their ability to continue to develop creatively, and thereby avoid the trap of repeating themselves, which can be the downside of success. This piece is gestural in its colour, texture and form, like a brush painting in three dimensions. The original wax is clearly the source of the movement and texture, being hand-modelled directly rather than cast from a model. Frolic regards the *Sprout* series as an important shift in her imagery.

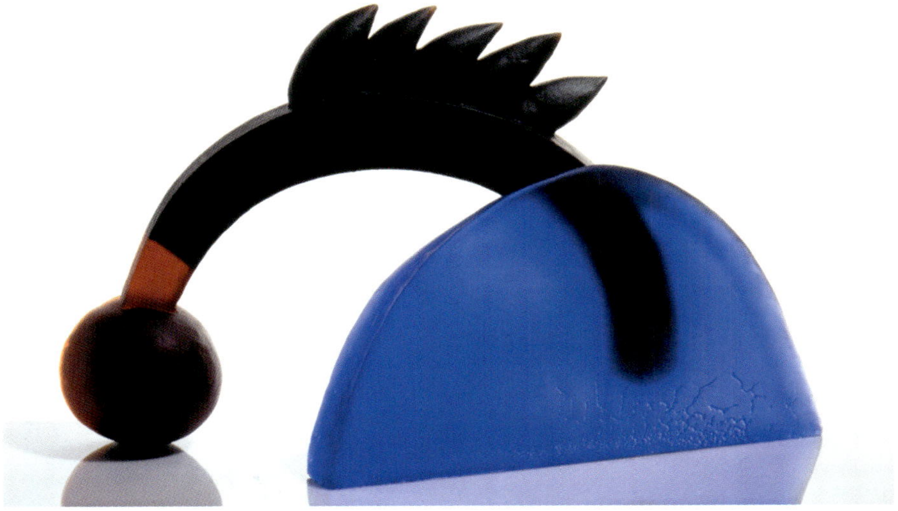

Vivid Blues with Black and Amber, Irene Frolic, 2004. Kiln-cast from wax original, H. 42 cm (16½ in.), W. 45 cm (17¾ in.), D. 20 cm (7⅞ in.).
The title indicates that the central theme of this piece is the colour contrasts expressed through forms. The connection between the main blue section and the linear one is achieved by physical means rather than fused.

she used this to explore personal history and express emotion through the figurative. In this early work she represented an interesting aspect of kiln-forming, a rejection of the glossy, light-manipulating qualities of glass in favour of a darker, more heavily textured personal palette. Given the premium put on the more conventional glassy qualities by galleries and collectors this represented an individual and courageous stance.

Having achieved international recognition with this approach, however, Frolic has more recently confounded expectations again by breaking new ground in her sculptural enquiry. Given that in today's climate it is risky to change the nature of one's work, particularly once success has been achieved, this again shows her artistic and creative integrity.

Artist statement

In my recent work I have begun to explore the purely formal aspects of glass, its ability to carry line and colour. The sculptures are flattened out, more calligraphic than in the round. The newer work refers to the wandering vivid line of Joan Miró. The sculptures relate to calligraphy in the sense of the vigorous mark made by the artist's brush.

Antoine Leperlier

With his brother Etienne, Antoine Leperlier stands alone in the kiln-forming world in the sense that they represent a living link to the origins of pâte de verre through their illustrious grandfather, Francois Décorchement. Leperlier was actually introduced to the process by his grand-father, working with him in his studio from 1968 to his death in 1971. Initially, his working methods were naturally based on what he had absorbed there, but he rapidly developed his own language and has built a reputation to match that of his great forebear.

Leperlier's main methods have centred around casting, with the accent being on multicolour gravity casts. However, he has always sought to use technique to express a personal aesthetic and, where he has found current practice to be insufficient for his formal language, he has developed fresh procedures to bridge the gap.

As a result his works evolve in their relationship to both the material and its creative range. Their allusions to a range of expressive formats – poetry and philosophy among them – make his pieces among the most intellectually layered in contemporary practice, and at the same time among the least dependent on the natural novelties of the material. This is not to say that his works lack these seductions – far from it; but these

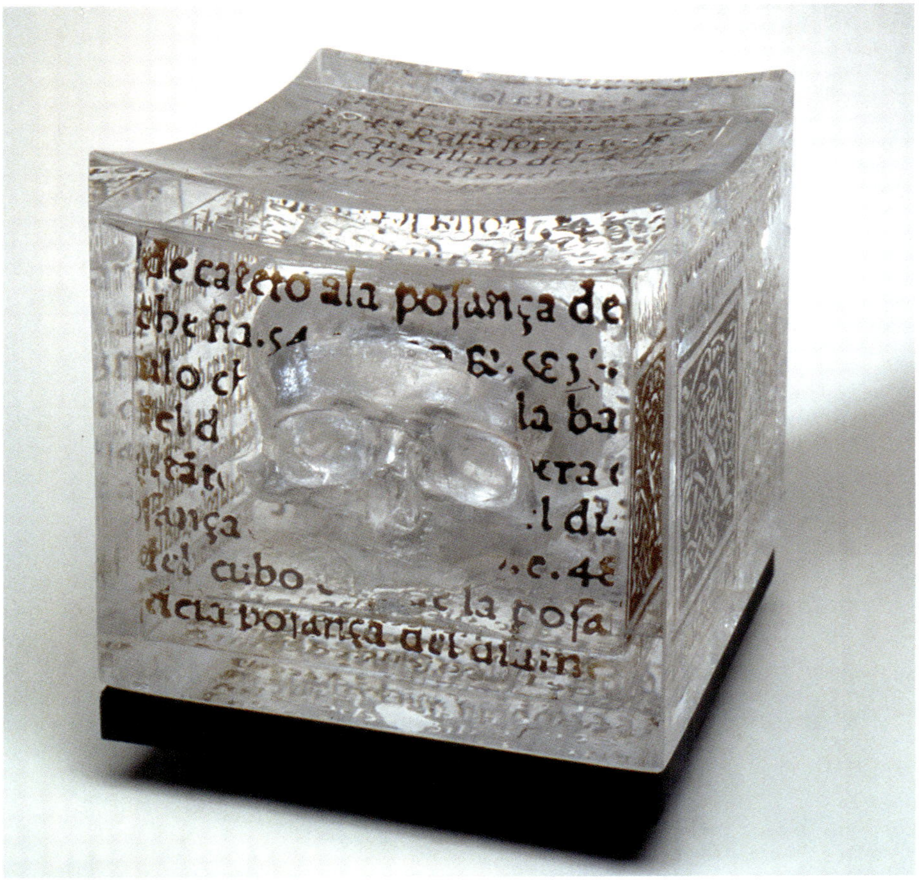

Effets de la Mémoire X, Antoine Leperlier, 2000. H. 25 cm (9⅞ in), W. 25 cm (9⅞ in), D. 25 cm (9⅞ in).
Photo: courtesy of the artist.

Clearly, Antoine Leperlier uses glass as a fully sculptural material, and he talks of inventing new techniques to facilitate the imagery he desires. Despite the complex methods he uses, including multiple cast sections and the controlled creation of internal voids, he can never be accused of seeking novel qualities for their own sake. The symbolism and literary references inherent in his pieces serve individual methods rather than ends in themselves.

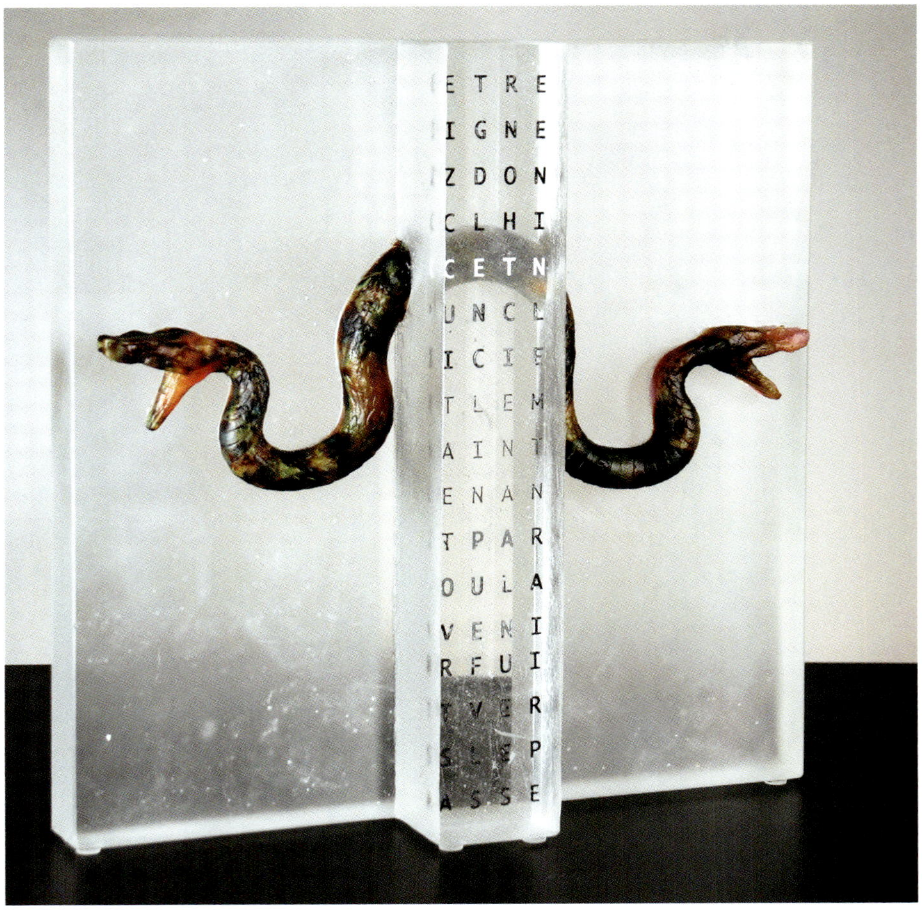

Hic et Nunc – serpent, Antoine Leperlier, 2007. W. 38 cm (15 in.).
Photo: courtesy of the artist.

Leperlier's recent work combines traditional multicoloured pâte de verre with clear glass. The technique involved in the creation of the serpent form that moves through the clear glass is a tour de force of kiln-forming.

are used as channels through which ideas flow, and are never allowed, despite their originality, to move to the foreground.

Antoine Leperlier's influence extends beyond his works themselves. He has helped a number of artists who have either sought his advice or worked in his studio. The list is impressive, and includes Diana Hobson and the next artist Marie-Aimée Grimaldi.

Marie-Aimée Grimaldi

On one level I could and perhaps should have included Marie-Aimée Grimaldi in the section devoted to pâte de verre, especially as she herself describes her work in these terms. I should therefore explain my reasons for not doing so. These are twofold, both based on the high temperature at which she casts her work. Firstly, the various glass grains that she employs to give the local colour in her casts have been heated to a point where the colour is the only record of the original grain. Secondly, she has devised a method of casting three-dimensional forms so that they interlock without being fused together. Taken together, these two innovations seem to me to move the more traditional pâte-de-verre process onto a different level – one that places it in the company of this particular group, at least in terms of its technical interest.

▼ *Pratique Derisoire*, Marie-Aimée Grimaldi, 2001. H. 14 cm (5½ in.), L. 22 cm (8⅝ in.), W. 15 cm (6 in.).
Photo: courtesy of the artist.

The theme of this group of pieces by Grimaldi involves that most human of images, the skull, but by interpreting it through the medium of delicately coloured glass and decorating it with delicate piercings she brings an extra range of visual references to bear.

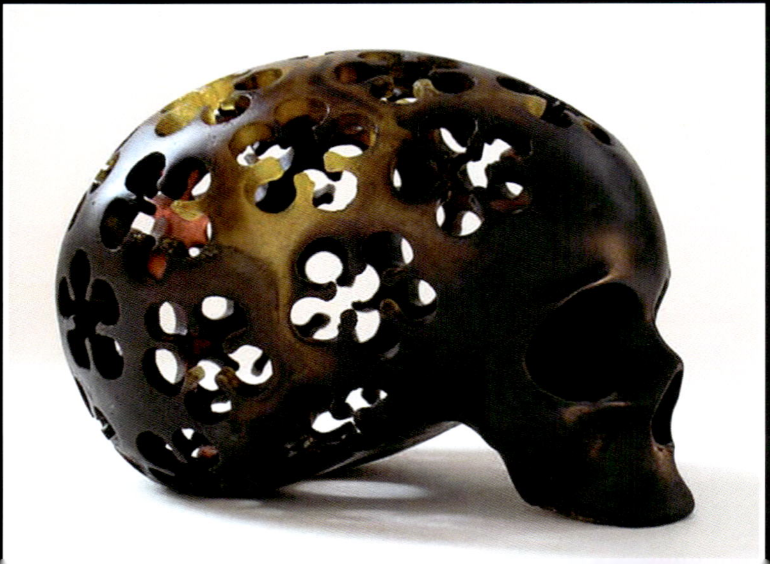

▼ *Yellow Submarine*, Marie-Aimée Grimaldi, 2006. H. 14 cm (5½ in.), L. 22 cm (8⅝ in.), W. 15 cm (6 in.).
Photo: courtesy of the artist.

The techniques involved in the casting of this skull form are inventive, and are used to great effect. The flowers were cast separately and attached to the wax prior to the casting of the host form.

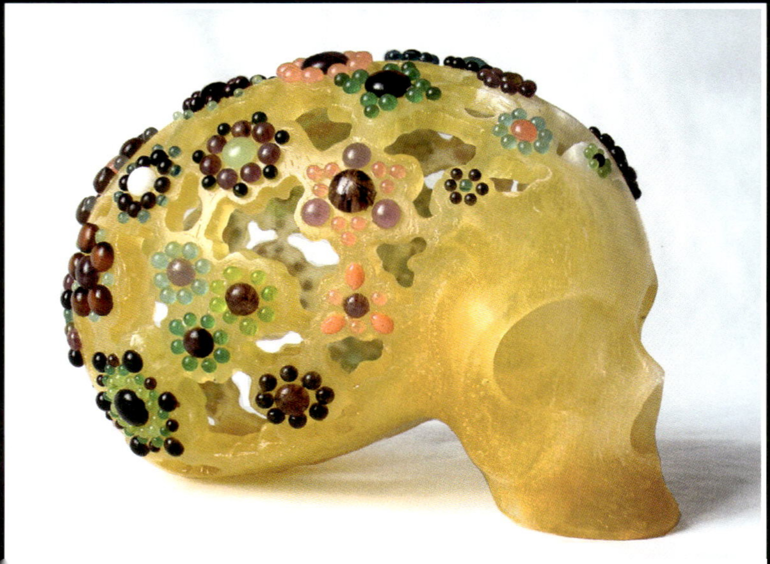

As an artist, Grimaldi uses some of the most powerful human images – particularly in the skull series – and yet combines them, through the use of colour and pattern, in a state of tension. The way in which the various elements react with one another creates highly personal pieces.

Artist statement

After my studies at the École des Beaux-Arts at Tours, I worked with Antoine Leperlier, who introduced me to the technique of pâte de verre. Fascinated by the possibilities offered by the material and the colours of this process, I began to research under his direction in his studio. These studies seldom exceeded the scale of jewellery, but permitted me to identify a personal vocabulary of material qualities and colour. I set up my own studio in 1990, and produced a series of masks in bas-relief on a large scale, which became my first coherent body of work.

The piece I made for the World Glass Now exhibition in 1994 was my first fully realised three-dimensional polychromatic piece. It was acquired by the Museum of Modern Art in Hokkaido, which was also the exhibition venue.

The theme of the skull is not intended as a symbol of death or human vanity, but was chosen by me to signify that once the mask of the flesh is removed there still remains the essence of an individual human being.

Mark Peiser

Mark Peiser has been involved with glass for over twenty-five years. The use of the word 'involved' is deliberate on my part, because it comes closest to describing his particular take on the material. He is, of course, an artist with a strong formal language, but to this he adds an ability to work with the material itself, exploring and extending its creative potential. He does this by an understanding of its physical make-up and unique behaviour. From this he devises ways of harnessing these characteristics in the invention of new ways of forming glass; his cold-stream casting system is a prime example.

Peiser's work is too diverse to be comfortably contained within a single category of glass-forming, but it is precisely this willingness and ability to push boundaries that made his inclusion in a book devoted to kiln-forming essential. I have always argued for cross-fertilisation to keep glass moving forward, and Peiser's attitude and example shows how this can be done. In his statement his description of casting speaks volumes.

Artist statement

I have been casting glass for over twenty-five years. I think of casting as how to get glass from one container to another. In doing that I have observed some curious things, most of which were unwanted, unexpected and presented problems for what I wanted to do at the time. Over the years I have had the interest and the opportunity to take another look at these phenomena and their implications.

When you choose to investigate a new process – a way of doing things that has no history, no examples – the only way to discover the possibilities is to do something and see what you get. Sometimes you can theorise what's possible, and it works, but more often something unexpected happens to show you possibilities you could not have imagined.

You build a vocabulary of possibilities, and if there are enough of them, and the process will allow you to combine them and allow the composition to grow, then perhaps beauty can evolve and take a new form.

▼ *Passing Thought*, Mark Peiser, 2004. Crucible cast, H. 26 cm (10¼ in.), W. 27 cm (10⅝ in.), D. 16 cm (6¼ in.).
Photo: Tom Mills.

The quality and colour of the glass he uses is important to the artist, and is one reason for his insistence on casting from freshly founded glass.

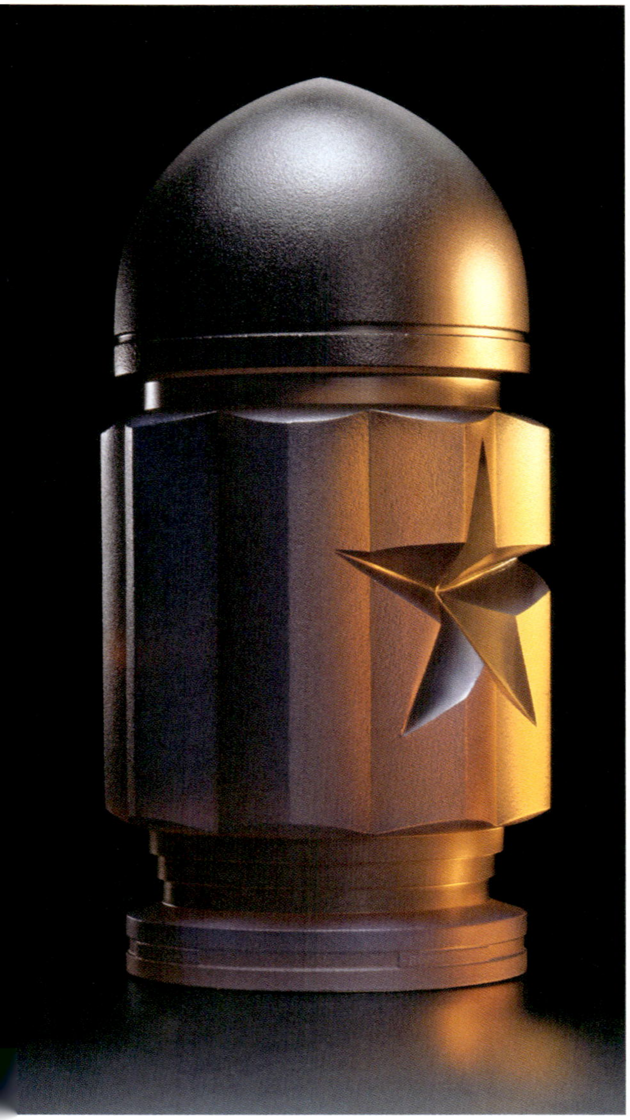

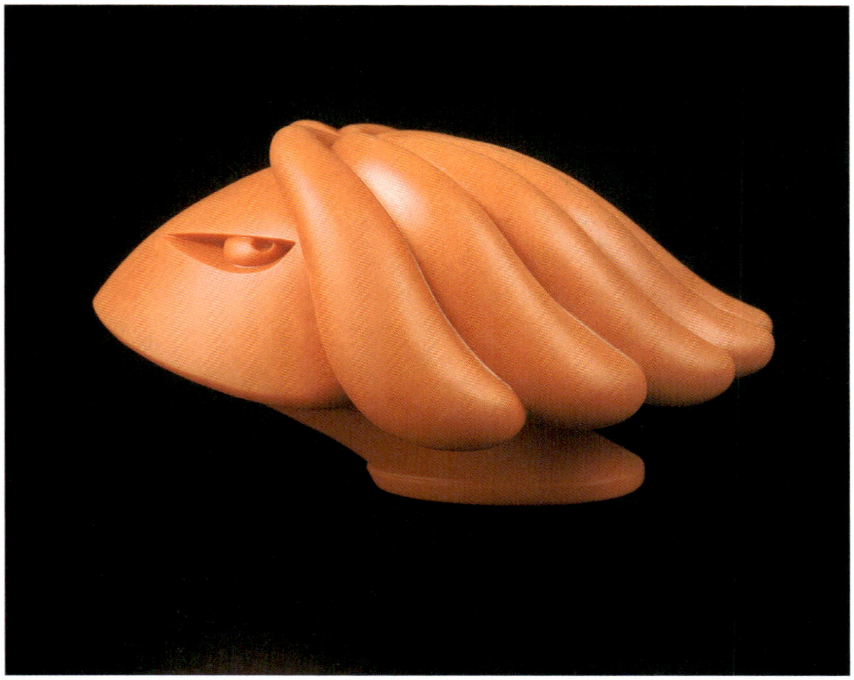

◄ *Bomb*, Mark Peiser, 2007. H. 50 cm (19¾ in.), D. 25 cm (9⅞ in.).
Photo: Tom Mills.

Mark Peiser has throughout his near thirty-year career moved between one glass process and another as his ideas have demanded. This piece is cast, but not inside a kiln. The hot glass is transferred to the mould by flowing through an aperture in the base of the furnace. His example shows that divisions between making methods are there to be crossed.

Steven Weinberg

As an artist who has been at the forefront of contemporary glass for over thirty years, Steven Weinberg has constantly extended his creative use of the material, despite the fact that his earlier work set standards for control and precision in the realisation of his pristine, often geometrically inspired cast sculptures. The language of these forms required technical excellence to do them justice, and Weinberg was among the first studio artists to pioneer the use of pure optical glass ingots to achieve the effects he required.

However, in his search for the ultimate, he has continually developed his control of process, material and finish in the evolution of new work. As his statement makes clear, he finds the demands of such perfection difficult – they are in some ways at odds with his natural inclinations –

2 Buoys, Steven Weinberg, 2004. ➤
H. 46 cm (18 in.).
Photo: Marty Doyle.

Steven Weinberg is another artist who extends his lifetime involvement with kiln-forming into crucible-casting, to ensure the highest-quality glass. In these pieces the optical quality of the glass is contrasted with the textured and coloured exteriors, created by spray-coating the crystal in metallised iron and copper, which are then patinated.

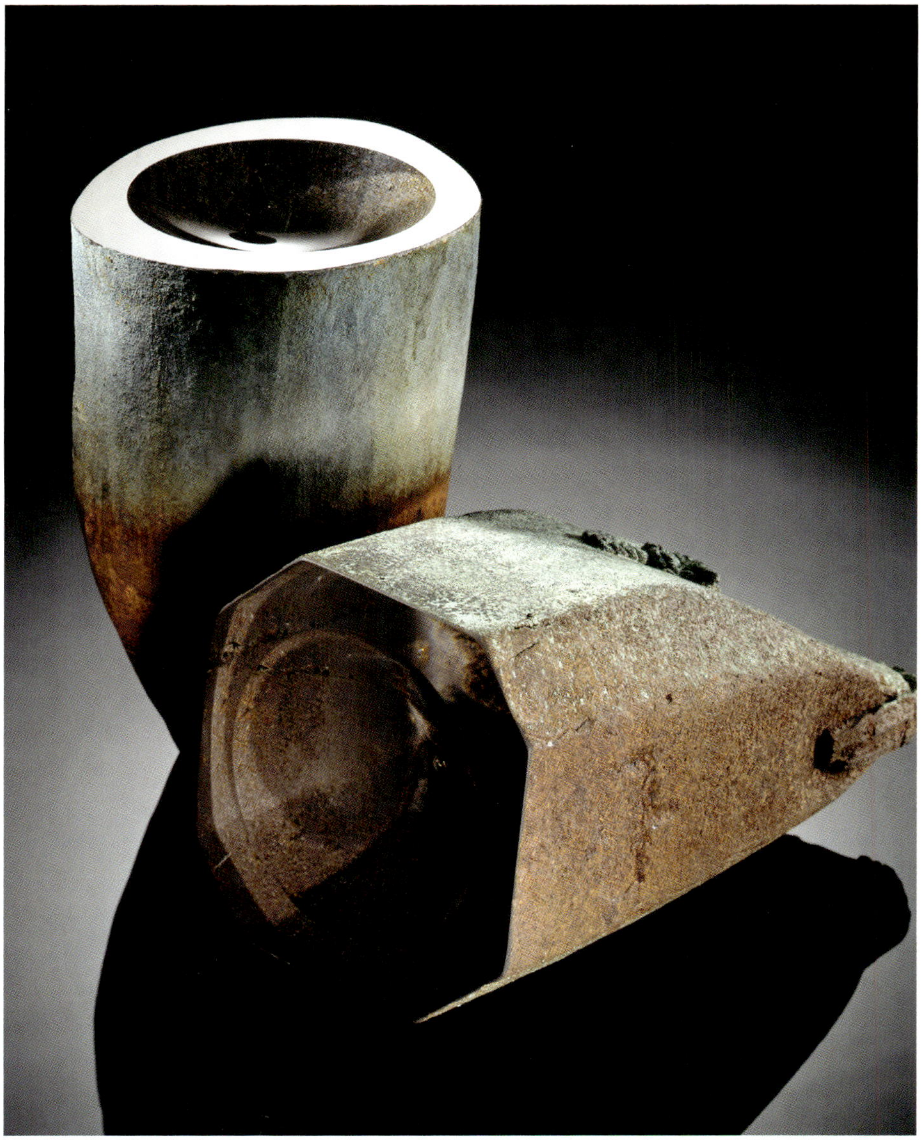

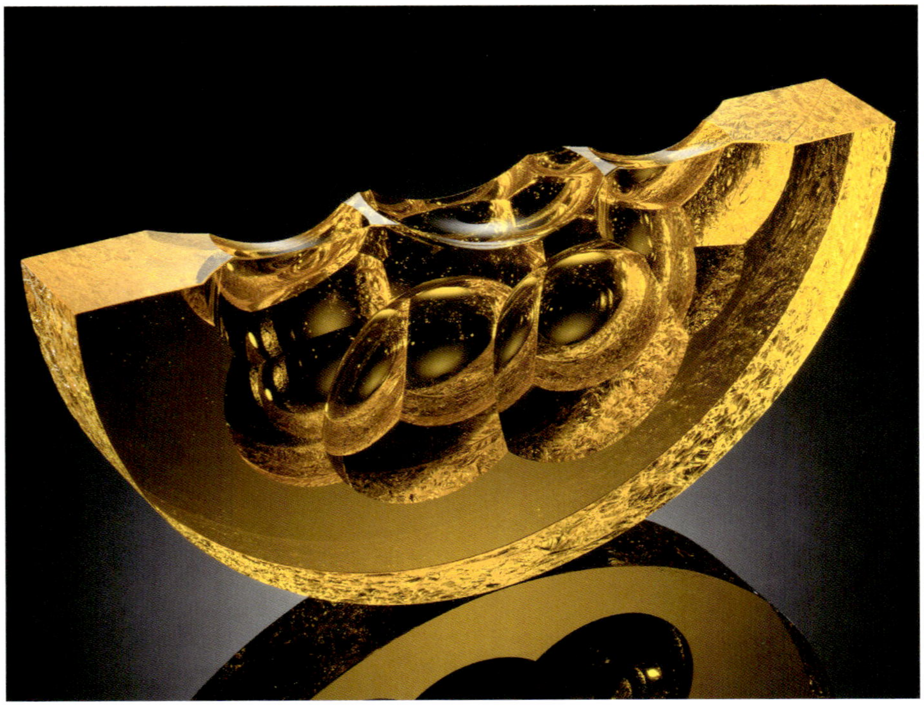

Misquamicut, Saffron Boat, Steven Weinberg, 2007. H. 29 cm (11⅜ in.), W. 60 cm (23⅝ in.), D. 4 cm (1½ in.). Photo: Marty Doyle.

In this piece the limpid glass is exploited with cutting. Absolute control over process to gain the highest-quality outcome has always been a major feature of Weinberg's work. The use of crucibles facilitates the production of small quantities of glass for specific casts. This allows maintenance of the highest standards and the use of a wider range of colours and glass types than reliance on larger furnaces or the use of standard off-the-shelf glasses permits.

but the realisation of the work overrides this reservation. In admitting as much, he gives voice to an often unsaid truth about kiln-forming: many of its stages are tedious and unrewarding in themselves. Yet truly successful artists like Steven not only give these stages their full attention, but often go out of their way to search for constant improvement, whatever the cost in terms of time and energy.

This has led him to the borders of kiln-forming proper, and beyond, in his development of casting through the use of crucibles, enabling him to produce casts of sumptuous clarity, and to show these to their best advantage through high-quality cutting and polishing. Despite this, his forms are never subservient to the glass; his formal vocabulary is always in control.

Artist statement

It makes no sense for a person like myself, who has always been addicted to immediate gratification, to work the way I do. Kiln-casting glass and then spending countless hours, weeks or months finishing surfaces is about as exciting as watching a cactus grow. I refuse to ask myself who is making my work, because that person can't be me. Yet it has been, for over thirty years. It would take a patient man to work to the degree of perfection that I demand of each piece, and those who know me know that I am far from patient. Chaos and clutter abound in everything I touch in life except my work.

The beauty of striving for perfection is that I know that I will never achieve it. As an object maker I am cursed with seeing where I could have done better, rather than being happy with a finished piece of work in front of me. Maybe what keeps me going is the voyage of seeking perfection through a balance of control juxtaposed with the haphazard nature of the material. Whatever it is, I will continue to watch the cactus grow.

David Ruth

In a career spanning three decades David Ruth has remained true to his original source, his interest in the internal space he can determine in his pieces. From this apparently simple starting point has emerged a creative journey that has been anything but simple, taking in as it does a wide range of technical development, and finding its expression in sculptural and architectural terms.

To achieve the scale and complexity of his 'inner space', Ruth has stretched the nature of kiln-forming to new levels, devising methods by which he can engineer the layered details in his monumental works. He is unusual in the way he is comfortable in a number of different contexts, producing both individual pieces of personally driven sculpture and large-scale architectural commissions. For kiln-forming to continue to develop, it needs constantly to extend its boundaries, and Ruth's work is a prime example of how this can be achieved.

Artist statement

My block pieces are the result of an evolution that started many years ago. One of the first things I was interested in seeing in glass was the paradoxical internal space of the rock-solid material. There are not many natural examples of such a thing, except maybe ice or rock crystal.

My first real glass teacher, Roger Darricarrere, was a Frenchman who brought the techniques of dal de verre (casting thick slabs of glass for setting in concrete) to the United States in the early fifties. Because he could not get the glass for the 'glass embedded in cement'-type stained-glass windows that he wanted to make, he made his own. The hand-pouring and small-scale melting led to pieces where the colours were streaked and bubbles embedded. When I worked with him in the early seventies, I gazed into these pieces and found my future.

A decade later, I was in graduate school, and when asked by one of the professors what I liked about glass, I replied 'the inside picture'. His comment was that the interior of the glass body could be seen as a metaphor for the internal life of mankind. I took that as my own internal life and

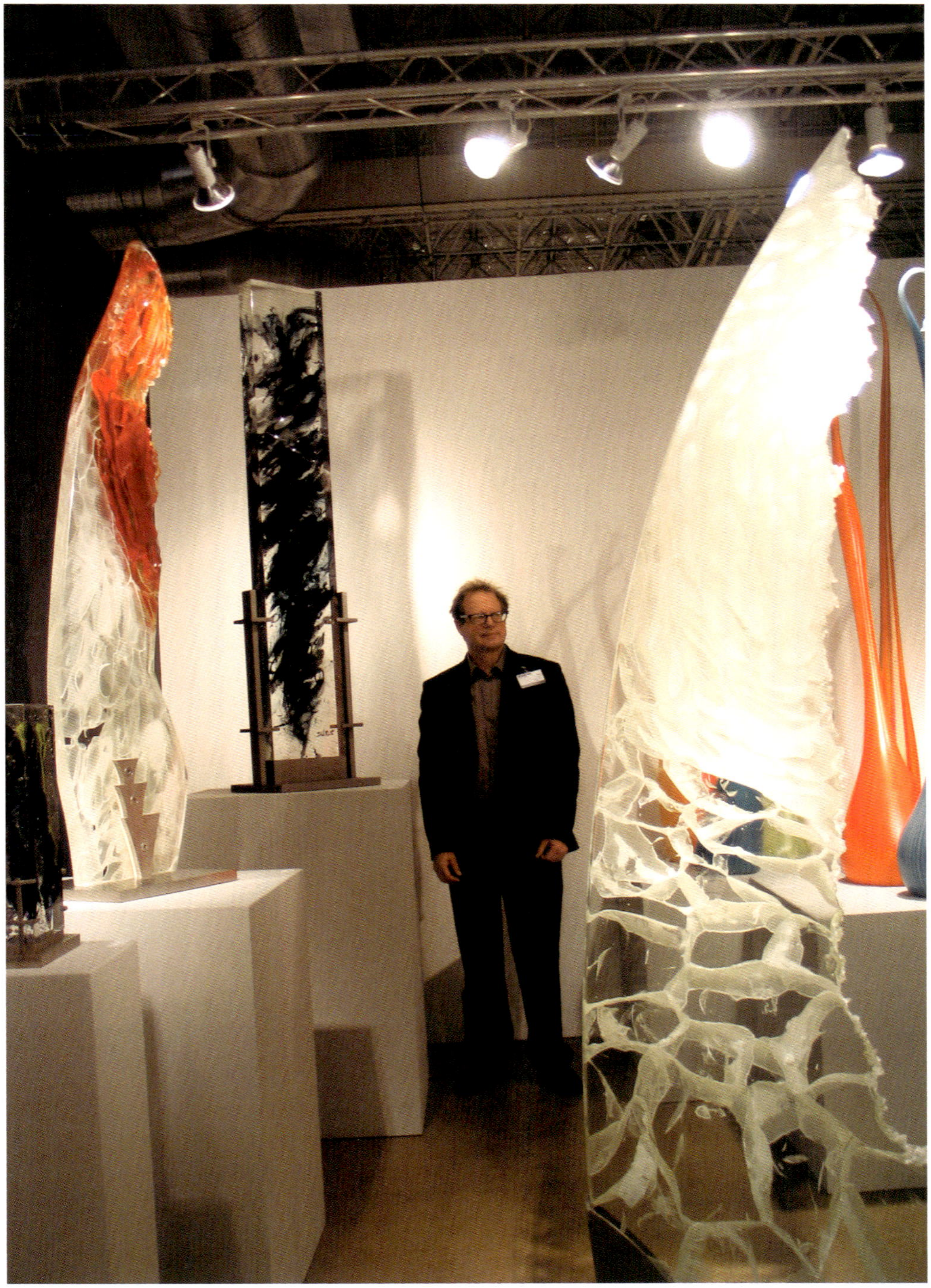

David Ruth in his studio, 2008.
Photo: courtesy of the artist.

David Ruth works on a large scale, producing architectural features and one-off free-standing pieces. He has always stretched the limits of kiln-forming to include his physical intervention in the fusing process to manually add coloured, pre-formed elements into the fused mass. In this way he achieves the layered, painterly effects that are such a feature of his work.

endeavoured to make that interior real and prominent.

Another decade and more later, a scene from Andy Goldsworthy's film *Rivers and Tides* caused me to ponder the idea of flow and the possibility of capturing an active moment in an anti-gravity mass. Goldsworthy is shown throwing balls of dirt or dust in the air. For one magic moment each ball takes on a three-dimensional, tumbling form before the particles

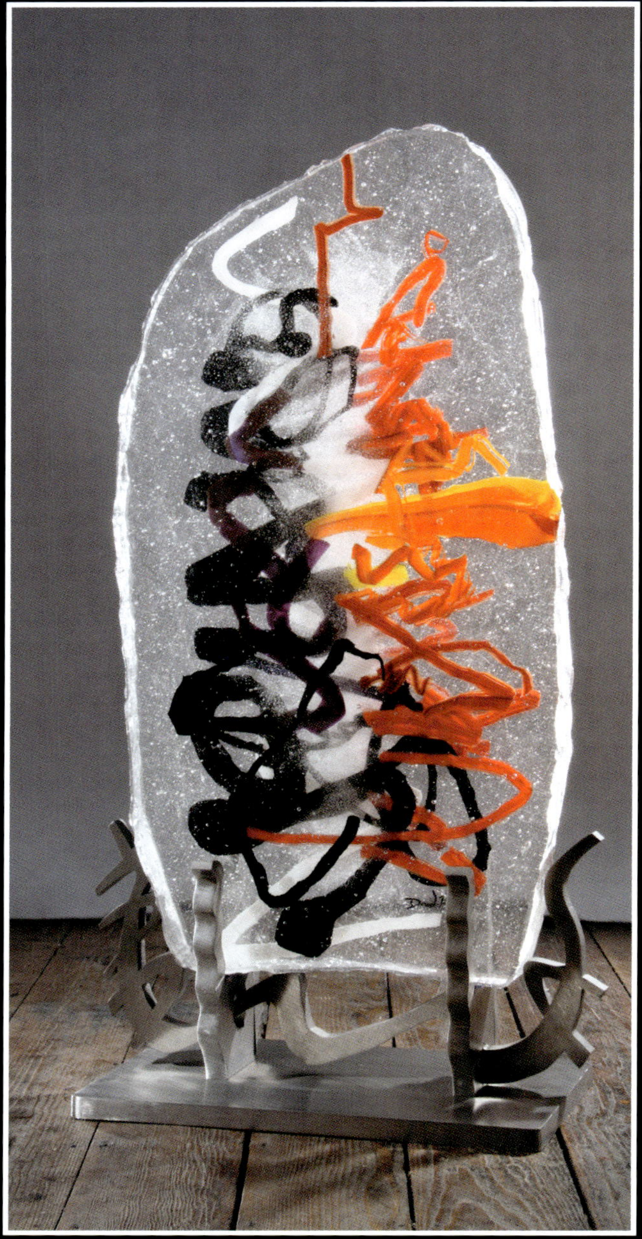

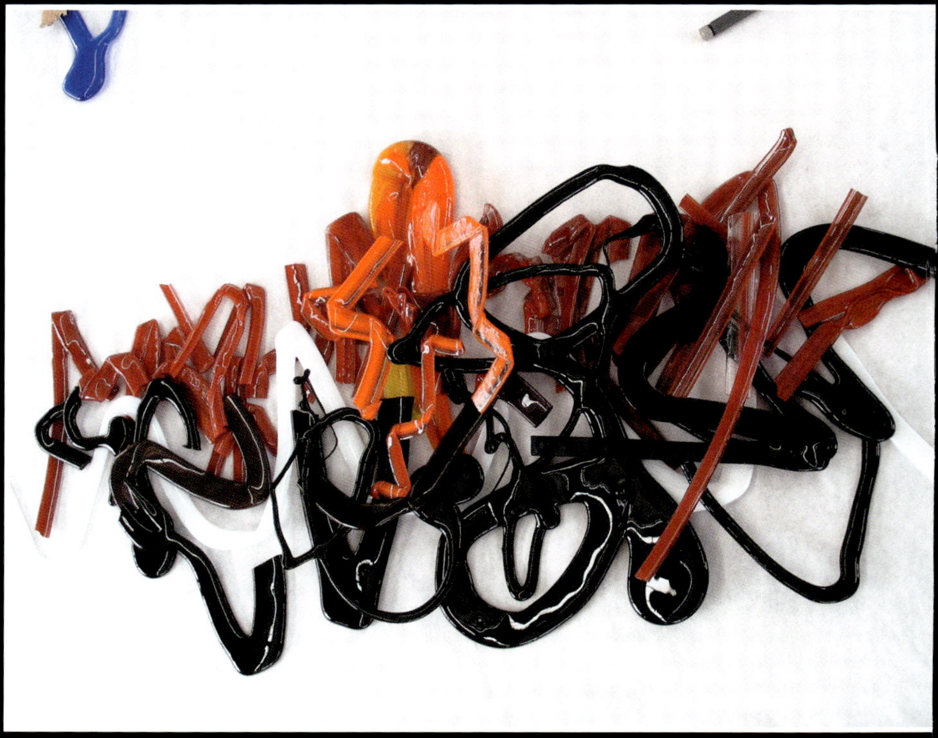

Tega, David Ruth, 2008. H. 120 cm (47¼ in.), W. 61 cm (24 in.), D. 35 cm (13¾ in.).
Photo: Scott McCue.

This monumental piece combines the gestural colour work of a painting with the physical presence of a sculpture. The scale of David's pieces is such that he employs lifting and moving equipment to handle the blocks of cast glass, and uses handheld grinding and polishing equipment to work on the static glass.

David Ruth. Trails for *Tega*.
Photo: the artist.

The individual hot-glass trails, ready to be placed into the clear matrix at different depths, and kiln-cast.

fall to earth. I feel like I can capture a flow of liquid for a long moment. Something in the randomness of the flow of hot glass can be set into these blocks, where we can freeze it and observe the universe inside the glass block. By now this has become a canvas upon which I can express my internal life, longings and sense of joy at being alive, bringing the eye into the world I have suspended inside the piece.

Over the years I have made many attempts to elucidate the interiors of the glass. The earliest pieces were cast as experiments. It took me several

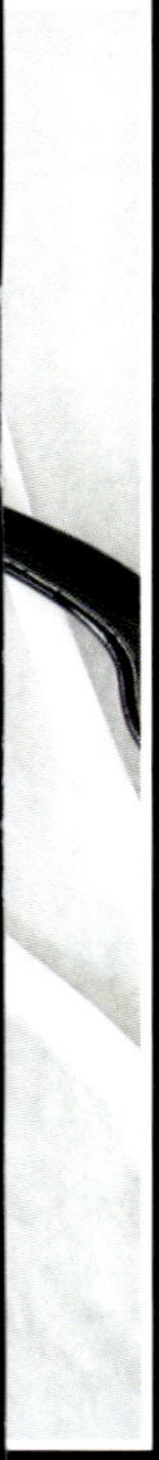

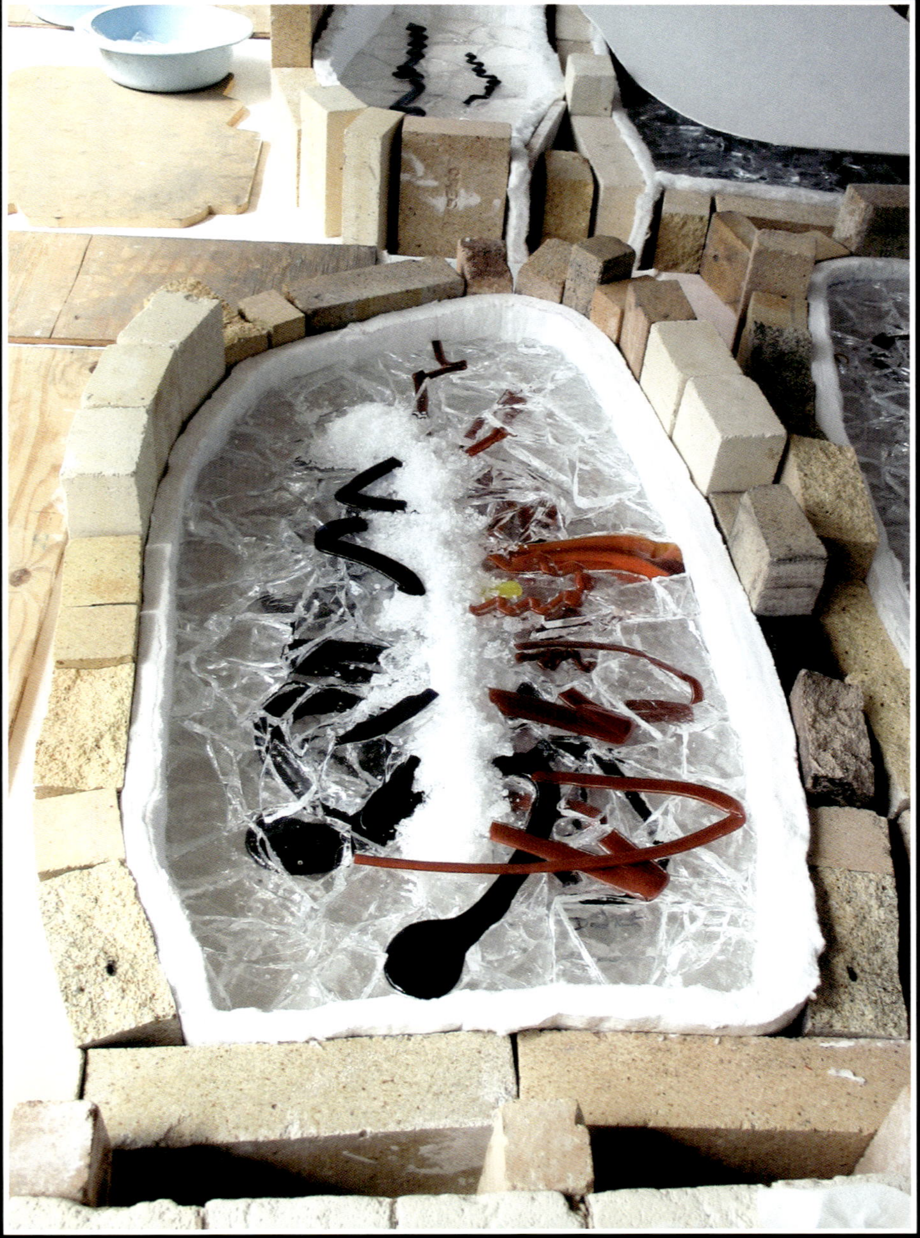

◄ David Ruth. *Tega* in position in the kiln.
Photo: the artist.

The trails are embedded in shards of clear glass in a mould made from ceramic fibre, held firmly in place with high-temperature bricks. After casting, extensive cold-working replaces the texture of the fibre with a flat polished surface except around the perimeter of the piece.

years after my first fused pieces before I gained the confidence to make them really thick. It was really the surface polishing that made my work come alive, generating the view into the internal space.

All of the names come from exotic places – among them, islands in the South Pacific or an Antarctic volcano near the American base at McMurdo.

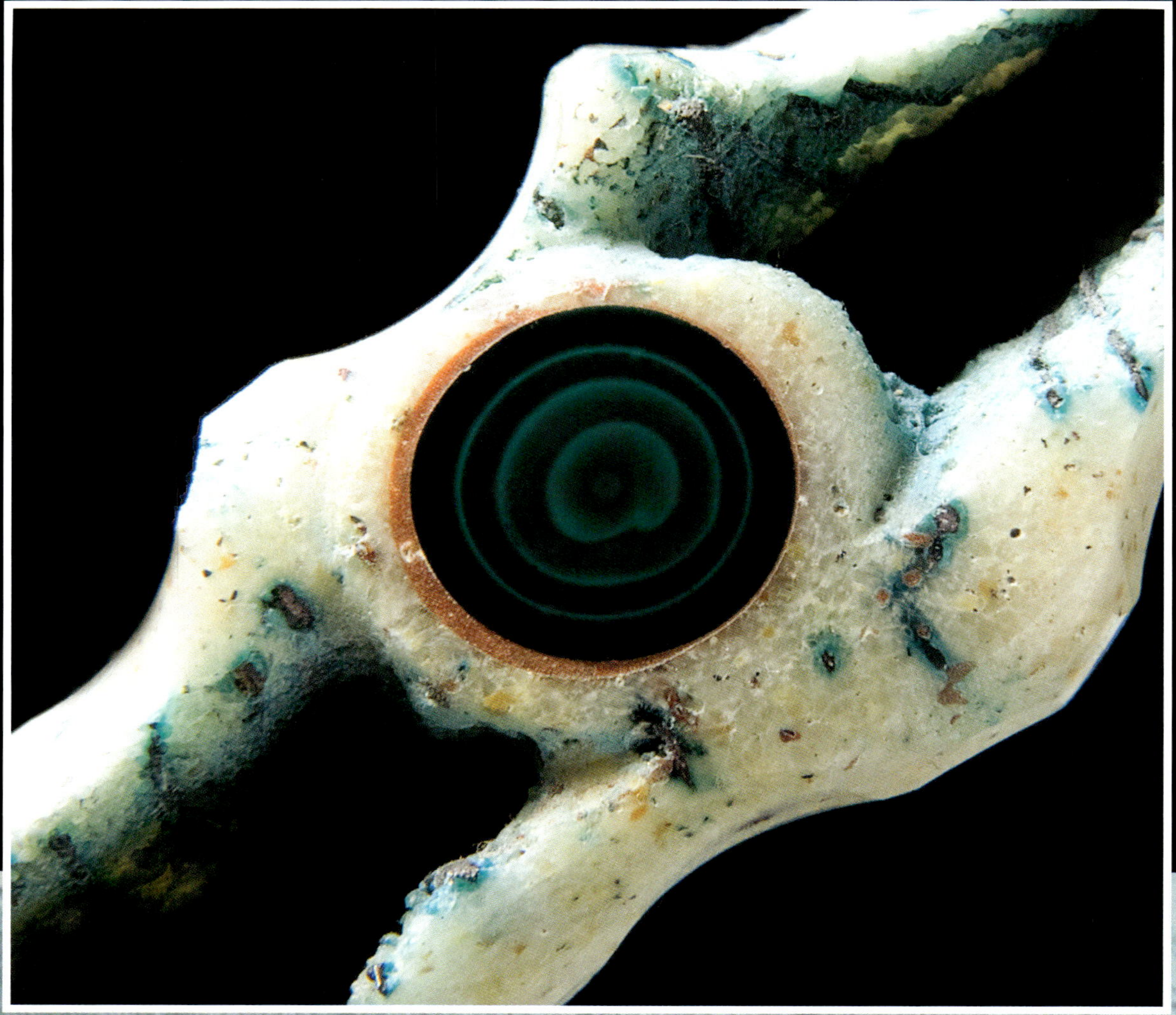

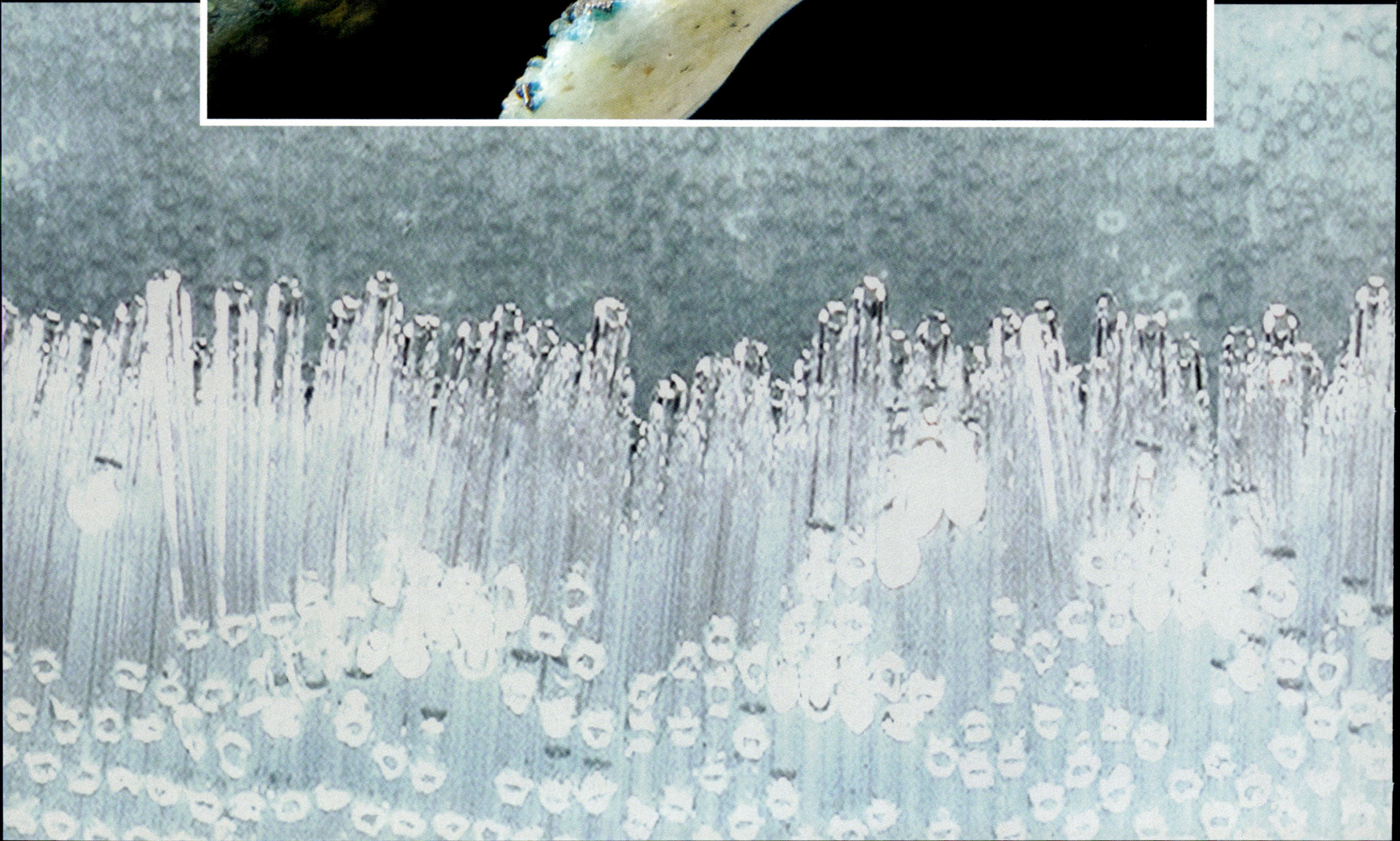

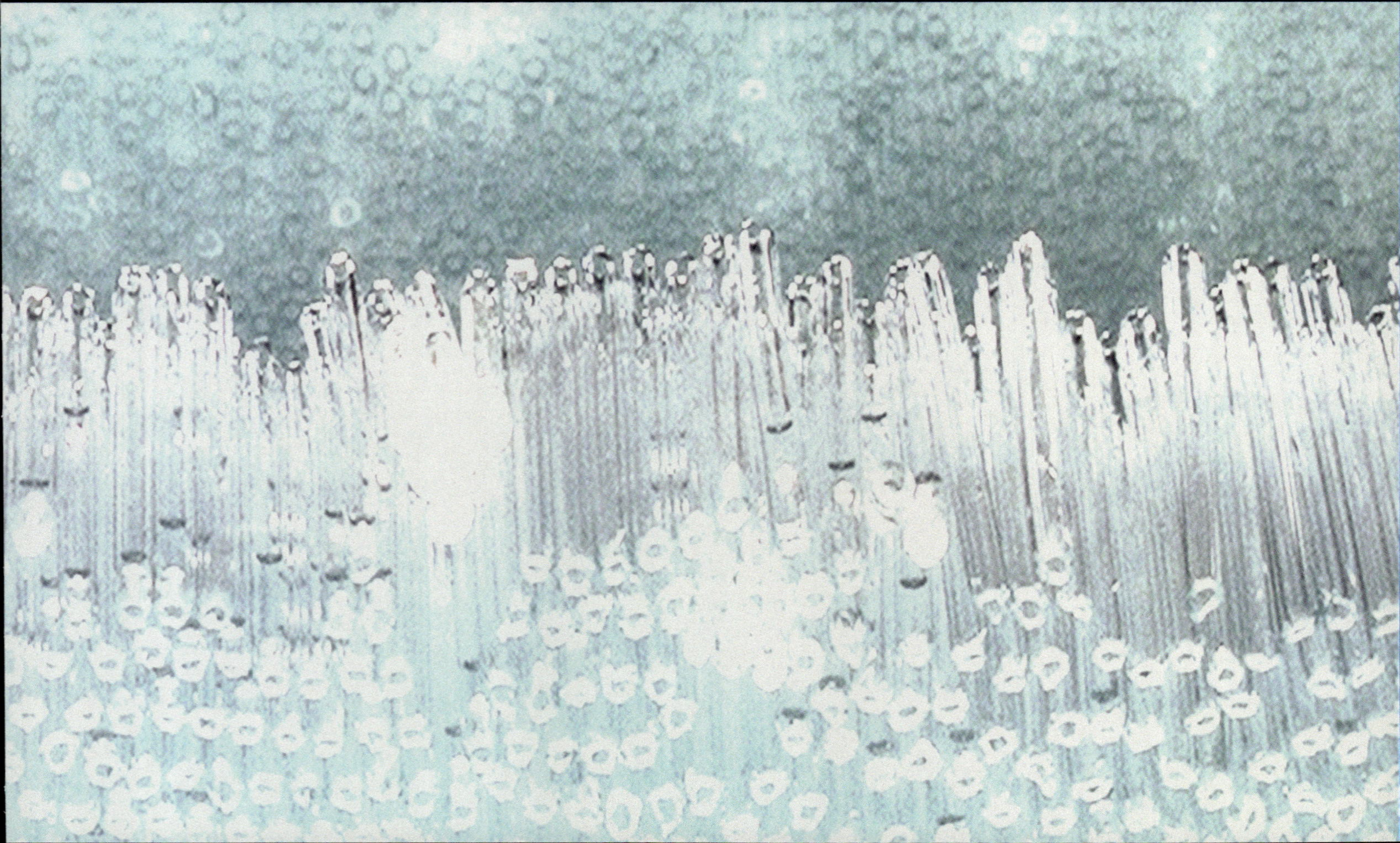

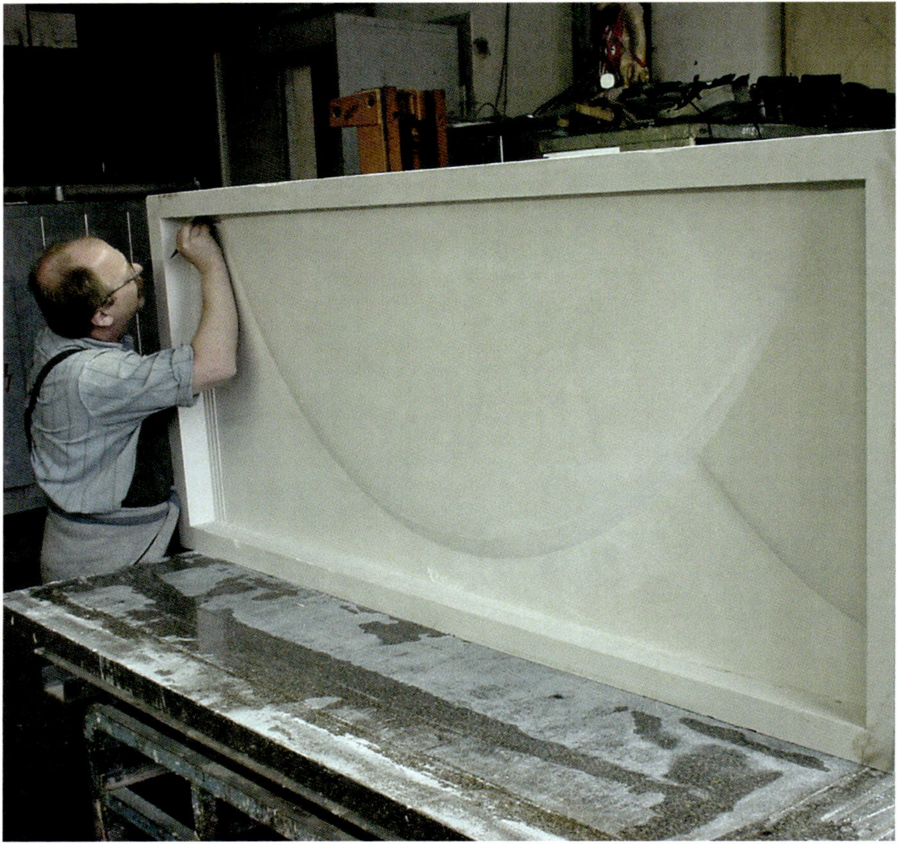

The general range of kiln-forming processes has not been significantly added to, in terms of major new procedures, in the last couple of decades, covering as it does a range from enamelling at the lower end of the temperature gradient to high-temperature casting at the other, with bending, slumping and fuse-casting in between.

There have been, nevertheless, changes in some of the techniques that make up these processes, many of them evident in the works of artists that I have chosen for this book. I have drawn attention to this when describing individual pieces, and evidence of such innovation was one of the criteria I used in deciding which artists to approach, with aesthetic quality and originality being the others. However, I thought it might be helpful to review some of the most significant areas of improvement in recent years, and to discuss their possible implications for kiln-working in general.

Perhaps the most universal observation that can be made about the contemporary scene is the dominance of casting as the pre-eminent kiln-forming method. It has during the past decade become more diverse and sophisticated, with much of this advance centred on the construction and composition of moulds.

There are clearly many more individual studio-based artists casting glass than ever before, and most of them appear to employ variations on the basic system, i.e. the use of a water-castable amalgam of plaster with modifiers and strengtheners. The variations employed depend on a number of factors and their interaction, namely: glass type, e.g. lead, soda, borosilicate, optical; size and complexity of the form; temperature range; glass format, e.g. sheet, billet, grain, powder; and the precise quality of surface desired for the finished cast.

A recent research project into mould mixes carried out at the Royal College of Art in London* yielded some interesting results, particularly in the responses that they received to their questionnaires. Many of their respondents were based in Eastern Europe, where it is clear that the influence of Stanislav Libensky, both as teacher and artist, is paramount. His large-scale casts using slump-casting, often in a single colour, provided an example that is still prevalent, despite the collapse of the state-controlled system.

* Thwaites, A., *Mixing with the Best* (digital-format research report) (London: Royal College of Art, 2002).

PREVIOUS PAGE
Pod (detail). *(See p.201.)*
Photo: Simon Bruntnell.

This detail was achieved by drilling the glass to a given depth, then breaking off the core of glass left by the drill to create an accurate depression. A coloured rod inside a metal casing of the same diameter as the drilled hole was set into the hole and then ground and polished to secure a flush fit.

◀ Casting at Lhotsky, 2001. H. 1.2m (4 ft), L. 1.6 m (5 ft).
Photo: courtesy of Lhotsky.

Preparing the mould for a section of an architectural feature designed by Libensky and Brychtová for the Mint Museum in Charlotte, NC, USA. (See overleaf.)

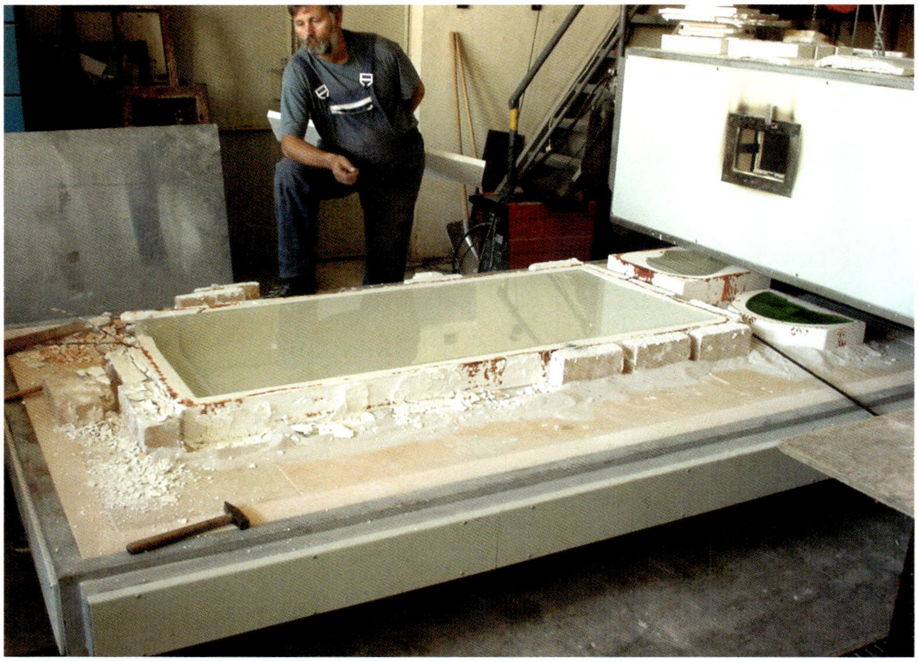

Removing the cast from the mould.
Photo: courtesy of Lhotsky.

The specialist nature of the commercial casting studio effectively creates a separation between the artists and the realisation of their work. The vast bulk of their creative decision-making has to end at the prototype stage, although the gain is made in the quality and scale of the finished product.

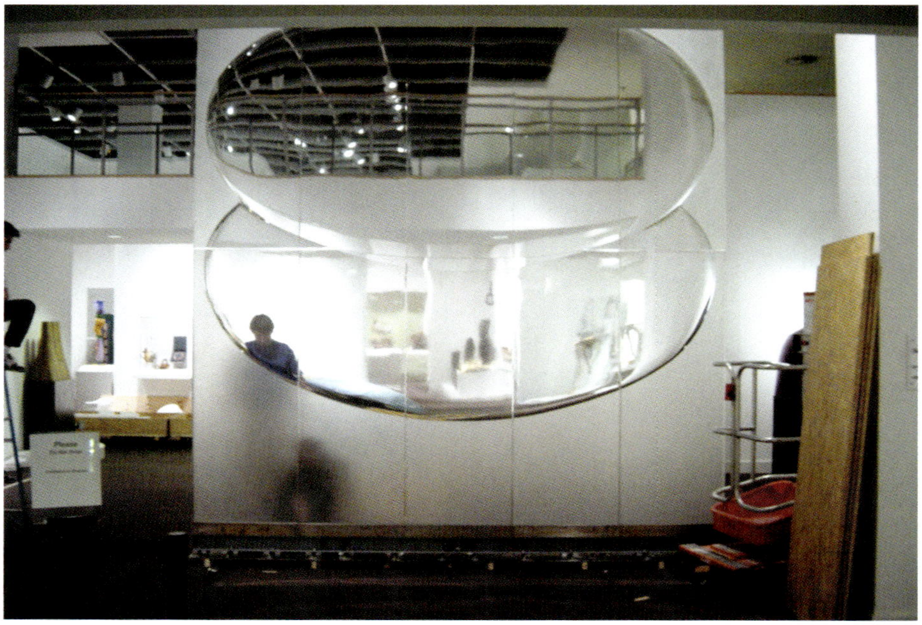

Installing the finished piece.
Photo: courtesy of Lhotsky.

The final feature, comprising ten sections and finished by cold-finishing, displays a level of control that is hard to imagine happening outside a professional facility like that at Lhotsky. The nature of their expertise, as well as their equipment – from kilns to moving, cutting and polishing machinery – is geared to the production of large-scale, professionally produced items.

This has given way to studio-cast specialists like Lhotsky who employ the same method but have adapted it to commercial use, producing high-quality casts of artists' models to precise specifications (see Ann Wolff, Peter Bremers and Brian Glassar). For this kind of cast a simple 2:1 ratio of plaster and silica is used, with strength provided by embedded metal mesh or custom-made frames. The sheer weight and thickness of the mould is relied on for basic strength, with the metal reinforcements as a back-up to prevent cracking.

The fact that generally the forms are large and open, and can be cast using large ingots, means that the process can be carried out at a lower temperature than is true of more complex forms; this itself puts less strain on the mould mixture.

The Czech system is reliable and cost-effective. Previously fired mould material (sometimes called ludo) is often used to save expensive, unfired mix, both in powdered form and, at Lhotsky, as blocks placed in the blank mould areas (although they are carefully positioned to avoid any contact with the glass as it casts). Large, simple, closed forms are often made in rubber, or sectioned so as to avoid the need to use lost wax to make the mould's cavity. Also, many of these forms are surface-worked after casting, through sandblasting, grinding, acid-polishing, etc. In such cases, where all, or virtually all, of the mould's imparted surface is removed by these methods, it is not necessary to use a more complex mould mix.

Mixes

It seems obvious that, given the wealth of materials and expertise in existence, mould mixes and systems can be devised that are highly sophisticated, can be tailored to meet specific requirements, and are capable of functioning within stringent limits. Such designer mixes come at a price, however, both in terms of their material cost, and also in the time needed to make them. The old engineer's adage comes to mind, that 'it only needs to be *just* good enough to *be* good enough'. My experience, as both practitioner and teacher, leads me to side firmly with this attitude, although, given the enormous variations within casting caused by high temperatures, different glasses, size and weight, complexity and, perhaps most of all, surface qualities, it is impossible to expect one mix to cover every possible angle.

A crucial factor in choosing the right mix is to appreciate the acute difference between the mould mix that comes into contact with the glass, and the mix that makes up the rest of the mould and any necessary strengthening. The mix that is actually used to impart the desired form and texture to the glass is almost certainly going to be the most complex and crucial of the mould's constituent mixes. It is extremely wasteful to construct entire moulds from such mixes when they only need to be a few centimetres thick. Such surface layers have to be well supported and held firmly in place by any one of a number of systems to prevent this from cracking. Providing this is done, the surface mix can be soft, the only criterion it has to fulfil being to remain firm enough to carry the form and texture yet soft enough to be easily removed from the glass after casting. Potters' plaster seems to be the near universal choice for its strength, modified by a softening material in powder form, which should be added to the mix before the water is added.

Silica, alumina and crystobolite are all in use as constituents of the mix with the specific function of softening the rigidity of plaster on its own, and there are clearly more possible variants; they all have the quality of remaining inert at temperatures up to 1000°C/1832°F (in terms of their function within the mould). However, they all have serious safety implications, for, once breathed in, the body cannot easily break them down, and thus they build up in organs like the lungs. All mould storage, handling and especially mixing must be carried out with this in mind. Work-surface extraction and the wearing of quality dust masks is essential; they must be used both while a mould is being made and when it is being removed after casting. Alternatives are being sought, such as the substitution of olivine sand for silica, but it seems highly unlikely, given that silica possesses the necessary qualities, that a totally safe type of mould mixture is feasible; and thus it is essential that health and safety issues are always taken extremely seriously.

Any mixture must take into consideration a wide range of variables, based on where they sit in the range from low to high temperature, and the relative complexity of form and texture required, which will necessitate not only higher casting temperatures, but also being held for longer periods at high temperatures. I still favour a 50:50 mix by volume of potter's plaster and Investrite for the few centimetres that come into contact with the glass itself. It is a soft, weak mix, but if well supported produces excellent results. In cases where a strengthening to this topcoat is required – where the piece is complex, large-scale or has a deep texture, for example – a finely sieved HT dust (High Temperature aggregate) added to the mould mix as 20% of the volume, imparts strength, though at the expense of some delicacy of surface. The research carried out at the Royal College of Art London, already mentioned, concluded that the inclusion of glass-fibre strands to strengthen the mix was not recommended, as the fibres did not function in this way, as had been previously thought.

These suggestions are based on a rigorous use of support to hold the surface mix in place. This can take many forms, and once again systems can vary from the simple to the complex and high-tech, from the expendable, single-trip cast jacket to a multi-use, stainless-steel container. (A cast jacket can be made from, for example, crushed HT and plaster, strengthened with metal in the form of chicken wire; a rod-frame, stainless-steel mesh; or, in my case, simple copper wire wound round the inner mould before casting the jacket – this works extremely well, and can be recycled many times.)

It is possible to use ceramic saggars, or their equivalent in metal, to hold the inner mould in place, filling the gap with tightly packed sand or even fired, broken-down mould mix. I cannot stress enough the importance of a strengthening layer. Once the function of holding the mould together is taken away from the mix that is actually in contact with the glass, it is possible to simplify this layer and make it softer and thus easier to remove from the glass after casting.

Mould coatings

These can have a number of functions, among them to stabilise the soft powdery mould surface, to encourage its removal from the glass after casting and to impart a particular quality, effect or colour to the glass. The use of shellac, a natural material – made from the carapaces of insects, rendered into a brushable liquid by methylated spirit – works well as a stabiliser and separator. Among the most important findings of the research into the practice of Amalric Walter was the discovery that he and other pâte-de-verre artists had used shellac for this purpose.

Graphite is a superb separator but is expensive and will burn away quickly; it can be applied as a liquid, or even in dust form, which can be brought to a polish. An area for experiment is the addition of a small amount of graphite powder to the surface mould mix, where it is integrated into the depth of the mould and will remain effective longer than

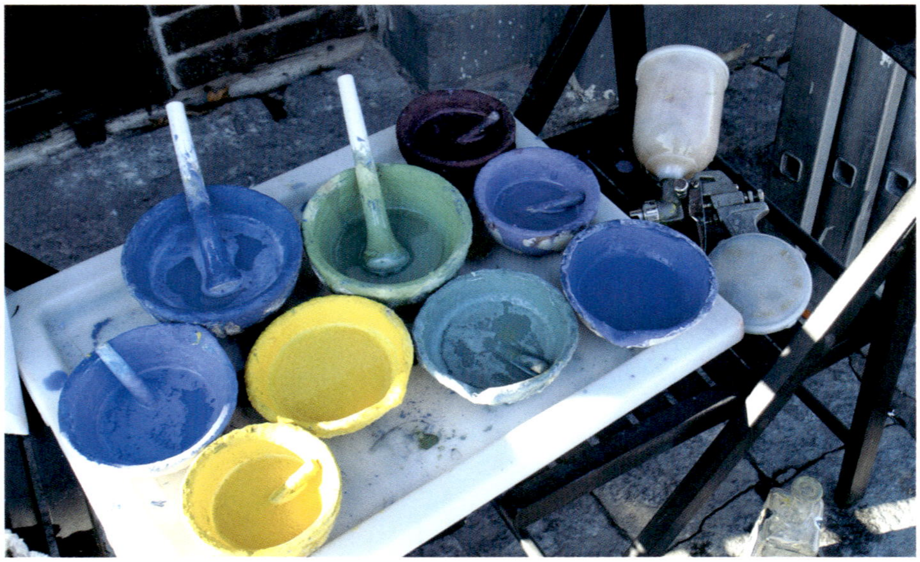

Tomasz Urbanowicz. Liquid-oxide paints.
Photo: courtesy of the artist.

Tomasz employs a range of methods to permanently colour the surfaces of his slumped architectural features. These involve oxides placed under and on the glass during firing, in addition to the spray-painting and firing of the slumped top layer in a separate operation.

Detail of a panel for a private residence in Poznan, Poland, by Tomasz Urbanowicz.
Photo: courtesy of the artist.

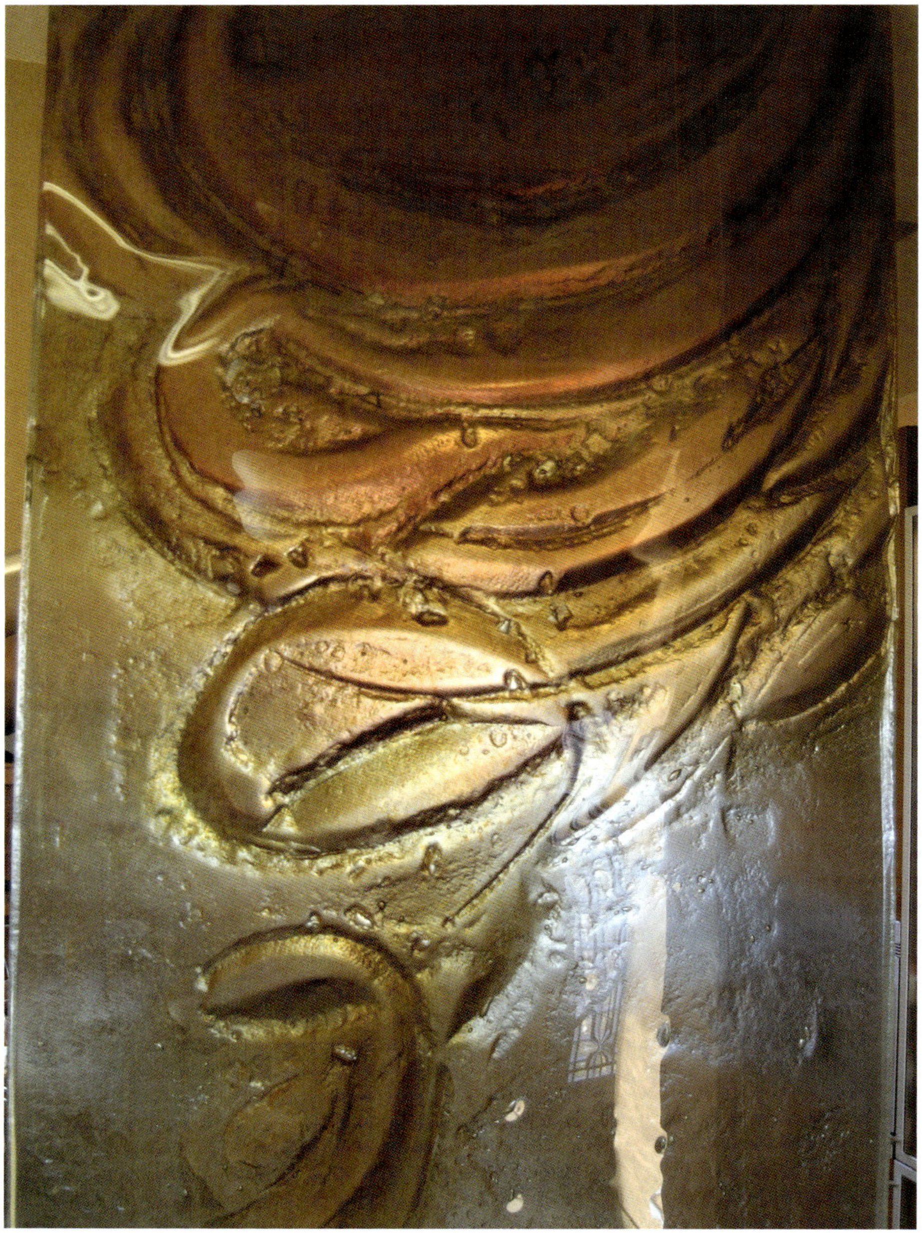

The use of oxides, and the ways in which they are applied and fired creates a range of subtle effects that complement the slumped images. The use of silver oxide to create the transparent yellow is a contemporary take on the original uses of yellow stain in traditional stained-glass windows, a practice dating from the 15th century.

a surface application. Another potentially rich area of research – that of including chemicals or metal powders in the surface mould mix to colour the glass – is indicated in the work of artists like Tomas Urbanowicz.

Mould removal

This problem obviously increases with the complexity of the mould surface, the granular nature of the glass, and the temperature. Single-piece slump casts (see Colin Reid, p.156) and multiple ingot casts manifest this problem much less than pâte-de-verre casts, for example. Using high-pressure water jets and a stiff brush can be effective, but I favour the use of a simple brick acid that can be obtained from hardware stores or builders' merchants. *It is, of course, a weak acid, and must be treated with caution and respect: goggles, gloves, good ventilation and careful disposal are all essential to its safe use.*

Extremely small glass casts can be immersed in a plastic container containing just enough of the acid to cover them; larger ones can be placed in a shallow container with a small quantity of the acid, and 'basted' like a joint of meat. Washing with water and brushing will loosen and remove the trapped mould debris. The duration of each immersion or application will vary according to the cast; it can be anything from a few minutes to several hours. Prolonged contact with the acid should not damage the glass, but it can affect any metal inclusions near the surface of the glass, particularly copper.

Mould thickness

Most practitioners pour their liquid or semi-liquid mixture into some kind of container set up round their model. This means that unless the surround follows the exact contours of the model – e.g. through the use of a hand-modelled clay outer wall – there will be some unnecessary build-up of mould thickness. This is clearly both wasteful and inefficient. A technique developed by Ann Robinson in New Zealand, and illustrated in the work of Galia Amsel, is to use the mixture at a later stage, when it is stiff rather than liquid, and to 'butter' it onto the model. This can be repeated a number of times to build up to a shell mould that exactly follows the model's profile. Once the initial layer starts to set, further layers with strengthening, in the form of additions of grog, sand or HT dust (High Temperature aggregate), can be applied.

Moulds built in this way are effective in three main ways: they are economical, and present less of a barrier to the heat; this in turn means that the glass will fire at a lower temperature; and during the annealing stage the reading of the kiln's pyrometer will be that much closer to the actual temperature of the glass.

The choice of electric kilns seems to be almost universal, as does the practice of thoroughly drying moulds prior to use. Vibrating moulds while the mixture is setting so as to release trapped bubbles is mentioned by a large number of artists.

Dr Gillian Burdett. Stages in the production of a cast with an internal, textured void.

Photo: courtesy of the artist.

Rubber moulds of the cores are used to cast soft kiln-mix positives onto metal armatures that will hold them in position during casting.

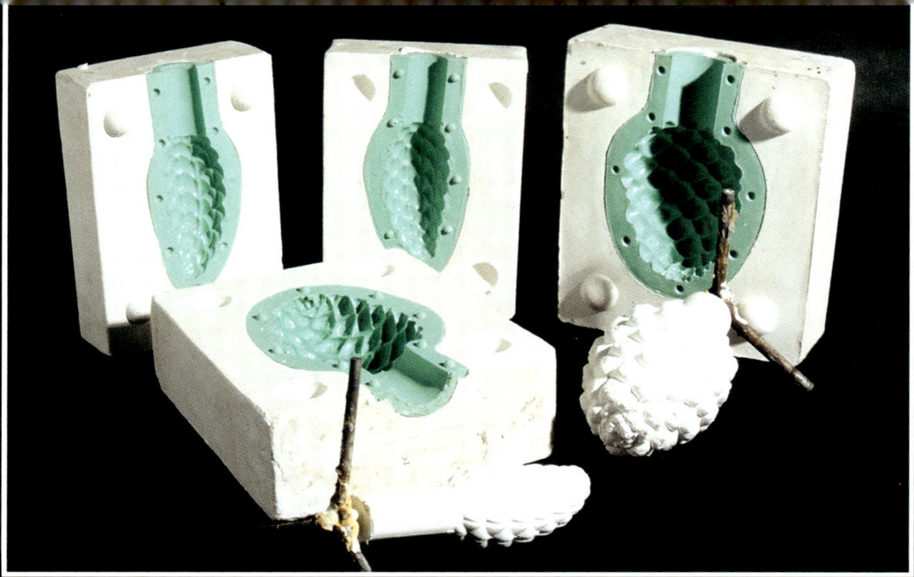

The cores covered in wax.

Photo: courtesy of the artist.

The cores are covered in the required depth of wax inside an exterior rubber mould. The depth allows for the loss of some thickness during the restoration of the outside surface by cold-working. The metal armature is designed to hold the core firmly in position inside the void created when the wax is steamed from the refractory mould. It must also allow for the removal of the wax and yet have no contact with the glass.

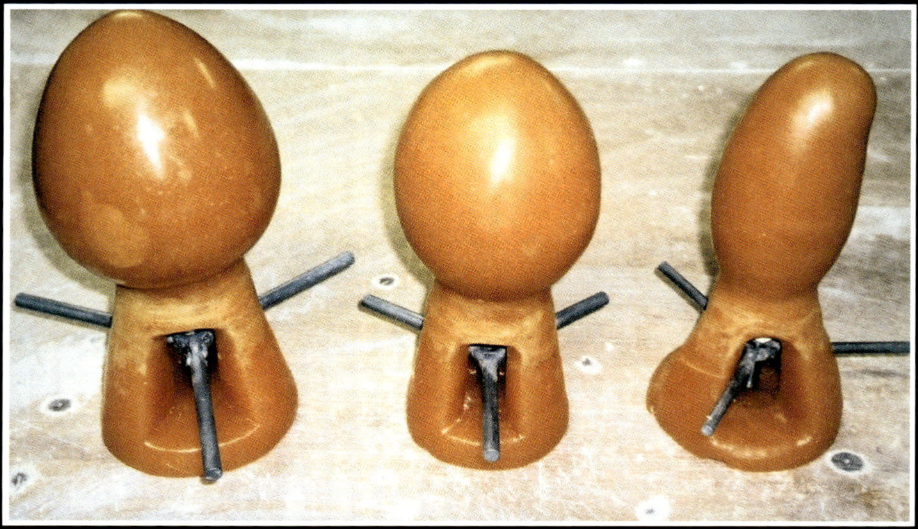

Casting complex forms

In the work of the featured artists in this book there are some prime examples of particular technical advances in the casting of complex and multi-piece forms. This is worthy of comment when discussing the individual artist's pieces, but, like so much else in this volume, each advance has implications for the vocabulary of kiln-forming as a whole. These can be summarised under the following headings:

1 The accurate casting of internal voids within the glass mass.
2 The casting of 'reverse' forms, in which a textured form is created as a void within a transparent solid.
3 The casting of two or more glass forms that physically interlock in a way that necessitates their manufacture together.

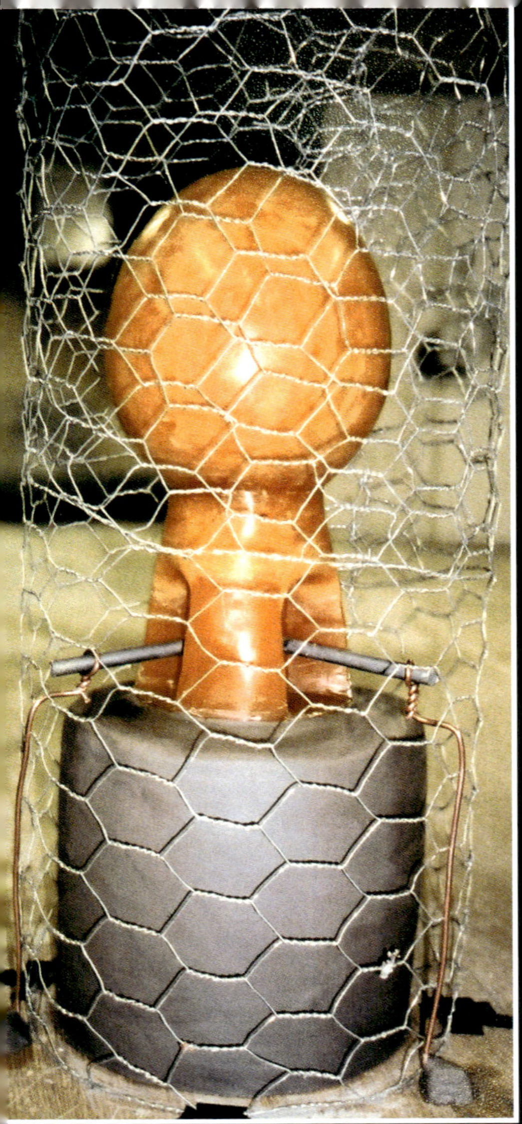

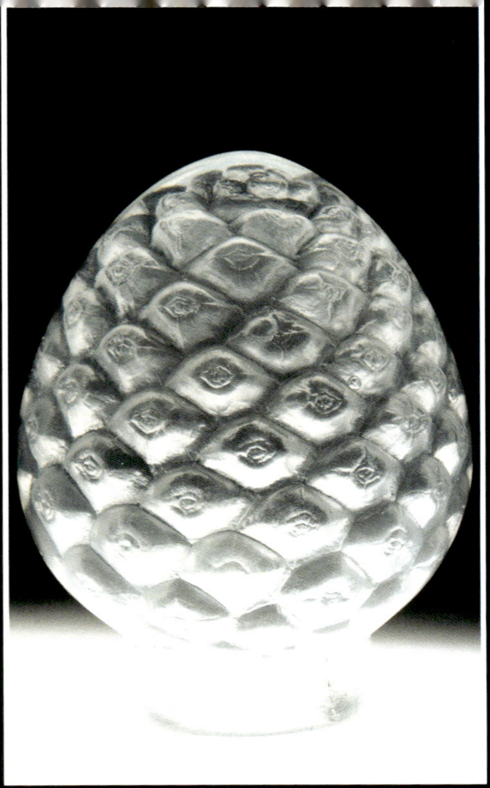

Ready for the casting of the refractory mix.

Photo: courtesy of the artist.

The wax, with the core inside it, stands on a clay form that will, when removed, act as a reservoir for the glass. The wire is there to strengthen the mould and prevent hairline fissures.

The finished piece.

Photo: courtesy of the artist.

After surface polishing, the full depth and quality of the internal void can be appreciated.

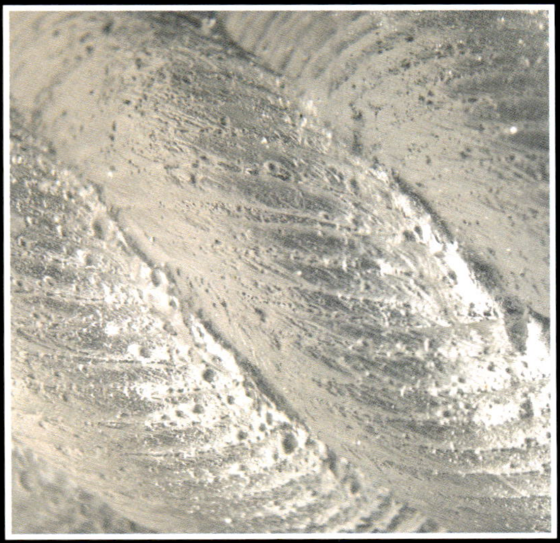

A further example.

Photo: courtesy of the artist.

In this example the form is cylindrical, with the internal void cast from a heavy rope, the full structure and texture of which have been captured by the process.

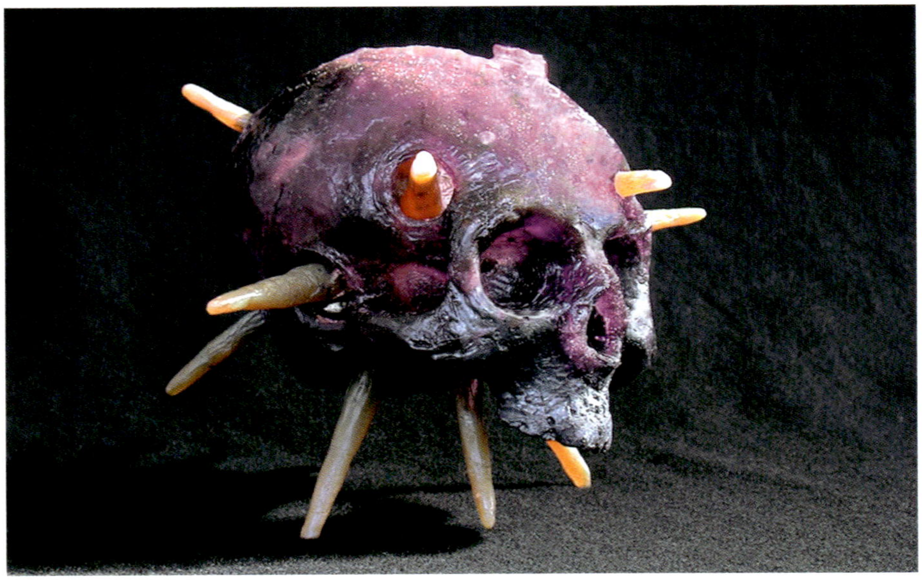

De minimis non curat, Scarface said, eating salt peanuts, cast by Marie-Aimée Grimaldi, 2001. H. 18 cm (7 in.), L. 22 cm (8⅝ in.), W. 28 cm (11 in.).

Photo: courtesy of the artist.

Two separate glass casts have been locked together to create a single sculpture. The procedure involves the placing of a previously cast section into a new mould with a wax form, but separate from it. This ensures that the first section remains in position while the new one is cast.

Items 1 and 2 are obviously linked and involve the use of a refractory core that is anchored inside the main void. This can be removed, along with any strengthening wires or armatures, after casting.

Item 3 involves casting in stages. First a section or sections are cast in glass, assembled in juxtaposition to a wax form, and the whole is embedded together in a refractory mould. Once the wax has been steamed out, glass can be introduced into the void created by the removal of the wax, while the original glass forms are held in position and are unaffected. Once the firing has taken place, the removal of all the mould mixture will reveal the different sections locked permanently together.

Pod, Keith Cummings, 2006. W. 26 cm (10¼ in.), H. 9 cm (3½ in.), D. 7 cm (2¾ in.). ➤
Photo: Simon Bruntnell.

The use of metals to create colour. This piece was cast in colourless soda glass in fine granule form. All the colour has been induced during firing by embedded metals. These took the form of copper and silver, both as powders and wire. The powders were added to the glass grains and appear as dots of colour in the mass of the glass; while the wire was added to the surface of the wax, resulting in linear detail.

Affecting the nature of the glass

Adding materials to the glass during firing to achieve a particular effect can be done in two main ways: either by mixing materials into the glass prior to casting, usually by the addition of small amounts of a variety of 'contaminants' to the grains used to fill the mould; or by joining extraneous materials to the top surface of the glass as it fuses. Different temperatures and different glass compositions result in different qualities being achieved, as do different conditions within the kiln. This is surely a fruitful area for further experiment.

Cold joining

The use of glues and resins has a long history, and it is not one I am in a position to expand on at length, as it lies outside both the general remit of this volume and the limits of my knowledge. I have long been suspicious of the use of glues to join areas of glass together, as in reality so many have proved to have a short lifespan. However, there do seem to have been some improvements in recent times, and some artists of note are using them in interesting ways; Tomáš Košt'ál, for example, whose adoption of them adds a new dimension to the uses of kiln-formed sections.

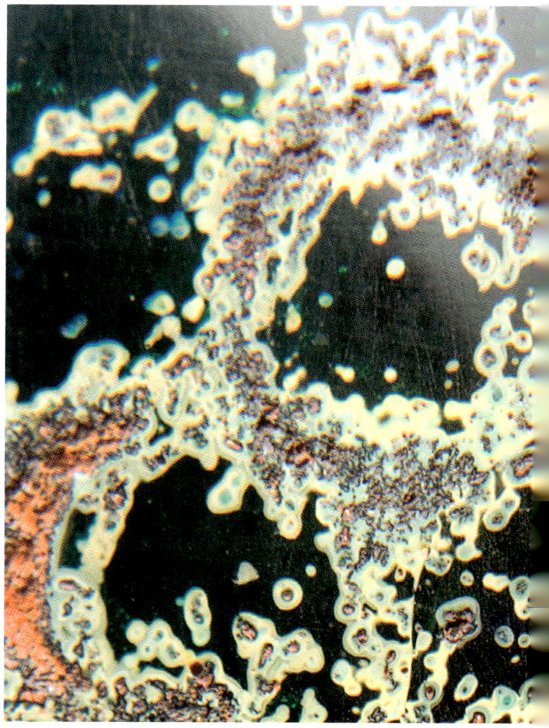

Copper and silver in conjunction with glass rods. ➤
Photo: Simon Bruntnell.

The mould was filled with cut sections of glass rod, and silver and copper powder was carefully poured down the intervals between them. Upon casting, the rods fuse into the familiar honeycomb pattern, but the metals mark their positions by overlaying an extra pattern of oxidised colour.

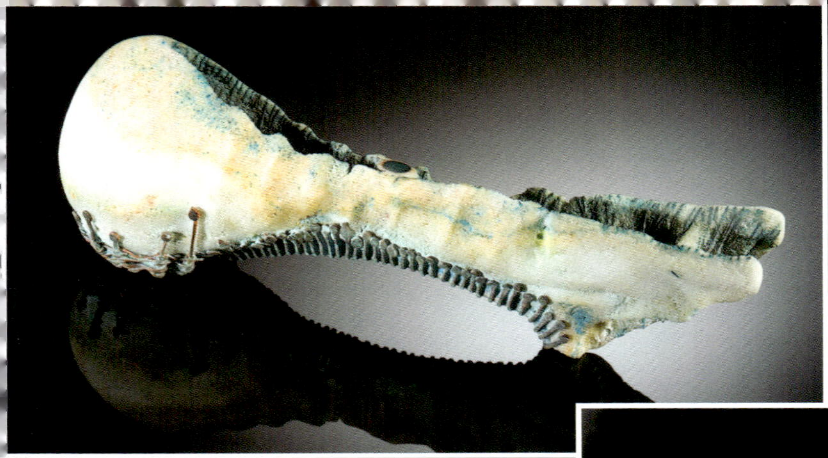

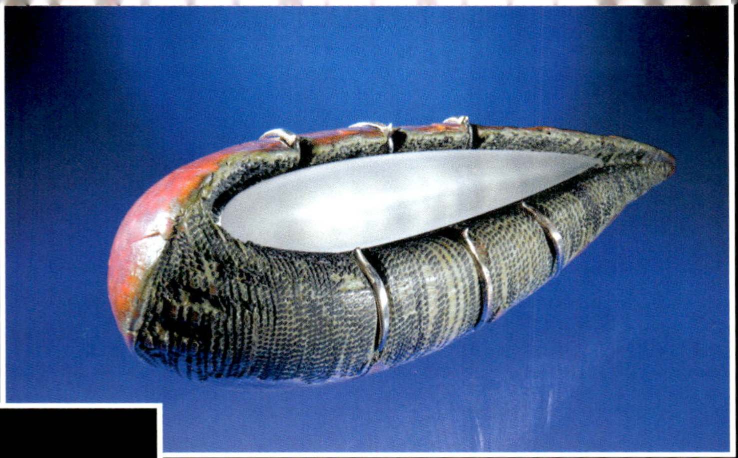

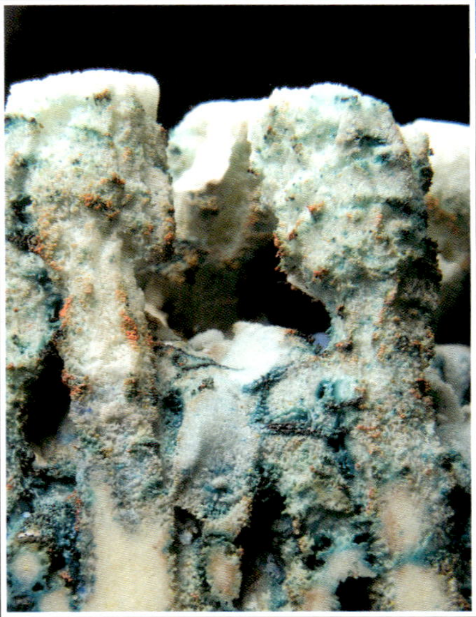

The effects of oxidation. ➤
Photo: Simon Bruntnell.

The colour caused by metals in the glass, or on its surface during casting, are largely the result of oxidisation. However, where oxygen is absent, a colour change occurs through reduction. In a normal kiln and mould, oxygen is present until continued heating at a high temperature drives it off; an example of what this reaction can produce is this shift of colour from blue to red.

▲ *Grenadier*, Keith Cummings, 2003. W. 12 cm (4¾ in.), H. 6 cm (2⅜ in.), D. 6 cm (2⅜ in.).
Photo: Simon Bruntnell.

Reaction between embedded metal and metals in the glass batch. The silver-plated copper wire was embedded in the wax model. When the wax was steamed from the refractory mould, the wire was left as part of its surface, to become integrated into the glass during casting. The glass was a gold ruby, and its high metal content has resulted in a strong reaction to the copper, and particularly the silver, creating a rich hybrid colour.

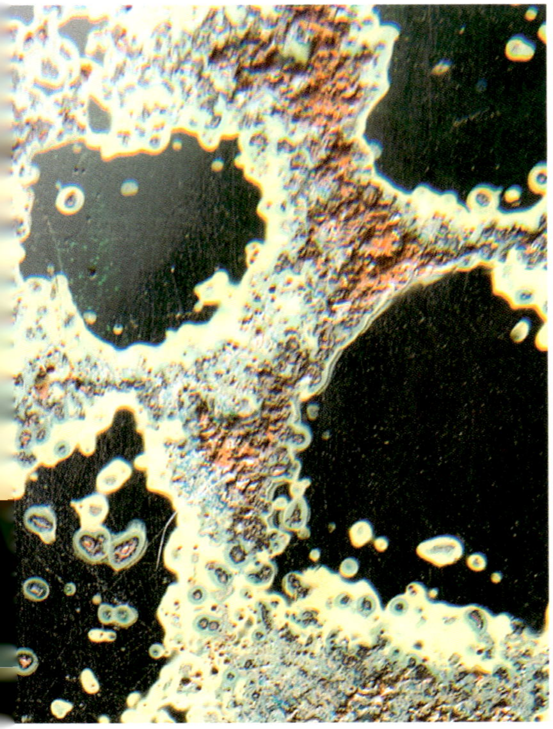

Electroforming and plating

Glass is a non-conductor of electrical current, a fact that allows it to be used in situations where this quality is needed, e.g. in the manufacture of electrical resistors. From the earliest days of the use of electricity this was exploited for decorative effect. By coating the surface of the glass with a conductive material, it is possible to successfully electro-deposit a range of metals onto the glass. By selectively applying the conductive coating – i.e. a solution rich in silver – a filigree of metal could be woven around the glass form. The Austrian factories of Loetz and Lobmeyr produced some beautiful silver and glass objects by this means in the early years of the 20th century. More recently, artists of the studio movement, notably Michael Glancy, have generated their own approaches to this procedure.

However, this would have remained a decorative technique with no real connection to kiln-forming had the work of a few individuals not extended the use of electroforming and deposition onto glass in a new direction. The work of Dr Gillian Burdett (see Bibliography) in

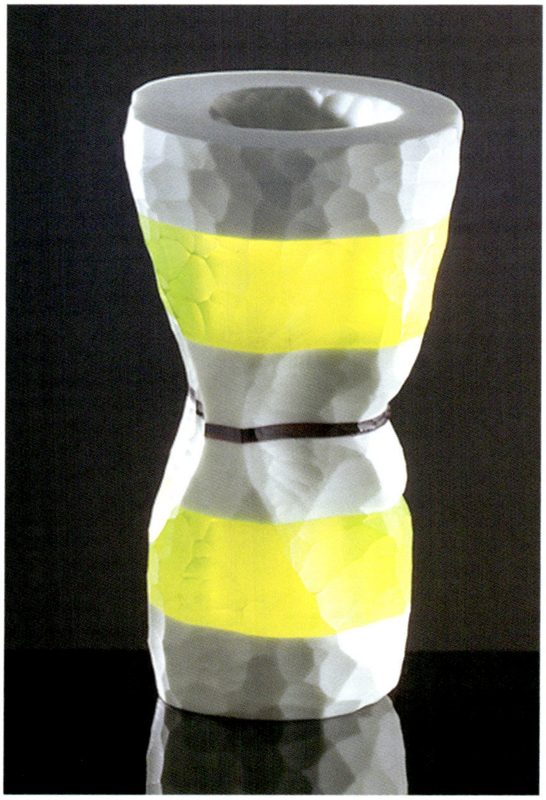

▲ *Uranic* vase by Tomá š Koš t'ál, 2004. H. 40 cm (15¼ in.), W. 20 cm (7⅞ in.). Photo: Jaroslav Kvitz.

The use of resins to combine sections of kiln-cast glass enables the artist to set off different colours and textures in the same piece. Once glued together, the piece was subjected to cold-grinding and polishing.

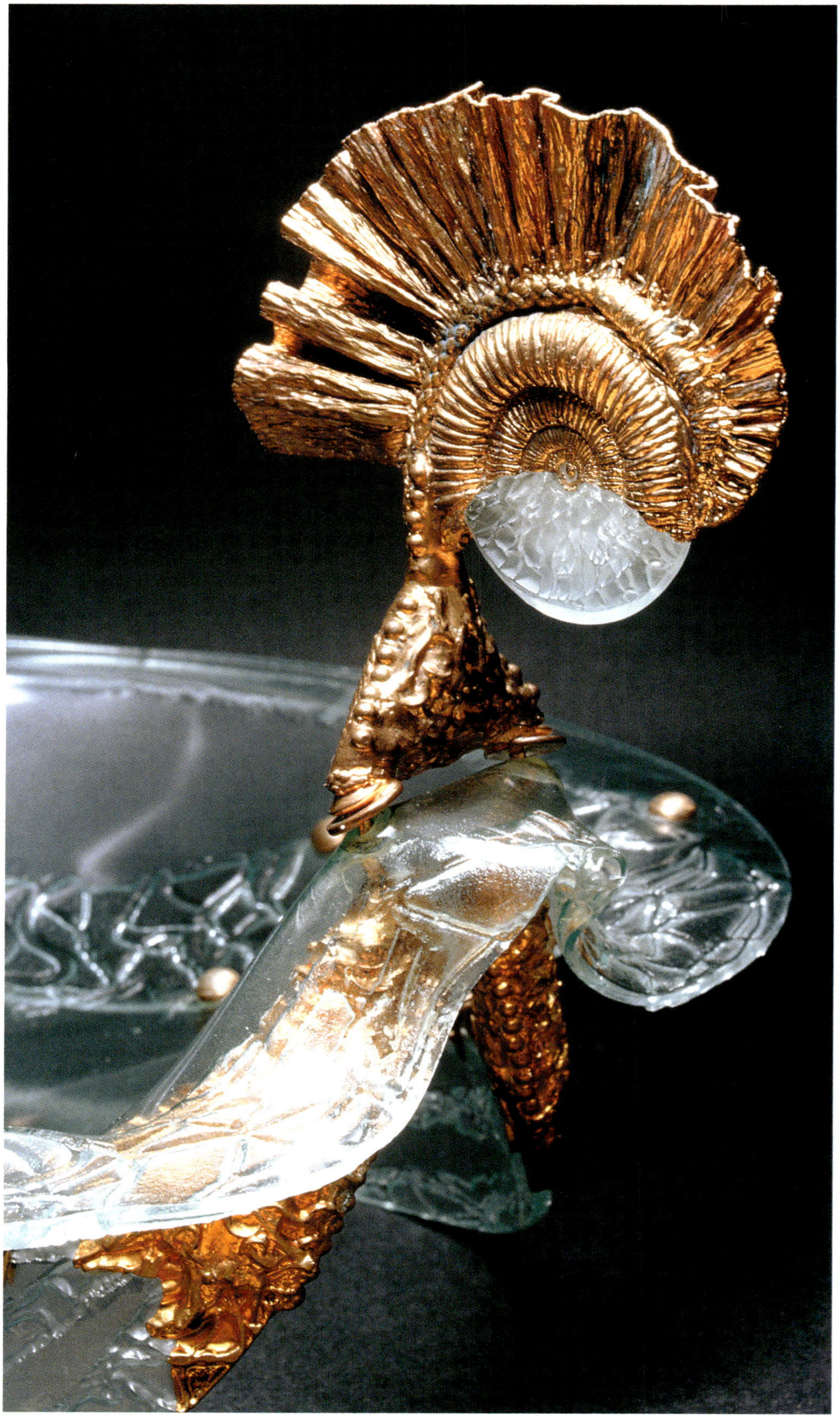

particular has suggested and demonstrated how it can be completely integrated into cast glass.

This involves the fusing of metal wires or powders into or onto the glass during firing, which can then be used as a conductive substrate on which, subsequently, further metal can be plated. Not only can this be used to make rich, decorative surfaces, it can also be used to create anchor points onto which other sections can be joined.

The use of cold-forming

The use of cutting, grinding, drilling and sawing equipment has long been a feature in kiln-forming. Usually, this has been to prepare glass for the kiln or to work the glass after firing. The development of sophisticated processes like laser-cutting, and the proliferation of handheld devices, suggests that important additions to the vocabulary of glass-forming are, and will become, increasingly available to artists and craftspeople seeking to use glass as a purely creative material. Often this requires a shift of emphasis and perception on the part of the artist, but one thing is clear: kiln-forming, for all its unique qualities, must continually seek to extend itself.

The future

Before ending this account of the current use of kiln-forming, I feel that it is worth speculating about the nature of kiln-forming's contribution to the plastic arts in general, and daring to imagine its possible future uses and progress. Consistent with my attitude throughout this book, no attempt would have any interest or validity unless it accepted the two

➤ *Keel* (detail), Dr Gillian Burdett, 1999. Dimensions of complete piece: H. 22 cm (8⅝ in.), W. 29 cm (11⅜ in.), D. 30 cm (11¾ in.).
Photo: courtesy of the artist.

Sandblasted and slumped glass and electroformed copper encapsulating separate glass detail. Engraved and polished. The selective electro-deposition of metals onto cast glass has enabled the artist to cover areas of the glass with layers of metal, which then act as anchors for the combination of other sections of metal and glass.

cultural layers within which kiln-forming operates and will continue to operate for the foreseeable future: namely, that as a method of forming glass it is very much part of the studio-glass movement, and that this in turn is part of the wider applied-art movement.

Two observations seem to suggest themselves immediately: that the secrets of kiln-forming are unlikely to disappear as easily as did those of the 19th-century pioneers; and that its palette of qualities are unique to, and embedded within, the studio movement. The sheer number of individuals who are dedicating their lives to its use, and the openness with which they are willing to communicate their knowledge, both within educational institutions and among themselves via the internet, conferences, organisations and publications, will ensure its long-term survival.

A feature of much of the work in this book, often expressed within the statements that accompany it, is the patience and dedication required to master and practise the multi-staged, slow route to form that is kiln-working. The fact is, many of us accept that much of the time we spend working with these techniques will be dull and repetitive, but equally the rewards will be great.

Bibliography

Bloch-Dermant, J., *G. Argy-Rousseau: Glassware as Art* (London: Thames and Hudson, 1991).

Bray, C., *Dictionary of Glass Materials and Techniques* (London: A&C Black/Philadelphia: University of Pennsylvania Press/Australia: Craftsman House, 1995).

Bremers, P., *Icebergs* (Netherlands: Peter Bremers, 2007).

Burdett, Dr G., *The Electro-deposition of Metals onto Glass* (doctoral thesis, University of Wolverhampton, 2000).

Cummings, K., *A Glass Menagerie: The Work of Amalric Walter* (exhibition catalogue) (Dudley: Museum of Glass, 2006).

Cummings, K., *A History of Glass-forming* (London: A&C Black/Philadelphia: University of Pennsylvania Press, 2002).

Cummings, K., *Techniques of Kiln-formed Glass* (3rd edn) (London: A&C Black/Philadelphia: University of Pennsylvania Press, 2002).

Frantz, S., *Particle Theories: International pâte de verre and other cast-glass granulations* (exhibition catalogue) (Wheaton Village, Millville, NJ: Museum of American Glass, 2005).

Klein, D. & Jancovicova, S., *Zora Palova & Stepan Pala* (Bratislava: FO Art s.r.o., 2007).

Lagier, J-F., *Udo Zembok: Spaces of light* (Chartres: Centre International du Vitrail, 2008).

Manhart, T. & M., *The Eloquent Object* (exhibition catalogue) (Tulsa: The Philbrook Museum of Art, 1987).

Opie, J., *International Sculptural Glass* (London: Victoria and Albert Museum, 2005).

Petrie, Dr K., *Glass and Print* (London: A & C Black/Philadelphia: University of Pennsylvania Press, 2002).

Thwaites, A., *Mixing with the Best* (digital-format research report) (London: Royal College of Art, 2002).

Weschenfelder, K. (ed.), *Coburg Glass Prize* (catalogue) (Coburg: Kunstsammlungen der Veste Coburg, 2006).

Index

Index of Contributing Artists –

Website or Contact Details

Akester, Karen	www.karenakester.com
Albert, Sean	seanalbert2001@hotmail.com
Aldridge, Lara	jon@lara.aldridge.com
Bremers, Peter	www.bremers.com
Bruce, Jane	www.janebruce.com
Dailey, Dan	studio@dandailey.com
Dong Hai Guan	www.guandonghai.com
Dam, Steffen	www.damkarslund.dk
Frolic, Irene	irenefrolic@hotmail.com
Fuller, Penny	penny@ pennyfullerglass.com.au
Glassar, Brian	brian@brianglassar.com
Grimaldi, Marie-Aimée	magrimaldi@yahoo.fr
Hiscott, Amber	www.amberhiscott.com,
Hlubucek, Martin	martinhlubucek@seznan.cz
Jacquard, Max	www.maxjacquard.com
Jarman, Angela	www.angelajarman.com
Kasper, Eeva	eeva@glass.ee
Kelman, Janet	www.janetkelman.com
Klimley, Nancy	nancyklimley@earthlink.net
Leperlier, Antoine	www.antoine-leperlier.com
Lepisto, Jeremy	infotravergallery.com
Lhotsky	www.lhotsky.com
Linn, Steven	info@habatat.com
MacNeil, Linda	www.lindamacneil.com
Odahashi, Masayo	www.morganglassgallery.com
Palova, Zora	glassresearch.sunderland.ac.uk
Pearl, David	www.david-pearl.com
Peiser, Mark	www.markpeiser.com
Petrie, Kevin	kevin.petrie@sunderland.ac.uk
Reekie, David	www.davidreekie.co
Reid, Colin	www.colinreidglass.co.uk
Romanelli, Bruno	www.brunoromanelli.com
Ruth, David	www.davidruth.com <
Shaffer, Mary	www.maryshaffer.com
Swinburne, Elizabeth	www.elizabethswinburne.com
Turrin, Daniela	info@danielaturrin.com
Urbanowitz, Tomasz	tomasz.urbanowicz@ archiglass.com.pl
Vandenhouke, Sylvie	www.sylvievandenhouke.com
Watson, Louise	louise@louisewatson.co.uk
Weiland, Julius	mail@juliusweiland.com mailto:mail@juliusweiland.com www.juliusweiland.com
Weinberg, Steven	www.weinbergglass.com
Wolff, Ann	info@annwolff.se
Yang, Loretta Hui-shan	liuli.us
Zembok, Udo	www.zembok.com

Moon Pool, Keith Cummings, 2007. Kiln-formed glass with fused metals. H. 15 cm (6 in.), W. 18 cm (7 in.), D. 17 cm (6¾ in.). Photo: Simon Bruntnell. ➤

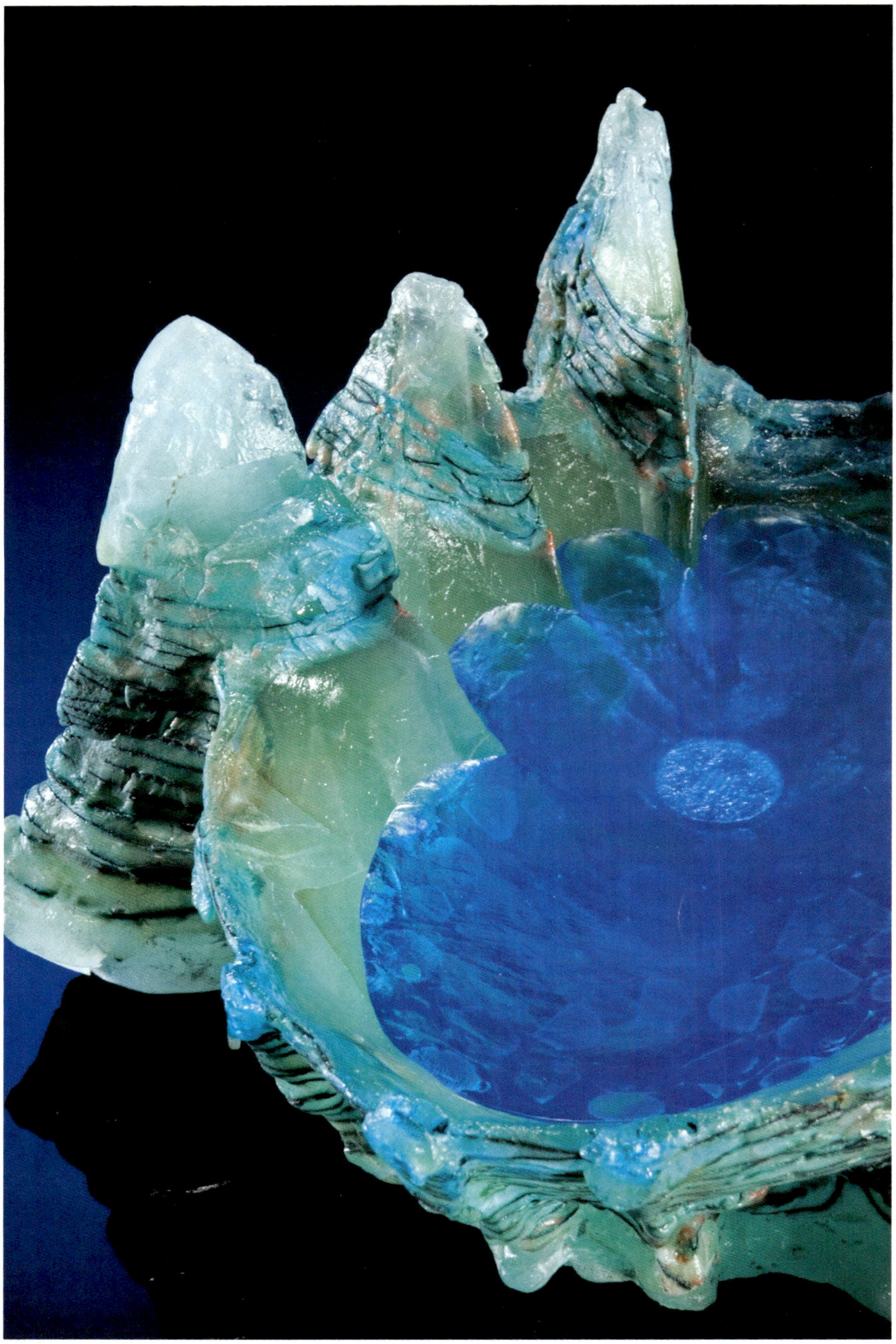